William Henry Lewis

The History of Methodism in Missouri for a Decade of Years from 1860 to 1870

William Henry Lewis

The History of Methodism in Missouri for a Decade of Years from 1860 to 1870

ISBN/EAN: 9783337326821

Printed in Europe, USA, Canada, Australia, Japan

Cover: Foto ©Thomas Meinert / pixelio.de

More available books at **www.hansebooks.com**

DEDICATION.

To the M. E. Church, South,

In which I was born and cradled—for it has been the same Church all the time before and after the division; in which I was reared and educated; in which I was "born again" into spiritual life, which is "hid with Christ in God;" in which I have endeavored to preach the pure gospel in its simplicity and truth for more than four and a half decades of years; in which my sainted father and mother lived and died after having reared twelve children, every one of whom is either in heaven or on his and her way to heaven, to which I owe all I am and have, and which I love more dearly than I do this natural life—is this book sincerely and affectionately inscribed BY THE AUTHOR.

PREFACE.

At the urgent request of my old friend, Dr. D. R. McAnally, I have consented to write the continued history of "Methodism in Missouri," from A.D. 1860, he having written said history to that date. I expect to continue it as long as I may have time and materials with which to do so. While it is a continuation of the same history, my part of it is distinct and complete in and of itself from date of its commencement. I have used extensive quotations from influential persons because I thought it would give greater variety and additional interest to the history, at the same time carefully preserving its unity by having the same line of thought to run through its entire extent. I hesitated, with no little reluctance, to undertake it, under a consciousness of my inability to produce a history that would measure up to my ideal of what it should be—not only a chronicle of facts, but also the philosophy of those facts, the causes that lie behind them, thus tracing the effect to its cause, and observing the operation of the cause in producing the effect, opening to the mind of the historian a vast field of logical and philosophical investigation and research, while endeavoring to reach the true causes of the facts and events contained in the annals of history.

As we understand it the history of "Methodism in Missouri" should be not only a narrative of what the M. E. Church, South, has done in preaching the gospel and saving souls, giving an account of the lives and labors of the men (clerical and lay) and consecrated women, who, indeed, should have a conspicuous place in this history; but it should also embrace what the Church has done: 1. In material progress, in the way of building houses of worship and parsonages for the homes of her ministers and their families. 2. In the all-important cause of education, what she has accomplished in establishing instititutions of learning throughout the State, from the primary school to the college proper. 3. In the work of organizing and building up Sunday-schools in all sections of the country. 4. In the part she has taken in the great missionary enterprise of sending the Word of God into all lands and countries destitute of the Bible. 5. In the distribution and circulation of our religious literature among our people, old and young.

We think the above formulated outline of specifications contains the legitimate subjects of Church history, though not an exhaustive analysis by any means. It has been our purpose to make this history, in relation to the foregoing particulars, what it should be, full and complete. Whenever it comes short of this purpose it is because we have not been able to obtain the desired information and suitable materials along these lines of Church history. The historian cannot manufacture these materials; should he do so, it would be fiction, and not history. Notwithstanding any deficiency resulting from the above cause, may we not indulge in the idea that the reader in perusing these pages will be repaid for his time and attention?

During the war period the operations of the Church in her various departments of usefulness were well-nigh suspended, and there is but little else than a sad history of the severe and cruel trials through which she was called to pass in the mysterious providence of God, and in which she maintained her fidelity to him. This history, however, is of paramount importance to know how she passed through the fiery ordeal of the fierce and destructive persecution of four years' duration, to know how she submitted to the dispensations of Divine Providence, uncomplainingly and without a murmur; how she took joyfully the spoiling of her goods; how they, like Christ and St. Stephen, prayed for their enemies in the agony of the last hour, while they were applying the instruments of torture and death. To pass over this history in silence would be great injustice to the cause of truth and righteousness, great injustice to those who lived and suffered and died in the Church and for the Church, great injustice to the relatives and friends of those who suffered martyrdom for Christ and his Truth, as well as great injustice to the present and future generations. Such an omission would call down the condemnation of all right-minded people upon the historian.

While we feel that we are under the highest obligations to give a true and faithful history of those times, we do so with no unkind, unchristian feeling toward the M. E. Church, many members of which no doubt condemned the conduct of others in the course they pursued during the Civil War. Indeed, we harbor no ill-will toward those who took an active part in the persecution of the M. E. Church, South; for Christ teaches that we must love and forgive our enemies or we cannot be his disciples.

In writing this history our motive has been to serve the cause of truth and thereby promote the interests of Christ's kingdom on earth. We know that it is imperfect, subject to criticism, like all other human productions. Of its literary character the reader must judge for himself. No effort at an ornate style of rhetorical embellishment has been attempted. We give it for what it is worth, and send it out upon its mission, praying that it may be successful in the vindication of truth and in the accomplishment of good.

Dr. D. R. McAnally has requested me to state that the second volume has been unavoidably delayed. The history of the third volume, however, is complete in itself, regardless of what may go before it or come after it. It embraces a very important period in the history of our Church. As a general thing it would be out of order for the third volume to make its appearance before the second, but in this case it can make no difference, as the foregoing reasons show.

I was expected to continue the history to 1880, but when I reached 1870 I found that my MS. would make a book large enough, and concluded to have it published, with the understanding that should it be desired the history would be continued by myself or some one else.   W. H. LEWIS.

St. Charles, Mo.

CONTENTS.

CHAPTER I.
MISSOURI CONFERENCE.

Our History Commences Simultaneously with the Civil War—The M. E. Church, South, Charged with Being the Cause of the Rebellion—A Malicious Purpose to Destroy Said Church—Cruel Persecution—Maintained Her Religious Integrity through the Severest Persecution—True Servants of God Always Persecuted—The Prophets, the Son of God, the Apostles, the Christians in the Dark Ages—The M. E. Church, South, Cannot Ignore Her History During the War; Others Make the History, the Historian Writes It—Forty-fifth Session Missouri Conference—Death of Rev. B. S. Ashby—Prosperous Conference Year—Preachers Non-political—*St. Louis Christian Advocate*—Fasting and Prayer for Our Common Country—Three Important Topics: Our Country, Our Government, and Our Religion—Great Suffering on the Border Line next to Kansas—Rev. N. Scarritt—Utterance of the *St. Louis Christian Advocate* 17

CHAPTER II.
ST. LOUIS CONFERENCE.

Signs of the Times Indicate Something Serious in the Near Future—Public Mind in a State of Excitement—The Annual Conferences of the M. E. Church, South, Recommend a Day of Fasting, Humiliation, and Prayer—Convocation of Ministers and Members of Different Christian Denominations at St. Charles to Promote Peace—Session of St. Louis Annual Conference—Death of Revs. J. A. Cumming and J. W. Hawkins—Ministers of M. E. Church, South, Special Objects of Persecution—Their Being Preachers of That Church the Only Charge against Them—Cannot Omit History of Our Church During the War—Persecution of Revs. D. J. Marquis, J. B. H. Wooldridge, J. Ditzler, the Great Debater, M. Arrington, and J. McCary 40

Chapter III.
MISSOURI CONFERENCE.

Seat of the Conference Changed from Hannibal to Glasgow—Orderly Session of Good-looking, Intelligent, and Happy Men—The Civil War Rages—Sad Parting in View of Threatening Danger—Great Consternation Prevails throughout the State—Persecution of Rev. Andrew Monroe—His High and Influential Character—Mrs. Monroe—Their House Plundered and They Robbed of All They Had—Rev. John McGlothin Cruelly Treated—Seizure of Our Church in Louisiana by the M. E. Church—Severe Trials of Rev. R. N. T. Holliday, as Related by Dr. Oregon Richmond, a Federal Officer.................... 54

Chapter IV.
ST. LOUIS CONFERENCE.

Session of the Conference Changed from Warrensburg to Arrow Rock, and from Arrow Rock to Waverly in Consequence of Great Excitement at the Two Former Places—Dr. W. M. Leftwich Captured by a Squad of Soldiers While on His Way to the Conference—His Account of It—Small Attendance at Conference Owing to War Troubles—Short Session, Leaving Much of the Work To Be Done by Presiding Elders—Persecution of Dr. D. R. McAnally—His Wonderful Life in Various Departments of Usefulness—Gives a Statement of His Troubles—Publishing House and Book Depository of the M. E. Church, South, in St. Louis—Rev. James M. Proctor Tells of His Trials—Rev. M. M. Pugh—His Useful Life—Tells of His Persecution During the War—Brutal Murder of Rev. Green Woods—A Detailed Account of That Dreadful Affair by His Own Daughter....................... 69

Chapter V.
ST. LOUIS CONFERENCE.

No Missouri or St. Louis Conference Session This Year—The M. E. Church, South, in a State of Consternation and Disorganization—Loyal State and Loyal Church—United and Concentrated Efforts at the Annihilation of the M. E. Church, South—"You Are the Man We Are After"—Seizure of the Houses of Worship Belonging to Our Church—Her Property, for Which She Paid Her Money, and in Which She Had the Sole Right and Title for Many Years, Contested by the M. E. Church—Church in Kansas City Taken Possession of by M. E. Church—Abuse of Southern Methodists for Not Uniting with Them—Some True Members Who Saved the Church—Murder of Rev. T. Glanville and His Son—Seizure of the Church at Independence—Independence Female College—Large and Costly House of Worship—Good Parsonage—Rev. H. N. Watts—The Church at Springfield—Report of Committee—Rev. J. M. Breeding. 93

Chapter VI.
MISSOURI CONFERENCE.

Conference at Fulton—No Bishop Present—Minute Business—History Confined Chiefly to the Persecution of Her Ministers and Seizure of the Property Belonging to the M. E. Church, South—The Unarmed and Innocent Persecuted at Their Homes and at Their Houses of Worship—Denying the History Does Not Change the Facts—Murder of Rev. John L. Woods, a Local Preacher—Local Preachers Fill an Important Place in the Church—Persecution of Rev. D. B. Cooper Given by Dr. Harris—Persecution of Rev. W. M. Rush—Troubles of Rev. Tyson Dines, as Given by Rev. R. P. Farris, D.D., Presbyterian Minister—Rev. James Penn and His Four Clerical Sons—Severe Trials of Rev. Jesse Bird, as Stated by Himself—Spiritual State of the Church, by Rev. F. A. Savage.. 121

Chapter VII.
MISSOURI CONFERENCE.

No Published Minutes of the St. Louis Conference This Year—Forty-eighth Session of the Missouri Conference at Mexico—Minute Business—Preachers Received Their Appointments—Imminent Danger Threatens Them in Every Direction—Their Trust Is in God—Reign of Terror—Cruel Murder of Rev. Thomas Johnson—Trials of Martin L. Eads As Given by Himself—Rev. W. M. Newland Arrested—Church at La Grange—Rev. J. H. Pritchett and His Work—The Palmyra Meeting Formed an Era in the History of Southern Methodism.......... 147

Contents.

CHAPTER VIII.
MISSOURI CONFERENCE.

Remove All Outside Restraints, and Every Man Will Show What He Is—Persecution Continues under the "Test Oath" of the New Constitution—Ministers of the Gospel Refuse to Take It—Forty-ninth Annual Session of the Missouri Conference at Hannibal—Minute Business—Six Deaths in the Conference During the Year: W. G. Caples, Edwin Robinson, William Ketron, John F. Young, George L. Sexton, and D. R. Smith—Biographical Sketch of Each One—Preachers Blessed in Their Work—Report of a Committee of the Missouri Conference on the State of the Church—Persecution of Rev. W. A. Tarwater—His Own Account of It—*St. Louis Christian Advocate* on the State of Things—Trial of Rev. J. A. Mumpower—Rev. John D. Vincil—Wise Counsel—The Church at Lexington.................. 180

CHAPTER IX.
ST. LOUIS CONFERENCE.

Wise and Judicious Advice of the *St. Louis Christian Advocate*—No Printed Minutes of the St. Louis Annual Conference—Statistical Information from Other Reliable Sources—The Preachers Received Their Appointments Uncomplainingly and Went Forth to Their Fields of Labor Joyfully—The Conference Proceedings Were Such as Properly Pertain to a Purely Christian Organization—The Voice of the *St. Louis Christian Advocate* in Relation to the Respective Prerogatives and Duties of Church and State—Statement of Rev. J. S. Frazier—Trials of Rev. J. C. Williams and Rev. H. M. Long—Document of Rev. W. S. Woodard—Seizure of Our Church in Boonville—Notorious Murder of Rev. Samuel S. Headlee—Pastoral Address of the St. Louis Annual Conference of the M. E. Church, South................ 206

CHAPTER X.
ST. LOUIS CONFERENCE.

The Sound of the Battle-cry Is no Longer Heard—Session of the Conference at Lexington—Bishop Doggett Presided—Statistical Business—Memoirs of J. T. Davenport,

W. H. Mobley, L. Riley, John McEwin, S. S. Headlee—Rev. L. F. Aspley's Trials in Time of the War—Church at Potosi Captured—Rev. J. C. Williams in Trouble—Origin and Early History of Methodism in St. Louis—Revival Notice of Rev. W. L. Powell and Other Ministers—A Description of the Different Charges in St. Louis in Connection with the Introduction of the Church Conference as a New Institution of the Church—Accounts of Revivals by Rev. D. J. Marquis, W. G. Horn, Rev. J. A. Murphy, and Others...................... 228

CHAPTER XI.
MISSOURI CONFERENCE.

The Fiftieth Annual Session of the Missouri Conference—Statistical Business—The Blessings of Peace in Contrast with the Evils of War—United as One People, the United States the Greatest Nation on Earth—Would Give a High Christian Civilization to the World—Is Not That the Divine Purpose?—Rev. J. A. Mumpower Speaks of His Work—Also Rev. Thomas Hurst and Rev. W. E. Dockery—His Usefulness and Persecution—Revival Notices by Other Preachers—Revival in a Sunday-school—Rev. Jesse Bird's Work—Church at Glasgow—Work of Rev. A. Monroe, Presiding Elder of Fayette District—Chillicothe Station, Rev. S. W. Cope, Pastor—Revival Notice by Rev. John D. Vincil—Work on St. Joseph District by Rev. W. M. Rush, Presiding Elder—Trials of Rev. Jesse Faubion During the Internecine War—Also of Rev. S. J. Burgin—Revivals Reported from All Parts of the Conference—Also a Revival of Building Many Houses of Worship in Different Portions of the Country 254

CHAPTER XII.
MISSOURI CONFERENCE.

Statistical Business—Increase of Membership—Eighty-seven Preachers Receive Their Appointments—Biography of Rev. W. G. Caples—Incident in the Early History of Bishop Marvin—A Good Report of Chillicothe District, by Rev. W. E. Dockery—Sketch of Rev. E. R. Miller's Life and Work, by Himself—Rev. T. B. King Gives a Good Report of His Field of Labor—Other Interesting Accounts of Revivals by Revs. D. C. Blackwell, J. R. Taylor, and Other Preachers........................ 284

Chapter XIII.
St. Louis Conference.

The Ministers Addressing Themselves Earnestly to the Work of Rebuilding the "Waste Places of Zion" in Missouri—Session of the St. Louis Conference Held by Bishop Marvin at Kansas City; W. M. Prottsman, Secretary—Usual Statistics—Memoir of Rev. H. E. Smith—Rev. J. S. Frazier Speaks Interestingly of the Church—Rev. J. W. Cunningham Visits the Southern Methodist Charges in St. Louis—South-west Missouri, by Rev. H. W. Webster—*Multum in Parvo*—Origin, in this Country, of the Different Christian Denominations, and Their Respective *Status*—What the Character of the Ministers of the Gospel Should Be.................................. 310

Chapter XIV.
Missouri Conference.

Fifty-second Session of the Missouri Conference Held by Bishop Kavanaugh at Weston; J. D. Vincil, Secretary—Our Church-house a Large and Splendid Edifice—Weston Is Full of Good Houses of Worship—Institution of Learning Founded by Rev. W. G. Caples, but Now Belongs to Rev. W. H. Lewis—The Conference Full to Overflowing—Influence and Popularity of the Bishop—Good Statistical Report—Increase of Members Nearly Thirty-five Hundred—Great Improvement in Sunday-school Work—Should Be As Many Scholars in Sunday-school As Members in the Church—Dr. W. G. Miller Reports Favorably of Weston Female College—Rev. D. A. Leeper's Funeral Preached during Conference by Bishop Kavanaugh—His Memoir—Rev. J. Devlin's Work on Carrollton Circuit—Rev. C. I. Van Deventer's Life and Work, by Himself—Our Church and Moberly—Rev. J. A. Mumpower's Life and Work, by Himself—Rev. George C. Light, D.D............................ 334

Chapter XV.
St. Louis Conference.

At Jefferson City, Bishop Kavanaugh Presiding; W. M. Prottsman, Secretary—Preaching at the Capitol on the Sabbath by the Bishop—An Occasion of Unusual Interest

—Statistical Reports Favorable—Increase of Membership 2,000—Missionary Anniversary a Success—Missionary Cause Growing in Interest—Also an Advance Movement in the Sunday-school Interests—One Hundred and Forty-six Church-houses—Dr. W. A. Smith Delivered an Address on Education in the Interest of Central College—Education on Upward Grade—Southeast Missouri—Also South-western Missouri—Same Country Spoken of by Alonzo Dante—Rev. J. A. Murphy on Revival Interests—Future Prospects of Kansas City—A Voice from South-west Missouri Again—New Madrid Circuit—Marvin Camp-ground, Near St. Louis. 361

Chapter XVI.
MISSOURI CONFERENCE.

Bishop Pierce, President; J. D. Vincil, Secretary—Schools and Colleges Doing Well—Interest in Missionary Cause—Sunday-schools Improving—Church Literature Circulated—Death of Rev. Henry H. Hedgpeth—His Memoir—District Reports of Presiding Elders Contain Historic Information—Report of Plattsburg District, by Rev. S. W. Cope—Report of St. Charles District, by Rev. A. Monroe—An Autobiographical Sketch of the Life and Labors of J. H. Ledbetter—His Position in the Ministry—A Biographical Sketch of Rev. George J. Warren, Given by Himself—The Life and Character of Rev. John Thatcher, by Rev. G. W. Hughes.......... 382

Chapter XVII.
MISSOURI CONFERENCE.

Rev. Abraham Millice, the Oddity, Known to This Present Writer as the Most Eccentric Person He Ever Saw—Humorous Incidents When Holding Meetings with Him—An Account of His Ministerial Life, by J. B. Landreth—Millice Forced His Landlord to Let Him Have Prayer with Him and His Family—His Cave Church—His Overshot Mill, etc.—M. E. Church, South, in Callaway County, Mo., by Rev. George W. Penn—Fulton Station—Pleasant Grove Church—Prairie Chapel—Miller's Creek Church—Prospect Church—Shiloh Church—Mount Pleasant Church—Williamsburg Church—Reedsville Church... 407

CHAPTER XVIII.

ST. LOUIS CONFERENCE.

The Minute Business and Statistical Reports—Bishop Marvin's Travels in South-west Missouri—Pleasant Hill—Church Dedication—Harrisonville—Nevada City—Red Oak Camp-ground—Granby District Conference—Reason for no More Missions on the District—The Editor of the *Advocate* Doctored—Reorganization in the South-west—The Strength of the Church in That Part of the State—Report of Lexington District, by Rev. J. R. Bennett—Warrensburg Circuit, Rev. W. J. Brown, Pastor—Warrensburg Station, Rev. C. C. Woods in Charge—Warsaw Circuit, Rev. R. C. Meek, Pastor—Clinton Circuit, Rev. J. B. Wooldridge, Pastor—Dover Circuit, Rev. N. M. Talbott in Charge—Saline Circuit, Rev. W. S. Woodard, Pastor—Waverly Station, W. F. Mister, Pastor—Lexington Station, Rev. W. F. Camp, Pastor—St. Louis District, Rev. Joseph Boyle, Presiding Elder—First Church, Dr. Clinton, Pastor—Centenary, Rev. C. D. N. Campbell, Pastor—St. John's, F. A. Morris, Pastor—Kirkwood, Rev. Robinson, Pastor—The Autobiography of Rev. W. S. Woodard—Rev. J. C. Berryman Gives an Account of the Charleston District—Fort Scott—Sedalia—Travels of Rev. L. M. Lewis through South-east Missouri.. 419

CHAPTER XIX.

EDUCATIONAL.

The Age in Which We Live Demands of the Church a High, Thorough, Christian Education, to Combat the False Theories of Scientific Infidelity and Materialistic Atheism—Historic Sketch of Central College, Located at Fayette, Mo.—Historic Sketch of Central Female College, Located at Lexington, Mo.—Historic Sketch of Woodlawn Seminary, Located near O'Fallon, Mo.—Brief Notices of Howard College, at Fayette, Mo., and St. Charles College, Located at St. Charles, Mo.—Other Institutions.. 444

METHODISM IN MISSOURI.

CHAPTER I.

MISSOURI CONFERENCE.

Our History Commences Simultaneously with the Civil War—The M. E. Church, South, Charged with Being the Cause of the Rebellion—A Malicious Purpose to Destroy Said Church—Cruel Persecution—Maintained Her Religious Integrity through the Severest Persecution—True Servants of God Always Persecuted—The Prophets, the Son of God, the Apostles, the Christians in the Dark Ages—The M. E. Church, South, Cannot Ignore Her History during the War; Others Make the History, the Historian Writes It—Forty-fifth Session Missouri Conference—Death of Rev. B. S. Ashby—Prosperous Conference Year—Preachers Non-political—*St. Louis Christian Advocate*—Fasting and Prayer for Our Common Country—Three Important Topics: Our Country, Our Government, and Our Religion—Great Suffering on the Border Line next to Kansas—Rev. N. Scarritt—Utterance of the *St. Louis Christian Advocate*.

IT is a source of sincere and deep regret that we are under the necessity of commencing and pursuing the history of the M. E. Church, South, through a long, sanguinary, and destructive civil war, which visited with wreck and ruin our once peaceful, prosperous, and happy State. It is marvelously strange, and subsequent developments make it more strange, that the M. E. Church, South, should have been charged with the cause of the rebellion, and consequently pursued during the entire internecine war with a malicious and vindictive intent to accomplish her utter overthrow and destruction, But while passing through the fiery ordeal of four years' cruel and unrelenting persecution, scourged, peeled, and scathed, she maintained her Christian character and unswerving fidelity to God, without compromising a single principle of her evangelical faith. She came forth out of it all, cleansed and purified, bright and burnished, like the pure gold to which the purifying power of fire has been applied—the better prepared for a holier life and a more complete consecration to the service of God.

Nor should we think strange of this persecution. Are not the true and faithful followers of our Lord Jesus Christ called to suffer with him in this wicked world? Indeed, has not the history of the true Church of God been written in blood through all the past ages? and has not his spiritual Church always been the object of the implacable hate and cruel persecution of the world, the flesh, and the devil? In the very nature of the case it cannot be otherwise. Did not the irrepressible conflict commence in Eden? And has it not continued with no abatement, but with increasing virulence, ever since Cain slew Abel? Let the Apostle Paul tell how the faithful servants of God were persecuted under the Old Testament dispensation: "They had trials of cruel mockings and scourgings, yea, moreover of bonds and imprisonments. They were stoned, they were sawn asunder, were tempted, were slain with the sword:

they wandered about in sheep-skins and in goat-skins; being destitute, afflicted, tormented; of whom the world was not worthy; they wandered in deserts and mountains, and in dens and caves of the earth." We see the three Hebrew children thrust into the fiery furnace because they would not bow the knee to the idol of Nebuchadnezzar. We see Daniel cast into the lions' den because he would pray to his God. Thus suffered the righteous people of God through the cycles of centuries until the advent of the Messiah, the Lord's Christ.

How did they receive the Son of God, who is "the brightness of his Father's glory and the express image of his person," and who came on the mission of divine benevolence for the redemption of a lost and ruined world? How did the Jewish nation receive him? With cordial welcome and demonstrations of joy and rejoicing? No. Did the people hail him their Prince and Saviour? No; he came to his own, and his own received him not. They gave him no place in their hearts, nor in their homes. They spurned him from their presence, saying: "We will not have this man to reign over us. Away with him!" And from that hour he was despised and rejected, maligned and persecuted with a hellish hate that culminated in his death.

That the people of God are hated and persecuted by the world, the flesh, and the devil is what might be expected, for they are in direct antagonism at every point, and between them there is a perpetual warfare; but that they should be despised and persecuted by those who claim to be the Church is an inexplicable mystery, something we cannot understand. Who slew the prophets? Jerusalem, representing the Church. Who falsely accused, condemned, and crucified our Lord? The Jewish Church, Annas and Caiaphas, the officiating high priests at the altar of God, and the great Sanhedrim, to whom the interests of the Church were committed, and the multitude of the Jewish people, all combined to make sure his death. Did not Pontius Pilate, the Roman Governor, who was not a Jew, manifest a disposition to release Jesus, calling him that innocent man, saying that he saw nothing in him worthy of death? But who were they that cried out the more: "Crucify him! crucify him?" The high priests, and the members of the Sanhedrim, and the multitudinous Jewish rabble. Again, by whom were many of the apostles killed? By whom was the sainted Stephen stoned to death? Was it not by the infuriated members of the Jewish Church? By whom did the pure, holy, consecrated followers of Jesus, in the dark and middle ages, suffer persecution and martyrdom by hundreds and multiplied thousands? Was it not by the Church of Rome? Coming to our own country, during the civil war, did not many faithful Christian ministers and laymen of the M. E. Church, South, suffer cruel persecution, the destruction of all their earthly possessions, banishment, imprisonment, and death by her sister Church of the same origin and name?

Here we would gladly let the curtain fall, if by so doing it would blot out forever the terrible history of the internecine war; but this it cannot do, for history is a true record of facts, and is as inextinguishable, indestructible as truth itself.

It would be unpardonable ingratitude to deny those faithful servants of God who withstood evil, and suffered persecution to the last and to the death, to refuse them a place in the history of that Church they loved dearer than life, and in whose cause they sacrificed their all. They deserve to have an imperishable monument as high as heaven in honor of their Christian heroism. Their names should live in the Church of Christ until time shall be no more.

While we have no disposition whatever to excite unkiud or unchristian feelings on the part of any person or persons, fidelity to truth and justice requires the statements of facts and events just as they occurred, uninfluenced by partiality or prejudice, though the facts may be very revolting to our feelings. Indeed, truth, and not feeling, should be the controlling principle of the historian. He should give a correct statement of things as they actually occurred—good or bad, right or wrong, virtuous or vicious. The bad should be told as well as the good, let the truth hit whom it may. Such is Biblical history. It records a man's vices as well as his virtues, his bad deeds as well as his good ones. The eminent position of the person, though highly distinguished for his moral rectitude and Christian character, does not protect him. When Abraham, the father of the faithful, and the friend of God, and the most illustrious person in the Old Testament Scriptures, under the pressure of very peculiar circumstances, prevaricated, the Bible did not withhold the fact, but published it to the world. When the pious and devout David unwarily yielded to temptation, and committed two of the worst sins in the moral code, the word of God exposed his guilt, and not until deep, thorough, and genuine repentance did he realize his restoration to the divine favor. Profane history should be no less impartial and truthful than sacred history.

Let it be understood that this historian did not make the bloody history of wail and woe, of carnage and death, but it becomes his duty to write it after it has been made by others, whose boastful language was: "We are making history." This, too, was in connection with the cruel persecution of the M. E. Church, South, which, as a Church, was unsectional, unpolitical, and loyal to the Constitution and government of our country. There were some exceptions, but most of them were driven by persecution to the necessity of joining the Confederates for personal safety. Yes, hundreds went to Price's army because it was death to stay at home. Their loyalty to the constitutional government of the country was no protection.

MISSOURI CONFERENCE.

Bishop Kavanaugh held the Forty-fifth Session of the Missouri Annual Conference at St. Charles, Mo., September 12-19, 1860. The Conference was opened with religious service, conducted by the presiding officer. Rev. E. K. Miller was elected Secretary. W. T. Luckey, O. P. Noble, Jacob McEwin, Adolphus Green, Isaac Kelsoe, Thomas F. C. James, William C. Martin, James M. Tutt, Samuel Alexander, Walter C. Fowler, E. McKendree Bounds, and Joseph Card were admitted on trial. William H. Albright, William Collett, O. R. Bouton, Edward H. Hudson, Jacob Agee, Henry B. Watson, Henry G. McEwin, and Henry H. Dodd remained on trial. Admitted into full connection: George W. Penn, Norman P. Halsey, John F. Shore, Robert M. Leaton, John Stone, John R. Taylor, Robert R. Baldwin. The following traveling preachers were elected and ordained deacons: George W. Penn, Norman P. Halsey, John F. Shores, Robert M. Leaton, John R. Taylor, Robert R. Baldwin, and Wesley W. McMurry. Traveling preachers elected and ordained elders: William A. Tarwater, David R. Shackelford, Jesse Faubion, John W. Penn. Local preachers elected and ordained deacons: Thomas F. C. James, Orin R. Bouton, William C. Martin. Local preacher elected and ordained elder: William White.

Rev. Benjamin S. Ashby was reported in reply to the question, "Who died this year?" and the following is his memoir as read before the Conference:

BENJAMIN ASHBY was a native of Kentucky. We know nothing definitely of his early history, except that he emigrated to Missouri in 1818, being then about twenty-one years of age. At this time he was a licensed local preacher, and came to Missouri with the intention of entering at once the traveling connection; but his aged, widowed mother coming soon after, he deferred entering upon the itinerant work until he had provided for her comfort. In 1823 he received his first appointment to the New Madrid Circuit; in 1824, La Mine; 1825, Cedar Creek; 1826, St. Louis Circuit; 1827 and 1828, Buffalo; 1829, Fishing River. In 1830 he received a superannuated relation, in which relation he continued until he located in the year 1834. In 1845 he was readmitted into the traveling connection, and was appointed to the Brunswick District. In 1846 and 1847 he traveled the Keytesville Circuit; in 1848 was stationed at Palmyra; in 1849, Portland Circuit; in 1850 and 1851, the Richmond District; in 1852 and 1853 he traveled the Savannah District; in 1854, stationed at Clarksville and Paynesville; in 1855, stationed at Canton. In 1856 he was appointed as supernumerary to Brunswick Station; in 1857 his strength was so far exhausted that he took a superannuated relation, which relation he retained until his death. He was a delegate to the General Conference in 1854, and was noted for the soundness of his judgment and the practical character of his views on all matters upon which he was called to deliberate. Brother Ashby was a zealous, faithful preacher; in the pulpit he was always sound, instructive, and sometimes powerful. He was a man of prayer, being much on his knees in private as well as in public. On Wednesday, August 29, 1860, he preached twice, delivering his last sermon on Matthew xi. 28, 29. Near the close of the sermon he was greatly blessed; related his experience, regretting all unfaithfulness; he affirmed that if he had a thousand lives he would give them all to the ministry; and that he would like to die at the altar of God. The following day he was apparently in the enjoyment of his usual health, attending Church morning and night. After the sermon in the evening he talked with the penitents for nearly an hour. It was intimated to him that it was time to close. He answered that it was, but that he wanted to pray first. The hymn being concluded, he called upon the congregation to join him in prayer. He led the prayer till near its close, when he was observed to pause a moment, and then to attempt to speak, but his voice was faint as one going to sleep. He fell to the floor. The attack was thought to be epilepsy. In twenty minutes he so far revived as to be able to swallow a little water, and with much effort to speak a few words, but was soon taken with another spasm, in which, for a few minutes, he appeared to be in great distress. But this soon passed off, and at fifteen minutes past twelve o'clock, on the morning of the 31st, he slept in Jesus without a struggle or a groan. His remains were interred at Keytesville.

The Conference session was a pleasant one. The preachers made encouraging reports from their respective fields of labor. God had been with them during the year, making the word preached by them his own power in the salvation of the people. Revivals were numerous and extensive throughout the bounds of the Conference. They reported a membership of 17,717, with an increase over last year of 1,516. God smiled upon them, and they had a prosperous and happy year in the delightful work of preaching the gospel and saving souls. But when the Conference adjourned they went to their new appointments with no little anxiety and forebodings. Future trouble was brewing. They saw a dark and portentous cloud rising in the political horizon of our country; already vivid flashes of lightning could be seen, and the roar of coarse and pealing thunder could be heard, louder and louder, indicating the approach of the war cloud. Nor were they mistaken. They soon realized their fearful apprehensions, as we shall see in the history of the Church during the internecine war. It is a well-known fact that the preachers of the M. E. Church, South, who had charge of Churches in Missouri did, during the Civil War, confine themselves to their pulpit ministrations and pastoral duties, and did all in their power to promote kind feeling, peace, and harmony in their congregations and among the people with whom they lived. So far as the knowledge of this writer extends, the subject of politics was not mentioned in their pulpits. Their influence in the Church and in the community was against disorder and strife, and in favor of public peace.

The following remarks of another will be read with interest:

The *St. Louis Christian Advocate*, edited by Rev. D. R. McAnally, D.D., contained a series of very able editorials, running through April and a part of May, 1861, on "The Times," "The Duty of Christian Men," "The Time for Prayer," "To the Ministers and Members of the M. E. Church, South, in Missouri and Kansas," "A Word to Our Patrons and Friends," and kindred topics, in which the people were warned of the character of the danger that threatened, advised to remain at home, cultivate their lands, and pursue their avocations of peace and piety in the fear of God as the best means of promoting good order in the State.

How much of suffering might have been prevented and how many thousands of valuable lives might have been spared to the country, to say nothing of the millions of treasure, had the advice of that paper been taken and the timely warnings of its honored editor been heeded!

Dr. McAnally's ideas of right and wrong, of truth and error, of justice and righteousness, were derived from the old standard. He had no patience with the new standard of virtue that grew out of party fanaticism and war expediencies; new-fangled notions, dissimulations, prevarication, and moral travesty "he could not away with it." He had not so learned the responsibilities of public journalism, and hence his simple-hearted appreciation of right led him to expose the wrong wherever it existed. His honesty required him to expose the wide-spread dishonesty of the times. His simple love of truth caused him to make honest and truthful reports of the " news of the week " according to the actual facts, without reference to the interest of this party or that party, this army or that, this commanding officer or that. In this his paper presented such a contrast with the press generally that it was sought and read by thousands of both parties, and accepted by the unprejudiced as the most reliable paper then published. But, *because* it was truthful, and honest, and candid, and popular, and reliable, it was pronounced disloyal and dangerous; and because it would not serve the cause of cruelty, confiscation, conflagration, desolation, and destruction; and, with the venom of a viper, hound on the barbarous hordes with fire and sword to the commission of the foulest deeds of war; nor with sanctimonious hypocrisy sanctify the implements and instruments of blood and death and canonize the vilest thieves, and robbers, and murderers— for these reasons the paper was set down by the enemies of the M. E. Church, South, as in the interest of treason and rebellion, and *by them* the military authorities were induced to suppress the paper, and arrest and imprison its editor. Of his arrest and long confinement in the Myrtle Street Military Prison, St. Louis, the reader will be more fully informed hereafter.*

The ministers of the Southern Methodist Church not only kept themselves aloof from the political strife of the country, but appointed days of public humiliation and prayer, that the evils of war might be averted and peace and tranquillity might be restored to the entire country. This writer directs the attention of the reader to the *St. Louis Christian Advocate* of June 13, 1861:

---

*Dr. Leftwich's book.

FASTING AND PRAYER.

To the Ministers and Members of the M. E. Church, South, in the Missouri and St. Louis Conferences.

Dear Brethren and Sisters: Whereas our once happy and prosperous country is now involved in the calamities of a civil war, which threatens ruin to all our cherished hopes and interests; and whereas God alone, in the exercise of his sovereign and gracious dispensations, can avert the terrible evil; and as he has promised to be inquired of by those that fear him, and to interpose for those who reverently and submissively supplicate his mercy and seek his divine interposition, it therefore becomes to every Christian community both a high privilege and solemn duty, in such times of serious and alarming trials, humbly and reverently to prostrate themselves before the mercy-seat and supplicate the aid and deliverance which God only can afford.

And as I have been requested by many ministers and laymen of both Conferences (in view of my seniority as a minister) to designate and recommend a day of fasting and prayer, I would, therefore, most respectfully recommend that Wednesday, the third day of July, be set apart and observed for this solemn purpose, and that appropriate religious services be held in all our places of worship; and, in accordance with the expressed wishes of many, and, as I think, in accordance with manifest propriety, I tender most cordially, and in behalf of the whole Church, an invitation to all Christian people of the State to unite with us on that day, humbly and devoutly to supplicate in behalf of our common country that God, who can turn the hearts of men as the streams in the South, would forgive our sins and in his merciful providence hasten the return of peace to our country, our entire country.

ANDREW MONROE.

Fayette, Mo., June 5, 1861.

The undersigned do most cordially approve the above proposition, and earnestly recommend its observance throughout the State.

JOSEPH BOYLE
E. M. MARVIN,
H. S. WATTS,
P. M. PINCKARD.

St. Louis, Mo., June 12, 1861.

The call of the ministers upon the Christian

people to earnest and importunate prayer all over the State of Missouri was repeated again and again. Nor was the call made in vain. There was a cordial and hearty response by the lovers of the Church and the true followers of Christ in every section of the country. What a sublime scene to contemplate! See the embassadors of Christ, who had consecrated themselves to the service of God, who had placed their lives and their all upon his sacred altar to *do* or to *suffer* the divine will, whatever that will might be, assembled with the religious people to whom they had preached the gospel of peace and with whom they had worshiped many years, for the purpose of supplicating mercy and invoking the favor of God, that he would turn back the war-cloud, speak to the belligerent elements, quell the infuriated passions of men, stop the war, and restore peace to Zion and to their beloved country. Was it not a sublime scene to contemplate? They were moved by the grandest motives, religious and patriotic, that ever stirred the human heart. Behold them in convocations throughout the State, with Christians of other denominations, met to pray for the salvation of the Church and of the country—the best country and the best civil government in the world.

The foregoing remarks have suggested to our mind three topics of the deepest interest to every Christian, to every patriot, and to every philanthropist—viz., our country, our government, and our religion—and as they are mutually dependent and clearly interwoven with each other, we ask the indulgence of the reader to speak of these topics respectively at some length.

In the first place, God has given us the best civil government in the world. Here the writer may premise that the government is one thing and the administration of the government is quite another thing. The government may be very much abused when it falls into the hands of selfish, ambitious, and unrighteous men. They may trample upon its laws and disregard its authority, and misuse its power. Let it be understood that this writer is speaking of the government and not of its administration.

The reader will no doubt assent to his proposition that it is incomparably superior to any other civil government in the world. That government which recognizes the sovereignty of God, and yields obedience to the divine authority of the Bible, and incorporates in its Constitution the cardinal principles of Christianity, is beyond all controversy the model government of the world. It is a government of truth, justice, and honesty, "rendering unto Cæsar the things which are Cæsar's, and unto God the things which are God's"—a government that recognizes the freedom of man and protects him in the exercise of his inalienable rights.

Nowhere in the world is civil liberty, which is the birthright of every man, enjoyed as it is in the

United States. Ours is not only the home of the brave, but also the land of the free. In no other country has the tree of liberty grown to such gigantic dimensions, sheltering beneath its widespread branches and shady foliage 65,000,000 people.

This government has no castes, but gives to every man an equal chance with every other man. It stimulates him to noble deeds and urges him onward to life's high aim and ends. He can advance from the humblest position in society to the highest office in the government. To be a citizen of the United States is enough to inspire in him the loftiest aspirations for what is noble and great. We admire the government that develops the manhood of its citizens and elevates them to their proper position in the scale of God's intellectual and moral creatures. We are happy to say that such is our government when not perverted by corrupt men and designing politicians. The danger that seriously threatens the safety of our government is in that direction.

The munificent donor of all blessings has also given us the greatest country in the world, a second Canaan, almost boundless in extent, stretching across the continent from ocean to ocean, measuring thousands of miles in all directions, with a rich and productive soil of incomparable fertility. In the precious metals and in rich mineral resources, where can you find such another country? The United States furnish one-half the gold and silver of the world. In one year they produced gold enough to make five car-loads and silver enough for one hundred car-loads. Coal is abundant almost everywhere, in mines inexhaustible. It seems to be imbedded under the surface of our entire country—fuel enough to meet all demands for many centuries to come. In this we see the good providence of God in providing for us in such great abundance that which is so essential to our present comfort and future prosperity. Iron, too, the most useful of all metals, is found in every State in the Union. In Missouri there are hills and mountains of iron, which can never be exhausted. The abundance of iron is another demonstration of the goodness of God. Lead is very plentiful in some of the States. Missouri produced in one year 63,000,000 pounds of lead.

Look at our magnificent rivers, one of which is the longest in the world, affording steam-boat navigation for more than three thousand miles. Look, too, at our vast prairies and woodlands, and grand and majestic forests, supplying the country with all kinds of timber. Look, too, at the agricultural productions of the country—grains, fruits, hogs, cattle, horses, and other domestic animals, in quantities defying all computation.

God has also exalted us as a nation, in many respects, above all the other nations of the earth. The English-speaking people, or the Anglo-Saxon race, is unquestionably in the lead of nations, while the American people, on account of their superiority, are in the lead of every other branch of the Anglo-Saxons. Great Britain herself must yield the palm to America, for the daughter has outgrown her mother. The American people have no equal in enterprise, energy, and push. They move rapidly, with an increasing momentum. Steam and electricity suit them exactly, because they are quick and powerful. Speed and power are the prime factors of their triumphant success. By steam they travel a mile a minute—faster than the wind, unless it be a tornado. By electricity they send their messages with the speed of lightning. Steam has taken the place of working-men and animals. It is harnessed and hitched to all kinds of machines, and does all kinds of work. It has thrown hundreds and thousands of men out of employment, and has taken the bread out of the poor man's mouth.

The progress of the United States, in developing the vast resources of this country, is without a parallel in the history of the world. How sluggish and inactive have other nations been—sometimes slowly advancing, sometimes stationary, and sometimes retrograding—each successive generation moving in the same groove and living as their ancestors did five hundred or a thousand years before them. China—fossilized and petrified China—claims an existence of several thousand years, and is now, with a few changes, what she always has been. The rapid progress of the United States has attracted the attention of other countries. Mr. Hatton, of England, says: "Ten years in the history of America is half a century in European progress." This shows the superiority of our people and of our country. In the first place, the country possesses all the resources they need to make them a great nation. In the second place, they are developing those resources with a speed and power hitherto unknown to the world. For their manufactories they have an exhaustless supply of coal to convert water into steam. The country also produces the raw material to be manufactured. They do not have to import them from distant countries. Dr. Strong says: "England has to travel three thousand miles for every cotton ball she spins." But we have the cotton at home; also the wool, the hemp, the flax, the metals, all kinds of wood. Indeed, it is difficult to tell what we have not.

Then, too, the mechanics and operatives in the factories and in all the industries of the country are a superior class of workmen. They are all the time improving machinery, and making important inventions and discoveries. It is stated that "at the International Electrical Exposition at Paris, a few years ago, five gold medals were offered for the greatest inventions and discoveries." In this contest the nations of the civilized world were represented. How many of the five gold medals do you suppose were awarded to those who went from this country? Just five! Yes, the United States, in competition with the world, took all the gold medals at Paris for inventions and discoveries! We stated that Great Britain must yield the palm to America. Now for the proof: We learn from reliable authority that our mining industries exceed those of Great Britain three per cent.; that the products of our manufactories in 1880 were greater than those of Great Britain by $650,-000,000; that the United States Government issues four times as many patents as the English; that our wealth exceeds hers by $276,000,000. To which, therefore, belongs the prize banner of the world? The question has already been answered. Well may the stars and stripes proudly wave over every land and sea to earth's remotest bounds!

All that has been said in the foregoing remarks relates to the material wealth and prosperity of our nation. At the same time the American people have not neglected their more important national interests of education and Christian civilization. Nowhere in the world is education more liberally patronized. Intelligence and virtue are the cornerstones of our civil government and the palladium of our country. In monarchical and despotic countries the people belong to the government. They are the mere serfs and slaves of their monarchs and despots, and the more ignorant they are the better subjects they make. But in this country it is just the reverse. Here the government belongs to the people. *Vox populi* is sovereign, to which all must yield obedience. The people appoint their officers from the village squire to the President. They make their laws through their representatives. In short, they make the government what it is. Hence the necessity of intelligence and virtue for the perpetuity and prosperity of our free institutions.

Though there is great corruption and wickedness in the country, yet we believe that we have the best type of Christian civilization in the world. Our religious ideas are more Biblical, purer, less mixed with rationalism, materialism, and the vain philosophy of wicked men. Our Christianity is more spiritual and less ritualistic. In many parts of Christendom religion has degenerated into ecclesiasticism and ritualism—nothing left but the shell. When Christianity loses its spirituality, all is lost—God, Jesus Christ, the Holy Spirit, and all saving power are lost. It becomes the religion of man without God—a name, a shadow, a fantastic farce!

The American people, however wicked, believe in a spiritual Christianity more than any other people in the world. Many of them not only believe in it, but possess it and enjoy it. God is with them to bless, renovate, purify, and exalt them to their proper position in the scale of his intellectual and moral creatures. Is not this the secret of our national elevation? Is not this the power behind the throne? Is it not righteousness that exalteth a nation? Then look not to material wealth, to gold and silver, to inexhaustible mines of mineral treasures, not to systems of railroads and telegraphy, not to steam and electricity for the perpetuation of our national greatness. For moral and political corruption will inevitably undermine the whole fabric without a spiritual Christianity—the only power in the world that can reconstruct man and make him good, honest, pure, just, and upright. Christianity is our only sheet-anchor.

Under the auspices of heaven and in the good providence of God we have become a mighty people. America is the brightest star that sparkles in the galaxy of nations, but our only safety is a pure, high Christian civilization, in which God is known, loved, feared, and obeyed. Then we shall not fear the surging billows of political corruption and strife; for God will say: "Thus far shalt thou go, and no farther." "Happy is that people whose God is the Lord."

The citizens of Missouri suffered perhaps more along the border line of Kansas than in any other part of the State. Some time before the war the people of Kansas manifested a strong feeling of prejudice against Missouri because she was a slave State. After the war began some of them gave unrestrained indulgence to their ill feelings. During the war they had an opportunity of showing their base character. Their meanness was no longer concealed. They were destitute of all principle and all human feeling, ready for the work of destruction and death. They were familiarly known by the name of "Red Legs" and "Kansas Jayhawkers." They organized into bands of freebooters and brigands, and made frequent raids in the border counties of Missouri, to rob, to plunder, and to kill. Destitution, suffering, and sorrow followed in their wake. They left behind them desolated hearts and homes. They seemed to take pleasure in persecuting Southern Methodist preachers, as you may learn from a letter to the *St. Louis Christian Advocate* by Rev. N. Scarritt, whose integrity cannot be doubted, and who was presiding elder at that time. He thus writes:

> In addition to this, some of our preachers in the southern portion of the Conference have been compelled to quit the field and leave their work for the present, on account of the violence of civil strife, so prevalent in that section.
>
> Our preachers there have taken no part in the political questions that are involving the country in so much trouble. They have been peaceable, law-abiding citizens, leaving politics alone and devoting themselves exclusively to the peaceable work of preaching the peace-making gospel of the Prince of Peace.
>
> Yet, though this has been their known and acknowledged character, it has not been sufficient to protect them from the rage of fanaticism and outlawed violence. Several of them have had their horses stolen from them by the "Jayhawkers." Repeated threats of hanging, shooting, etc., have been made against them; though no attempt, so far as we know, has been made in the form of any overt act.

There is a brief editorial in the *St. Louis Christian Advocate* of July 25, giving information of the sad state of affairs already existing in the country. It reads as follows:

> TRAVELING PREACHERS.
>
> We are sad, sad indeed, when we think of the privations and

sufferings of many of the traveling preachers of our Church in Missouri during these troublous times. The treatment some of them have received has been severe, not to say cruel. Bad men have sought to implicate them in measures with which they have had nothing to do, and have them annoyed and distressed merely that private *piques* and personal animosities might be gratified. A number have been driven literally from their work, either by the malice of their enemies or by want. We have at present only a word to say: We hope the preachers will remain at their work to the fullest possible extent, reproving, exhorting, comforting, etc., with all long-suffering and kindness. In these times we must all suffer more or less, and let us suffer with our people, and be sure that we suffer for righteousness' sake, and not as evil-doers. God rules, and they that serve him in spirit and in truth shall find him a very present help in time of trouble.

CHAPTER II.

St. Louis Conference.

Signs of the Times Indicate Something Serious in the Near Future—Public Mind in a State of Excitement—The Annual Conferences of M. E. Church, South, Recommend a Day of Fasting, Humiliation, and Prayer—Convocation of Ministers and Members of Different Christian Denominations at St. Charles, to Promote Peace—Session of St. Louis Annual Conference—Death of Revs. J. A. Cumming and J. W. Hawkins—Ministers of M. E. Church, South, Special Objects of Persecution—Their Being Preachers of That Church the Only Charge against Them—Cannot Omit History of Our Church During the War—Persecution of Revs. D. J. Marquis, J. B. H. Wooldridge, J. Ditzler, the Great Debater, M. Arrington, and J. McCary.

THIS Conference, as well as the Missouri Annual Conference, met in the fall of 1860 preceding the commencement of the Civil War in the spring of 1861. Of course evidences of the coming trouble existed everywhere throughout the country, and the public mind was in a state of feverish excitement. The signs of the times certainly indicated something serious in the near future; therefore the Annual Conferences of the M. E. Church, South, in the fall of 1860, recommended to all Christian people the observance of a " day of fasting, humiliation, and prayer" for the peace of the country and the amicable adjustment of existing difficulties. This fact of itself shows unquestionably that the ministers of the M. E. Church,

South, as a body or class, were in favor of peace and against war; that they were unsectional, unpolitical, and non-combatant. We need not say that they sustained this character during the entire war. They never desecrated their pulpits with the discussion of political questions.

This unpolitical spirit not only existed among the preachers of the M. E. Church, South, but also among ministers of other Christian denominations as well. In order to give an expression of their harmony and unanimity of feeling on this subject they assembled with the ministers of the M. E. Church, South, in the city of St. Charles, Mo., May 21, 1861, and after religious service they adopted the following:

Whereas in the providence of God our country is now involved in a civil war, which has already brought upon us many calamities, and still threatens to introduce a state of ill-will, discord, and desolation utterly inconsistent with our condition as a Christian land; therefore,

1. *Resolved*, That we together on this day, in the fear of God and with a firm reliance on his divine providence as a Christian people, members of the respective Churches in this city, observe such means as will at least tend to promote good-will among ourselves during the continuance of the war.

2. That we regard all war as a sore calamity, contrary to the spirit and teaching of the gospel; and more especially a civil war, as revolting to our Christian teaching, unnatural, abhorrent to all our religious instincts, and subversive of the cause of Christ, whose blessed mission was to establish peace on earth.

3. That as ministers of the Christian Churches, irrespective of private opinions, we hereby pledge ourselves one to another, ministers and people, to abstain as far as possible from all bitter and exciting controversy upon the questions now agitating the public mind; but will, each within the sphere of our influence, endeavor

to promote a spirit of brotherly love, and by calm and judicious counsel, animated by the spirit of Christ our peaceful Master, suppress every act among ourselves which may have the tendency to increase the present difficulties.

4. That we call upon the Christians of our land to band together to stay, if possible, the further shedding of fraternal blood, etc.

5. That we will not forget our best refuge—prayer, and therefore humble ourselves before God, and supplicate our heavenly Father to quell the madness of the people, and put away from us "all bitterness, and anger, and clamor, and evil speaking," and animate us with the gentle spirit of "peace on earth and good-will toward men."

We have given the above because we believe that it expressed the general sentiment and feeling of all the Churches in Missouri, and we are satisfied that if they had had their way, and could have controlled the affairs of the country, there would not have been a civil war. And just because they preferred peace to war on Christian principles they were denounced and proscribed as rebels, secessionists, and enemies of the Government, and without trial, judge, or jury sentence of condemnation was passed upon them; and we shall see, in pursuing the history of the M. E. Church, South, in Missouri during the Civil War, how they were treated. We cannot do otherwise than follow our Church through the days and years of her fierce and fiery persecution.

The session of the St. Louis Annual Conference was held at St. Louis, Mo., October 10–20, 1860, Bishop Kavanaugh presiding. Rev. W. M. Prottsman was elected Secretary.

George Schaffnit, William M. Patterson, John

Campbell, Charles C. Woods, William M. Williams, Stewart C. Stratton, William C. Godbey, James H. Dulany, John H. Wade, David I. Harris, Norval Davis, and Calvin C. Wright were admitted on trial. Stephen A. Blakey, G. W. Horn, T. M. L. Bedsworth, and A. C. Morrow remained on trial. Leonidas H. Boyle, Theophilus G. Atchison, J. C. B. Renfro, David M. Proctor, Jacob H. Cox, Turner W. Davis, and Wiley B. Quinn were admitted into full connection, and were elected and ordained deacons. John P. Barneby, M. M. Pugh, John R. Hall, James Copeland, and William F. Lowe were re-admitted. William M. Compton, John A. Murphy, Stephen A. Ritchie, Turner W. Davis, George C. Knowles, Lucilius F. Aspley, and William D. Stewart were deacons of one year. The local preachers—John D. Kruse, David J. Harris, Calvin E. Wright, J. H. Bottom, J. H. Wade, and J. D. Davison—were elected and ordained deacons. The following traveling preachers were elected and ordained elders: Joseph W. Lewis, Henry W. Webster, John P. Phelps, E. H. White, and John F. Pearson.

The Committee on Memoirs read the following two:

James A. Cumming was born in Buncombe County, N. C., November 23, 1826. Of his early opportunities and boyhood peculiarities we know but little. His father being a preacher, it may be inferred that his mind was early impressed with religious truth, and that his home education gave to his character the elements of that eminent personal piety which matured in after life. He embraced religion at an early age, and became a member of the Methodist Church. In 1849 (July 14) he was licensed to preach, and was admitted into the Indian Mission Conference on October 28 of the same year. His first work was among the Indians on the Shawnee and Delaware Mission. He speaks frequently in his journal of the embarrassments and difficulties of his work, arising from his want of experience and the process of reaching the Indians through interpreters. By the change of boundary lines he fell into the St. Louis Conference, in which he ended his days. Having given himself to the itinerant work, and feeling the spirit of a divine call to the ministry, he ever stood before the Conference, saying: "Here am I; send me." How willingly and cheerfully he went to his work, and how patiently and heroically he endured hardness and suffered affliction, those who labored with him and knew his spirit can testify. His labors were blessed to the Church on West Point Mission, Osceola, Columbus, Neosho, Deep Water, Potosi, and Ste. Genevieve Circuits, and none rejoiced more than he when the Lord prospered the work of his hands. Brother Cumming was everywhere acceptable to the Church, and labored efficiently for the advancement of all her interests. He inherited much of the spirit of his father, the Rev. David B. Cumming, and tried to do all the work of a Methodist preacher. His personal piety was deep, earnest, and consistent. Indeed, to lead a holy life himself, and teach others so to do, was the controlling principle of his character. He was prudent and discreet in all his intercourse with the world, and sought studiously to give none occasion to offend, feeling that "while all things were lawful to him," yet "all things were not expedient." If one term could distinguish his character and describe it to the world, that term is "love." He approximated as nearly the fulfillment of the law and prophets as any man perhaps of the St. Louis Conference. As a preacher he was successful. Turning not aside for the accommodation of any false or corrupt tastes, and catering not to the vagaries of popular fancy, he expounded the word of God faithfully and pointedly, making it "quick and powerful" upon the sinner's heart and hopefully inspiring the Christian's faith. He "studied to show himself approved unto God, a workman that needeth not to be ashamed." He was just making character as a *preacher*, under discouragements and afflictions, when the hand of death marked him for its victim; and ere the strength of maturity had crowned the *preacher* an inscrutable

Providence removed the *saint*. He left a journal of his ministerial career, which confines its records mostly to facts that may be gathered from the published Minutes of the Conference, except the spirit of humility and resignation to the will of God under severe and protracted afflictions.

John Wesley Hawkins was born in Gibson County, Ind., December 3, 1826. He emigrated with his father to Gasconade County, Mo., in the autumn of 1841. In 1844, under the ministry of J. R. Burk, he professed faith in Christ and joined the Methodist Church. He was licensed to preach in July, 1848, and in the autumn of the same year was admitted on trial in the St. Louis Annual Conference. Having voluntarily entered the itinerant ministry, he sought no favors at the hands of the Conference, but was ever ready to go whither the appointing power might direct. The Church was blessed with his godly labors on Thomasville Mission, Steelville Mission, Charleston Circuit, Benton Circuit, Ste. Genevieve Circuit, Wolf Island Circuit, Cape Girardeau Circuit, Christy Chapel Station, St. Louis, and Springfield Station—at the latter place two years. He was always well received and highly appreciated as a preacher and as a Christian gentleman. On the 9th of May, 1858, while in his pulpit in Springfield, preaching "Jesus Christ and him crucified," in the holy effort of warning sinners to "flee from the wrath to come," he felt his nervous system give way and sat down, assured that his work was done. He traveled South, and wasted away slowly with consumption until December 3, 1858, when he calmly fell asleep in Jesus. He died at the residence of Dr. J. W. Sullivan, in Monroe County, Ark. He was a true son of John Wesley, not only inheriting his name, but much of the spirit of ardor and consecration to the work of the ministry which characterized that great man. He was a sound, practical, gospel preacher, depending not upon the showy tinsel of ornament to attract, but the power of gospel truth to enlighten, convict, and convert the sinner's heart. In his hands the gospel was "the power of God unto salvation," and the day of eternity will disclose the success of his ministry in every field of labor in the conversion and salvation of souls, that will be his crown of rejoicing forever. He combined the elements of a humble, intelligent, courteous, Christian gentleman in all the private walks and relations of life; with the dignity, urbanity, and catholicity of an evangelical Christian minister.

With the beginning of the Civil War, in the spring of 1861, commenced the persecution of the ministers of the gospel. It seems to have been the fixed purpose of those in authority, and who had the management of the war, to rid Missouri of all the preachers who did not take sides with them in that sanguinary and destructive conflict. You would infer from the way they acted that their idea was to exterminate the last one of them. With a well-concerted plan their special aim seemed to be against the preachers of the M. E. Church, South. With no mercy, no relenting, but with cruel hate, they persecuted them in every way their inventive genius could devise. This is very strong language, but the facts are much stronger than the language. Indeed, language is wholly inadequate to do the subject justice. These persecuted preachers, too, were all the time law-abiding and peaceable citizens, and the only charge they brought against them was that they were ministers of the M. E. Church, South, and *would preach the gospel without their permission*. As already stated, their names certainly merit a prominent place in the history of "Methodism in Missouri." Some persons may be ready to ask: "Why don't you pass over the troubles of the war, and leave them out?" If we were to do so, our Church would have but little history for that period of time, because the persecution of the M. E. Church, South, constitutes the major part of her history during the Civil War.

Revs. D. J. Marquis and J. B. H. Wooldridge, of

the St. Louis Conference, had the honor of being among the first to suffer persecution for Christ's sake, an account of which is given by another as follows:

In 1861, soon after the occupation of Jefferson City by the Federal forces, these two men were arrested by Col. Boernstein's order, or by his officers, at Tipton, in Moniteau County; taken to Jefferson City, abused by the officers, kept in the dungeon under the State Capitol over twenty-four hours without a mouthful of food, taken out, abused, put on board a steamer, and sent up to Boonville. They were put into the hands of Col. Stevenson, who had them closely guarded in the fair-grounds for ten days, and then sent to St. Louis. Here they were kept for two days in the guard-house in the old arsenal, and then released unconditionally, by order of Maj.-Gen. Fremont.

The only charge against Marquis was that he was a minister of the Southern Methodist Church, and kept company with Wooldridge. They charged Wooldridge with keeping company with Southern Methodist ministers who were known to be disloyal. The old adage that "evil communications corrupt good manners" is scarcely a criminal law, and the associations of ministers of the gospel in their legitimate work can hardly be considered a criminal offense, involving the safety of the Federal government. And yet these humble ministers were subjected to arrest, insult, imprisonment, hunger, abuse, and various tortures of body and mind, for no other reason than their ecclesiastical connection and ministerial association in promoting the kingdom of Christ on earth.

While Mr. Marquis was attending the Warrensburg-Arrow Rock-Waverly Conference, in the fall of 1861, his home was taken and used for a hospital and literally stripped of every thing of any value—even the clothing of himself and family—leaving not a single change of raiment for any of them. This act of plunder and robbery was done by Gen. Fremont's men, upon the charge that Marquis was a Southern Methodist minister, and had no rights.

Believing that his life was not safe in Moniteau, he removed to Jefferson County; where he was still subject to persecution during the war, and where he had the honor of an indictment from the grand jury, after the war closed, for preaching the gospel without taking the oath prescribed by the new Constitution of the State, which was pronounced illegal by the Supreme Court of the United States.*

In 1860 and 1861 the Rev. J. Ditzler, the great debater, who was stationed at Jefferson City, found himself very unexpectedly in the hands of the military authorities, as the reader may see in the following statement:

After Gov. Jackson and Gen. Price had evacuated the State capital, and the United States forces under Gen. Lyon had taken possession, Mr. Ditzler remained as a non-combatant, supposing that he would not be molested. In this he was mistaken. He was not allowed to remain long in his quiet study at the Ferguson House, or to attend to his pastoral duties. An "orderly," with a guard of seven men, called on him at the Ferguson House, arrested and marched him through the city, and put him with others in an old meat-house. He was taunted and sneered at by his guard—the Dutch—through the cracks of the old log house. Mr. Ditzler talked back to them in German, Italian, Spanish, French, Greek, and Hebrew, quoting freely from Schiller, Goethe, and other German authors of note, for his own relief and their amusement, until he was reported to Col. Boernstein, post commander, and by him unconditionally released, solely upon literary grounds. No charges were preferred against him, nor could he ever find out why he was imprisoned. His father fought at Tippecanoe in 1812, and his grandfather at Valley Forge under Washington, and this treatment was not borne without some little indignation.

Brig.-Gen. Brown succeeded Col. Boernstein, and Mr. Ditzler was apprised of the purpose to re-arrest him. He was advised by his friends to flee, and accordingly took the train late Saturday night for St. Louis; and at noon the next day (Sabbath) a posse of ten armed soldiers entered his church to arrest him, but he was gone. They followed him to St. Louis, only to find that he had taken a train on the Ohio and Mississippi railroad.*

---

*Dr. Leftwich's book.

Rev. Marcus Arrington

was for many years a faithful and useful member of the St. Louis Annual Conference, M. E. Church, South. He endured hardness as a good soldier of Jesus Christ. In the Lord's service be bore the heat and burden of the day uncomplainingly and without a murmur. When he put his hands to the plow in the cultivation· of Immanuel's ground he did not look back. Through heat and cold, wet and dry, he pressed forward in the prosecution of his ministerial duties, regardless of trials and difficulties. Such being his life, of course he gained the confidence, the esteem, and love of all persons, saints and sinners.

Read his own account of his sufferings:

When the troubles commenced, in the spring of 1861, I was traveling the Springfield Circuit, St. Louis Conference. I was very particular not to say any thing, either publicly or privately, that would indicate that I was a partisan in the strife. I tried to attend to my legitimate work as a traveling preacher.

But after the war commenced, because I did not advocate the policy of the party in power, I was reported as a secessionist; and in the midst of the public excitement it was vain to attempt to counteract the report.

At the earnest solicitations of divers persons I took the oath of loyalty to the government. This, it was thought, would be sufficient. But we were mistaken. Soon after this my life was threatened by those who were in the employ of the Federal government, but they were, as I verily believe, providentially prevented from executing their threat.

After the battle of Oak Hills, or Wilson's Creek, July 10, 1861, it became my duty to do all I could for the relief of the sick and wounded, and because I did this I was assured that I had violated my oath of allegiance. I was advised by Union men (so called) that it would be unsafe for me to fall into the hands of Federal soldiers. Believing this to be true, when Gen. Fremont came to Springfield I went to Arkansas, as I think almost any man would have done under the circumstances.

While in Arkansas I met Brother W. S. Caples, who was acting chaplain to General Price. He requested me to take a chaplaincy in the army, informing me at the time that by an agreement between Gens. Fremont and Price all men who had taken the oath of loyalty as I did were released from its obligations.

In December, 1861, I was appointed by Gen. McBride chaplain of the Seventh Brigade, Missouri State Guard. In this capacity I remained with the army until the battle of Pea Ridge, March 7 and 8, 1862. On the second day of the battle, while in the discharge of my duty as chaplain, I was taken prisoner. Several chaplains, taken at the same time, were released on the field; but I was retained. I was made to walk to Springfield, a distance of eighty miles. We remained in Springfield one day and two nights; and while many prisoners who had previously taken the oath, as I had, were paroled to visit their families, I was denied the privilege.

We were then started off to Rolla, and although I had been assured that I would be furnished transportation it was a sad mistake, and I had to walk until I literally gave out. I cannot describe what I suffered on that trip. When we reached Rolla I was publicly insulted by the commander of the post.

From Rolla I was sent to St. Louis on the cars, lodged one night in the old McDowell College, and the next day sent to Alton, Ill. Whilst I was in Alton prison a correspondent of the *Republican*, writing over the name of "Leon," represented me as a "thief and perjured villain." I was kept in Alton prison until August 2, 1862, when I was released by a general order for the release of all chaplains.

I then went to St. Louis, and thence South, by way of Memphis, Tenn., in exile. I would have returned to Missouri after the war closed but for the restrictions put upon ministers of the gospel by the new Constitution.

Eternity alone will reveal what I have suffered in exile. The St. Louis Conference is properly my home, and her preachers have a warm place in my affections. They are very near my heart. May they ever be successful!

Rev. Josiah McCary

was also a member of the St. Louis Conference, M. E. Church, South. With many others he entertained the idea (which seems to have been a correct idea) that there was a well-understood arrangement to oust every Southern Methodist preacher in the State, particularly the most prominent and influential. He speaks for himself:

In my own case, some time in May, 1861, just before I reached one of my places of preaching, I was met by a friend who inquired if I was going to fill my appointment. I answered: "Yes." Said he: "I am informed that you will not." My answer was: "Your informant don't know." I went to the place, and delivered my message to a large and attentive congregation, which, when dismissed, retired peacefully from the house. Several of the people informed me that many threats had been made against me, and thought, from the tone of some, that an effort would have been made that day to take me out of the house, or to prevent my going into it. "What is the accusation against me?" I inquired. "Southern Methodist preacher and a Southern man" was the answer. "If this is my crime, I am ready to answer. If a man is to be punished for being born in any particular part of these United States, or to be condemned for belonging to any religious body whose sole aim is to benefit mankind, who, then, is safe when law and liberty are at an end? If he goes North, they kill him because he did not go North to be born; if he stays at home, or goes to the house of God to worship, they will kill him, and then rob his family."

At my next appointment every thing was ready, I was informed, for an assault upon me. Some young men requested me to permit them to arm themselves for my defense. This I refused. I went and preached the gospel of peace and salvation to the people, but no man rose up against me. The mob no doubt thought they were too weak to be successful, as the congregation was large.

In a short time after a company of about forty came to my house to hang me, so a messenger who informed me of their coming said. I plainly saw that there was but one hope or chance left me: that was to get out of their reach, which I did. I was driven away from my own house. In a short time my house was robbed of every thing valuable, breaking open trunks with axes, and carrying off their contents and blankets. In the dead of winter, in December, 1861, an armed band came in the night and burned my house to ashes. Then came the militia and tore down the corn-house and corn-pens on the premises, and carried off about two thousand bushels of corn, for which I have never received one cent. Mine was not the only case. The wrath and fury of the enemies of our preachers fell heavily on us all; in which many lost not only their property, but their lives, upon whose moral character no stain can be found. I have often remembered the word of the Lord to Cain: "The voice of thy brother's blood crieth to me from the ground."

After the close of the war I attended the Annual Conference of the M. E. Church, South, held at St. Louis, and was sent to Georgetown Circuit. I came at once, and got off the Pacific railroad at Dresden, Mo., where I was informed that very night by one who was dubbed "Governor of Pettis County" that if I attempted to preach on the circuit I would get into difficulties that I would not get out of very soon. I understood that my life would be taken. I went to my farm (or where my farm ought to have been), on Warrensburg Circuit, and under the test oath, as it was called, I was arrested for preaching the gospel.

Who would, who could have believed, until it actually did take place, that such instruments of torture should ever be invented in the State of Missouri by authority of law, so called, as have been put in operation to punish men for opinion's sake? One would have thought that not one man could be found who would be willing for his name to go down to posterity in the history of the times stained with so foul a blot as must forever rest upon the names of the men who took part in getting up and carrying forward the wicked schemes contemplated by the test oath. I have often thought, since many in our land have engaged so earnestly in plotting destruction against their countrymen, of the old Greek poet, who says:

> The eagle saw her breast was wounded sore;
> She stood and weeped much, but grieved no more;
> But when she saw the dart was feathered, said:
> "Woe's me, for my own kind hath me destroyed."

Yes, our own countrymen! There is one comfort to me after

all. I would rather lose all I have lost and suffer all I have suffered than to be the man of such wicked contrivance to bring suffering on others. Little and unknown let me live, and let me die rather than go down to the grave with the consciousness of having lived to inflict injury upon others who never injured me.

The intelligent reader cannot fail to perceive that the trials and sufferings inflicted upon the Southern Methodist preachers were nothing else than sheer malicious persecution for righteousness' sake. They were not punished for disobedience to the Constitution and laws of the civil government; they were not punished for outrageous crimes—such as theft, robbery, arson, murder; they were not punished for taking by violence that to which they had no claim whatever, nor for burning and destroying the property of others amounting to multiplied thousands of dollars. They were persecuted because they were righteous and would maintain their Christian integrity and fidelity to God. Noble set of heroes! they are not dead, but will live when sun, moon, and stars are no more.

CHAPTER III.

MISSOURI CONFERENCE.

Seat of the Conference Changed from Hannibal to Glasgow—Orderly Session of Good-looking, Intelligent, and Happy Men—The Civil War Rages—Sad Parting in View of Threatening Danger—Great Consternation Prevails throughout the State—Persecution of Rev. Andrew Monroe—His High and Influential Character—Mrs. Monroe—Their House Plundered and They Robbed of All They Had—Rev. John McGlothin Cruelly Treated—Seizure of Our Church in Louisiana by the M. E. Church—Severe Trials of Rev. R. N. T. Holliday, as Related by Dr. Oregon Richmond, a Federal Officer.

THE session of the Missouri Annual Conference, M. E. Church, South, was to have been held at Hannibal, Mo., but in consequence of the great political excitement and war troubles in that section of the country, and on account of strong prejudices caused by designing persons making false representations, it was thought best to change the place of meeting. Therefore it was held at Glasgow, Mo., September 11-16, 1861. In the absence of a bishop Rev. William G. Caples presided. Rev. E. K. Miller was elected Secretary. Marshall McIlhany, John W. Atkisson, James S. Smith, James B. Short, George C. Brown, and Samuel J. Huffaker were admitted on trial. O. R. Bouton, Jacob McEwin, J. T. Tutt, Samuel Alexander, Walter G. Fowler, and E. McKendree Bounds remained on trial. E. H. Hudson, Henry B. Watson, H. G. McEwin, and Charles W. Collet were admitted into full connection. H. A. Bourland, John F. Shores, Wesley W. McMurry, Roderick D. Baldwin, John Stone, John R. Taylor, George W. Penn, and George H. Newton were deacons of one year. No bishop being present, there were no ordinations. William Penn, O. R. Bouton, Richard Minshall, Horace Brown, Jesse Faubion, Joseph H. Pritchett, L. Baldwin, R. A. Austin, and Samuel J. Catlin were supernumerary. L. R. Downing, R. P. Holt, D. C. Blackwell, R. C. Hatton, J. F. Young, and William Ketron were superannuated.

The session of the Conference differed in nothing from that over which a bishop presides. In the transaction of business perfect order prevailed, and the deliberations and discussions were conducted in a dignified and respectful manner. This writer has frequently thought that it would be difficult to find such another body of good-looking and dignified men. He has heard the same sentiment expressed by others. The preachers are so joyous and happy in their annual convocations, how could it be otherwise? They are brethren—one in Christ Jesus—baptized into one and the same spirit, preach one and the same gospel, made partakers of the same divine nature. They love, too, to tell each other of the labors and toils, the trials and temptations, the conflicts and battles, the defeats and victories of the past year.

But now comes the sad scene of parting. They

have received their appointments, and are off in a hurry to their respective fields of labor, asking themselves many questions about their appointment. One thought, however, saddens their hearts very much. They may never meet again, as they are going into the scenes of sore and fierce persecution.

Let not the reader forget that we are writing in the Conference year 1861–62; that the war is fiercely raging; that we are amid the scenes of the battle-field; that we can see the ascending columns of smoke; can hear the thunder of the cannon, the shrieks of the wounded, the groans of the dying. While the great armies are in battle array against each other, there are those who are parading through the country, fighting, killing, and robbing the unarmed, the innocent, and the helpless, producing panic and consternation all over the land.

Rev. Andrew Monroe.

We now approach the history of the troubles and sufferings of him who has been very appropriately styled "the venerable patriarch of Methodism in Missouri," the Rev. Andrew Monroe. No attempt to give a true description of this noble man of God can be a success; language falters, words are inadequate. There are thoughts and truths language cannot express, words cannot tell. An approximation is all that language can do. He was the embodiment of Methodism, about as good as the Discipline; was a strong and able advocate of the cardinal doctrines of the M. E. Church, South—which are the fundamental doctrines of the Bible. He was at home on the gospel truths essential to salvation—true repentance, saving faith, thorough conversion, or spiritual regeneration through the operation of the Holy Spirit, a consecrated, righteous life, the resurrection, a future judgment, the eternal reward of the righteous, and the everlasting punishment of the wicked. We are favored with an interesting notice of his trials during the war, which we give below:

In the winter of 1862 the Rev. A. Monroe was traveling the Fayette Circuit, Missouri Conference, M. E. Church, South, and living in the town of Fayette, Howard County. Fayette, like all other towns of importance in the State, was a military post, with one Maj. Hubbard in command.

"One day of that winter Mr. Monroe and his family were surprised by the appearance of a Federal officer and a squad of men entering his humble home, placing him and his wife under arrest, and marching them off to head-quarters, for what offense they never knew.

The soldiers arrested many other gentlemen and ladies at the same time, and they had plenty of company when they reached head-quarters, among whom were Rev. W. H. Lewis, President of Howard Female College, and Rev. Dr. W. H. Anderson, President of Central College.

When Maj. Hubbard came in, and saw the number of ladies present under arrest, he affected surprise, and said that he had not ordered their arrest; that his subalterns had transcended his orders, and at once informed the ladies that they were released, remarking at the same time that when he wished to see them he would not send for them, but do himself the pleasure of calling at their homes. To which Mrs. Monroe promptly replied that they were obliged to him for releasing them so early, but as for seeing him, she had no desire whatever to see him at her house or anywhere else.

Many a true and modest woman had occasion during those troublous times to call upon her ready wit to reply to the various impertinent inquiries and demands of a ruffian soldiery; and while Mrs. Monroe was surprised at her own courage, her indignation was somewhat appeased when she observed the cutting effect of her retort. Not many days afterward she had occasion again for her ready wit and Christian fortitude and forbearance. Very early in the morning five soldiers called and demanded breakfast. Mr. Monroe was at home, but he soon retreated from the front door and called upon his wife to meet the issue. She had no help, and the idea of cooking for so many, and those, too, whom she believed to be her enemies, and who would not hesitate to do her any injury, was very repulsive. But to get rid of them was a difficult question, as many ladies know. By the time she had reached the front door and heard their request, her answer was ready. She replied: "My Bible teaches me, 'If thine enemy hunger, feed him; if he thirst, give him drink.' Upon these terms and no other you can get breakfast." To her surprise one of them said: "Madam, we will accept breakfast upon those terms, for I profess to be somewhat acquainted with the Bible." She thought they would turn and go away in a rage, but, on the contrary, she had to turn and get breakfast, with the best grace she could.

It turned out that the spokesman was a local preacher in the Northern Methodist Church, and at the table he remarked to Mrs. Monroe that his father was as great a rebel as she was; to which she replied that it was a thousand pities that he had so far departed from the ways of his father as to be a degenerate son of an honored sire. Whereupon he said: "As a loyal man, I would hate awfully to have to live with such a rebel. Gen. Price could well afford to issue a commission to you, madam."

Not many days after this Mr. Monroe was just ready to mount his horse one morning for a tour of appointments in the country, when a soldier appeared with orders to arrest him and take him to the head-quarters of Capt. Hale, then commanding the post. The venerable man of God was then marched up to head-quarters at the point of the bayonet and required to take the military oath and give bond, with good security, for his future loyalty to the government, and for the loyalty and good order of his family, the captain remarking: "The Secesh talk of the women of his family should be stopped.' Mr. Monroe replied that he could take the oath if he would let him go about his Master's work, but as for the bond, he must excuse him, as he did not wish to involve his friends, and he had but little property. If it was this little property he was after, he might as well go and take charge of that at once, and let him go about his business. The Captain saw the point, and told him to take the oath then, and "go preach the gospel to every creature."

In 1864 Mr. Monroe was living on a farm about six miles east of Glasgow, in Howard County, when Gen. Price made his famous raid into Central Missouri, and took Glasgow among other places. The day before the battle of Glasgow Mr. Monroe was out in a field on his little farm, and his family all away from home except a servant, when a company of Kansas soldiers passing along the road halted, entered the house, and robbed it of every thing of value they could find. The house was literally pillaged. Mr. Monroe's watch, a fine cloth coat, several pairs of bed-blankets, quilts, comforts, and, indeed, every thing of any value to them. While thus engaged, they saw a young man who lived near approaching the house, all unconscious of what was going on. He was arrested and relieved of all his money, seventy-five dollars. One rough-looking Dutch soldier rode out to the field and accosted the venerable man with an imperative demand for his money. When he found he had but two dollars in the world, he would not take it, but rode back in disgust. A young man—Mr. Monroe's nephew—was met near the house on his uncle's only riding-horse, with his only saddle and bridle. The young man was arrested, and the horse and equipments taken to Glasgow and never heard from afterward.

Thus in one single hour the faithful servant of God stood alone in his field, stripped of every thing he had—his horse, watch, clothes, blankets, bedding—every thing of any value. What must have been the feelings of Mrs. Monroe on returning home after the absence of just one hour to find her house plundered by ruffian soldiery, and her husband beggared! To complete the work, a small squad of soldiers passed along soon afterward, and when they could find nothing else to steal or appropriate, a rough, drunken Dutchman demanded of the old man his woolen mittens, which a lady had recently given him. He gave them up, and considered himself fortunate to get off so easy.

With such petty annoyances, involving privation and suffering, this faithful minister of the gospel—this pioneer and patriarch of Missouri Methodism—passed through the dark and trying scenes of the Civil War, always hopeful and joyful and ready to rejoice that he was counted worthy to suffer for a cause of which he himself was the finest type, and for which he would go even to prison and to death. To the struggling cause of Christ and his suffering friends he was a tower of strength; to the discomfited and disheartened hosts of the Methodist Israel he was "our Moses." When "these calamities were overpassed," and the shock of the war had expended its fire and force; when the smoke of battle had cleared away and the storm-cloud hung low upon the horizon, he surveyed the field, marked the desolations, measured the extent of the wreck, discovered some remains of Zion's former beauty, while others, with indecent haste, sounded her funeral knell; and his voice, like that of a mighty chieftain, was heard over the prairies, along the railroads, and in the cities of Missouri, calling the faithful to duty, and rallying the scattered forces for counsel. Upon his call a few ministers and friends convened in Palmyra, June, 1865, and decreed the life of the Church, the resuscitation of her vital powers, the recovery of her lost ground, and the rehabilitation of her distinctive institutions.*

REV. JOHN McGLOTHIN.

The intelligence of the persecution of the preachers comes to us from every direction, and we cannot pass them by unnoticed without doing violence to our conviction of duty. Their names should be perpetuated in the annals of history to the latest generation.

The Rev. John McGlothin was a useful local preacher of the M. E. Church, South, exemplary in life and of an unimpeachable character. Hear of his trials:

In 1862 he was residing in Ray County, Mo., when Maj. Biggers, the commander of the post at Richmond, issued an order that

---

* Dr. Leftwich's book.

no minister of the gospel should preach the gospel who did not carry with him the Union flag. A few days after the order came out Mr. McGlothin was called upon to go to Knoxville, Caldwell County, to procure suitable burial clothing for a Mrs. Tilford, a widow, who died in his neighborhood—as he was the only man available for that service. After the purchases were made and he was ready to return, a Capt. Tiffin, of Knoxville, stepped up and asked if he had "reported." He answered in the negative, and convinced the captain that there was no order requiring him to report, as he had license to preach. The officer then asked him if he had a "flag." He told him he had not. "Will you get one?" "No," said he; "I will recognize no State or military authority to prescribe qualifications for the work of the ministry." The officer at once arrested him. Mr. McGlothin acquainted Captain Tiffin at once with the peculiar character of his business in Knoxville and the necessity of his speedy return, offering at the same time his parole of honor to report to him at any time or place he might designate. This he promptly refused, and the officer said he would ride out part of the way with him. When they arrived within a few miles of the house where the dead lay waiting for the interment, the officer pressed a boy into service and sent the burial clothes to their destination, after detaining them three or four hours on the way. The minister was not released, even to attend to the burial service, but was kept in close confinement, dinnerless, supperless, bedless, and comfortless.

The next day, with over twenty others, he was taken to Richmond and confined in the fair-grounds and in the old college building for five weeks, and then unconditionally released. The only charge they could bring against him was that he would not take the oath of allegiance, give bond in the sum of one thousand dollars for his good bevavior, and buy a flag to carry about with him as an evidence of his loyalty and a symbol of authority to preach the gospel of Jesus Christ.

Few instances of petty persecution in the exercise of a little brief authority can surpass this. It needs no comment except to add that the minister who was thus made a victim of the narrowest and meanest spitefulness was a high-toned gentleman of unblemished character, against whom even the petty military officers and their spies could never raise an accusation.*

---

* Dr. Leftwich's book.

The Church in Louisiana.

The M. E. Church tried to take forcible possession of the property of the M. E. Church, South, in which effort she did not finally succeed. Let us in this case hear from one who has thoroughly investigated the subject:

In 1853 a deed to a lot of ground in the city was made by Edward G. McQuie and wife to Edwin Draper, John S. Markley, John W. Allen, Samuel O. Minor, John Shurmur, Joseph Charleville, Ivey Zumwalt, David Watson, and Thomas T. Stokes, as trustees of the M. E. Church, South, to hold in trust for the use and benefit of said Church. Consideration, $500. Soon thereafter a commodious church-edifice was erected on the lot and dedicated to the worship of God, in the name and for the benefit of the M. E. Church, South. It was occupied and used by them unmolested until 1862. In the meantime vacancies had occurred in the original Board of Trustees by the death of David Watson and the removal from the State of Thomas T. Stokes.

These vacancies had been filled by the regular authority of the Church, and according to law, by the appointment and election of Samuel S. Allen and William A. Gunn, as seen in the records of the Quarterly Conference for Louisiana Station. But this fact did not prevent the tools of the M. E. Church (North) from devising a bold scheme that would put them in the possession of the Church property. They could not claim that the property was originally deeded to the M. E. Church, and was afterward wrested from the rightful owners, as in the cases of Lexington, Independence, La Grange, Boonville, etc. That subterfuge could not serve them in this case, and to accomplish their purpose they devised another. It was this: An *ex parte* petition was filed in the Louisiana Court of Common Pleas, setting forth the fact of the above-mentioned vacancies in the Board of Trustees, and praying the court to fill the vacancy occasioned by the death of David Watson by the appointment of Charles Hunter, and to appoint Robert S. Strother to fill the vacancy occasioned by the removal of T. T. Stokes. This petition, as it now stands on the records of the court, was signed by Edwin Draper, John S. Markley, John W.

Allen, Ivey Zumwalt, Samuel O. Miner, Joseph Charleville, and John Shurmur, and was granted July 21, 1862.

On the second day thereafter (July 23, 1862) Samuel O. Minor, John W. Allen, Ivey Zumwalt, William A. Gunn, and S. S. Allen filed a petition, asking the court to vacate the order appointing Hunter and Strother, and set forth the following facts why the order should be set aside: They admitted the vacancy occasioned by the death of Watson and the removal of Stokes, but set forth from the Church records that on the 21st day of January, 1861, Rev. W. M. Newland, then preacher in charge, nominated, and the Quarterly Conference elected, W. A. Gunn to fill the vacancy occasioned by the death of said Watson; and that the other vacancy was filled by the nomination and election of Samuel S. Allen April 23, 1862, Rev. W. G. Miller then preacher in charge. They therefore allege that at the time of the appointment by the court of Hunter and Strother no vacancy existed, the same having been filled, according to the law of the Church made and provided, and therefore the order of the court ought to be vacated.

They further represented that the names of John W. Allen, Samuel O. Miner, and Ivey Zumwalt were used in the original petition without their knowledge or consent, and insisted that the order should be set aside for that reason.

Both the petitioners and community were astonished when the court refused to vacate the order, and the only recourse was an appeal to the Supreme Court of Missouri on a writ of error. It may not be improper to state in this place that Judge Gilchrist Porter, then on the bench of that judicial district, presided; and Thomas J. C. Fagg, then Judge of the Louisiana Court of Common Pleas, was counsel for the M. E. Church (North) in his own court.

The case was argued July 24, 1862, and the petition was overruled. The petitioners filed a bill of exceptions, and the case went up to the Supreme Court. The case was not heard in the Supreme Court until January 10, 1866, when the judgment of the court below was reversed and the case dismissed upon the ground of irregularity and informality.

The suit for title was stricken from the docket without being heard, and those who bought the lot and built and paid for the church are again in possession of their own; albeit they were kept out of the use of it for nearly five years, and then received it in a condition that required extensive repairs, for which those who had used and damaged it had no disposition to pay one dollar. Thus, one by one the property that was taken from the Church, South, was restored, after being used and abused by "our friends, the enemy."

Pending this case Mr. Allen, counsel for plaintiffs in error, made a very able argument upon the relation of the Church to the civil government. He took high ground upon the separate and distinct jurisdictions of Church and State, as understood by our fathers and as developed in this country under the genius of our government. He characterized severely the efforts made by partisan fanatics to confound in fact what was distinct in law, and to unite the Church with the State for purposes of ecclesiastical power and political corruption.*

Rev. R. N. T. Holliday.

A sketch of the persecutions and sufferings of this eminently good and useful man was written by his personal friend, Dr. Oregon Richmond, who was a Federal officer and desired to see their cause successful and triumphant; but he detested the persecutors of the defenseless, the helpless, and non-combatant citizens of the country. We admire his character very much; there is something noble in it. Read what he says:

At the request of Rev. R. N. T. Holliday, I have consented to put together and transmit the somewhat remarkable events of that period of his life connected with the late war troubles. His request is the result of an antipathy on his part to acting the part of a self-eulogist. In my judgment no greater eulogy can be written of a minister of the gospel than that of a calm, unvarnished recital of the persecution to which that class of our citizens was subjected during the prevalence of and immediately subsequent to the late war.

And perhaps, after all, it is but simple justice that these facts should be written by one who was an officer in the Federal army,

---

* Dr. Leftwich's book.

but can thank God that his military life is unstained by a single act of cruelty or persecution; and above all is he thankful that he never made use of his military power to war against the institutions of heaven or the chosen instruments ordained for their establishment among men. In other words, he was not attached to a Missouri regiment, is not a son of Missouri, and hence has never been instructed in the mysteries of that department of military tactics that teaches the wonderful doctrine that the truest patriotism consists in the abuse of defenseless women and children, and subversion of the sublimest precepts of religion by the persecution and murder of its chosen apostles.

In September, 1860, Rev. R. N. T. Holliday, the subject of this sketch, was appointed by the Missouri Conference of the M. E. Church, South, of which he has long been a member, to Rushville, in Buchanan County, Mo. In the ensuing spring the war commenced; but it was not until May, 1861, that he received the first intimation of the approaching trouble that would draw him into its clutches, and ultimately make him a wanderer and an exile from his chosen field of usefulness.

About that time a Union meeting was held near Rushville, and addressed by Hon. Willard P. Hall and others, from St. Joseph. Mr. Holliday was urged to be present and reply on behalf of the South. This he declined to do. He was not even present at the meeting, believing that ministers of the gospel should keep themselves unspotted from the political strifes of men. Yet his enemies said he staid away through personal fear, and he was henceforth the subject of various kinds of annoyances and petty persecutions.

The Conference of September, 1861, returned Mr. Holliday to Rushville. He was not molested until March, 1862, when Brig.-Gen. W. P. Hall issued a proclamation requiring all men subject to military duty to enroll themselves in the State militia. Mr. Holliday refused to enroll, upon the ground that ministers were exempt from military duty. Gen. Hall sent him word at once that if he did not enroll he would have him arrested. Mr. Holliday replied that, being exempt from military duty by the laws of the State, he could not but consider the demand extra-official, and if an arrest must be the result of non-compliance with an illegal demand he preferred to be arrested. Upon this Gen. Hall addressed a note to Mr. Holliday in the politest terms, requesting an interview to arrange the difficulties. Trusting the general's honor, Mr. Holliday complied; but, upon presenting himself at headquarters, the general refused to see him, and ordered him taken to the provost-marshal's office for enrollment. Gen. Bassett, the provost-marshal, had the entrance to his office securely guarded after Mr. Holliday was admitted, and informed him that he must enroll under Order 19, as a Union man, and submit to a physical examination; or under Order 24, as a rebel sympathizer, and pay a commutation fee of $30. Finding submission inevitable, or something worse, Mr. Holliday registered under Order 24, but refused to pay the commutation as an unlawful and an unauthorized exaction, and demanded his exemption papers as a minister of the gospel, at the same time producing his ordination parchment. Gen. Bassett, after some delay, gave him exemption papers; and, after considerable annoyance, he gave him a pass also, which enabled him to travel back and forth and fill his appointments without further molestation than an occasional petty persecution—the instigation of malice—and an occasional threat of being shot.

During the summer of 1862 Mr. Bassett was superseded in the office of provost-marshal by a Mr. W. Tool, who had been up to that period a minister in the M. E. Church, South. He had, however, apostatized and joined the M. E. Church (North).

Mr. Bassett's brief apprenticeship in villainy fitted him for, and he was appointed to, a higher office. Mr. Holliday was requested to fill the pulpit made vacant by the military prohibition upon Rev. W. M. Rush, of St. Joseph; and the ladies of the Church in which Mr. Rush had been silenced waited on Provost-marshal Tool, and requested permission for Mr. Holliday to fill the silent pulpit. Mr. Tool, who was acting in the interest of the Northern Methodists, refused to permit Mr. Holliday to come to St. Joseph to preach the gospel.

In September, 1862, Mr. Holliday was sent to Platte City, and there remained unmolested until the following June, when soldiers from Kansas took his horse, which he never saw afterward. He borrowed another, which was also stolen and carried off. He thus lost two horses in as many weeks.

About the middle of July, 1863, Col. Jennison, of Kansas, went to Platte City and burned the town. His men were ordered to shoot Mr. Holliday at sight. Knowing the character of Jennison's men, and being apprised of the order by a Union man, Mr. Holliday made good his escape, leaving his family at Mr. Redman's. On the evening of his flight his house, containing all he had in the world except what they had on, was given to the flames. His family were thus made destitute and reduced to beggary.

The next day, at 3 P.M., Mr. Holliday was arrested, by order of a Clinton County militia captain, and taken to Plattsburg. He was there subjected to some indignities, until Mr. Cockrell informed Capt. Irvine, commander of the post, of the facts, who, being a gentleman and a Mason, ordered the instant release of Mr. Holliday.

The next day Capt. Irvine was killed in an engagement with the rebels. This very much enraged the militia, and again an order was issued to shoot Mr. Holliday on sight. He again made his escape by flight and concealment. He remained ten days at the residence of Mr. Powell, of Clinton County; but, upon hearing of the order to shoot him, he, with two other ministers (Messrs. Tarwater and Jones), took refuge in the woods, and made their way on foot to Osborn, where Mr. Holliday met his family, and all took the train to Quincy, Ill. They remained in Illinois till the war closed, in 1865, doing the best he could as a minister of the gospel. Returning to Missouri in 1865, he met the Conference at Hannibal, and was appointed to the Shelbyville Circuit.

By this time the new Constitution had been declared the fundamental law of the State, and under it all ministers of the gospel were required to take the iron-clad test oath as a qualification for the work of the ministry, or subject themselves to arrest, indictment, fine, or imprisonment.

Actuated by the same motives of conscience that impelled all true ministers of the gospel, he promptly refused to take and subscribe said oath. He was therefore arrested and indicted by the grand jury of Shelby County for preaching and teaching as a minister of the gospel without having, under oath, attested his past and present loyalty to the government of the United States. A copy of the indictment is in Mr. Holliday's possession, to be handed down to his children as a memento of his sufferings and triumphs in the cause of his Master. It will doubtless make their faith doubly strong in the principles of that holy religion for which he endured so much privation, persecution, and personal danger.

The facts above narrated I have received from Mr. Holliday's own lips. He was so reticent of matters concerning himself personally that I cannot but regard this as a very meager epitome of all he was required to do and to suffer in the performance of the work his Master gave him to do. He evidently is already richly rewarded in the depth of his own consciousness, and justly decided that nothing man may say for him can serve in the smallest degree to increase his reward.

[Signed]   OREGON RICHMOND.

The reader will readily agree with this writer that there is something magnanimous in the character of the author of the foregoing sketch.

CHAPTER IV.

St. Louis Conference.

Session of the Conference Changed from Warrensburg to Arrow Rock, and from Arrow Rock to Waverly in Consequence of Great Excitement at the Two Former Places—Dr. W. M. Leftwich Captured by a Squad of Soldiers While on His Way to the Conference—His Account of It—Small Attendance at Conference Owing to War Troubles—Short Session, Leaving Much of the Work To Be Done by Presiding Elders—Persecution of Dr. D. R. McAnally—His Wonderful Life in Various Departments of Usefulness—Gives a Statement of His Troubles—Publishing House and Book Depository of the M. E. Church, South, in St. Louis—Rev. James M. Proctor Tells of His Trials—Rev. M. M. Pugh—His Useful Life—Tells of His Persecution During the War—Brutal Murder of Rev. Green Woods—A Detailed Account of That Dreadful Affair by His Own Daughter.

THERE are no published minutes of the session of the St. Louis Annual Conference for the year 1861. We learn that the appointment had been made to meet at Warrensburg, but in view of the great excitement and political troubles at that place it was thought advisable to meet at Arrow Rock, Saline County. There the Conference organized September 25, 1861, with D. A. Leeper in the chair and W. M. Prottsman Secretary. Danger threatening them at Arrow Rock, the Conference adjourned to Waverly. Dr. W. M. Leftwich made a vain effort to reach it. He says:

I was prevented from attending on that occasion only by the untimely interference of a small detachment of Col. Nugent's command, then posted at Kansas City.

I had announced on Sabbath to my congregation that I would start to Conference next day, stating where it would be held, and about how long I expected to be absent.

On Monday morning early, in company with Mr. H. B. Conwell, a brother-in-law and a steward in the Church, I started for Conference. Just as we were passing out of the city, on the main road to Independence, we discovered a small squad of soldiers riding slowly about half a mile ahead of us. To avoid molestation and detention, we took a by-road that would intersect the Westport and Independence road, on reaching which we discovered the soldiers still ahead of us, and we began at once to conjecture some designs upon us. They had halted by a peach-orchard, and were helping themselves when we drove up. They very politely gave us of their peaches, and requested us not to go ahead of them.

We traveled on behind them for some little distance, when the officer in command stopped to talk with a farmer by the roadside who knew me well, and asked when we drove up if I was on my way to Conference.

"What Conference?" asked the officer.

"The Conference of the M. E. Church, South, at Arrow Rock," I replied, quite indifferently.

"What! that Secesh concern? I'll see to that. No such body of traitors can meet in this State." And with the last words he spurred his horse up with his command and detailed four men to put us under arrest and guard us to Independence. With "two behind and two before" we were ordered to "drive." Thus we traveled until we reached Rock Creek, two miles from Independence, when an orderly was sent back, who dismounted and ordered us to "halt." "I want you men to get out of this," he said.

"For what?" I asked, mildly protesting against the proceedings.

"I want to send this buggy back to camp," he replied. "We have use for such things sometimes to ride our wives and children out a little."

"Where is your camp?" was asked by Mr. Conwell, at the same time declaring that the horse and buggy belonged to him. And when informed that their camp was in Kansas City, at Col. Nugent's head-quarters, he asked: "Then why can't you send us back to Kansas City in the buggy, under guard if you like. We live in Kansas City."

"No," said he; "no use talking. If you are loyal men, you can afford to walk ten miles for the sake of the government; and if you are disloyal, we are not around hauling rebels. Get out!"

We did not wait for another invitation, but got out; and when we found it was not *us* but *ours* they wanted, we felt somewhat relieved, took a luncheon to stay the appetite, and then the roof of the stage an hour after, which safely landed us back whence we started.

Mr. Conwell soon obtained his horse and buggy, and a message came to me that, if I would stay at home and attend to my own business, I would not be arrested; but it would not be well for me to make another attempt to go to Conference.*

It was a source of great regret that so few of the preachers could reach the seat of the Conference—particularly from St. Louis and the southwestern part of the State. Indeed, the troubles were well-nigh at their worst. No safety anywhere. It was unsafe to be at home, and equally unsafe to be away from home. It was death to stay, death to go. Many of the preachers felt that if they should start to Conference they would fall by the way. Under these circumstances only a few of the ministers were able to attend the Conference. Not only so, but those who were present found themselves in no proper state of mind to transact important business. They were in great suspense, expecting every mail to bring them intelligence of some great disaster at home. With such thoughts and feelings it would be very difficult to attend properly to the business of the Con-

---

*Dr. Leftwich's book.

ference. They expedited matters as rapidly as possible, and after a short and unsatisfactory session the Conference adjourned, leaving many of the appointments to be made by the presiding elders as best they could under the unfavorable circumstances. How any person can oppose the office of presiding elder this writer cannot imagine. In his judgment it is much nearer being the center wheel than the fifth wheel of the Church.

THE TROUBLES OF REV. D. R. McANALLY, D.D., DURING THE CIVIL WAR.

It would seem to be an act of supererogation in this writer to give to the reader a delineation of the life and character of Dr. D. R. McAnally—a man so well and extensively known throughout the length and breadth of this vast country, from the Atlantic to the Pacific coast. But "honor to whom honor is due" is both just and right. There is no flattery in telling the truth, and the truth cannot hurt a truthful man. If he has reached a position of eminence and distinction in the elements of goodness and greatness, should not the fact be made known for the good of others, that they may be inspired with a laudable ambition to attain similar renown in every thing that is good and great? It is the duty and the pleasure of the historian to hold up such characters before the public, that they may catch the inspiration and do likewise.

Dr. D. R. McAnally holds a front position, side by side with the ablest, wisest, and greatest men of the Church and of the country as well. He has filled every place to which he has been assigned in the providence of God with marked success and ability. For scores of years he has been a telling power in the pulpit as an able minister of the Lord Jesus Christ. Always entertaining the idea that simple truth is the greatest power, he has preached the gospel in its clearness, simplicity, and purity, accompanied by the Holy Spirit, making it the wonderful power of God in the salvation of sinners, by hundreds and by thousands. His voice has been heard in the proclamation of the glorious gospel for more than half a century, in the Middle, the Southern, and Western States. Thank God that voice is still heard on the walls of Zion, proclaiming salvation to a lost world!

For many years he was engaged in the cause of Christian education, which must accompany the preaching of the gospel to give it durability and perpetuity. Education is the handmaid of Christianity, and must go with it wherever it goes. Thus was he employed in institutions of learning, educating the youth of the country and qualifying them for the responsible stations of life they were destined to fill, in society, in the Church, and in the State. In this, as in other fields of usefulness, he distinguished himself as a competent and successful educator.

It is our conviction that no truer patriot ever

lived in America; that no one has studied the science of civil government more thoroughly; that very few, if any, understand the principles of the Constitution and the laws of our country better than he. What is still better, his patriotism is practical as well as theoretical. He conscientiously obeys the laws of his country, and always has done it. He has been outspoken and loud-spoken on this subject in trying to persuade others to follow his example of loyalty. For years he has been a faithful sentinel, standing upon the watch-tower of our country sounding the alarm through the " News of the Week," that very important department of the *St. Louis Christian Advocate.* Had his voice been heeded, there would not have been a civil war.

About thirty-nine years ago he was appointed editor of the *St. Louis Christian Advocate.* When he came to this State to fill the editorial chair of that paper he identified himself with the interests and destiny of the M. E. Church, South, in Missouri. Ever since that time he has used all his resources and employed all his energies and powers in advancing the interests of said Church. But the important enterprise which has engaged his undivided attention and received his indefatigable and ceaseless labors is, and has been for many long years, the *St. Louis Christian Advocate.* He came West for the purpose of establishing a Church paper of the highest order. Let his many thousand readers tell how well he has succeeded.

Has it not been the popular religious paper of the West for more than thirty-five years? At the present day it has a circulation in almost every State in the Union. Has he not a name in journalism equal to that of any editor in this country?

He had, too, a noble Christian object in building up a first-class paper in Missouri. Through that medium he could teach and preach to many thousands at the same time. How many families all over the country, who are deprived of sanctuary privileges, hail with pleasure the weekly visitation of the *St. Louis Christian Advocate!* In it they find much to cheer and comfort them, and many sound and instructive religious lessons. He is also a man of ripe scholarship and high literary attainments. As an author, he has contributed several valuable books to our Church literature. Yet this pre-eminently useful and good man did not escape the severe ordeal of fierce persecution during the Civil War.

By the request of his friends he has given the following statement of his trials and troubles:

On the 21st day of April, 1862, I was arrested by the order of the provost-marshal at St. Louis, and immediately imprisoned in what was then called "Myrtle Street Military Prison." No reasons were given; none were asked, as arbitrary arrests were then matters of every-day occurrence; and in most cases if reasons were asked none were given.

From the first hour of my imprisonment I calmly but firmly determined that, with a perfect consciousness of the purity of my motives and rectitude of my conduct, I had violated no law, either civil or military; that in my heart, in my conduct and conversation, I had been true to the real interests of my country; I would take no oath, give no bond, nor ask any favors, either directly or indirectly. Nor did I do any of these things from the first to the last. I never asked why I had been arrested, what were the charges, what the military intended to do, or what they wanted me to do. I knew there were no grounds for any charges whatever; that the whole procedure, in regard to myself and others, was a low, cowardly effort to intimidate and humiliate men who formed their own opinions, preserved their own self-respect, and refused to be swayed to and fro by the influence or mere *dicta* of blind passion; so that, without any thing like stubbornness, and in the entire absence, I trust, of all unchristian or ungentlemanly feeling, I resolved to make no concessions—having none to make—ask no favors, nor do any thing else that might be construed, either directly or indirectly, into an acknowledgment on my part of the right of the military to institute and carry out such proceedings.

Besides, I was satisfied that it was not against me personally so much as against me as the representative of a Christian denomination—the M. E. Church, South—that this warfare was to be waged. Many of the ministers of that denomination had even then been driven from their flocks and from the State; others had seen the storm coming, and had left; while many others, in different parts of the State, had been put under heavy bonds by provost-marshals; and then, or soon after, some six or eight had been shot down as if they had been ferocious beasts. Some of those arrested had been told by military commanders that the fact of their being ministers of the M. E. Church, South, was "enough to hang them;" and many of our members were put under bonds or sent to prison for no other ostensible reason than that they had subscribed for and paid for and read the *St. Louis Chris'ian Advocate*, an official organ of the M. E. Church, South, then and for more than ten years previously under my editorial management. I was not a *blatant abolitionist*, and had thrown some serious impediments in the way of ecclesiastical radicalism; hence the determination to be rid both of the paper and its editor.

At various times during more than three months previous to the arrest I had been warned of my danger, because of the *religious* rather than the political opposition to me; and some of my friends advised me to leave, which I could have done any day previous to the arrest.

On Sunday, the thirteenth of April, there was a consultation among the "faithful" as to what course had best be pursued in reference to the *St. Louis Advocate* and its editor. At this consultation it was proposed:

First, to incite the soldiers, and let them tear down the building and demolish the office of publication. But that proposition was rejected, because it was thought the influence on the minds of the people of the State would be bad; that it would be going further than would be safe to their own cause.

Second, it was then proposed and agreed to that an indictment for conspiracy—conspiring with others against the government of the United States—should be drawn up for the action of the grand jury of the United States District Court, which was to sit the next day; and, in the event of the jury failing to find a true bill, why then I must be summarily and arbitrarily arrested by the provost-marshal, sent to prison, and the paper suppressed. Accordingly the next day (Monday, the 14th) the court met and the grand jury was empaneled. Soon after a bill was presented them. Diligent inquiry was made; witnesses were summoned and examined; day after day the matter dragged on, until finally, on Saturday, the 19th, the jury, having completed their work, were discharged, and no presentment was made against the *Advocate* or its editor. Partisans as they were, and corrupt as I knew some of them to have been, they would not say on their oaths that a true bill for conspiracy could be found. Hence, in accordance with the programme previously prepared, on Monday following the paper was arbitrarily suppressed, and I arrested and imprisoned by order of the provost-marshal, as already stated. The marshal was one Capt. Leighton, a man whose intellectual, social, and moral qualities and whose early life and associations seem to have eminently qualified him for the work he was called on to perform.

The keeper of the prison placed me in a room twelve or fifteen feet square, with ten other persons, all of whom were genteel, worthy men, and some of them highly intellectual and cultivated. So far, therefore, as they were concerned, my situation was altogether agreeable and pleasant. They uniformly and invariably treated me with respect and kindness, and really seemed to vie with each other in manifestations of kindly feeling.

In the same prison, in different parts, there were perhaps from a hundred to a hundred and fifty persons, a few of whom had been regularly in the Confederate service and captured; others had been in the Federal service, and were there in prison for crime; while the great majority were citizens from different parts of the State, arrested on mere suspicion, and in some cases had been imprisoned for weeks and months with only the scant clothing they happened to have on when arrested. Some fifty or sixty such as these were in a miserable condition. But under the rags and dirt that covered them there were some as noble hearts as ever throbbed. These, too, after I had been but a few days in prison, all treated me with respect and kindness; nor did any of the officers of the prison ever use to me a disrespectful or an unkind word. I endeavored to deport myself in a dignified, respectful, gentlemanly, and Christian manner, and was everywhere met with a corresponding course.

It was my understanding at the time that the keeper of the prison was allowed a *per diem* for feeding the prisoners; but whether that was so or not he evidently drew rations for all, but allowed some twelve or fifteen to have their meals sent regularly from the Virginia Hotel, and I verily believe the hotel keeper sent the "best his house could afford." My meals were sent regularly three times each day by an estimable family living close by.

On the 20th the officer of the prison was directed to release me on my verbal parole to report forthwith at the office of the provost-marshal, which I did, and was there informed that charges and specifications had been drawn up, to which I would be required to answer before a military commission on the 23d, and on my verbal parole I was released till that time.

23d. Reported accordingly, when the parole was extended to Monday, the 26th.

On Monday, the 26th of May, I appeared before what was called a "military commission," composed of Col. Merrill, Maj. Straw, and Capt. Howard, the latter of whom acted as Judge Advocate. These were all of the volunteer service, and, except the colonel, were, perhaps, in the service more in name than in reality. The charge I was required to answer to was that of having violated the articles of war by the publication of sundry specified articles in the *St. Louis Christian Advocate*. It was a little remarkable that a number of the articles complained of had been copied from the foreign quarterlies, or from *Blackwood's Magazine*, which publications had been freely circulated in the city from one to three weeks before I made the extracts. I objected in form to being tried by that tribunal, alleging that if I had committed an offense at all it was an offense against civil and not military law, and claimed as a citizen and civilian to be tried by the civil laws. I further objected on the grounds that many, if not all, the articles complained of were published before the proclamation of martial law in St. Louis; and, as no war had been formally declared, I could not, under the circumstances, be justly tried by the articles of war. Several other exceptions were regularly filed, but all were overruled, as, indeed, I supposed they would be, and only entered them to make a fair and full record.

The trial proceeded. The Judge Advocate threw on the table a number of copies of the *St. Louis Christian Advocate*, with certain articles therein marked, but did not read them openly; and if either he or other members of the "commission" ever read them, the fact was and is unknown to me. The fiscal agent of the publishing house whence the *Advocate* was issued was examined at great length and with great care, and to all questions asked he gave distinct, prompt, and truthful answers. This ended the first day's proceedings.

On the second day a number of gentlemen were introduced, some who were well known to be among the most "loyal of the loyal," and others who were suspected of having Southern sympathies," when my manner of life, public and private, my manner of preaching, and the character and tone of my public prayers, were all diligently inquired into, but no one was found who, upon his oath, would say that he ever saw or heard me say or do aught that was inconsistent with the character of a peaceful, law-abiding citizen and Christian minister.

I continued to introduce witnesses on these points until the Court expressed their entire satisfaction.

It was then ordered that what defense I might choose to make be prepared and presented to the Court on the next day. Accordingly, on the opening of the court on the third day, I read a short paper setting forth the grounds on which I thought I was entitled to be released from the prosecution. This closed the trial. I was then remanded to the care of the provost-marshal, who, upon my verbal pledge "not to give aid and comfort to the enemies of the United States, nor to leave the County of St. Louis, and to report myself at the office whenever required," allowed me to go. This parole was kept hanging over me until the 19th of November 1865, three years and six months from the time of the trial. The decision of the court by which I was tried I have never had nor ever known to this good hour!

I kept the parole faithfully, because it was a parole of honor. To be sure I suffered many inconveniences and discomforts because of it, but still kept it, and did it uncomplainingly.

On Sunday, the 10th day of May, 1863, while preparing for the evening service for the Church, I was again arrested, this time by order of Provost-marshal Dick. The arrest was made at my house. After gathering a bundle of clothes, and having prayers with my motherless children, commending them to "Him that judgeth righteously," I accompanied the officer and was by him delivered to the keeper of "Gratiot Street Military Prison." Here there were a great number of persons, many prisoners of war, and many citizens from different parts of the State, some of whom had been long confined, and there were many others, residents in the city, who had a little while before been brought in.

On the next day, Monday, 11th, quite a number of us were notified that we would be sent South beyond the Federal lines, and would be started at 12 o'clock on Wednesday, the 13th. We accordingly made what preparation we could. I was informed that I would be allowed to carry a limited amount of clothing and two hundred dollars in money. The clothing I had. The money I had not; had but a very few dollars in the world, and was leaving my children not only motherless, but penniless and helpless. Some friends outside the prison learned my condition, and the two hundred dollars were quickly furnished. One-half the sum was sent by a high-toned gentleman who was then serving as a colonel in the Federal service, a man whose every sense of justice, honor, and fairness was outraged by the proceedings against me. Had the sum been needed, I believe two thousand or ten thousand dollars would have been furnished me.

On Wednesday, the 13th, those of us who had been ordered into banishment were paraded and marched between two files of soldiers through some of the principal streets in the city to the steamer which was to bear us South. The whole number of persons on the boat was, perhaps, one hundred or more, including men, women, and children.

Just before the boat left the landing an order came countermanding the order for my banishment, and directing that I should be sent to the office of the provost-marshal. This was done, and the other prisoners went South. At the marshal's office I was directed to report there in person at 11 o'clock the next day, and in the meantime I might do any thing not inconsistent with the parole I had given more than a year before.

At the appointed hour next day I reported myself at the office of the provost-marshal, Col. Dick. He expressed a desire for a long conversation, and commenced in a sort of apologetic way by stating how much pleasure it gave him to rectify any mistake he might make, or undo any wrong he might happen to commit; and, as he had been led into a mistake in regard to my arrest and order of banishment, he had much pleasure in countermanding the order, etc. The conversation was protracted and very plain. The colonel was reminded that the old ideas regarding civil rights, civil law, etc., were not entirely exploded, and that it might be well for persons temporarily in power to remember that orders for the arrest, imprisonment, and banishment of persons, and the confiscation or destruction of property, ought to be based on something else than mere suspicion or vague rumor. Finally, the conversation was ended by the colonel's suddenly remembering that he had some important business just then, and requested me to call the next day, that the interview might be renewed. I did call the next day, and the next, and the next, and many succeeding days, but from the day of that interview to the present never found the colonel at leisure. Soon after that he was relieved of his position and duties as provost-marshal, and not a great while afterward, no doubt for good and sufficient reasons, he left the city and State.

The colonel gave no reason for my arrest, nor was he asked for any. Perhaps he was not aware that I had learned his order for my arrest had been issued at the instance of a couple of ignorant and bigoted old women connected with the "Loyal League," and who had been instigated by two men who, for private reasons, desired I should be banished. These two men have since developed the very unenviable character which then I knew they possessed. And perhaps he was not aware that I had learned his order countermanding the order for banishment had been issued on the peremptory command of the general (Curtis) then in command, or that Gen. Curtis had acted on the representation of at least two of his own colonels, who had assured him: (1) that the order was in itself wrong, unjust, and an outrage; and (2) that to let it be carried out would do great harm to the "Union cause." One of them told the general that the very fact of my being in the South, under the circumstances then existing, would do as much harm to their cause "as could be done by a thousand armed men," and added: "I do not know what he may do in the South, but I do know that if he exerts himself as I know him capable of doing you might as well send five thousand armed men to help the rebels as send him. However peaceably disposed he may be now, we cannot expect him to continue so if this outrage is carried out."

Perhaps the colonel was not aware I had learned all this, and much more; still he may have thought of it when he asked me what I would do if sent South, and in reply simply received: "You may rely upon it I will eat no idle bread!"

In all this I allude only to the arrests which were followed by actual imprisonment, saying nothing of an arrest made in September, 1861, not on a charge of any thing having been done, but on a supposition that something might be done. I was quite ill at the time, but taken in my office, carried before the provost-marshal, where, defenseless and surrounded by armed men, I was coarsely harangued, villified, abused, and lectured as to my editorial and ministerial duties, during a half-hour or more, which was at length terminated by my plainly informing the provost-marshal that, as I was in their power, the military could do with me as they chose; that they had the power and could suppress my paper when they chose, but until it was suppressed it should contain just what I might think fit to put into it—neither more nor less. That provost-marshal was one John McNeil, of Palmyra-prisoner notoriety.

Nor have I alluded to the fact that in July, 1861, a mob of "Home Guards," so called, threatened to destroy my dwelling house and church because I had publicly baptized a child whose parents chose to name it Harry Beauregard, which mob desisted from their purpose only a few short hours before that purpose was to have been accomplished, and then not until one of the principal men had been told there were not less than thirty or forty men who would, at the risk of their lives, hold him personally responsible for all harm that might befall me from the mob.

Nor yet have I alluded to the fact that in July, 1861, a company of armed men, forty-four in number, wearing the uniform of United States soldiers, and acting professedly under orders from head-quarters, surrounded my house and ransacked it from cellar to garret. What they expected to find, or were looking for, I never asked—I never knew. Nor to the ransacking of my editorial office, the destruction of my private papers, etc., which was done in April, 1862, when I was absent; nor the almost numberless unlawful and unjust indignities, disabilities, etc., that were put upon me during the three years and more that I was a prisoner.

In the following statement, given by another, the reader will see that an effort was made to take possession of the Publishing House and Book Depository owned by the M. E. Church, South, in St. Louis:

Certain parties in the interest of the M. E. Church (North) managed to get hold of many of the heaviest claims against the concern, with a view of forcing a financial crisis and crash. They could invent no plea or pretext that would libel the property for confiscation, and they undertook to break down the concern by forcing collections. This scheme was discovered and defeated by the timely sagacity of the Agent, Rev. P. M. Pinckard. He called together the Joint Publishing Committee, presented the facts, and, after mature deliberation, they proposed to sell the whole concern to the Agent, at an appraised value, if he would with his own personal resources meet its liabilities and save the property from the clutches of the enemy. A *bona fide* sale was made, and the purchaser subsequently filed a written pledge to sell the property to the Church again upon an equitable valuation, should the Conferences ever be able to buy it. The property was saved by the sacrifice of his wife's personal property and by the most skillful management.

It was an hour of the darkest and most dangerous trial, and perhaps not another man in the Church had the nerve to meet the responsibility and brave the danger. The property was saved. The concern was run in the interest of the Southern Methodist Church, and was ready when the war closed to republish the *Ad-*

vocate, resupply the Church in Missouri with books, and enter with the Church upon the great contest for religious liberty which has been so heroically vindicated by the non-juring ministry of the State.

The services thus rendered to the Church by Mr. Pinckard in her time of greatest need will never be fully appreciated until the power of a religious press shall be measured upon the augmenting interests and vital issues of the crowded future, when the Mississippi Valley and the great West shall throng with a population as dense as that of Europe; while the Church owes a debt of gratitude equal to the sacrifices made, the trials endured, and the interests subserved.

True to his pledge, he preserved the property, declined often the most advantageous offers made for it by private parties, lest it should be alienated from the Church, and when the time came passed it into the hands of the "South-western Book and Publishing Company," authorized and organized by the St. Louis and Missouri Annual Conferences, upon an appraised valuation.

It is perhaps proper to state that when Dr. McAnally was arrested at the depot of the Iron Mountain railroad the officers came up immediately and took forcible possession of the printing department of the concern and announced that they would hold the entire establishment. The next morning an order was made confiscating the property, but for some reason it was not promulgated. Mr. Pinckard, the Agent, saw Col. Leighton, provost-marshal, and asserted his right to the job office and Book Depository, affirming that they did not belong to and were not part of the *St. Louis Christian Advocate*, and demanded that they be given up to him. After a very spirited interview, much delay—going back and forth from the city provost-marshal's office to the head-quarters of the general commanding the department and the office of the provost-marshal-general—and many sharp contests for rights, the keys were finally given up to Mr. Pinckard, and he was permitted to run the establishment, especially the job printing, with all the front doors closed, and then only to finish the jobs on hand. He was distinctly prohibited from receiving any new business. When persons came to purchase books they were required to bring a special permit from the provost-marshal. Two pious ladies from the First Church desired to purchase books for the Sunday-school, but they were required first to go before the provost-marshal and state their desires before they could get a permit to supply the Sunday-school children with good books. Such petty tyranny and oppression characterize the cruelties of war and the corrupt hearts of mean men.*

Rev. James M. Proctor speaks of his trials thus:

I was arrested by W. Hall at Brady's Chapel, on the Sabbath, July 6, 1862. Hall, with his company, reached the chapel before me, and had the "stars and stripes" placed just above the church door. He said that he had been informed that I would not preach under the Union flag. After preaching, and just as I was coming out at the door, near which he had taken his position, he accosted me and said: "You are my prisoner." He trembled like an aspen leaf.

I said to him: "Why this emotion, sir? Show yourself a man, and do your duty."

He replied: "I hate to arrest you, but I am bound to do my duty." He said I must go with him to his father's then, and the following morning he would take me to head-quarters at Cape Girardeau.

I could not go with him that night, as I had been caught in the rain that morning, and had to borrow a dry suit on the road which I was under obligations to return that evening.

After some parley he granted me permission to report at the Cape in a few days, which I did promptly, to Col. Ogden, the provost-marshal. Col. Ogden paroled me, to report at his head-quarters every two or three weeks. On the 29th of September, 1862, I reported to him the fifth and last time, when I was tongue-lashed at a fearful rate by Lieut.-Col. Peckham, of the Twenty-ninth Missouri Regiment, and by him sent to the guard-house.

I asked this irate colonel "if the front of my offending was not my connection with the M. E. Church, South."

He replied: "Yes, sir; and the man who will belong to that Church after she has done the way she has ought to be in prison during the war."

"It is a hard sentence for such an offense," I said.

He replied: "I can't help it, sir; all such men as you are must be confined so that they can do no harm."

---

* Dr. Leftwich's Book.

I remained in the guard-house at the Cape until Thursday, October 2, 1862, when, in company with thirteen other prisoners, three of whom died in a few weeks, I was sent to Gratiot Street Military Prison, St. Louis. In this prison I met several very worthy ministers of different denominations, and also Brother J. P. Boogher and two of his brothers, nobler men than whom I have not found anywhere in the world.

October 20, 1862, I was released on parole, there being no crime alleged against me. The little man who first arrested me was a Northern Methodist. He wrote out and preferred two charges against me, which were so frivolous that the officers in St. Louis would not investigate them. I furnish them as items of curiosity.

"1. He [the said J. M. Proctor] threatened to hang Mr. Lincoln.

"He said that the Federal soldiers were horse-thieves."

After my release from Gratiot Street Prison, St. Louis, I went to the town of Jackson, where I was again arrested at the special instigation of a Northern Methodist preacher named Liming. I continued to preach during and after my imprisonment. When the notorious test oath was inaugurated I continued to preach, and was indicted three times before Judge Albert Jackson, Cape Girardeau County. Rev. D. H. Murphy and A. Munson were also indicted for the same offense.

I never took the test oath, nor any oath of allegiance during the war. It was plain to all that the Northern Methodists were our worst enemies during that long and cruel war.

Rev. M. M. Pugh.

The present writer, when in charge of the Independence Female College prior to the Civil War, had the pleasure of making the acquaintance of Mr. Pugh—not a slight acquaintance, but one somewhat long and familiar—an acquaintance cultivated into personal friendship and Christian love.

Ever since our first knowledge of him he has been the same uniform, active, zealous, able, and successful embassador of Christ—on the circuit, in the station, and on the district. He has pursued the even tenor of his way through the past years, going straightforward in the prosecution of his ministerial duties, overcoming all difficulties and defying all antagonisms. Such a life of consecration is worthy of imitation. Preaching by example is more forcible than preaching by precept; but when a man does both, his influence for good is duplicated.

He was performing the duties of pastor and preacher in the station at Kansas City when he became involved in the troubles of the war, of which he has given the following statement:

> I was first arrested in Kansas City in the latter part of 1861, at the instance of a Northern Methodist, and confined in Fort Union for a short time, perhaps for not more than an hour, then released on parole and granted city limits.
>
> In the summer of 1862 I was greatly annoyed and frequently threatened by a Northern Methodist preacher, who had command of a company in Kansas City at that time. To avoid the relentless opposition and persecution of this man I left home two or three weeks. He said his Church was largely represented in the Federal army, and to a considerable extent influenced the United States forces, and that Southern Methodist preachers should be hunted and punished. I mention this to show that we were not persecuted for evil-doing, but simply because we were Southern Methodists. This, in their eyes, was a crime of the greatest magnitude.
>
> In the fall of 1862 I was ordered to pray for the President of the United States by name, for the United States Congress, and for the success of the Union army so called. This I refused to do; and said, among other things, that no man, or class of men should dictate my prayers.
>
> In the winter of 1863 I was assessed as a Southern sympa-

thizer. I refused to pay the unjust assessment. For this refusal I was arrested and put in the guard-house in Kansas City. Here I was kept in close confinement about twenty-four hours, when, in company with nine others imprisoned for the same offense, I was sent to Independence in a greasy wagon guarded by twenty men, and lodged in an exceedingly filthy prison. Col. W. R. Renick, then in command, refused to let us have our meals from the hotel or from our friends. We were kept in this filthy place about twenty-four hours, when we were unconditionally released by order of Gov. Gamble.

Believing that I could do no good, opposed as we were, and that cruel men were seeking my life, I left Kansas City in April, 1863. Soon after I left the Northern Methodists took possession of our Church.

In March, 1866, I was indicted in Independence for preaching without taking the oath of the new Constitution. I was arrested by the deputy sheriff, a man who before the war would not have been thought of in connection with that office. I gave bond for my appearance at the next term of court.

In the fall I appeared in court, when the case was continued. The next spring, the United States Supreme Court having decided the so-called "test oath" unconstitutional, my case was dismissed.

How willful, how malicious, and how unprovoked was the vexatious persecution of Mr. Pugh. He was cautious and prudent, gave offense to no one, studiously abstained from the strife and every thing partisan and political. But these things were no protection in those times. The Northern Methodist preachers who were his persecutors were no doubt enraged against him because he had left the M. E. Church (North) and united with the M. E. Church, South, some years prior to the war. His having deserted their Church would have a tendency to exasperate their feelings and make them more determined to give him all the trouble they could, and had he not left Kansas City he no doubt would have fallen a victim to their wrath.

REV. GREEN WOODS.

The fate of the man whose name appears just above is sad beyond description. It is enough to chill the reader's heart and make the blood congeal in his veins while he reads it. Why did they seek the destruction of the purest and best men in the country—men distinguished for their moral rectitude and Christian character; men whose hearts were pure, whose lives were righteous, whose influence was for good and against evil; men who were the salt of the earth, preserving it from moral putrefaction and death; men who were the religious and spiritual light of the world, without whose light darkness would cover the earth and gross darkness the people; unselfish men, who lived for God and humanity, who like their Lord went about doing good, preaching the gospel of salvation to lost sinners, transforming their character from evil to good, from wickedness to righteousness, from hatred to love, from vice to virtue, from falsehood to truth, from corruption to holiness—in short, from bad men to good men, who love God supremely and their neighbors as themselves? In this way they promoted the highest and best interests of humanity, and were benefactors of their race. Mr. Woods belonged to the class of Christian philanthropists who live for the good of their fellow-men. He was presiding elder of the Greenville District, St. Louis Conference. A description of his suffering and death is given by his eldest daughter, and will no doubt be read with intense interest:

> In the spring of 1862 the excitement in the country became so intense that my father could no longer travel his district; so he thought he would stay at home, and try to make enough to support his family on his farm. As the people in the neighborhood desired him to preach to them, he made an appointment to preach about three miles from home the second Sunday in May. He filled this appointment, and announced another at the same place for the second Sunday in June. Before that time arrived he was advised by some of his friends not to go to his appointment, as they believed he would be taken prisoner, and perhaps killed, that day by the soldiers if he attempted to preach. But he told them that he would go and preach, and if the soldiers wished to arrest him they could do so; that if necessary he could go to jail. He said he did not believe they would kill him, as he had not done any thing to be killed for.
>
> A man by the name of Silas Hamby, a member of the Methodist Church (North), had said some time before that no Southern Methodist preacher should preach at Mount Pleasant again. But my father thought it was an idle threat, as he had heard of no preacher being killed because he was a preacher.
>
> When Sunday morning came, father and my sister, younger than myself, went to Mount Pleasant, and he preached to a small congregation, the people being afraid to turn out on account of the soldiers, and returned home the same evening unmolested. The next morning he took my sister (just thirteen years of age) and two little boys that he had hired, and went out to a field one mile from home, to finish planting corn. While they were at work the mother of the boys came by the field, on her way to our house. She saw that they were nearly done, so she thought she would wait until they finished, and come along with them. By this means there was one grown person present to witness his arrest. I think that it was about the middle of the forenoon of that Monday, June 9, 1862, when sixteen men,

armed and uniformed as Federal soldiers, came to our house and surrounded it. They inquired for father. Mother told them that he was not at home, but out in the field. (Father told her if they came and called for him to tell them where he was.) They made a general search, and then huddled up out in the yard and held a council for a few minutes. Five of them were sent to the field, and while they were gone those at the house were stealing every thing they could get their hands on that belonged to father, leaving very few things behind.

When the five soldiers got to the field father was not quite done planting. They rode up and asked if his name was Green Woods. He told them it was. They told him that he was the man they were after, and ordered him to alight over the fence. He asked them if they could not wait until he finished planting, as he had then but a few short rows; but they told him with an oath that they were in a hurry, and kept hurrying him while he was getting his horse ready to start. When they started from the field my sister asked them what they intended to do with father. They told her with an oath that it was uncertain where he would get to before he came back. They brought him to the house, and allowed him to eat his dinner; but when he went to dress himself he could not find a change of clothes, as the soldiers had taken all that he had and would not even give him his pants and hat. They took him about three miles from home, to a man's house by the name of Jones, and pretended to get evidence against him. They then took him about three miles from home, in another direction, to where a man lived named Peter Skiles, who kept a blacksmith shop. They stopped and staid there awhile, and searched the house. Skiles was a Southern man. They then took father about half a mile and killed him, and left him lying out in the woods away from the road, no one knew where except those who placed him there. Two guns were heard after the soldiers left Skiles's.

This was done on Monday, and his body was not found till the next Monday. We did not know that he was killed until his body was found. When found he was lying on his back, with his overcoat spread on the ground under him. One arm was stretched out one way, and the other stretched out the other way; his hat drawn over his face; his coat and vest and left glove lying on the ground near him; his right glove on; his left shirt-sleeve torn off, and his left hand off and gone. He seemed to have been dragged some two or three hundred yards before he was shot, as there was but little blood along the trail, and was found, as above described, near a large tree and among some low bushes.

We have heard several times that the Northern Methodist presiding elder, by the name of Ing, sent the men to kill my father. All the evidence we have that Ing sent the men is that he was their commander at the time; and it has been told by those who said they saw it that father's hand was carried to Ing as proof that they had killed him; and that he still had it in his possession a year or two ago.

[Signed] JOSEPHINE M. A. M. WOODS, Eldest Daughter;
E. A. WOODS, Wife; and
MARY LOUISA WOODS, Daughter of Rev. Green Woods.

CHAPTER V.
St. Louis Conference.

No Missouri or St. Louis. Conference Session This Year—The M. E. Church, South, in a State of Consternation and Disorganization—Loyal State and Loyal Church—United and Concentrated Efforts at the Annihilation of the M. E. Church, South—"You Are the Man We Are After"—Seizure of the Houses of Worship Belonging to Our Church—Her Property, for Which She Paid Her Money, and in Which She Had the Sole Right and Title for Many Years, Contested by the M. E. Church—Church in Kansas City Taken Possession of by M. E. Church—Abuse of Southern Methodists for not Uniting with Them—Some True Members Who Saved the Church—Murder of Rev. T. Glanville and His Son—Seizure of the Church at Independence—Independence Female College—Large and Costly House of Worship—Good Parsonage—Rev. H. N. Watts—Seizure of the Church at Springfield—Report of Committee—Rev. J. M. Breeding.

THERE are no published minutes of the Missouri and St. Louis Conferences this year, from the simple fact they did not hold their usual annual sessions. This they could not do in consequence of the cruel and fierce persecution through which the M. E. Church, South, was passing at that time. The Church was thrown into the greatest confusion and disorganization. Both shepherds and sheep were separated and scattered in every direction—hundreds, and some of them thousands of miles from their State and from their homes and families. A wide-spread scene of suffering and sorrow, dreadful to contemplate!

It is generally admitted as an historic fact that no class of men suffered during the war like the ministers of the M. E. Church, South. There are two reasons which make this a very singular fact: Missouri did not secede; she was not a secession State, and the ministers in Missouri, the history of whose persecution is now being written, had not seceded and did not secede. They were loyal citizens in a loyal State. No better patriots, no truer friends to the Constitution and Government of our country ever lived. Had they not the right, therefore, to expect and claim the protection of that government they loved so dearly, and whose laws they had never violated? Yet, as we see above, they were not allowed to hold their Annual Conference to transact the religious business of the Church.

Judging by the extensiveness and destructiveness with which was executed the well-arranged system of persecution, one would conclude that the object was the annihilation of the M. E. Church, South.

Their places must be vacated for others who expected to be their successors. But for the interposition of Divine Providence, it appears, in view of all the facts, that they would have accomplished their purpose. No doubt they themselves thought victory was certain and that possession was an assured fact. By taking an active part in the internecine war, by manifesting an active zeal for the safety of the country, and by wearing Federal uniform and insignia of military authority, they ingratiated themselves with the war department of the government. Thus gaining the confidence of the Federal officials and soldiers, they had no difficulty in prejudicing their minds and making them believe that the M. E. Church, South, was the cause of all their trouble, thereby securing co-operation in the overthrow and destruction of said Church. Indeed, did not some of their preachers vacate their pulpits and seek position and office in the Federal army, that they might more effectually accomplish the aforesaid purpose? With the sanction of the Federal authorities and with the forces of the Federal army, did they not make a direct raid upon the M. E. Church, South —upon an unarmed, defenseless, peaceable, loyal Church? Was it not their first object to get rid of the ministry of that Church, knowing that that would be a grand step toward her ruin?

While in eager pursuit of her preachers all over the State, whenever they met a person they supposed belonged to that class they would ask him: "Who are you?" or "Are you a Southern Methodist preacher?" Should he answer in the affirmative, they replied: "Well, you are the man we are after." They did not ask him: "Are you loyal? are you a peaceful and law-abiding citizen? Do you subscribe to the Constitution of the United States? and are you a supporter of our civil government?" He might easily have answered all the above questions in the affirmative; and if he were a Southern Methodist preacher, "he is the man they are after." The one unpardonable crime of being born on the south side of the Mason and Dixon line and being a Methodist preacher was enough to bring him under condemnation and subject him to the sorest persecution of confiscation, suffering, and death.

Nor were they satisfied with the persecution and discomfiture of her ministers; but did they not devise and put into practical operation a scheme of Church seizure by which they expected to come into the possession of all the property belonging to the M. E. Church, South?

After the property question between the two great branches of Methodism in the United States had been thoroughly litigated and settled by the highest judicature of the country, and after the M. E. Church, South, had enjoyed the peaceable and indisputable possession of her property for many years, did not these same persons conceive the idea and project a plan to contest the claims and dispute the titles of the original owners of that property, for every cent of which they had paid their own money? If they had invested any amount of money in said property, however small, or if they had had the merest shadow of a claim, upon the basis of justice and equity, do you suppose they would have remained silent all those years? Did they not know just as well as we did that they had no just claim, no equitable right to said property? Had they not already contested the title of the property of the M. E. Church, South, on several previous occasions, not only in violation of the "Plan of Separation" agreed to by both sides, and adopted by the General Conference of 1844, but also in violation of every principle of justice and equity? Did they not contest this right not only upon a large scale involving hundreds of thousands of dollars, but also on a small scale involving houses of worship along the border line between the two Churches?

The reader will recollect that according to the "Plan of Separation" the Methodist Societies living on the border line were allowed to choose to which Church they would attach themselves. In deciding the question the Society would belong to the Church, North or South, which received the majority of votes. This was the plan to which both parties assented—a very correct way in which to adjust the difficulty. And yet it seems that the M. E. Church was disposed to ignore the agreement. Did they not dispute the right of property in several places where the majority voted to adhere to the M. E. Church, South? This of course was prior to the decision of the Supreme Court of the United States in favor of the Church, South, One of the most notable instances was the Church in Maysville, Ky. The Methodist Society there numbered two hundred and fifty-six. When the question came up ninety-seven cast their votes to adhere North, while one hundred and fifty-nine adhered South. Notwithstanding this fact, the M.

E. Church sent their adherents a preacher and entered suit for the Church property. If the reader is at all acquainted with Church history, he already knows the decision in the case. It was taken to the State Court of Appeals. Chief-justice Marshall, an eminent jurist and noted for his probity, decided that the property justly and rightfully belonged to the M. E. Church, South. In making known his decision, among other things, he said: "There are now two distinct Churches in the place of the M. E. Church of the United States—the one the M. E. Church, North, the other the M. E. Church, South—these two differing from the original and from each other only in locality and in extent; each possessing in its locality the entire jurisdiction of the original Church." On this same basis of justice and equity the Supreme Court of the United States settled this whole question of Church property. And it was thought that this matter never would be agitated again, that it had been disposed of finally and forever. But all the courts in the United States, from the lowest to the highest, cannot change the ambitious and covetous disposition of the human heart, whether in individuals or Churches. The large fish naturally loves to swallow the small one, and realizes its own augmentation thereby, while the little fish loses its identity altogether; but in this case the little fish has never been willing to be swallowed, until it has grown into such large dimensions that deglutition would be a very difficult operation.

When the war broke out did not the identical ambitious spirit manifest itself in the same Church, which showed that prior to the war it was latent and lurking in their hearts, anxiously waiting for a suitable time to accomplish its selfish designs? and was not the Civil War hailed as a favorable opportunity? They knew that what could not be gained by courts of justice and equity might be accomplished by military power. For this purpose did they not, as already stated, form an alliance with the military department of the government? Did they not wear Federal uniforms, become captains and colonels, and fill many important offices in the army? All this gave them positions of influence and power among those who were engaged in quelling what they called the rebellion. Is it not known how they used their influence and power with intent to annihilate the M. E. Church, South? With their armed forces did they not pounce upon her as the hungry vulture pounces upon its devoted prey, proclaiming, as published in the papers, that "the Southern Methodist Church was the cause of the rebellion?" Hence destroy her, and the rebellion will soon disappear. A falser charge could not have been made; yet, believed, it had all the force of truth. Was not that the impression throughout the entire Federal army? and did they not prove it by their conduct of killing our preachers without *trial, judge,* or *jury,* giving them no opportunity of exonerating themselves from false accusations—prejudged, pre-condemned, indicted, imprisoned, banished, killed, without allowing them to say one word? Was not the order given, on some occasions, when they knew he was a Southern Methodist preacher, to "shoot him on sight?" and was it not done in some instances? Read this history, and you will ascertain for yourself.

Let it be understood that we bear no ill-will toward the M. E. Church. Like Saul of Tarsus, that conscientious man who thought he was doing God service in persecuting the infant Church of Christ unto strange cities and to death, so the M. E. Church was perhaps following the conviction of what she conceived to be her duty; but in view of existing facts and developments since the war will she not discover that she made a great mistake, though she then thought that she was doing the will of God in persecuting his people even unto strange cities and to death? And will she not, like Paul, repent of her wrong-doings? Then true fraternization would be established upon the honorable basis of justice and righteousness.

During this Conference year there appears to have been a general understanding among them to take possession of the property in Missouri belonging to the M. E. Church, South. There was a movement in that direction in all parts of the State—to seize, to hold, to possess, to use her houses of worship, her parsonages, her seminaries, and her colleges.

The following interesting account is given of

THE CHURCH IN KANSAS CITY.

In the fall of 1862 Rev. M. M. Pugh, then stationed at Kansas City, was forced by persecution to abandon his Church and charge, and fleé for protection to a neighboring military post. Mr. Pugh was watched by enemies and warned by friends. The threat, oft repeated, of arrest and imprisonment did not deter him; but to know that his steps were dogged, that detectives were on his track, that his life was threatened, and to be told by military officers that they could not be responsible for his life any night, and to be advised that there were liers-in-wait to assassinate him, put his life in too great a peril to remain with his people.

As soon as his absence was known the Northern Methodists took possession of the Church, and held it under military protection. They organized a Society, composed of a few Northern fanatics and a few renegade and weak-kneed Southern Methodists. They pronounced the M. E. Church, South, dead, and beyond the hope of resurrection; tried to get possession of the Church records, and to absorb all the former Society of Southern Methodist members, *nolens volens*. When they found that but few would accept the transfer they pronounced the rest disloyal, and threatened them with confiscation. "But none of these things moved them," and they maintained their fidelity to the Church of their choice, notwithstanding all the abuse and slander and threatenings and slaughter that these religious loyalists could bring to bear upon them.

After the occupancy of the church for some months, they became conscious of wrong-doing and of guilt, and in shame and humiliation turned the property over to the rightful owners. They found that m litary orders did not confer letters of administration. If the Church, South, were dead and buried, what right had they more than others to administer on the estate?*

In the *St. Louis Christian Advocate* of June 13, 1866, the subject is spoken of by the writer in the following language.

After Brother Pugh was run off the church was occupied for

---

* Dr. Leftwich's book.

some time by the Northern Methodists, who assumed that the Church property was theirs, to have and to hold, with all the appurtenances thereto belonging to them and to their successors forever. They abused Southern Methodists roundly, threatened them much, and with all the prestige of power assaulted the gates of our Zion until they became so offensive that all true friends of our Church and of the government gave them a wide berth and left them alone in their shame.

Some who in name only had been with us went out from us, to take shelter under their political banner, prove their loyalty to the government, and, as they were told, save their property and their lives, and be fitted, as it proved, to enjoy the product of others' labor and the spoils of pious conquest.

The faithful of our Church pursued the even tenor of their way, and when refused their own house of worship met in private houses to worship; and when denied this means of grace they kept up the sewing circle and mite society, and in this way the "faithful women not a few" preserved an organization, a name, and a life. While their harps were upon the willows they often sat down together and wept when they remembered their Zion, once so beautiful for situation, the joy of our hearts. They suffered all that the betrayal of Judas and the denial of Peter could inflict upon them; yet, believing truth and right, though nailed to the cross and buried in the tomb, would, like the divine Redeemer, rise again, leading captivity captive and conferring gifts upon men, they waited patiently and hopefully till their change should come. And it did come, and that by a way they knew not. They were, like their Lord, "despised and rejected of men," yet their faith failed not. They had confidence in the Church and the pledges of her risen Head. Their faith grew sublime as the darkness increased and the troubles multiplied about them. They heard in the thick darkness the promise, "The gates of hell shall not prevail against the Church;" and, bowing to the storm, they sheltered themselves in the clefts of the everlasting Rock "until these calamities be overpassed."

There were some men in authority who loved the right and hated the wrong. There were also "good men and true" in the Church, whose loyalty to the government was only equaled by their fidelity to the Church; and neither could be shaken by all the libels and slanders of ecclesiastical hirelings. When such men have the adjustment of the rights of property, truth and righteousness will prevail, and justice will be reached in the end. To such are we indebted for our Church property in Kansas City.

Whenever persons think and act under the dictation and impulsion of an enlightened conscience—a Bible-taught conscience—you may be sure they will think and act right. They adhere unswervingly to the principles of truth and righteousness, of justice and equity, and no motive, however strong, could induce them to violate any one of these divine principles. It is true they are fallible, and may do wrong through ignorance or mistake; but their intention is right, their motive is pure. It seems to this writer that the case of the Southern Methodist Church in Kansas City fell into the hands of just such persons. Ascertaining the facts in the case—who purchased the property, who paid their money for it, who met the annual expenses of keeping it in good repair for lo! these many years past—with these facts before them, they hesitated not to turn the property over into the possession of those to whom it rightfully belonged. If other Church property seized by the M. E. Church in other places in this State had fallen into the hands of such good men as were at Kansas City, how much of anxiety and trouble and expense it would have saved the M. E. Church, South! While some of them were seizing the Church property of the M. E. Church, South, in Missouri, others, with swords and bayonets, with pistols and guns, were eagerly pursuing and killing her ministers. We shall not stop with the mere mention of such startling facts, but will give examples, as they were quite numerous during the Civil War.

Rev. Thomas Glanville and Son.

This useful minister of the gospel and true servant of God might have used the language that was once applied to Christ: "The zeal of thine house hath eaten me up." Though his life was in imminent danger, he could not refrain from preaching the glorious gospel of salvation. He was told of his perilous condition, and he knew that his life had been threatened; but there were destitute portions of the country in which sinners were perishing for the bread of life, and souls were being lost because the word of God was not preached to them. The fire seemed to be shut up in his bones, and he felt that he must preach though it might cost him his life. The following notice of his tragical end was furnished by a personal friend:

It was the privilege of the writer to be intimately acquainted with the subjects of this sketch for more than a score of years. Without reference to official documents, or private papers, I write mostly from memory, hoping thereby to preserve the precious memory of two worthy men.

Rev. Thomas Glanville was born in England about 1811 A.D., and came to America when about sixteen years of age. He was converted to God in early life, and after much mental agony yielded to the conviction that it was his duty to preach.

Soon after he began to preach he joined the St. Louis Conference, M. E. Church, South, and traveled several years. But family afflictions came upon him—his wife died and left him three children. He married again, and soon after located.

Time rolled on, and ever found him diligent in business, fervent in spirit, serving the Lord, and laboring efficiently as a local preacher. In the fall of 1852 a camp-meeting was held in his neighborhood by the lamented Leeper, Anthony, and Bond. Brother Glanville's three children were at the altar as penitents. All the tender sympathies of a father's heart went out after them. How pointed his instructions! and O how fervent his prayers! He told the writer that he had made a vow that if the Lord would accept his three children at that meeting he would rejoin the Conference and travel and preach as long as his way seemed open. The Lord did mercifully accept his three children; and, true to his vow, he rejoined the Conference and remained in it till the day of his death.

When the late Civil War commenced, and the flock in Southwest Missouri was left for the most part without a shepherd, he and the local preachers of his neighborhood met in council and went out "two and two" and held meetings in the most destitute neighborhoods. After a time he was ordered by a militia captain to discontinue his meetings. This grieved him much, but he yielded and remained silent for almost a year.

In February, 1863, a meeting was appointed in one of those destitute neighborhoods, which he attended. The "fire was shut up in his bones," and in company with a friend he waited on the captain then in command in that vicinity, and requested permission to resume his duties as a minister. To his great joy, he received a written permission, and the next night he preached a sermon full of joy and comfort.

In July or August following three men called at his gate one dark night and ordered him to leave the country on pain of death. A few days after he remarked to the writer that he would like to live to see peace restored to the country, and he hoped he would, and then added: "Those fellows may kill me, but I think not. Of one thing I am certain: they can't harm me; death has no terrors for me, and has not had for fifteen years."

He was a bold and fearless man. Conscious innocence knows no fear; but through the entreaties of his friends he left home for a month or more; and it is to be regretted that he made up his mind to return, and did so, saying that he would risk the consequences.

He published an appointment for preaching, and a few hours before the time came two militia soldiers waited on him and informed him that he would not be permitted to hold the service. He remained at home that Sabbath, and remarked to a neighbor: "Those fellows will kill me, I believe; but they shall never have it to say that they shot me in the back." That holy Sabbath was his last on earth.

When night came on, and good men laid them down to peaceful slumbers, his murderers approached his quiet dwelling. A ball discharged from a revolver passed through the window, entered his face, and he fell to the floor. To make sure of their victim, the murderers raised the window and, reaching in, shot him through the chest. They then went round and forced open the door, and three men entered. After a few words with Brother Glanville's son, one of them remarked that he had better finish the old man, and so saying shot him again. Thus died Rev. Thomas Glanville in the fifty-third year of his age.

After threatening to burn the house and ordering the family to leave on short time, they rode two miles to the residence of Brother Glanville's eldest son, Mr. A. C. Glanville, a man of fine mind and respectable literary attainments, with a meek and quiet spirit, and a member of the M. E. Church, South. They called him up, and, entirely unconscious of his father's fate and his own danger, he made a light. No sooner was the light made than a ball passed through his window, entered his head, and he fell lifeless on the hearth. Thus perished father and son in one night.

Brother Glanville had for many years been an ordained elder in the M. E. Church, South, and while as a preacher he was neither profound nor brilliant, yet he possessed a sound mind, a good understanding in the things of God, was a good sermonizer, and improved every year, so that his future was quite promising. Peace to his memory! JOHN H. ROSS.

SEIZURE OF THE CHURCH AT INDEPENDENCE.

The following account of the seizure of the

Southern Methodist Church at Independence is given by a competent and interesting writer, and no doubt will be read with lively interest:

In company with a number of lady friends I paid a flying visit to Independence, Mo. Rev. W. H. Lewis had the students of his college out in a beautiful grove, with hundreds of friends enjoying a May-day celebration in which the Queen of Spring was coroneted with very interesting exercises in which the young ladies of the college took an active part, making the occasion highly entertaining and enjoyable. There were many of that happy band of young ladies who had met me on Saturdays for religious instruction, now so grown and changed that even a few short years had strangely counterfeited the *seventy-nine* beautiful, innocent faces that still hang in one picture-group in my library-room. That picture I have, for it perpetuates what they *were then;* yet, glad as we were to meet after so long a separation, I had to be told who many of them *are* now. Some are grown and married, others far away, and some are gone to the brighter world for which they made such early preparation.

There were also many old, familiar faces who had stood by the Church and country during all that long reign of terror. Time has been kinder to them than war, and they look happy and hopeful on this festive occasion. Brother Lewis, who was President of the Howard Female College at Fayette during the war, has returned to Independence, now that the war is over, and re-occupies his splendid buildings with a large and flourishing school, appreciated by the people, and deserves an extensive patronage.

There, too, stands that elegant church with its stained windows and tall, graceful spire, at once the pride and ornament of the city; but its aisles are trod by other feet, its cushioned pews are occupied by other worshipers than those who built, paid for, and owned the property. The pulpit and altar, so tastefully fitted and furnished by the young men in 1857, are served by other hands and other tongues.

The parsonage, which has housed so many good men and their families of our Church, for whom it was built, is now oc-

cupied by another, and the spacious yard, once so tastefully
and usefully ornamented with shade and fruits and flowers and
evergreens, by the writer, is laid waste and almost bare, now
the common resort of horses, cows, hogs, dogs, and children
which have no right there.

Sadly I turned away from a scene of wrong and desecration
to reflect upon the moral condition of the hearts that could perpetrate such sacrilegious injustice. What right have the Northern Methodists to this property? Did they build it, buy it,
pay for it, or even give one dollar toward it? What claim do
they set up? If there be a higher standard of justice and right
than civil law or inspired gospel, these men may find some
claim.

For twenty years that property had been held by trustees,
regularly appointed, for the use and benefit of the M. E. Church,
South, and no one questioned their legal right, or sought to
disturb their peaceable possession. But during the "reign of
terror" in 1862-64, under which so many people lost their lives
and so many more their property in Jackson County, and under
the oft-reiterated threats of Northern Methodists and their hirelings, the property passed out of our hands without the formal-
ities of bargain and sale, or legal transfer of title. A Rev.
James Lee, of the M. E. Church (North), made his appearance
and demanded possession of the church. He first demanded
the key, which the rightful owners refused to give up. He
then appealed to the military commander of the post. This
officer ordered the trustees of the M. E. Church, South, to report the key to his head-quarters under pain of confiscation and
banishment. The key was surrendered to him, and he gave it
to Mr. Lee with his authority to hold and use the Church.
After Mr. Lee got possession of the house of worship he, as if
to "add insult to injury," went through with a formal dedication service, setting the house apart to the worship of God as
though it had been a pagan temple; after which it was used by
the Northern Methodists as though it belonged of right to them,
and without any seeming compunctions of conscience.

In 1864 Rev. Mr. De Mott was sent by his Church to hold
possession of and use the property. Not content with the
church, he demanded the parsonage. He already had the coat,
and he wanted the cloak also. But the trustees of the M. E.

Church, South, had rented the parsonage to a poor widow, Mrs. Brazil by name. Mr. De Mott asked her to vacate the house; this she declined to do. He demanded the key; she refused to give it up. He then appealed to the commander of the post, and returned with a military order for her to vacate the parsonage, giving her a short time in which to do it.

To turn a defenseless and helpless widow, with her children and household effects, into the streets to make room for a Northern Methodist minister to occupy and hold property that belonged to others was, perhaps, a military movement of great strategic importance to the cause of the Union and the restoration of the government; but in the sight of moral honesty and Christian decency the military maneuver becomes a pious fraud which the perpetrators were forced, after using its opportunities for several years, to confess before men.

The church and parsonage were occupied and used by Mr. De Mott when, in the fall of 1865, Rev. M. M. Pugh was appointed by the St. Louis Annual Conference, M. E. Church, South, to the Independence Station. On his arrival he made a formal demand of Mr. De Mott for the property. This was just as formally refused, the occupant declaring at the same time that he had been sent there by his Church to hold that property for the use and benefit of the M. E. Church, and he intended to do it. Recourse was had to the law, and suit for possession was instituted.

The ladies, believing that they had the first and best right to the property, and chagrined at this refusal, entered the Church one day with their knitting and sewing, to the number of thirty, and conducted themselves in a peaceable, quiet, and orderly way, to spend the day in the house of worship built and paid for by their fathers, husbands, and brothers. The Northern Methodist preacher, soon apprised of the fact, hastened to a civil magistrate and made affidavit that these ladies were "disturbing the peace," procured a peace warrant and a constable and proceeded to the church, where he found these orderly ladies "assembled, neither with multitude or tumult," and had them arrested and dragged before the civil officer for trial. With all of their "false witnesses" nothing was found in them "worthy of prison or of death;" and binding them over to keep the peace, they were released.

The suit spoken of was called in the Circuit Court for the spring of 1866, when Mr. De Mott made affidavit that important witnesses were absent and he was not ready for trial. The case was continued. The following fall term of the court was held, and the defendants again swore that they were not ready for trail. Again the case was continued, but it was apparent that the motive for continuing the case so often was the further use of the property of which they knew the law would deprive them. They were never ready for trial, but began to feel the force of public sentiment and the shame of fradulent dealing, if the sense of shame still remained; and the wiser and abler of them began to fear the penalty not only of fraud, but of rents and damages, and advised a compromise. In February, 1867, they proposed through their counsel, one Col. Hines, to surrender the property and pay all costs if the M. E. Church, South, would withdraw the suit. To this Messrs. Sawyer, Chrisman & Hovey, counsel for plaintiffs, agreed. The suit was accordingly withdrawn, the property vacated, and the rightful owners took possession.*

In the first part of the above narrative we are carried back in memory to the place where we spent twelve years very pleasantly in charge of Independence Female College prior to the war. After the war we returned to Independence and had a large and flourishing school until we sold the college buildings to the city for a public school. It was there and then before the war that we enjoyed the pleasure of making the acquaintance of Dr. Leftwich, who was preaching near enough to visit Independence frequently. So that our acquaintance was cultivated into genuine friendship, which has known no abatement through more than three decades of years. How much does this writer admire that true Christian friendship that

---

* Dr. Leftwich, in *St. Louis Christian Advocate.*

nothing changes—the same through the mutations of days and weeks, of months and years, and will be the same through the revolving cycles of eternity. Such friendship is more valuable than silver and gold, more precious than pearls and diamonds.

REV. H. N. WATTS.

The oldest, the most influential and useful ministers were the special victims of the persecutors of the M. E. Church, South. Mr. Watts was one of the excellent of the earth—a holy, consecrated man; active, zealous, energetic, persevering, and indefatigable in the performance of his ministerial duties. He occupied a high position in the St. Louis Conference, filled various offices in the Church with fidelity and success, and perhaps has accomplished as much good as any intinerant preacher in said Conference. His whole mind was absorbed in the one work of preaching the gospel; while the politics, secularities, and temporalities of this world did not trouble him much. His conversation was in heaven. The following is authentic:

In 1863 Mr. Watts was living in Charleston, Mississippi County, Mo.; and on the 23d of July was arrested at his house by a squad of soldiers, accompanied by Meeker Thurman, Aaron W. and John Grigsby, and taken to Columbus, Ky. He was charged with no crime, and no offense against the laws and peace of the government was ever alleged against him. In vain did he plead the protection of the Constitution of the United States. He was threatened with banishment or imprisonment during the war, unless he would take and subscribe a military oath, which was as repugnant to his feelings as oppressive to the rights of conscience. After taking the oath to secure his liberty, and receiving some personal abuse as a minister of the gospel, he was released and permitted to return to his home, after an absence of several days.

In the spring of 1864, and while Capt. Ewing's company of militia were stationed in Charleston, and Lieut. James A. Reed was assistant provost-marshal, Mr. Watts was prohibited from preaching the gospel for several weeks by military authority. He continued, however, to travel his circuit and hold religious services. He would read the word of God, sing, pray, and exhort the people to "flee from the wrath to come," and "lead peaceable and quiet lives in all godliness and honesty.*

He was very fortunate indeed in passing through the troubles of these perilous times as well as he did.

THE CHURCH AT SPRINGFIELD.

Prior to the war the members and friends of the M. E. Church, South, erected a costly and magnificent house of worship in Springfield. It was perhaps the finest church in the State outside of the metropolis. It was an object of strong temptation to those who were seizing churches *vi et armis*. While they burned to ashes cheaper houses of worship through that part of the State, they took care to preserve the elegant edifice in Springfield for their own use. Their title to the cheap churches was just as good as to the costly ones. Strange they burned their own houses (?)!

In the report of the committee appointed by the St. Louis Conference to investigate the matter the reader will find satisfactory information concerning it:

---
* Dr. Leftwich's book.

St. Louis Conference.

To the Bishops and Members of the St. Louis Conference.

The committee to whom was referred the subject of your Church property at Springfield, Mo., and instructed to take such measures as they deemed proper to recover the property, beg leave to submit the following report:

One member of your committee (R. P. Faulkner) residing at Arlington, Mo., and two members in St. Louis, and the property in question and parties holding it being in Springfield, Mo., have had to labor at considerable disadvantage and loss of time, owing to these distances.

Yet we have endeavored to give the matter all the attention that so important a trust deserved, and for the sake of common justice and our sacred Christianity we regret to state that our house of worship at Springfield is not yet in our possession.

But we are happy to state that we have reason to believe that we shall soon regain that which is justly our own.

A part of your action on this subject at your last session was "that the presiding elder of the Springfield District should see that the Board of Trustees of our property at Springfield be immediately filled, according to the Discipline."

We take pleasure in stating that your instructions in this matter have been complied with by Rev. G. M. Winton, P. E., and the following-named gentlemen appointed trustees: Lawson Fulbright, Elisha Headlee, Thomas W. Cunningham, Adam C. Mitchell, and William Montgomery.

Parsonage Property.—In the examination of this question we found that the house was taken possession of about the middle of the year 1863 by the authorities of the M. E. Church, under the idea that it would be destroyed as an enemy of the national government if not protected by them, and was subsequently held and used by them under the discovery that it was deeded to the M. E. Church, a Church without representative or existence in that part of Missouri at the date of said deed.

The facts in regard to the title of this property are best explained by reference to a letter herewith submitted (marked A), from Rev. B. R. Johnson, formerly a member of your Conference, now of California.

Thus it appears that the title of the M. E. Church to this property is from a clerical mistake (?) and a strong desire to protect our interests from destruction.

We would further state on this point that our examinations satisfy that the rental for the use of this property should be at least $25 per month for the whole time (four and a half years) it has been saved from destruction by our friends (?). As will be seen in a subsequent part of this report, a claim equal to the sum of the rental is made by those who have possessed and protected this property for "needed repairs." We will recur to this subject again in its place.

House of Worship.—We regret exceedingly to have to report a sad disappointment to our friends—the occupants—who were deprived of the use of this house after great preparations had been made for a fair, festival, and feast of fat things, by a thunder-storm whose lightning struck the church and well-nigh settled the controversy in regard to it.

As soon as practicable your committee convened at the St. Nicholas Hotel, St. Louis, and among other things determined that it was necessary for one or more of the committee to visit Springfield.

Shortly thereafter R. P. Faulkner went to Springfield and, on an inquiry into the matter, elicited from the authorities of the M. E. Church a proposition for settlement which will be presented presently.

Just previous to this William C. Jamison, a member of your committee, received the following letter from Judge Baker, of Springfield (marked B).

We here present the proposition referred to above (marked C), with a letter from R. P. Faulker to the committee (marked "one"). On receiving this communication your committee convened at Arlington, and on due consideration of the propositions, made to them the following answer herewith submitted (marked D).

This, our answer to the committee on the part of the M. E. Church, we inclosed to the Hon. John S. Phelps, of Springfield, with the following letter of instructions (marked E).

Immediately after closing its session at Arlington your committee received the following letter from Rev. J. J. Bently, presiding elder of Springfield District, M. E. Church (North), relating to the parsonage (marked F). This communication was immediately sent to Hon. John S. Phelps, our counsel.

Thus we have given you all that we have been able to do

St. Louis Conference.

in this matter, simply adding our opinion that we will ultimately recover our property.

The condition of the church at Springfield, as will be seen by reference to the letter of R. P. Faulkner, who examined it, requires immediate attention.

The damage done to the house on the occasion of the *defeat of the religious fair* is thus reported on by R. P. Faulkner: "Though seriously damaged, yet it can be repaired for much less than I had any idea of until I visited it. I had a builder go and examine and make a rough estimate of the cost to repair the damage, including every thing but seats, pulpit, etc.; who reported to me that if a thousand dollars would not do it, twelve hundred would."

The committee submitted the following resolutions:

1. *Resolved*, That the bishop be requested to station one of the most efficient pulpit and business men at Springfield.

2. That the Missionary Society be requested to make as liberal appropriations as they are able for the support of the preacher stationed at Springfield.

3. That with the approval of our counsel at Springfield and the recommendation of the Board of Trustees, the preacher in charge be authorized and requested to visit such places as he may see proper to raise means to pay debts and repairs on the church.

4. That the whole matter pertaining to the church and parsonage at Springfield be referred to the presiding elder of Springfield District, the preacher in charge of the station, and the trustees of the Church.

Respectfully submitted.   W. M. PROTTSMAN,
W. C. JAMISON.

We have a striking instance of the fierce and fiery persecutions to which the ministers of the M. E. Church, South, were subjected in the experience of

REV. J. M. BREEDING,

an account of which is taken from a very authentic source:

In March, 1863, Mr. Breeding was residing on Barker's Creek, Henry County, Mo. His wife was very sick: not able to raise her head from the pillow. When they were alone, and at midnight, three armed men opened the yard gate, rode rapidly up to the house, and called for Mr. Breeding to come out. This he declined to do, telling them that he could hear what they had to say where he was. He saw from the door, which he held ajar, that they held their pistols well in hand, as if awaiting an object to shoot. They ordered him to come out a second time, and in no genteel language. He refused, saying to them that if they would come to see him in the day-time he would see and talk with them like neighbors.

They asked him if he was armed. He told them that he was a civil man, and had some plows with which he expected to cultivate the ground in the summer; and did not let them know that he was wholly unarmed. They asked his politics, and were informed that he never meddled with the politics of the country; that his only platform was "repentance toward God and faith in the Lord Jesus Christ." "You are a preacher, then?" "Yes, I belong to the M. E. Church, South." "Well, that is just what we have understood, and we don't intend to let such a man live in this country. We have come with authority to order you to leave in six days, and if you are here at the expiration of that time it will not be well with you. We want to know whether you intend to leave or not."

Mr. Breeding asked for their authority, which they declined to give, whereupon he told them that as he had not meddled in any way with their political strife he did not think any sane officer would send them at such a time on such business. They remarked that he could either obey or risk the consequences, and turned and rode off.

A few days after this occurrence Mr. Breeding learned from the nearest military post, through a friend, that no such order had been issued; but that the commander of the post, Capt. Galliher, would not be responsible for what his men did from under his eye.

During the following summer there were very few nights when one or more of these lawless men was not seen prowling about the premises and keeping the preacher in constant dread of arson or assassination. He had no peace and felt no security.

In July his appointment in Calhoun was attended one Sabbath by a Lieut. Combs, with his company of men, whom he stationed at convenient places about the church and along the road near the church, as though they expected to encounter a desperate enemy.

As he approached the church and began to comprehend the situation he discovered what he afterward learned were signals. When these signals were made the whole force moved out to the road and advanced rapidly toward the preacher. He was halted and his name demanded.

"You pray for bush-whackers, I learn," said the officer.

"No more than for other sinners," the preacher answered.

"But," said the officer, "some of the boys tell me they have heard you pray for the success of bush-whackers. They say they have known you long, and that you are an original secessionist; that you have always believed in secession."

The preacher appealed to those who had known him the longest, if they ever heard him utter disloyal sentiments or knew him to attend a political meeting of any kind. He was no political partisan, and never had been. They finally told him that he was a Southern Methodist preacher, and that was enough, as they were all rebels.

While this conversation was going on, and most of the company were in disorder, a squad of men were drawn up in line in front of the preacher with their guns ready for use. Lieut. Combs stepped up in front of these men, when the conversation closed with the preacher, and talked to them some time in a subdued tone of voice. At the close of the interview one of the men said in a low voice, "Well, if you will not let us shoot him, we will egg him," and started off to a barn near by, from which he soon returned with his hands full of eggs. The officer would not let him use the eggs, and, after some further conversation, he dismissed the preacher and took his company back to headquarters.

In a few days after this Mr. Breeding had occasion to go to Windsor for medicine for his afflicted wife. There he again met these Calhoun soldiers. They were very annoying and insulting. A mounted squad of them started off before Mr. Breeding was ready, and took the road leading to his house. When he started home, and had reached the forks of the road, he was going to take the plainest and best road, but his horse pulled so obstinately for the other that he finally yielded and reached his home in safety. The next day a friend came to see if he was safe, and informed him that the squad of soldiers that left Windsor before him waylaid the road to assassinate him. What a providential deliverance!

The next Sabbath Mr. Breeding had a regular appointment to preach at Windsor. With the Sabbath morning came a foraging party to his house demanding breakfast. They staid and detained the preacher until it was too late to reach his appointment. This detention saved him from further trouble, and perhaps his life. He afterward learned that a band of twenty men were all that morning on the road that he was expected to pass. When it became so late they supposed that he had gone some other way, they went to the Church, surrounded it, and entered, but to discover again their disappointment. The preacher was nowhere to be found; and in consultation, some wanted to go immediately to his house and inflict summary punishment, but other counsels prevailed, and they determined to try him again the next Sabbath at his appointment at Moffat's school-house.

The Sabbath came, and with its earliest rays came a messenger from Mr. Owen, a Baptist friend, requesting Mr. Breeding to come to the house immediately, as his son was at the point of death. Mr. Breeding went without delay several miles in a direction from the church. After detaining him as long as he could, Mr. Owen informed him of a trap set for him that day, and that he must remain at his house all day. The preacher was not aware of any evil designs, and only yielded to much earnest solicitation to keep out of harm's way.

After having so often and so narrowly escaped, Mr. Breeding thought it best to seek safety elsewhere. Accordingly, he disposed of his effects, packed up, and journeyed to Macon County, in North Missouri, and settled down near the old Hebron Church. He found at his new little home a faithful band of men and women who met every Sabbath where prayer was wont to be made. To these he gladly joined himself.

By this time religious privileges were few and religious liberty greatly abridged by the operation of the "new Constitution." Ministers were afraid to preach, and the membership discouraged and depressed. The party in power were very vigilant in hunting out and dragging before the civil courts all non-juring ministers.

Mr. Breeding could not take the oath, and he contented himself for some time with an occasional exhortation to the faithful few who still kept the altar fires burning in a quiet way.

The prayer-meetings began to attract the attention of those in authority. They concluded that Mr. Breeding must be preaching, as the meetings were so regular and so well attended. The superloyalists determined that if such were the case they would take the law into their own hands and see what virtue there was in powder and ball.

The next Sabbath found eight armed men on the front seat to enforce the new Constitution. There appeared an equal number of orderly citizens prepared to protect the peaceful worship of the congregation. For a time matters wore quite a menacing aspect.

The prayer-meeting exercises were had, and Mr. Breeding closed up with a warm and earnest exhortation. The services were somewhat abbreviated, that the unfriendly parties might the sooner be separated.

The next Sabbath the same armed superloyalists were present, but the friends of peace and order were absent. The preacher had great liberty in the service, and felt no way intimidated by the presence of armed men on the front bench. During his earnest exhortation, founded upon a favorite text, the men became somewhat excited, but they had either not chosen a leader or the leader showed the white feather. They kept calling one upon the other to start. "You start, and I will follow!" "No; you start, and I will follow!" were expressions, though whispered, that could be heard by those near them. Such things did not deter the preacher. They could not browbeat him, and finally, in their shame, they vented their pique on a luckless dog that lay stretched out on the floor near them.*

Thus by the guiding and protecting hand of Divine Providence Mr. Breeding was brought safely through all his trials and persecutions. On several

---

* Dr. Leftwich's book.

different occasions, and at different times, and in different places death seemed inevitable, and yet in every crisis deliverance came in a way that he knew not. No one can read the foregoing narrative of his sufferings without seeing the direct and positive interference of Providence in his rescue from danger and from death. He could very appropriately have made a personal application of David's language: "The Lord is my rock, and my fortress, and my deliverer; my God, my strength, in whom I will trust; my buckler, and the horn of my salvation, and my high tower."

CHAPTER VI.
MISSOURI CONFERENCE.

Conference at Fulton—No Bishop Present—Minute Business—History Confined Chiefly to the Persecution of Her Ministers and Seizure of the Property Belonging to the M. E. Church, South—The Unarmed and Innocent Persecuted at Their Homes and at Their Houses of Worship—Denying the History Does Not Change the Facts—Murder of Rev. John L. Woods, a Local Preacher—Local Preachers Fill an Important Place in the Church—Persecution of Rev. D. B. Cooper Given by Dr. Harris—Persecution of Rev. W. M. Rush—Troubles of Rev. Tyson Dines, as Given by Rev. R. P. Farris, D.D., Presbyterian Minister—Rev. James Penn and His Four Clerical Sons—Severe Trials of Rev. Jesse Bird, as Stated by Himself—Spiritual State of the Church, by Rev F. A. Savage.

THE Forty-seventh Session of the Missouri Annual Conference was held at Fulton, Mo., October 14-20, 1863. No bishop being present, Andrew Monroe presided, and John D. Vincil was elected Secretary. After the usual committees were appointed, the regular minute business was taken up.

James O. Swinney was admitted on trial. John W. Adkisson, Samuel Alexander, S. J. Huffaker, and George C. Brown remained on trial. M. McIlhany, James S. Smith, and Jacob McEwin were admitted into full connection. W. W. McMurry was deacon of one year. James S. Smith, M. McIlhany, and J. McEwin were traveling preachers who were elected and ordained deacons. The traveling preachers, H. A. Bourland, George Penn, John F. Shores, C. W. Collett, and Henry G. McEwin were elected and ordained elders. C. W. Pritchett, Thomas Demoss, N. P. Halsey, T. Hurst, George Fenton, Joseph Devlin, Jesse Sutton, L. R. Downing, A. P. Lynn, S. J. Huffaker, Jesse Faubion, W. W. McMurry, and E. H. Hudson were supernumerary. John F. Young, R. P. Holt, D. C. Blackwell, W. M. Wood, and M. L. Eads were superannuated.

The destructive Civil War was moving forward with increasing momentum, devastating the country and spreading wreck and ruin in its course. The Church papers being suppressed, the St. Louis Annual Conference having no published minutes, the Missouri Conference meeting only long enough to transact its minute business and make the appointments, and all other means of information being cut off, leave the historian with very scant materials for writing history outside of the war troubles.

Therefore during the war period the history of "Methodism in Missouri" is necessarily confined mostly to the persecution of the ministers and the seizure of the property of the M. E. Church, South, by their "friends (?) the enemy." The questions may be asked: "What better could have been expected? Were they not secessionists, and in favor of the rebellion?" Their lives during the war sufficiently answers these questions. Let it be understood that we are now speaking of them as a *class*. We readily admit that some of them, on their own individual responsibility, did espouse the Confederate cause, but not a sufficient number to brand the *whole Church* with secession. If they had persecuted only those who took part in the rebellion, the case would have been very different. The fact is, they were not the ones they persecuted. They eagerly pursued the destruction of those ministers who refused to join the Confederate army, who did not participate in the rebellion, who staid at home as loyal, peaceable, and good citizens, and who gave their undivided time and attention to their one work of preaching the gospel of peace and salvation to lost sinners. They realized all the time in their consciousness that they were called of God to preach his word, and every one of them truly felt " Woe is me if I preach not the gospel." With some their conviction of duty was so strong that they would rather die than not to preach. See one with Christian heroism standing in the pulpit as the messenger of heaven, confronted by ten or twenty or thirty armed men, looking vengeance at him, and with drawn and presented muskets and bayonets, pistols and swords, ready at the slightest signal and as quick as powder to dispatch their devoted victim! But behold him unmoved, self-possessed, undaunted, preaching to his persecutors in a calm, clear, strong tone of voice, calling them to " repentance toward God and faith toward the Lord Jesus Christ!"

Where did the persecutors go to find the victims of their cruelty? Did they go to the Confederate army, to the ranks of those who were arrayed against the Federal cause, or to those who were engaged in recruiting the Southern forces? Had they gone there, they would have met an enemy in arms, and would have had to do some fighting. They preferred to carry on their warfare among non-combatant, peaceable, and law-abiding citizens, particularly among ministers and Churches whose religion teaches them that their weapons are not carnal, but spiritual; and tells them to put up their sword in its place, that they who use the sword shall perish by the sword, and to follow peace with all men. Hence to find the objects of their pursuit they went to their peaceful and quiet homes in the dead hour of midnight; found the inmates sleeping soundly and sweetly in the arms of innocence and domestic happiness. But O how quickly does the scene change into an awful tragedy! They awaken the man of the house with the shrill and loud whoops of midnight assassins. As the man, who is somewhat alarmed, but not knowing that there is any thing wrong, strikes a light, a pistol is fired, sending a bullet through the man's head, and he falls dead on the hearth. When the persecutors fail to find them at home they follow them to their fields, where they are at work cultivating the ground to make a support for their dependent families. They hurry them from their fields into the woods, and cruelly murder them in the first thicket they come to. Sometimes they penetrate the woods several miles, and for many days their families are in ignorance of their fate, and when found the bodies have been mutilated by the hogs. Again, these wicked persecutors go to Church where the people are assembled in worship, to kill the preacher—go there on the Sabbath. What a singular time and place for men to go armed and equipped for battle! They unceremoniously drag the minister out of the pulpit, and carry him off to do just what they please with him; and history tells what they did with many of them. It not only tells what they did with them, but also tells who did it—who were the prime movers, instigators, and actors in it. No intelligent person can read carefully the history of the persecution of the M. E. Church, South, during the war without understanding the source from whence all their trouble came. History cannot fail to reveal this truth, because it deals in facts and makes those facts known; and to deny the facts of history only proves the guilt of the persons to whom the facts relate. The Roman Catholics' trying to repudiate the history of their cruel persecutions of the true followers of Christ, in the days of the inquisition and martyrdom, does not change the mind of any one acquainted with their history. They would gladly expunge the abominable record that they have been making, running back for more than a thousand years, but they had just as well try to blot the sun out of the heavens. That history will live as a testimony against them when marble monuments shall have crumbled into dust.

Rev. John L. Wood.

He was a local preacher of the M. E. Church, South, in Sullivan County, Mo. He occupied an honorable and useful position in the Church. The local ministry is a power for good in the Church. It is impossible for the itinerant preachers to visit every neighborhood and preach in every community throughout the entire country. It is as much as they can do to give proper attention to the most important places in their circuits and stations, and if there were no local preachers in the Church the sparsely settled neighborhoods and remote sections of the country would be destitute of Methodist preaching, and in some places of all kinds of preaching.

Hence there are many fields of usefulness in which they may accomplish great good in the salvation of sinners. Without the occupancy of those neglected and destitute places by the local preachers, many precious souls would be lost. Then too, by an harmonious arrangement with the itinerant preacher, the local preacher can render him important assistance by co-operating with him in his work, and by helping him in his special meetings and protracted efforts; can also preach for him when sick or absent.

Local preachers frequently have interesting revivals of religion in which many persons are converted and unite with the Church. In this way they are useful in helping to build up the Church by increasing her numbers. All this, however, depends upon their zeal, activity, and faithfulness in the cause of Christ. From these and other considerations, we cannot do otherwise than view the local ministry as an important part of the Church.

Mr. Wood served the Church with fidelity in the capacity of a local preacher, but being a Southern Methodist preacher was enough to make him a victim of the wicked and reckless persecution which was raging all over the country. While in Unionville, Putnam County, he was deliberately shot in the back by a small band of soldiers of the Eighteenth Regiment of Missouri Volunteers. They knew nothing about him; never saw him before, never spoke to him. He was pointed out to them by a spy as a Southern Methodist preacher, and they walked up without saying a word and shot him in the back, the ball passing through his body and lodging in the skin on the opposite side.

Hear what a reliable person says about him— one who knew him well.

> Brother Wood was a good man—a man that I loved and that I *loved* to love. He had the confidence of all before the war; but when the war came it was considered by some a great crime to be a Southern Methodist, and a Southern Methodist preacher was thought by a great many to be unfit to live and enjoy the blessing of the best government under the sun. Brother Wood's only crime was that he was a Southern Methodist preacher. He lived a good man and died a good man. He died in imitation of his Master, praying for his murderers: "Father, forgive them, they know not what they do."
>
> The man who shot him and the rest of the mob who abused him

and threw brickbats at him were all strangers to him. They certainly *could not* have murdered him had they known him. Who it was that pointed him out to them I know not, but somebody did it.

After he died the same bloody hands put his body in an old box that had been used as a watering-trough, and buried him beside a bush-whacker who had been killed there some time before. His home was only twenty miles distant, in Sullivan County; yet before his wife could reach the spot he was buried. His remains were disinterred, taken home, and decently buried in the family grave-yard; there to await the sound of the archangel's trump. Peace to his ashes! . S. S. HARDIN.

Thus this good man was murdered by a band of ruffians in a most brutal manner. They assigned no other cause for their outrageous conduct than that he was a Southern Methodist preacher. The Constitution and laws of the United States guarantee to every man liberty of conscience and the right to worship God in his own way and in the Church of his choice. Religion is a matter between man and his God; and no human authority, individual, corporate, or governmental, has any right to interfere with the claims of God and man's corresponding duties to his God. Our great and glorious government recognizes this truth, and therefore secures to every man religious liberty. Then, in this case, who were disloyal, the savages who killed the man because he was religious, or the man who died a martyr for the truth? Would not the highest judiciary of the country pronounce them murderers in the first degree?

REV. D. B. COOPER.

This pious and useful clergyman was preaching

one Sabbath in Laclede, Mo., when the congregation was disturbed by the appearance of a squad of soldiers seen on the outside of the church. They had devised a scheme to give Mr. Cooper a ride on a rail that day. They were at that time stopping at Brookfield, and they went up to Laclede to execute their scheme and have some fun at Mr. Cooper's expense.

Dr. Harris, noted for his truthfulness and integrity, furnished an interesting account of the affair, which was published in a newspaper. The Doctor was not a member of the Church—not a professor of religion, but had the confidence of the community in which he lived. He used very strong language and forcible expressions, more so than we would have done, in giving utterance to his convictions. Read what he says:

In the summer of 1863 Rev. D. B. Cooper, now of Mount Sterling, Ky., was on the circuit in Linn County, Mo. He is one of the purest men I have ever known, and remarkably reticent. I knew him intimately and well, being his physician and personal friend. He never preached or talked politics, even to his most intimate friends and acquaintances. If there was but one man in Missouri during those wicked years of horror walking humbly before God and acting uprightly before his fellow-men, that man was D. B. Cooper.

On Sunday he was preaching at Laclede, my then residence. Some one whispered to me that some soldiers were outside intending to ride the preacher on a *rail*. I went out, and sure enough there were some half-dozen soldiers who had come up from Brookfield, had gone into a "loyal" doggery, imbibed freely, and, meeting some "loyal Methodists," were told that a rebel was preaching. Under the *stimuli* of whisky they had come to the Church with a fence-rail intending to commit an outrage upon this gentleman. But "man proposes and God disposes."

I tried to dissuade them from their purpose, but could not, and went back into the church to a lieutenant of Col. McFerrin's regiment, then stationed in Laclede, and told him to go to Col. McFerrin and tell him to send a file of soldiers immediately. I knew McFerrin could be relied on, as he was a Democrat and a gentleman. There was no time to lose; service was nearly over, and neither Mr. Cooper nor his congregation knew any thing of the impending outrage. The upper floor of a "loyal Methodist" house near by was full of "God's elect" to witness the fun. Just before the service closed the braves crowded into the house, and when the congregation was dismissed, they, the soldiers, were so situated that they had to leave the house last. When they came out and were about to lift their rail at the side of the house and seize Mr. Cooper, who was yet in ignorance of their designs, they and all but myself were surprised to see two files of soldiers, with fixed bayonets, marching down on us so as to encompass the entire crowd. As no violence had been done, no arrests were made. The miserable tools of the bad-hearted fanatics slunk away like whipped curs, leaving their pious(?) instigators gnashing their teeth and calling down curses upon McFerrin and myself. I don't think their prayers have ever been answered.

These maudlin soldiers were not to blame. They were tools in the hands of the base-hearted men and women who instigated the outrage. This act is only a type of the general conduct of this people during the war, who are now whining union with you. I am no professor of Christianity, but if such people are Christians, or your union with them would compose a Christian body, I pray the Giver of all good to incline my heart to heathenism rather than such a mongrel abomination.

I was living in Boonville when they committed the theft of your church there, and know all about it; but you will get the particulars of that honest (?) act from others.

I have given you the facts, but have taken no pains, as you see. You may have to re-write it. You are at liberty to insert in your book over my signature if you wish.   N. W. HARRIS.

REV. W. M. RUSH.

This name is a household word in the Methodist homes within the bounds of the Missouri Conference. Indeed, this good and great man—great in goodness—was known and loved throughout the State of Missouri. Distinguished for his sound doctrines and sterling principles, and for a faithful life continually exemplifying said doctrines and principles, as sound in practice as he was in theory, solid as a rock, firm as the mountains, he turned not aside either to the right or to the left. He could very appropriately have used St. Paul's language: "Forgetting those things which are behind, and reaching forth unto those things which are before, I press toward the mark for the prize of the high calling of God in Christ Jesus." We love to contemplate such a character of Christian excellency, but as a biographical sketch of him is given in the Minutes of the Missouri Conference, and will appear in its proper place, we need not extend our remarks along this line, but direct the attention of the reader to that part of his history embraced in the Conference year of 1862–63, and relating to his war troubles. The information comes to us through a very reliable source, and the reader may find it given below:

Rev. W. M. Rush was stationed in St. Joseph in 1861, the year the war broke out. He was deeply impressed with the necessity of caution and prudence in the conduct of his pulpit and public services, as the people to whom he ministered were divided on the questions at issue in the war. He was so careful not to give offense to any that he framed a somewhat formal prayer to be used in public services touching the troubles of the country. It was about as follows: "O Thou who art infinite in wisdom, in goodness, and in power, we pray thee so to direct the affairs of this country that the events that are now transpiring may all result for the glory and well-being of humanity. We pray that those in authority may have wisdom to direct them in adopting such measures as shall be promotive of the best interests of all the people."

To this form of prayer and the sentiments that it contained he thought all good citizens of either party could say "Amen." He carefully abstained from every expression that would be offensive to the sectional feelings and views of any of his congregation. In this he was particular and, he thought, successful. Matters passed on well enough until early in February, 1862, when, after preaching on Sabbath, he called on the Rev. W. C. Toole, a local preacher, to close the service with prayer. He was a strong partisan, and his language in the prayer was extremely bitter toward those in rebellion against the government. Though the congregation was much divided in sentiment, they were at peace among themselves. This prayer was like a firebrand. It excited a good deal of feeling, and people of opposite views thought it much out of place. Upon reflection and consultation with his leading brethren, he determined thereafter to close his own services with prayer, which ministers should always do, unless other ministers are present and in the pulpit. He pursued this course but one Sabbath afterward, and then a brother minister (the Rev. S. W. Cope) preached for him, when, during the week following, Brig.-Gen. B. F. Loan, then in command, sent for Mr. Rush to report himself at his head-quarters. This he did, and Gen. Loan told him that he had concluded to close his church. Mr. Rush asked on what account. He replied: "Because of disloyalty." He was then asked in what respect they were disloyal, and answered that he was informed that a prayer for the government could not be offered in that church without giving offense.

The whole matter of the prayer of Mr. Toole and the general character of the service were then explained to Gen. Loan. Mr. Rush was careful to give the reasons for avoiding the introduction of any thing savoring of sectional views into the public service: that they could not settle the troubles of the country in the Church service; that such an effort would only destroy the peace of the Church without in the least benefiting the country; that no prayer savoring of secession had ever been offered in the church, or would be tolerated on any account; that the course pursued was the only proper one; and that if all the Churches in the land would attend to their appropriate work and let politics alone, it would be far better for the country. To all of this the general replied that the time had come when there must be a distinction in the Churches between patriots and traitors. Mr. Rush told him that he could not discriminate in his Church on account of political opinions; that he had been in the ministry for more than twenty-five years, and in all that time he had not in a single sentence, in prayer or sermon, given utterance to a word or sentence by which his opinions could be known upon any political questions at issue before the country, and that he did not expect in the future to depart from that course. The general replied that his mind was made up to close the church. The interview ended, and the church was closed.

Soon afterward the general directed a general order to be issued forbidding Mr. Rush preaching or conducting any kind of religious service within the bounds of his military district. Thus he was silenced, deposed from the ministry, and his ordination credentials revoked by a military satrap; an embassador for God stricken down by one stroke of a pen to which bayonets imparted power; a messenger of salvation to dying men silenced by the caprice of shoulder-straps; and one to whom the risen Messiah by his Spirit said, "Go into all the world and preach the gospel to every creature," suspended from his divine commission by the decree of human power; a "legate of the skies" at the feet of a miserable specimen of human weakness clothed with a little brief authority!

After Gen. Loan was dismissed from the military service by Gov. Gamble, and Gen. W. P. Hall had succeeded him in command of the district, Mr. Rush addressed a note to Gen. Hall, calling his attention to the order of Gen. Loan, and asking its revocation. Mr. Rush hoped for much consideration at the hands of Gen. Hall, from a somewhat intimate acquaintance of sixteen years, and the further fact that at the beginning of the troubles their views were in perfect harmony. He had no doubt whatever but that the silencing order of Gen. Loan would be revoked. But for once he had mistaken the man. Mr. Rush did not then properly estimate the power of the German Radicals of the district nor the ambition of Gen. Hall—the necessity for him to manufacture a character for extreme loyalty, in doing which he would sacrifice any man or any principle that stood in the way of his personal promotion.

Gen. Hall not only refused to revoke the order of Gen. Loan, but published in the *St. Joseph Herald*, a paper that circulated extensively in the military camps, his letter to Mr. Rush, in which the latter was denounced as a traitor and unworthy the protection of the government. While Gen. Loan, in his personal intercourse with Mr. Rush, was courteous and gentlemanly, Gen. Hall was abusive, ungentlemanly, and tyrannical. His published letter unveiled his true character, while it subjected its helpless victim to suspicion, insult, and attempts at brutal assassination.

Mr. Rush, in the midst of such trials and dangers, had to give up his charge and return to Chillicothe. Here he found his beautiful home laid waste: the fencing destroyed, the house broken up, horses stabled in three rooms on the first floor, and soldiers quartered on the second floor, and the fruit-trees and shrubbery all destroyed.

He rented a house for his family, and while the officers of the post always treated him with courtesy and kindness, Gen. Hall's letter had stirred up the common soldiery until his life and the lives of his family were in constant peril. When he discovered this state of things he wrote Gen. Hall a polite letter, protesting against his published letter, representing the injustice he had done him, and the danger to his person and life caused by it. Gen. Hall returned his letter, and in reply threatened him with a military commission.

About the first of May, 1863, a bold attempt was made to assassinate him in his own house. His house was first assailed with stones and brickbats, by which the windows were crushed in and the doors battered. Pistol shots were then fired through the doors and windows, but a kind Providence protected him and his family from serious injury. On reporting the facts to the officers in command, protection was promptly furnished, and a guard stationed at the house. But at the same time the officers advised him to seek safety elsewhere; that with all their efforts to protect him the assassin's missile might any moment put an end to his life.

On Wednesday evening, just at dark, his son William, while

feeding, was shot at by some one who had secreted himself but a few yards from him. The bullet entered his cap just above his forehead, and passed out behind. An inch lower would have killed him. The shot was no doubt intended for his father.

Mr. Rush found it necessary for the safety of himself and family to remove to St. Louis and remain there until the close of the war. He found the Mound Church without a pastor, and by the appointment of the presiding elder took charge of that Church, and there remained until the quiet and safety that succeeded the war were restored to the State.*

It is astonishing how few, if any, ministers of the M. E. Church, South, escaped persecution in Missouri during the Civil War and the reign of terror which continued some time after the war. The persecutors had a perfect system of espionage, and their spies were everywhere throughout the length and breadth of the State. Wicked men would report on ministers through personal pique and animosity because their gospel preaching and their righteous lives of self-denial and cross-bearing constantly rebuked them for their outrageous wickedness. Jesus truly said, "All that will live godly in Christ Jesus shall suffer persecution;" and we might add that if they persecuted and crucified the immaculate Lamb of God they will take great pleasure in persecuting and killing his true disciples. If, by the utmost discretion and precaution and a judicious course of living, any Southern Methodist preacher could have passed through the war undisturbed and without molestation, that man was

REV. TYSON DINES.

But even this non-combatant, quiet minister of

---
* Dr. Leftwich's book.

the gospel, who, like his Lord and Master, was a peace-maker wherever he went, was not allowed to live in peace.

The editor of the *Missouri Presbyterian*, Rev. R. P. Farris, D.D., through great kindness, has given an account of Mr. Dines's disturbances and troubles in time of the Civil War, as follows:

When the war began this esteemed brother was in charge of the M. E. Church, South, in St. Charles. The writer of these lines, not belonging to his denomination, knew him well and loved him as a child-like Christian, a faithful preacher of the gospel for twenty-five years, a high-minded man, a most prudent pastor. Determined to know nothing but Christ and him crucified, not only did he keep politics and the exciting topics of the day out of his pulpit, but also he sedulously kept aloof, as far as was at all possible, even from his own parishioners, so as to avoid conversing about the war, and refrained absolutely from reading newspapers, so that he might be ignorant of, and uninfluenced by and unable to talk of the current, terrible events. Yet this man, because he pursued this course, and would not prostitute his office and influence to the schemes and passions of the hour, was accused, in a public speech July 4, 1862, by Walter W. Edwards, then prosecuting attorney, now circuit judge, of praying in his Church publicly for "Jeff Davis and the success of the Southern Confederacy." Of course the design of this lying vilification was to make Mr. Dines obnoxious to the military authorities, and thus to secure his removal and the closing of his Church, or its perversion to the purpose of the party in power.

In September, 1862, Mr. Dines was arrested on the charge of "general disloyalty." (Does anybody know what that is?) He was arraigned before one Lewis Merrill, brigadier-general commanding the district—a profligate and a poltroon. The following conversation was held:

Merrill: "Mr. Dines, are you a minister?"
Mr. Dines: "Yes, sir."
Merrill: "Of what denomination?"
Mr. Dines: "Methodist Episcopal."

Merrill: "Methodist, South?"
Mr. Dines: "Yes, sir."
Merrill: "Well, sir, that of itself is enough to condemn you." And during the interview the licentious coward presumed to say, in a rough, brutal manner, to the meek and venerable servant of Jesus: "Mr. Dines, you have read the Bible to little purpose; you are ignorant of the Scriptures."

Mr. Dines was held to be guilty of "general disloyalty," and Merrill sentenced him "to be confined during the war," and soon sent him under guard to Gratiot Street Prison, St. Louis. Here a friend and fellow-prisoner, who was well acquainted with Judge H. R. Gamble, then the Governor of the State, wrote to that functionary, detailing the facts in Mr. Dines's case—his age, his devoted piety, his long service as a minister, his feeble health, his dependent family, his prudence, his quiet walk, his outrageous treatment—suggesting that if the government must have sacrifice and not mercy, the writer, who was young and stout, asked no favors for himself, and was willing to endure the imprisonment, but entreating the judge to interfere for Mr. Dines's release. Gov. Gamble heeded the request, and secured a hearing for Mr. Dines before the provost-marshal, who immediately released Mr. Dines on parole.

The evening of that same day found Mr. Dines at his home in St. Charles, in the midst of as happy a family as the sun ever shone on. Praise and thanksgiving went up from full, grateful, glad hearts around the family altar that night. But alas! some son of Belial had informed Gen. Merrill by telegraph of Mr. Dines's return on parole, and next morning before breakfast a telegram came from Merrill ordering Mr. Dines to leave the district in twenty-four hours. Mr. Dines was compelled to obey, and for more than eight months was kept an exile from his home and flock.

REV. JAMES PENN.

No member of this Conference has made a better record and has served the Church longer and more faithfully than this venerable man of God. His voice has been heard in the proclamation of the gospel through North-east Missouri and elsewhere for scores of years, and sinners by hundreds, if not by thousands, have been induced to forsake their sins and seek the salvation of their souls. He is still publishing to a lost world the glad tidings of great joy. How bright will be his crown of rejoicing in glory sparkling with so many stars of happy souls saved forever through his instrumentality!

Nor is this all. He has quadrupled his usefulness by giving to the Church four clerical sons who have for many years followed the noble example of their worthy sire in the Christian ministry. They seem to have inherited the virtuous qualities and religious character of their consecrated father. The field of their usefulness has been extended. While preaching the gospel of salvation in its purity, simplicity, and power throughout the country, great success has attended their ministerial labors, and eternity alone can reveal the amount of good accomplished by that priestly family.

We would suppose, on account of his advanced age, his quiet and peaceable disposition, his purity and innocency of life, his devotion to the cause of morality and religion, that he would have escaped the troubles of the war. But no; he must suffer the ban of being a Southern Methodist preacher, irrespective of position or character. The ordeal through which he passed has been given to the public by himself as follows:

First, I was arrested in August, 1862, and carried to Keokuk, Ia., and there detained about a week. As there were no well-founded charges against me, I was released.

Second, in August, 1863, I held a meeting in Williamstown, Mo. There were present at that meeting a minister of the M. E. Church, whose name, I believe, was Moody. On Sunday morning, during prayer-meeting, this man, while we were kneeling in prayer, arose and began to read in a very loud tone of voice. The people got off their knees. The man who had thus disturbed an unoffending company of praying men and women was armed, as were some fifteen others whom he brought with him. I walked toward the door, and the congregation followed me and took a position in the street. I then preached to a large concourse of people, the armed minister and his valiant company retaining possession of the house. I continued the meeting until the next Sabbath, when this preacher with his armed band came again and drove us out of the house the second time. I preached out-of-doors as on the preceding Sabbath. The meeting resulted in much good, there being about forty accessions to the M. E. Church, South.

On another occasion flags were brought and placed on and around the pulpit, and a company of armed men sat near to prevent any one from taking them down. Seeing that this did not deter us from the discharge of Christian duty, a lot of wicked men raised a fight and fought like savages, so we were compelled to leave the house and ceased to preach at that place. Moody was asked why he did so. His reply was: "Because I can." He is now, I believe, a minister of good standing in the M. E. Church, but many responsible people regard him as a very bad man.

At Winchester, Mo., we had a very good house of worship, but they ran us out as they did at Williamstown, until our people were unwilling to attend divine services in the town. Then the house was almost destroyed, so that we had no place there in which to worship.

They seized our house in La Grange, a Mr. Stewart and others of the M. E. Church (North) being the chief actors in this matter. After three years they relinquished their hold upon that splendid house.

In addition to all this I have suffered personal wrongs, in various ways, at the hands of these people: but I have tried to keep a conscience void of offense toward God and men. Their wrong-doing is upon themselves. I leave them to be judged by him who is too wise to err and too good to do wrong. May he forgive the wrong done!

Thus speaks as true a man as ever lived.

Rev. Jesse Bird.

This good man was for many years a standard-bearer in the Church, and was a faithful member of the Missouri Conference, M. E. Church, South; was distinguished for his integrity and unswerving fidelity to the cause of Christ. He was an able defender of the doctrines of his Church, of which he had a clear, correct, and intelligent understanding. His preaching was positive, forcible, and impressive. His favorite themes or topics were the essential doctrines of the gospel, which he presented with a telling effect. He was a solid man—nothing superficial, artificial, or fanciful about him. Indeed, he was the embodiment of a living Christianity. Yet withal he was a Southern Methodist preacher, and must come under the condemnation of those who made it their one business to persecute Southern Methodist preachers. But let him speak for himself:

> In the fall of 1861 I was appointed by the President of the Missouri Conference to the St. Joseph District. On my first round I went to my quarterly meeting for Rockport Circuit, at Spencer's Chapel, in Atchison County. Arriving at the chapel at 11 o'clock, November 9, I found that a pole had been raised by the door with a rope fastened to it, with the purpose of hoisting a flag. There was no one present. I waited a little, and

saw two men approaching. They informed me that a burial was going on in the neighborhood; that the preaching was postponed until 3 o'clock.

In the evening I returned to the church in company with a few persons. As we approached the house I saw two men hoisting the flag in great haste. Fastening the rope as quick as possible, they ran and hid themselves inside a field. Coming up to the house, and seeing what had been done, I declined going, stating that I would preach under no political flag; that I should not mix my religion with politics. I was invited to preach at a private house, and I did so. I was not interrupted again until on my second round.

On the 6th of February, 1862, I commenced a quarterly meeting at Oregon, Holt County. The meeting went on quietly and properly until Monday morning, when the flag was hoisted over the door of the Church. I again declined going in for the same reasons. In the course of two or three hours I was arrested, cursed, and abused in various ways, and threatened by some men who styled themselves soldiers. I was then sent in charge of two young men to Forest City, and requested to "take the oath," which I also declined. But in order to get off and out of the hands of the law, I agreed to go before a magistrate and take a civil oath to observe the Constitution and laws. From Oregon I returned home and found a notice in my post-office at Rochester from Ben Loan, the commander at St. Joseph, requiring me to appear before him immediately. I went down and inquired for what purpose he sent for me, when he replied: "You are not to preach any more in this district." "Is this all?" I inquired. "You must go and take the oath," he replied. I informed him that I should not take the oath; that he could put me in prison or banish me from the State, as he had others. He immediately made out an order for me to leave the State within thirty days. This was done in the City of St. Joseph February 14, 1862. I was not restricted to any particular bounds. The ground was then covered with snow and ice to the depth of six or eight inches. I had no money to bear expenses, save about fifty dollars. I gave about two prices for a wagon, put what I could in it, and, leaving my house and crop of corn in the prairie, I started on a cold, stormy day, with my wife in feeble health, to go I knew not whither, and that for no other reason than that I was a Southern Methodist preacher and would not swear falsely.

This move made it necessary to sacrifice my little grain and stock my little boys had worked for, together with our furniture and a good portion of my library. I was accompanied by my daughter and two little sons, and also by Benjamin Bird, his wife, and two young children. We started South, and traveled four days, reaching the river opposite Lexington; and finding the ice giving way, and there being no boat, we turned up the river to Camden, Ray County, stopping at Brother Menefee's, a most excellent family, where we remained some three or four days. Leaving Camden, we went up the bottom to a point opposite Napoleon, in La Fayette County, where we remained in camp two or three days, when, the ice clearing away, we crossed the Missouri River and proceeded through cold and storm until we had passed the town of Clifton, in Henry County.

Here we met some men who told us, as others had the day before, that we could not proceed beyond the Osage. The Jayhawkers and Home Guards were robbing all who attempted to go through. We turned around and came back to La Fayette County, and finding an empty house near Greenton, stopped and spent the spring and summer there.

In a few days I went down to Lexington, saw the commander of that post, and got a sound cursing for my trouble. Returning to my family and finding the people of the neighborhood very kind and generous, we remained until the latter part of August, when we returned to our home in Andrew County.

I will say nothing of my trials from that time till the close of the war, except that I preached but little. A part of this time I was nominally the presiding elder of St. Joseph District.

About Christmas, 1865, I was employed by the presiding elder, H. H. Hedgepeth, to take charge of the Savannah Circuit. I commenced my work immediately, and continued preaching regularly until my last appointment to Savannah, in August, 1866. I had been threatened at different times during the summer by mobs, and sometimes I thought it quite likely that I should be put to death by the lawless rabble, but I was left unmolested until I was about to finish my work on the circuit. On Sunday the people expected an interruption while I was preaching, but all continued quiet till night. While in the pulpit I noticed some men come in and whisper to each other and go out, and presently return. When the services closed I heard a lady say: "They are at the door." I quietly walked out and went to my room, nobody disturbing me. Next morning I was told they were preparing to arrest me.

After I had adjusted my affairs, about 10 o'clock I went home. Having proceeded about two hundred yards, I saw the deputy sheriff coming at full speed. Knowing what it meant, I stopped until he came up. He said that he was authorized to arrest me. I was taken before a justice of the peace, who had issued the warrant for my arrest, upon the affidavit of one of the party that came into the church on Sunday night. The said justice inquired if I pleaded guilty or not guilty to the crime of preaching the gospel to the people, in violation of the fundamental law of the State of Missouri. I pleaded guilty; whereupon the said officer required me to give bond for my appearance at the next session of the court, which I declined to do. Consequently I was taken by the sheriff of Andrew County and lodged in the jail of Buchanan County, in the city of St. Joseph, there being no jail in Andrew County. This was done on August 27, 1866. I remained in prison about three hours, when the sheriff of Buchanan County, accompanied by Judge Woodson and others, of St. Joseph, came and opened the door of the jail and let me out. On Monday following the Circuit Court of Buchanan County came on, and the judge declining to try the case, I gave bond for my appearance at the next term of the Circuit Court of Andrew County, at which time and place I was indicted for preaching the gospel. I took a change of venue to Buchanan County, and before the sitting of the court the decision of the Supreme Court of the United States had set aside the test oath, and that ended the matter with me.

Mr. Bird recognized that his authority to preach the gospel was divine; therefore, that no human authority had any right to interfere with it; and it seems that the Supreme Court of the United States thought the same.

The following interesting information of the spiritual state of the Church this year is from the pen of Rev. F. A. Savage, from the *Canton Press:*

I shall not attempt an extended notice of the great work which God has wrought within the bounds of our Conference; but simply give a brief sketch. I term it a great work; and when we consider the terrible ordeal through which our country is passing, and the dreadful Civil War which is so extensively raging, and the consequent distrust and alarm that everywhere prevails, it is truly a great work. Notwithstanding the exciting and alarming scenes through which we have been passing, and by which we have been surrounded, yet in the main we have peace and prosperity in all our borders, and God has visited many of our charges with most gracious and powerful revivals. This is a matter of thanksgiving and praise to God, and with gratitude to him do I record it.

1. *Hannibal District.*—In this district are Hannibal and Palmyra Stations. Hydesburg and Monticello Circuits were blessed with interesting and, in some respects, powerful revivals. These seasons of refreshing were especially beneficial to the Church in quickening believers, reclaiming the backslidden, and restoring confidence and hope in reference to the future. My information enables me to state that within the bounds of this district there have been over two hundred conversions, and not less than three hundred additions to the Church.

2. *Bloomington District.*—A number of the charges in this district have received most gracious outpourings of the Holy Spirit. Paris and Bloomington Circuits have been abundantly blessed. Huntsville has shared largely in the revival influence. There have been about as many conversions and additions to the Church in this district as in the Hannibal. In reference to the revivals on Paris Circuit I am informed by letter that the work was extensive and powerful. In Callao, on Bloomington Circuit, where I labored with the brethren several days, the work was manifestly of God. At Bloomington, five miles distant, the work was equally great.

3. *Brunswick District.*—This district has been more abundantly blessed than any other portion of our work. Indeed, I

am informed that the work has been most extraordinary, especially that on Keytesville Circuit, in Chariton County. One who has been over twenty years in the ministry, and who has passed through many revivals, said to me: "In all the course of my ministry I have never seen more clear and manifest displays of the presence and power of God in convictions and conversions than I have witnessed in these revivals." It would be impossible to describe them. Such was the divine influence and power present that it seemed as a mighty avalanche bearing down all before it. The gracious influence spread from appointment to appointment, until the whole country seemed one continued flame of revival. Glasgow Station and Carrollton Circuit have been greatly blessed. The result has been over four hundred conversions and additions to the Church in Keytesville Circuit, and near seven hundred in the district.

4. *St. Charles, Fayette, Gallatin, Weston, and St. Joseph Districts.*—Of these districts I cannot speak with confidence, as my opportunities for information have been limited. I can say, however, from verbal information, that several of these districts, in a number of their charges, have been wonderfully blessed, and many sinners have been converted and added to the Church. So that within the bounds of our Conference there have been over fifteen hundred conversions and more than two thousand additions to the Church. To God be all the glory!

You have heard the outcry against our Church of disorganization, "rebel concern," "gone under," "played out," etc., and also the prediction that our Conference would never assemble again in Missouri. You have also heard the terrible bellowing of the great "bull of Bashan," whose fearful roaring in sounding alarm was heard throughout the land. Notwithstanding all this our Conference did assemble in Fulton, on the 14th of October, the time fixed by Bishop Kavanaugh, and organized under the law of our Discipline on the 16th, and proceeded to businesss. We had a very pleasant, harmonious, and profitable session. Moreover there were no "plottings or treason against the State," nor "measures concocted for the overthrow of the government," but a preamble, and resolutions, and pastoral address were by a rising vote unanimously adopted, in which we avow our fidelity and loyalty to the government, and enjoined this as a cardinal duty upon every member. We also declared our "unqualified disapprobation and censure" upon any of our ministers who have been involved in the affairs of civil polity or politics.

And now the "Old Ship" still floats. Her broad pennant is still to the breeze; Judah's Lion is her captain, her decks are crowded with happy sailors, her keel and rigging all sound, her sails all unfurled; and may God give her a successful voyage and bring her safely into the heavenly port!

CHAPTER VII.

MISSOURI CONFERENCE.

No Published Minutes of the St. Louis Conference This Year—Forty-eighth Session of the Missouri Conference at Mexico—Minute Business—Preachers Received Their Appointments—Imminent Danger Threatens Them in Every Direction—Their Trust Is in God—Reign of Terror—Cruel Murder of Rev. Thomas Johnson—Trials of Martin L. Eads As Given by Himself—Rev. W. M. Newland Arrested—Church at La Grange—Rev. J. H. Pritchett and His Work—The Palmyra Meeting Formed an Era in the History of Southern Methodism.

THERE are no published minutes of the St. Louis Annual Conference for this year. Those of the Missouri Conference are very meager and confined to the minute business of the Conference.

The forty-eighth session of the Missouri Annual Conference was held in Mexico, Mo., September 14, 1864.

In the absence of the bishop, Andrew Monroe was called to the chair by the Conference, and presided during the session. John D. Vincil was elected Secretary.

J. S. Allen, D. R. Smith, Thomas Penn, J. A. Mumpower, and B. F. Zumwalt were admitted on trial. S. J. Huffaker and James O. Swinney remained on trial. John W. Adkisson and Samuel Alexander were admitted into full connection, and were elected and ordained deacons. J. R. Taylor, W. W. McMurry, and E. H. Hudson were elders, but not ordained, as there was no bishop present. T. Dines, George Fenton, Jesse Faubion, C. W. Pritchett, W. M. Sutton, J. R. Downing, N. P. Halsey, L. T. Catlin, Walter Toole, Thomas Hurst, Samuel Alexander, James L. Smith, P. M. Pinckard, George Penn, William Penn, William F. Bell, Alex. Spencer, and W. Warren were supernumerary. John F. Young, D. C. Blackwell, Martin L. Eads, and William M. Wood were superannuated.

It was with great difficulty that the ministers could meet to hold an annual session of the Conference while the whole country was in commotion. Having received their appointments, they returned home with anxious hearts about the results of the ensuing Conference year. Looking from a human stand-point the prospects were very discouraging. Their own lives were in jeopardy all the time, not knowing what day or what night might be their last, not knowing when the desperadoes might visit their homes, burn their houses, and leave their families in the world without any thing upon which to subsist; for such instances were frequent and occurring in different parts of the State. Yet their trust was in God, who had brought them safely thus far through the war, and they felt encouraged to believe that as he had been with them in the past so he would continue with them in the future. He had given them success in their past ministry, had accompanied the word preached by them with the power and demonstration of the Holy Spirit, making it "quick and powerful, sharper than any two-edged sword, piercing even to the dividing asunder of soul and spirit, of the joints and marrow, and a discerner of the thoughts and intents of the heart." Under their preaching sinners had been convicted, penitents converted, and believers strengthened and established, while the work of saving souls was to them dearer than life itself.

When a civil war reaches its culmination the very elements, infernal and supernal, seem to collide—wrong against right, vice against virtue, error against truth, wickedness against righteousness, atheism against the Bible, and the kingdom of Satan against the kingdom of Christ. No orator could describe, no artist could paint the terrific scene, the fearful tragedy in Missouri during "the reign of terror." The very blackness of darkness covered the heavens, obscuring sun, moon, and stars; and the earth, crimsoned with human blood, was draped in mourning and death. May God save our glorious country and government from another civil war!

If the reader thinks we have drawn the picture in colors too dark, let him read the following narrative of the persecution and death of

REV. THOMAS JOHNSON,

a patriot, a philanthropist, a Christian, and a benediction to the Church and to the State. We knew him when a boy, was taught by him in school, and never knew a better man. But we have not the space to give a portraiture of his character here—would direct the attention of the reader to the following narrative:

Thomas Johnson was born in Nelson County, Va., A.D. 1804. In the fall of 1825 he emigrated with his parents to Missouri. In September, 1826, he was received on trial into the Missouri Conference during the session of the Conference which was held at McKendree Chapel, Cape Girardeau County, Mo., Bishop Roberts presiding, and John Scripps acting as Secretary. The Conference, which at that time embraced all the State of Missouri and Arkansas, numbered just twenty traveling preachers and three thousand three hundred and sixty-four members, all told.

With Mr. Johnson there were also admitted on trial into the Conference this year John Curitan, Parker Snedecor, John Wood, and John W. Yorke.

Mr. Johnson's first appointment was to Mount Prairie, in the Arkansas District, with Jesse Hale as his presiding elder. The next year he was returned to Mount Prairie, which was considered in those days quite a compliment to a young preacher. At the Conference of 1828, held at the old Fayette Campground, Bishop Soule, President, and James Bankson, Secretary, Mr. Johnson was admitted into full connection, with Parker Snedecor, J. W. Yorke, and A. Norfleet, ordained deacon and appointed to Fishing River, with Jesse Green, presiding elder, and John Trotter, junior preacher. The next year he was sent to Buffalo. At the Conference of 1830, in St. Louis, Bishop Roberts ordained him elder and sent him to the "Shawnee Mission." This was his first appearance on the border and among the people with whom so many years of his subsequent life were spent. The next year he was appointed to what was called the "Kansas Mission," with his brother, William Johnson, junior preacher.

In 1832 the "General Minutes" contain the following: "Indian Mission District, Thomas Johnson, Superintendent. Shawnee Mission and School, Thomas Johnson and Edward T. Peery."

In 1833 he was again appointed to the Indian Mission District, and his brother William to the Shawnee Mission and school. He was continued as superintendent of the Indian Mission District and in connection with the Shawnee Mission and school until 1841. For several years after this date he filled other important appointments, and labored in other parts of the vast territory then occupied and cultivated by the Missouri Conference.

He was frequently and extensively spoken of in connection with the highest office and honors in the gift of the Church; and yet he was so quiet, so humble, so approachable, and so generous in his feelings for the low and the poor and the suffering that, with his benevolent countenance and his frank, open manners, the savage Indian was awed into reverence, the lonely wayfarer felt drawn toward him, the poor, the sick, the dying found him a counselor, a friend, a brother, and the dirtiest and lowest Indian child learned to rejoice in his coming and hail with many expressions of pleasure the notice of the "Big Chief," a patronymic which the tribes gave him wherever he was known

He kept himself aloof, with great propriety and prudence, from the Missouri-Kansas broils of 1856, and when the Civil War broke out in 1861 he was found loyally and positively on the side of the Union. He took no part in politics, and determined to keep out of the war; but a man so well, so long, and so extensively known, living on the very borders of strife, and between the two opposing sections as it were, could not keep from the public nor did he care to conceal his sentiments on the great issues that were convulsing the country from one end to the other. He opposed secession on the one hand and coercion on the other. Yet he loved the Constitution and the Union of our fathers, and rather than see the one destroyed and the other dismembered he would favor a resort to arms. His loyalty to the government was never called in question, nor was his love for and loyalty to the Church of his choice— the M. E. Church, South—ever doubted. He was a living and sublime refutation of that oft-repeated falsehood that Southern Methodism and secession were one, and that a Southern Methodist preacher was, *per se*, a rebel and a traitor. Mr. Johnson loved the Union of these States, and was loyally and earnestly and notoriously in favor of its preservation; but he loved his

Church, her discipline, her doctrines, her principles, and was just as loyally, earnestly, and notoriously in favor of the preservation of her distinctive identity. He was equally opposed to secession in the South and abolition fanaticism in the North, and he believed that they were alike dangerous to the peace and safety of the country—that the ultimate of either would break up the government bequeathed to us by the patriot fathers of '76 and '87.

With such sentiments it was not surprising that he was harassed first by one party and then by the other party during the early part of the war. He was often required to provide for and feed soldiers; and his horses, wagons, feed, and provisions of every kind were pressed into the service of the army.

At this time he was living on his own farm and in his own elegant residence, two miles south-west of Westport, in Jackson County, Mo., three miles from the Kansas State line, and five miles from the old Shawnee Mission, which had ceased to be a manual labor school for the Indians. The whole property had been donated to Mr. Johnson by the Indians, and purchased by him from the government, and was now occupied as a residence by his eldest son.

After the first two years of the war Mr. Johnson was molested very little, and yet such was the reign of terror along the border that he never felt entirely secure. So many good men had been murdered, and so much property had been destroyed, and panic and consternation had been so often created during the war in the country, and he had passed through it all so safely, compared with thousands of others, that by the close of 1864, after Price's army had made the boldest and last raid into Missouri and had passed away from the borders of Kansas, he began to feel pretty secure.

His suspicions of foul play had often been aroused, but just as often allayed. During the Christmas holidays that closed up the year 1864 he was again induced to believe that he had enemies who might possibly be plotting his destruction; but who they were, and why they wished to molest him, he had no means of knowing. His suspicions again passed away, while he retained his caution.

On January 1, 1865, and while the younger members of the family were from home enjoying the festivities incident to the day, a squad of militia rode up to the house, dismounted, and walked in to warm (as they said), for the weather was bitter cold. It was nearly night, and Mr. Johnson, his wife, one son, and two little girls composed the family circle that evening. The soldiers were civil and pleasant, and sat around the fire until nearly 11 o'clock at night, when they arose, bowed themselves out, and rode away. Mr. Johnson felt relieved, had family worship, and all retired. Just at midnight, and before Mr. Johnson had fallen asleep, he was roused by the tramp of horses, the clashing of sabers, and the voices of men at the gate. He arose, and saw through the window thirty mounted men. They first asked the way to Kansas City, five miles distant. They then asked if they could come in and warm. He told them there was no fire, and his family were all in bed. They then wanted water. He told them where the cistern was. By this time a number of them had dismounted and walked up to the porch, Mr. Johnson meanwhile remaining in the hall, with the door opened just enough for him to put his head out and talk to them, *en dishabille*. When he saw them approaching, after so many expressed wants, he feared that they meant mischief, and he went in and shut the door. They then demanded admission, and began to force the door in. They swore that if the door was not opened they would break it down, and just as Mr. Johnson turned the key to lock the door they fired, the balls passing through the door, and one of them taking effect in the region of the heart. He sunk down speechless, and in a few minutes expired in the arms of his grief-stricken wife. He never spoke after the fatal shot. The fiendish murderers still demanded entrance. They were refused. They tried to break down the door, fired several shots into the house, and finally set the house on fire. The heroic woman firmly maintained her rights, and protected the lifeless body of her loved husband, as well as the sacred shrine of her cherished home, from the sacrilege and profanation of a brutal soldiery. She put the fire out, and maintained herself in her own home.

The soldiers, satisfied with their bloody work, or defeated in their efforts to commit other outrages, mounted and rode away, leaving to a darkened home and a broken-hearted widow the legacy of a martyred minister of Jesus.*

---

* Dr. Leftwich's book.

Murderers seek the hour of midnight, when good and honest people are sound asleep in their quiet homes, to perpetrate their inhuman and diabolical atrocities—the darkest hour for the darkest deeds. Demons as they were, they could not commit such an outrage in the light of day; they could not face the open, frank, majestic, awe-inspiring countenance of that good, great, grand man, whom they so brutally murdered at midnight. One look from him in the daylight would have made those thirty armed and equipped men skulk away self-condemned and confounded.

Rev. Martin L. Eads.

This generous and noble-hearted gentleman and Christian minister possessed those sterling virtues that constitute a good moral character, and was noted for the soundness of his principles—his inflexible integrity. Let the reader add the Christian graces to these moral qualities, and he can form a very correct idea of him concerning whom we are writing. He may see his true character in the following account, given by himself in a letter to his friend, Mr. Pinckard, of his experience in time of the war:

> I have been wandering up and down in this world for more than forty years, trying to preach Christ's gospel to my fellowmen. I have always been an ardent lover of popular liberty and a great admirer of the free institutions of our common country. I have often devoutly thanked Almighty God, on my knees, in the pulpit, and around the family altar, for the sacred privilege of worshiping God "under my own vine and fig-tree, none daring to molest or make us afraid." And as I have wit-

nessed the rise and progress of Christianity and liberal principles in this country, I never conceived the thought that I should live to see the day when those liberal principles would be violated, and the progress of the gospel impeded and trammeled by an iron-clad oath which no Christian minister of the gospel could take, according to my view, without doing violence to his conscience and prostituting the sacred office of the Christian ministry to corrupt political party ends. Yet I have indeed lived to see it. In September, 1865, Constable Glenn came to my house, with a writ for me to appear before Esquire Aubry, of Wellsville, to answer to the charge of preaching the gospel without taking the oath. When I appeared before him he required me to take an oath and sign a bond, both of which I refused to do. Esquire Aubry insisted on it, though in a mild and gentlemanly manner. I told him that I was seventy-four years of age, and before I would do it I would spend my few remaining days in jail. The reason I acted thus was because I could not take the oath without doing great violence to my conscience. I could never have gone before a congregation to preach the gospel with a commission from a County Court that supplanted a commission from the "King of kings," under which I had been preaching for more than forty years. During my trial a Rev. Mr. Dowler, of the Northern Methodist Church, who was the instigator of my arrest without any provocation, said to me: "Mr. Eads, do you know that I am an officer of the government?" I simply replied to him by saying that I thought the government had made a poor selection in an officer. There seemed, after refusing to take the oath, no alternative but to go to jail. I was on the eve of starting to Conference when I was arrested. I suggested to the esquire to wait until I had returned from Conference, to which he readily acceded.

On my return from Conference I started to report myself to Esquire Aubry, according to promise. I overtook Constable Glenn on the way there, by whom I sent the word that I was of the same mind—I could not take the oath—and that he might issue his *mittimus* as soon as he pleased. A few days after this, in Montgomery City, Constable Glenn came up to me, and said: "Mr. Eads, I suppose nothing more will be done with that matter." Why they did not enforce the law against me I know not.

M. L. EADS.

Rev. W. M. Newland.

As there are two kinds of preaching, so there are two classes of preachers, differing essentially and in many respects from each other. One class are known as popular preachers, by which we mean those who are preaching for worldly popularity—for the praise of men. Their object is to build up a reputation for superior talents and pulpit oratory, to be among those whose names are in all the newspapers, and are made the topic of conversation in all the circles of society. Their special aim is to be in favor with the influential, the rich, the great, the rulers of the synagogues, to whom they look for their appointments and special favors. The other class are honest, conscientious men, and preach because the love of Christ constrains them; and they feel that not to preach would be worse than death itself. "Woe is unto me, if I preach not the gospel," which woe means the loss of the soul, and banishment from the presence of God and the glory of his power forever. Their object being to save souls, they preach in the power and demonstration of the Holy Ghost. To this class our lamented Brother Newland belonged.

He was a prominent member of the Missouri Conference, M. E. Church, South; a sound theologian, and an able expounder of the word of God. He filled various positions in the Church successfully, but did not escape persecution. The following notice of his arrest appeared in the *Canton Press* October 7, 1865:

ARRESTED.—We learn from a communication in the *Palmyra Spectator* that Rev. Mr. Newland, presiding elder of the Hannibal District, was arrested at Newark on Sunday, the 2d instant, at the close of sacramental service, and held to answer at the ensuing term of the Circuit Court in Knox County, for exercising the function of his sacred office without having taken and filed the oath of loyalty. The arrest appears to have been made at the instigation of a son of a Presbyterian elder at that place, whose name is not given in the communication referred to.

The Sabbath seemed to be their favorite day for arresting preachers, thus desecrating the sanctuary and disturbing the worship of God in his own house and on his holy day.

CHURCH AT LA GRANGE.

This is an unusually interesting case, and shows how adroitly they maneuvered in trying to accomplish their purpose. They asked permission to preach in the Southern Methodist Church, and thereby got possession, and they manipulated in every way to hold it. We give below a full statement of the facts, furnished by a very reliable person. The reader will no doubt peruse the narrative with deep interest.

In 1838 two lots in the town of La Grange, Lewis County, Mo., were deeded to B. W. Stith, C. S. Skinner, John Lafon, Middleton Smoot, and others, trustees, for the use and benefit of the Methodist Episcopal Church, as then constituted. In the following year a small brick house was erected on the lots, and used by the Church in an unfinished condition until 1844. It was then finished, and upon the division of the Church passed into the hands and ownership of the M. E. Church, South. The membership of 1845 voted to adhere South, with only three or four dissenting voices, and they acquiesced in the will of the majority and remained in the Southern Church until after the repudiation of the Plan of Separation by the General Conference of 1848. Up to that time the Northern Church attempted no organization in La Grange; but soon after that event the Church (North) sent a Rev. Mr. Chivington (the same who made himself notorious a few years ago in the indiscriminate massacre of Indians near Fort Union) to that place. He sought and obtained permission to preach in the church. After the sermon he organized a class, and publicly thanked the members of the M. E. Church, South, for the use of *their* house.

The members of the Church (North) recognized the validity of the decisions of the courts in the Maysville (Ky.), and New York and Cincinnati Church property cases, and set up no claim whatever to the property in La Grange, or elsewhere in Missouri, until after the beginning of the war.

In 1853 the old church was displaced by a new and more commodious structure, erected and paid for by the members and friends of the M. E. Church, South, at a cost of over six thousand dollars. In this the M. E. Church (North) took no part, and paid no money, and claimed no interest. In 1863, ten years thereafter, a Rev. Mr. Stewart was sent to La Grange by the M. E. Church (North). This man professed great friendship for Southern Methodists, and made himself free and easy in their homes. The church was only occupied two Sabbaths in the month, and Mr. Stewart applied for the use of it when it was unoccupied. To this the owners objected at first. Mr. Stewart was offered the use of the German Methodist Church, but it did not suit his purpose, and he urged his application for the Southern Methodist Church. It was objected to by a large number of the members, on the ground that other churches in the State had been seized and possessed by them—some in one way, and some in another—and they feared that this might be a *ruse de guerre*.

Mr. Stewart finally pledged his honor as a Christian gentleman and minister to return the key every week to the trustees. This he did regularly until January, 1865, when his quarterly meeting was held in the church, and the Quarterly Conference appointed a Board of Trustees, and authorized them to hold possession of the property. Upon this action Rev. Mr. Stewart went out in town, purchased a lock, employed a carpenter, and had it put on in the place of the old one. He could then return both lock and key with impunity.

The trustees thus raised and authorized to act for the M. E. Church (North) served the following notice on the M. E. Church, South:

"LA GRANGE, LEWIS COUNTY, MO., Feb. 13, 1865.

"To John Munn, J. C. Goodrich, and Others, Trustees of the M. E. Church, South.

"*Gentlemen:* Having a just and legal claim to the property of the Methodist Episcopal Church in La Grange, as trustees of said Church, we hereby notify you that we intend to hold said property for the use and benefit of the ministers and members of the Methodist Episcopal Church in the United States of America, according to the Discipline and rules of said Church and the provisions of deed recorded in Book C, page 431, Lewis County records. We have accordingly taken possession of the herein mentioned property.

"Done by order of the Board of Trustees of La Grange M. E. Church.

"W. M. REDDING, *President Board of Trustees;*
"W. C. STEWART, *Secretary pro tem. and Preacher in Charge.*"

They had either been waiting a suitable opportunity or a new light had suddenly dawned upon them from some episcopal, military, or other throne of light and power, that they had been using, by gracious privilege and courtesy, property to which they had "a just (?) and legal claim," and they acted accordingly.

Possession is said to be nine points in the law, and if the adage is true the manner of gaining possession will not necessarily raise any curious questions of casuistry. The how will not vitiate the nine points when a new lock and key with an extra share of loyalty can make up and meet every other point in the legal decalogue. It only remained for them to serve the usual notification to save the form of the thing, and appoint Col. W. M. Redding, President of the Board and colonel of a regiment of Lewis County militia—not a member of any Church—to hold the property in peaceable possession. This duty he performed faithfully, for which service he received, in the *Central Advocate* (North) of December 20, 1865, the title of "the faithful guardian of the interests of the M. E. Church in La Grange, Mo."

A member of the La Grange Quarterly Conference, M. E.

Church, South, from whom much of the above information was obtained, writes as follows:

"To keep step after taking possession and serving notice was the exhibition of Christian charity (?) to us of the M. E. Church, South, by a polite offer to loan us the use of their (?) house for our religious worship. But we 'had not so learned Christ.' How could we be partakers with thieves and robbers? 'My house shall be called the house of prayer, but ye have made it a den of thieves.'

"Our house has been solemnly dedicated to the worship of Almighty God by Bishop Marvin when there was no name or membership of the M. E. Church (North) in the place; we say let the consecration abide and let God defend the right. We can worship there no more until the law with the whip of justice shall drive those who trouble us to their own place."

A letter in the *Central Christian Advocate* of December 20, 1865, from Rev. W. C. Stewart contains the following paragraph:

"When I was in La Grange I had the honor to organize a Board of Trustees of the M. E. Church, and by their authority to take possession of the valuable house of worship there, previously in the hands of the Church, South. In this movement Col. W. M. Redding took a prominent and most efficient part. He is still the faithful guardian of our Church property in La Grange."

This Col. Redding was once a member of the M. E. Church, South, but withdrew some time before this transaction, declaring when he did so that the time would come when a Southern Methodist could not live in that county. He was a prepared instrument of the M. E. Church (North), and well fitted for their special work, as he had once been a negro trader to the South and had the price of that human chattel in his pocket. A little power makes good radical leaders and instruments of such men.

Mr. Stewart exults in "the honor of organizing a Board of Trustees, and by their authority taking possession of the valuable house of worship formerly in the hands of the Church, South." The said "*honor*" is now made permanent and transmitted to posterity. This same Stewart left the M. E. Church (North), and went over to the Congregationalists.

The trustees of the M. E. Church, South, brought suit for possession in a civil magistrate's court. It was appealed to the Circuit Court for Lewis County by defendants, and then by the same party, upon a change of venue, taken to Shelby County. When called in the Circuit Court in Shelbyville they were not ready for trial. Before the session of the court in November, 1866, they asked the Church, South, to compromise by referring the whole case to three men for arbitration. When this was agreed to both parties gave bond in the sum of $500 to abide the decision. February 1, 1867, was set for hearing by the arbitrators. When case was stated by the Church, South, the other party asked leave to withdraw the bond. To this objections were made, and they wrangled over it till 4 o'clock P.M. The Church, North, asked a continuance till 9 o'clock next morning. This was granted, and at the appointed time they appeared and revoked their bond, saying that they preferred to have the case tried by the Supreme Court of the United States, and would make it a precedent for Missouri. Whether this course was intended only for delay their subsequent declaration that they did not expect to be ready for trial for ten years is the best interpretation.

Wearied out of all patience with such miserable tergiversation, the trustees of the M. E. Church, South, headed by their pastor, Rev. T. J. Starr, prepared to bring suit again, believing that their only hope was in the civil courts. As soon as Col. Redding and those who acted with him found that they would have to meet the case in the civil courts they proposed a compromise, which, during the absence of their preacher in charge, was accepted. This compromise gave the M. E. Church, South, a quitclaim deed to less than half the two lots with the new church, and the M. E. Church (North) a similar deed to the old church with the rest of the two lots.*

This shows what pertinacity can do. The M. E. Church, South, made them a present of the old church and the ground on which it stood just to get rid of them. They knew very well from what the civil courts had done in other cases that they

---

* Dr. Leftwich's book.

could recover all their property, but they were worn out and tired of litigation, and hence accepted a compromise. This may be regarded as a representative case, and will give the reader a very correct idea of their course of procedure in the seizure of other churches. Knowing that in law, in justice, and equity they had no claim whatever to the property, they were under the necessity of resorting to subtle chicanery to gain their point.

REV. J. H. PRITCHETT AND HIS WORK.

We take great pleasure in calling the attention of the reader to the following interesting sketch, given by Rev. J. H. Pritchett, of his ministerial life and work from the time he entered the itinerant ministry to A.D. 1867. The ministry and the Church are inseparable. Indeed, the ministry constitute an important part of the Church, and in giving an account of their work they necessarily furnish the annals and materials for the history of the Church. This fact the reader will readily see in this narrative.

I was admitted on trial in the Missouri Annual Conference during its session at Richmond in September, 1855, Bishop Early presiding. I was transferred at once to the Kansas Mission Conference, and was appointed junior preacher at Tecumseh Circuit, Lecompton District, L. B. Stateler preacher in charge, and W. Bradford presiding elder.

The session of the Kansas Mission Conference for 1856 was held at Kickapoo, Kan., Bishop Pierce presiding. I was appointed in charge of Council Grove Circuit.

In 1857 our Conference met in Leavenworth City. No bishop. I was returned to Council Grove Circuit. Met Bishop Andrew at Glasgow, Mo., and was ordained deacon.

In 1858 Shawneetown was the seat of our Conference. Bishop Early presided. He sent me to Leavenworth City, with Thomas Wallace as my presiding elder.

Bishop Paine presided at our Conference at Tecumseh, in 1859, and I was ordained elder and returned to Leavenworth City, but spent the last half of the year on the Council Grove District, Brother Bradford, presiding elder, having been sent to Denver, Colo., to look after our interests there.

Bishop Kavanaugh held our Conference for 1860 at Wyandotte, and I was transferred to the Missouri Conference, and appointed to the Sturgeon Circuit, Fayette District, with Edwin Robinson as my presiding elder.

I began work as soon as I could move and settle my family. There being no parsonage upon the charge, I took my family to my father's old farm in Warren County, where they remained through all the radical changes that followed until 1868. As then constituted, the Sturgeon Circuit embraced Sturgeon, Centralia, Mount Zion, Mount Moriah, Hallsville, and Union, together with Cook's, Bishop's, Green's, and one other schoolhouse. I found the people in the midst of a political campaign of a most heated and uncompromising character. Everybody was interested and everybody took part. This only passed away to be followed by the breaking up of the foundations of society and the long and bloody Civil War.

To one who had been through five years of Kansas troubles these things were neither strange nor unexpected; but they were none the less real and terrible. I preached this year to large and eager congregations all around the circuit; but such was the political followed by the military excitement that religion seemed put away for the time. We had some good meetings, however—notably at Mount Zion, Mount Moriah, and at one or two school-houses. Some revival and increase among those to whom I preached, and who labored with me in the Lord that year. A few still remain in my knowledge. John P. Horner, of Columbia, was then a merchant at Sturgeon. His house was my home, and he and his now sainted wife went a great way to constitute the Church at that place. Maj. Rucker, now of Sturgeon, was then a young man just from Virginia, and was clerking for Brother Horner. Jonn Reed still lives on his farm near Mount Zion Church. He must have been sixty years old when

I first met him in the old church in the fall of 1860. He was then and is now the patriarch of the congregation. His history in the Church there, personal and official, has been a remarkable one.

The old church which was built in 1848 was burned in December, 1861, by the Federal troops, after a hard-fought battle in and around it, with two or three companies of recruits on their way to join Gen. Price in South-west Missouri. A much better house, built since the war, now marks the old site.

The financial receipts of this year barely paid my traveling expenses.

The Missouri Conference for 1861 was held at Glasgow. No bishop was present. Owing to the general and intense excitement many of the preachers were absent, myself among the number. Our circumstances and wishes being unknown to the brethren, we were as a rule put down as supernumeraries on those charges where our families were known or supposed to reside. My name thus appeared in connection with the Flint Hill Circuit, in the St. Charles District, B. H. Spencer being presiding elder, and Charles Babcock preacher in charge. The circuit consisted of Flint Hill, Mount Zion, Paulsingville, and Pleasant Hill, churches, and Salem, Rockingham, and Young's, school-houses. My father's old farm, a part of which I had purchased, was within the bounds of the charge, and I was at home so far as residence was concerned. The Board of Stewards insisted that I should do full work, and I being perfectly able and willing, arrangements were made to support as well as possible two preachers' families. No Conference being held in 1862, the same arrangement was continued. Considering all the circumstances, it is wonderful how regularly our appointments were filled, how well the Church was kept together, and how many were persuaded to be religious.

Besides the general excitement created by the war, the presence and constant terrorizing of the "Dutch Home Guards" made life an uncertainty and a burden to all the better class of citizens in that region. During this time, while I alternated with my colleague in filling the regular appointments of the circuit, and bore my part in all special meetings, the greater part of our material support came from tilling my land and teaching school in my own house, the brethren often helping to take care of my crop and stock while I carried on or helped at meetings at a distance.

In 1863 Conference was held at Fulton. Comparatively few of the members were present, and no bishop. I was appointed in charge of Flint Hill Circuit, so that I really traveled that charge three years in succession. It was at that time a strong circuit. Mount Zion especially, as I remember it, had a remarkable congregation. In my thirty-five years' ministry, I do not recollect that I ever served its equal. The Campbells, the Pittman's, the Dorseys, the Ferrils, the Healds, the Keithleys, and their large family connections made an assemblage to be marked anywhere for intelligence, piety, sterling integrity, and worth. They had all been for a score of years the companions and co-laborers of my then sainted father. I felt toward them as I never felt toward any other body of men. What an inspiration it was to preach to those grand old pioneers of Methodism in that part of the State, knowing as I did that I had their sympathies, their prayers, and their hearty co-operation! Only a small remnant of the noble old guards of that troublous time is left, and I feel like taking off my hat and bowing my head whenever I meet Father D. K. Pittman, whose presence and counsel still linger with us.

During 1863 Brother Tyson Dines, who was stationed at St. Charles, was arrested, taken to St. Louis, put under bond, and was compelled to remain under military surveillance there. Our presiding elder, Brother B. H. Spencer, was also arrested and banished from the State. Brother Horace Brown was sent to the district and Brother Dines's charge was added to mine, and Brother H. B. Watson was sent to assist me on the work. These were times that tried men's souls, especially the souls of those who presumed to preach under the auspices of the Methodist Episcopal Church, South. The lay brethren, however, were eminently loyal to the Church, and not only stood by the men who preached for them, but out of their increasing poverty did what they could to feed and clothe the family of their banished presiding elder. The year, I trust, was not altogether a fruitless one.

In September of 1864 quite a number of the members of the Conference met in Mexico, and after a great deal of trouble with the military popinjay who had been dignified with the title of provost-marshal, by a special order from St. Louis we were allowed to proceed with our business. There was no bishop present, and Father Monroe was elected President. The doings of the Conference are of record. I left, by the advice of older brethren, early in the session. Not having taken the oath prescribed for preachers, I was not only excluded from my place in the Conference, but also threatened with military arrest.

I was appointed to St. Charles Station, and went to my work at once. Considering every thing, the Church was in a hopeful state, the congregation large, and but for the constantly recurring waves of military and political excitement which harassed, alarmed, and unsettled the minds of our people the results would have been *vastly* different. The Church, however, was considerably strengthened both in numbers and influence by parties who sought refuge in St. Charles from worse evils elsewhere.

Early in November our house of worship was badly wrecked by a storm, and for some time the propriety of repairing was a question of serious debate. Our congregation in the meantime occupied the Episcopal church, which was generously tendered us, that congregation being for the time without a pastor. Many of our people despaired at that time of the future of our Church, and felt little disposed to build or repair property for the use and benefit of those who were known to be waiting only for the *consent* of civil power to enter in and possess *our all*. The indications, too, were ominous that "Herod would not fail his Herodias," nor Ahab his Jezebel, when the proper time for the murder and transfer should arrive.

Besides, about this time quite a number of the best citizens of St. Charles and vicinity organized an association for the purpose of settling a colony in Brazil, and Judge E. A. Lewis went to Washington City to confer with the representatives of that government in regard to a location. The report made by the judge on his return divided the association, however, and the project was abandoned. Our people now saw nothing better for them than to repair their church, and with the hearty co-operation of a few such men as the three Overalls, McDowell, and Evans, together with a half-dozen irrepressible women, such as Sisters Dr. Overall and Rogers, the house was soon as good, if not better, than it had ever been; and we were again worshiping in it with full congregations.

The energy of those brethren in their discouragement was only equal to their liberality in their poverty. Nor was the Lord of the vineyard unmindful of their sacrifices, for his presence and blessing were clearly manifested in all their services in the newly repaired house. The Sunday-school, the prayer-meeting, the public service—all showed that the Lord was in his house. So passed the winter of 1864, and so came on the spring of 1865.

Having made all my arrangements, even to the purchase of gold, to go as *avant-coureur* of the colony to Brazil, and being disappointed by the failure of that enterprise, I determined early in the spring to go West and seek a new home for my family.

I surrendered my charge to Bishop Kavanaugh, and asked for a work in Montana. He supplied my place, but gave me no work. From April, 1865, to June, 1866, I was a wanderer, traveling by almost every conceivable means of locomotion, working at almost every available occupation, dealing with almost every known kind of people. I was able, by the help of God, to make a living, maintain my Christian integrity, do some good, I trust, and get back to my family. I found no place to which I felt disposed to transfer my family, though if I *had no* family I should certainly have remained in Montana. I think some of my best ministerial work was done in Helena, in that Territory.

When I arrived at home in June, 1866, I found Church affairs still much disordered. I applied to Brother B. H. Spencer, who was again presiding elder of St. Charles District, for work, and he gave me what had *once* been Warrenton Circuit. It had formerly embraced Warrenton, Troy, Marthasville, Ebenezer, and six or eight school-houses. The house at Warrenton, having been turned into a military stable during the war, was now unfit even to shelter horses. The church was disorganized and scattered. At Troy the house was out of repair and hopelessly in debt, the few members dispirited and divided. At Marthasville what had been a strong Church was now reduced to almost nothing. I went around the circuit twice, and learned at least what I have stated.

The presiding elder came round, and we held the fourth quarterly meeting in a *hay barn* at Wright City. We had a large attendance, a good meeting, and hopes were kindled that something might yet be done in the old home of E. M. Marvin.

Conference was held this year at Richmond, where eleven years before I had been received on trial. In one sense it seemed an age; in another, but a few days. Bishop Doggett presided. I was returned to Warrenton Circuit, with Horace Brown as my presiding elder. I had known him when a boy as the pastor of my father and mother, only to dread his long sermons, which I did not understand, and avoid his personal interviews, which I did not appreciate. I had known him a short time as my presiding elder during the war, but under circumstances which failed to bring out any thing for *me*, except the preaching power that was so hugely in him. In this new relationship I became strongly attached to him, finding in him not only one of the most powerful preachers that Missouri Methodism ever had, but one of the truest and warmest hearts that ever beat in *any* man.

This was a year of remarkable development on Warrenton Circuit along every line. The house at Warrenton was repaired at once, and a revival soon put us in possession of more than all we had lost. At Marthasville we soon repaired, paid the debt, and had a good congregation. At Troy the debt of fifteen hundred dollars troubled us for several months, but Bishop Marvin came to our help. We paid the debt, and have been moving a *little* ever since. Then lastly, at Wright City, the old home of Marvin, where we have never had any thing except a few scattered members, worshiping sometimes in a school-house and sometimes in a private house, we had a revival that took in almost every prominent family in the community, and ended in the erection of a beautiful and commodious house of worship which the bishop dedicated at the beginning of the next year. The presiding elder stated in the District Conference, which Bishop Marvin held for us that year at High Hill, that in his long and varied ministry he had never seen such a "resurrection of spiritual power" as was witnessed during this year, particularly on Warrenton and Williamsburg Circuits. Brother G. W. Penn was in charge of the latter circuit.

THE PALMYRA MEETING.

The most noticeable event in the history of the M. E. Church, South, during the war was the Palmyra meeting. Its importance cannot be adequately estimated. Did it not involve the destiny of the Church, which was at that time vibrating between life and death? It was indeed a fearful crisis in the history of Southern Methodism. The Church was wrapped in the most anxious solicitude, realizing that something must be done. For three long years she had suffered one of the most violent and destructive persecutions that ever visited the people of God. Some of her most intelligent friends entertained fearful apprehensions that she could not live through the ravages of the war. By the M. E. Church she was pronounced dead, hopelessly dead, beyond recovery. They spread the news all over the country, and gave it extensive publicity through their press and pulpits.

They may have thought she was dead, as she had suffered enough to cause death. Her homes had been desolated, her houses burned, her furniture, carpets, beds, bedding, silver plate, clothing of all kinds, had been captured; her farms laid waste; her wagons, loaded with her own goods, and drawn by her own horses and mules, driven away; her barns emptied of corn and wheat and oats and hay, and her stock of all kinds carried off; her ministers proscribed, banished, imprisoned, and put to death; her houses of worship, parsonages, seminaries, and colleges seized and taken possession of; her congregations disorganized and forbidden to assemble; her newspapers suppressed, and all means of intercommunication cut off.

In view of the foregoing facts, they might very naturally have come to the conclusion that she was dead. They must have believed it, for they proceeded to administer on her estate. The settlement of so large an estate was a matter of no little importance, for their idea was to embrace the entire M. E. Church, South. To manipulate the business successfully, and to reach the desired results, required their best talents and ablest men. It is not at all surprising that some of their prominent bishops took the lead in an enterprise of such vast magnitude. It was a big thing. The prospect opened before them grandly. Then there would be but one Methodist Episcopal Church in the United States, whose jurisdiction would extend to the utmost boundary of our country. What a grand and magnificent Church they would have! So Bishop Ames thought. Invested with the highest ecclesiastical and military authority and under the commission of Stanton-Ames order, he went South as minister plenipotentiary and administrator of the estate of a dead Church, with full authority to take possession of her property, *vi et armis*. Well might justice hide her blushing face, and equity retire from the scene of usurpation and oppression!

As has been already intimated, the M. E. Church,

South, scarcely knew, under existing circumstances, whether she, as an ecclesiastical organization, was alive or dead. Yet she was silently trusting in God, and earnestly praying for deliverance, that God would be merciful and come to the rescue of his distressed and persecuted people. Nor did she pray in vain. The God of infinite benevolence and boundless mercy answered her prayer in his own way. As he chose Moses to deliver the children of Israel out of the cruel bondage and servitude of Egypt; as he chose Martin Luther to break the power of the papal hierarchy, and expose the abominable superstitions of Romanism; as he chose John Wesley to save true, spiritual, experimental Christianity from the ritualism of mere formal worship, so he chose his aged servant, "the pioneer and patriarch of Missouri Methodism," Rev. Andrew Monroe, to lead in a movement for the deliverance of the M. E. Church, South, from the persecution, oppression, and usurpation of those in power. He called a meeting of the preachers and official members of the M. E. Church, South, within the bounds of the Missouri Conference, to be held at Palmyra June 22, 1865, for the purpose of ascertaining the real condition of the Church, and to take under consideration important questions appertaining to the vital interests of the Church, and the best measures for advancing her highest welfare.

The call was made as general as practicable, chiefly through private correspondence. This was attended with no little difficulty, as the mails were irregular and uncertain. Many and serious difficulties were in the way of responding to the call. There was great peril in traveling through the country. Some felt that if they should start they would not reach Palmyra. Others were so impoverished by the war that they did not have the means to defray their traveling expenses. Others, again, were too timid to face the music.

Twenty-four preachers, two of whom were local, and about half as many laymen, presented themselves at the time and place—a noble quorum of first-class business men of grit and pluck, and not afraid to follow their convictions. Rev. Andrew Monroe was elected President, and Rev. John D. Vincil Secretary. The following preachers enrolled their names: Revs. A. Monroe, C. I. Van Deventer, F. A. Savage, B. H. Spencer, W. M. Rush, R. G. Loving, James Penn, H. H. Hedgepeth, W. M. Newland, W. W. McMurry, John D. Vincil, R. P. Holt, A. P. Linn, Louis Downing, H. A. Bourland, E. A. Hudson, Jacob McEwin, L. Rush, W. Warren, P. M. Pinckard, S. H. Huffaker, and W. M. Leftwich; also Revs. W. D. Cox and W. O. Cross, local preachers, and a number of laymen were present.

This writer would rather have his name on the above roll than to have been one of the signers of the Declaration of Independence; for while he loves his country much, he loves his Church more. Did those patriots immortalize themselves by signing the Declaration of Independence? So did those ministers immortalize their names by adopting an important paper for the liberation of the M. E. Church, South, from the tyranny of ecclesiastical oppression more galling than the yoke of Great Britain. Will the names of those patriots live in the history of their country forever? So will the names of those ministers live in the history of the M. E. Church, South, as long as she has a history, and then will live on in heaven through the perpetual cycles of an unending duration. The Church now pays a grateful tribute to their memory.

The meeting was unique, *sui generis*, unprecedented—nothing like it had gone before. Hence it was characterized by originality. They had no previously established forms and usages to guide them. It was a new kind of meeting—new questions to be considered, new measures to be adopted, new life to be infused into the organization of the Church in all her departments.

The circumstances of the meeting were peculiar, delicate, critical, perilous. One mistake, one wrong word, one improper act might prove fatal to the meeting. Detectives and armed enemies were present, wide awake and watching with all diligence to get hold of something by which they might justify themselves in breaking up the meeting. Then, too, the abominable "test oath" of the new Constitution, which was all the talk at that time, was staring them in the face with its threats of arrest, proscription, indictment, banishment, imprisonment, and death to all Southern Methodist preachers who would not perjure themselves by violating their conscience and their obligations to God. It seems that the "test oath" was an instrument of persecution fabricated for that very purpose.

Notwithstanding these facts, which were calculated to intimidate them, they boldly proceeded with the business of the meeting as though there was nothing unusual. That they might obtain the necessary information from the different parts of the State, each preacher was called on to make a report of the state of the Church in the bounds of his work and the condition of things in his section of the country. To hear them tell of the trials and troubles, the privations and sufferings of themselves and of their people moved the congregation to tears, and was enough to melt a heart of stone.

Very much to the gratification of the preachers, Bishop Kavanaugh, of Kentucky, arrived on the second day about 12 o'clock M. They felt the inspiration of his presence and that his coming would be a benediction to them; that his judicious counsel and wise advice would be just what they needed.

After the preachers had made their reports and each one had given an account of the condition of the Church in his field of labor the whole matter was committed to the "Committee on State of the Church" to take what had been said under consideration and report to the meeting the results of their deliberations. Was there ever a committee charged with weightier and more important duties? The earnest prayers of the Church ascended to heaven in their behalf that God would guide them to right thoughts, right words, right actions, and to right conclusions. Let the reader give attention to the report of the committee as found below, and he will be satisfied that the prayers of the Church were answered:

Your committee, in considering "the importance of maintaining our separate and distinct ecclesiastical organization," beg leave to present the following resolution and accompanying paper:

Resolved, That we consider the maintenance of our separate and distinct ecclesiastical organization as of paramount importance and our imperative duty.

The reasons are many and obvious. While we have maintained a separate and distinct ecclesiastical organization for twenty years, yet we claim original paternity and co-existence as a Methodist Church with the other branches of the great Methodist family in the country. Facts will not permit us to yield to any other Church of that name priority of age; nor in any other light than as an attempt to deceive the unsuspecting among our people can we regard the specious claims urged to the confidence and patronage of the Methodist public under the name of "Old Church."

In contravention to the Plan of Separation agreed upon by the General Conference of 1844—the legitimacy and binding force of which were recognized by the Supreme Court of the United States—the Northern wing of the Church has acted in bad faith toward us in many ways.

And since that Church was forced by law to give to our Church her *pro rata* division of property—which she was too mercenary to do without an appeal to the highest judiciary of the country—she has persisted in an unprovoked and undesired war upon us—a war which has aggravated the questions of difference, widened the breach, and produced an estrangement of feeling and a destruction of fellowship for which she alone is responsible, and which we cannot even seek to remedy without compromising principles and yielding all self-respect.

Those who publish to the world that all differences between us are swept away with the institution of slavery are either ignorant of the facts or are trying to mislead the public. The question upon which the Church divided was not whether the institution of slavery was right or wrong, *per se*, but whether it was a legitimate subject for ecclesiastical legislation. The right or wrong of the institution, its existence or non-existence, could not affect this vital question. It is now abolished by Federal and State legislation, which event we accept as a political measure with which we have nothing to do as a Church. And it remains for us to demonstrate our ability to exist without the institution of slavery, as we have existed with it, which we have already done in California and other places.

Now, if we go into the Methodist Episcopal Church, we will by that act yield the position we have so often taken, admit the charges we have so often refuted, and, by accepting political tests of Church-fellowship, stultify ourselves and compromise the essential principles of the gospel. If we seek an alliance with or permit our Church to be swallowed up by any other ecclesiastical body so as to destroy our separate existence as a distinct organization, we admit the charge that with the institution of slavery we stand or fall.

The subject of Church reconstruction or consolidation has been widely discussed by the press and the ministry of the Methodist Episcopal Church (North), and reasons, both political and ecclesiastical, are urged with an ill-disguised pertinacity why we should consent to an absorption of our entire ecclesiastical body by that Church.

It cannot be disguised that what they failed to accomplish during the war by military order and authority they now seek to effect by ecclesiastical strategy and diplomacy—that is, to get possession of our Church property, and rather than recognize us now as a Christian Church entitled to their ecclesiastical fellowship and Christian fraternity (which they by formal vote of their General Conference refused to do in 1848) and in that way, and with a Christian spirit, seek to offer negotiations upon the subject, they prefer to ignore our existence, or, which would suit their purpose better, pronounce us disloyal to the government, and per consequence not entitled to an existence at all; then invade us and by misrepresentations seek to disaffect our people, disintegrate our Church, and inaugurate an ecclesiastical strife that will involve the third and fourth generations.

The only consolidation or reconstruction they would accept would be that we turn over to them our Church property and interests and influence; yield the whole field; confess that we have been in the wrong; indorse the politics of their Church as a condition of membership; and become political hucksters instead of gospel ministers; then even our motives would be suspected, and we looked upon with contempt for our cowardly truckling to party and power.

Again we affirm that our itinerant system has become a great moral agency in elevating the masses of the people, preaching the gospel to the poor and "spreading scriptural holiness over these lands." Under its wide-spread operations we have gathered the people together, planted Churches, organized Sabbath-schools, acquired Church property, built up and endowed institutions of learning, and become a moral and religious element of the country at least equal to any other Protestant Church.

The people have learned to look to our ministry for the gospel, to our Churches and Sunday-schools for religious instruction, and to our influence in restraining vice, encouraging virtue, maintaining law and order, and promoting the well-being of society. We cannot, therefore, abandon our Church and people, or betray the interests and trusts committed to us as a Church, without a plain and culpable disregard of duty that would subject us to the contempt and derision of the Christian public.

We are not at liberty to dissolve our ecclesiastical organization or permit our Church to be absorbed by any other, even should we desire to do so, for our people have been consulted as far as practicable, and they are unwilling to seek any other Church connection, but with great unanimity demand at our hands the maintenance of our Church organization intact.

It is, therefore, due the great mass of the people who oppose the prostitution of the pulpit to political purposes, it is due to our large membership who have been converted and gathered into the fold of Christ under our ministry, and who love our Church doctrines and discipline too fondly to seek any other fold now—it is due every principle of self-respect and ecclesiastical propriety that we maintain, with firm reliance upon the help of the Great Head of the Church, our organization without embarrassment or compromise.

While these are some of the many reasons why we should adopt the above resolution, we desire most ardently to cultivate fraternal relations with all the evangelical Churches, and "as much as in us lies live peaceably with all men."

Wm. M. Leftwich, *Chairman;*
John D. Vincil,
Wm. M. Newland.

After proper investigation, rigid criticism, and animated discussion, the resolution with the accompanying paper was almost unanimously adopted. The influence of the action of the meeting was very great indeed, and extended throughout the entire Connection. As formerly stated, the whole Church was anxiously waiting and looking and praying for something of the kind; and when it came it was like the voice of God among his people saying to them, as he said to Joshua, "Get thee up; wherefore liest thou thus upon thy face?" and as God went with Israel's hosts leading them forth from conquest to victory and from victory to triumph, so he has been with the M. E. Church, South, ever since the war, investing her with divine power and clothing her with salvation. See what a history she has made since A.D. 1865!

The glad tidings of great joy went from Palmyra on the wings of the wind and with lightning flash. Sooner than you could imagine it was all over the South and West, like the rising sun, with his golden beams of radiant light, dispelling darkness and driving away all gloom and sadness.

"Bishop Kavanaugh reported that the people of the whole South felt and acknowledged the power of the Palmyra meeting upon the tone and spirit of the Church, and that it did much to shape the policy of the bishops and leading men of the Church. Bishop Marvin said that the report of the Palmyra meeting was to Southern Methodism in Texas like the clarion notes of a mighty chieftain calling the scattered knights to duty and to danger, and inspiring the courage and confidence of the Church throughout the whole South. In Virginia and the Carolinas, according to the *Episcopal Methodist*, of Richmond, Va., it was like 'life from the dead.'"

Yes, indeed, it was "life from the dead," causing the great heart of Southern Methodism to throb with joy unutterable.

> Daughter of Zion, from the dust
> Exalt thy fallen head;
> Again in thy Redeemer trust;
> He calls thee from the dead.
>
> Awake, awake! put on thy strength,
> Thy beautiful array;
> The day of freedom dawns at length,
> The Lord's appointed day.

CHAPTER VIII.

MISSOURI CONFERENCE.

Remove All Outside Restraints, and Every Man Will Show What He Is—Persecution Continues under the "Test Oath" of the New Constitution—Ministers of the Gospel Refuse to Take It—Forty-ninth Annual Session of the Missouri Conference at Hannibal—Minute Business—Six Deaths in the Conference During the Year: W. G. Caples, Edwin Robinson, William Ketron, John F. Young, George L. Sexton, and D. R. Smith—Biographical Sketch of Each One—Preachers Blessed in Their Work—Report of a Committee of the Missouri Conference on the State of the Church—Persecution of Rev. W. A. Tarwater—His Own Account of It—*St. Louis Christian Advocate* on the State of Things—Trial of Rev. J. A. Mumpower—Rev. John D. Vincil—Wise Counsel of the *St. Louis Christian Advocate*—The Church at Lexington.

WE have followed the history of the M. E. Church, South, through the fierce and fiery ordeal of an internecine war and reign of terrors—Such times as tried the principles and souls of men and revealed to the world their true character. Remove all extraneous restraints, civil, social, and religious, from a man, and you will see exactly what he is. His base, vile, and wicked nature is concealed from public view because he is afraid of the civil law, of public sentiment, and of the righteous influence of Christianity. Let these restraints be taken away, and there will be an outward manifestation of the malicious passions of his heart. The reader certainly did not fail to see a verification and exemplification of this truth during the war. Some who were considered good, moral, and religious men before the war manifested a very vindictive spirit of cruel persecution during the war. This they did very much to the astonishment of their friends and acquaintances.

There is no difficulty, however, in the explanation. The war gave them an opportunity of developing their true character by removing the restraints of which we have just spoken. The war itself was wicked. It violated the principles of the gospel and the example and teachings of Christ. It contained the elements of diabolism, and antagonized Christianity at every point. It called forth the most degraded passions of fallen humanity; emnity, malice, hatred, revenge, taking pleasure in the shedding of blood and the work of destruction. The devil incarnate is under no restraint in a civil war. Nothing is so demoralizing, and its demoralization, deep and wide-spread, has continued in our country ever since the war.

Though the Civil War has ended and peace has been declared, yet there is a continuation of strife, of serious trouble, and malignant persecution in Missouri, caused by the ministers refusing to take the "test oath" of the new Constitution. As they could not take it conscientiously, they would not take it at all. As they had not been called on to take such an oath before the war, and as their loyalty to the government could not be called in question since the war, they saw no sense or propriety in taking it. They knew, furthermore, that the Constitution of the United States as well as that of their own State protected them in their preaching and religious worship. Hence the Supreme Court of the United States pronounced said oath unconstitutional. More than all this, they recognized the great fact that they received their authority to preach the gospel from God, who said to them: "Go ye into all the world, and preach the gospel to every creature." Under the sanction of high Heaven and fully invested with the authority of God to preach the word, they could not let themselves down so low as to ask for man's authority; and because they would not take an unconstitutional oath they were persecuted and some of them put to death.

On the 16th day of August, 1865, the forty-ninth annual session of the Missouri Conference was opened by Bishop Kavanaugh at Hannibal, Mo. John D. Vincil was elected Secretary. The long and disastrous war having terminated, the members of the Conference congratulated one another on the occasion of meeting once more through the protection and guardianship of a kind and merciful Providence. All joined in the voice of prayer and praise and thanksgiving to Almighty God for having brought them safely through the perils of the past, and for the encouraging prospects of the future, though they might yet meet with trouble and persecution in some of their fields of labor.

Joseph Metcalf and George Primrose were admitted on trial. Thompson Penn, John A. Mumpower, James Smith, J. S. Allen, and B. F. Zumwalt remained on trial. The following traveling preachers were elected and ordained deacons: Samuel J. Huffaker, James O. Swinney, Samuel Alexander, John W. Atkisson, and Charles W. Collet. The following local preachers were elected and ordained deacons: J. Metcalf, John Stephens, and F. R. Milton. The following traveling preachers were elected and ordained elders: J. R. Taylor, George Penn, Charles W. Collet, John F. Shores, B. N. T. Holliday, and A. Albright. One local preacher, Samuel Briggs, was elected and ordained elder. The following were supernumerary: P. M. Pinckard, Tyson Dines, S. J. Catlin, A. Albright, George Fenton, Jesse Faubion, N. P. Lynn, W. M. Sutton, R. A. Claughton, R. H. Jordan, C. W. Pritchett, William Warren, Walter Toole, S. J. Huffaker, James Penn, M. R. Jones, D. Mason, and H. G. McEwin. The superannuated were Martin L. Eady, W. M. Wood, and D. C. Blackwell.

There was unusual fatality in the Conference during the past year—not less than six deaths: W. G. Caples, Edwin Robinson, William Ketron, John F. Young, George L. Sexton, and D. R. Smith, some of whom died a natural death, while others died martyrs for the truth of the gospel. All these faithful embassadors of God deserve a name in history, and our notice of them shall be in accordance with the best and most reliable information we can obtain.

The report of the Committee on Memoirs, as published in the Conference Minutes, is exceedingly brief, and gives but little information concerning these ministers. The information is good as far as it goes, but it does not go far enough. A satisfactory and condensed history of the ministers of the M. E. Church, South, is very desirable. We shall be compelled to confine ourselves to the Minutes when we can find no other source of information. This last remark will enable the friends to understand why some of the biographies are so short and inadequate to the importance of the subject:

William Ketron, presiding elder of the Gallatin District, a veteran itinerant and indefatigable servant of the Church, has passed away. He fell at his post, his face to the foe, with his armor on. He died as he lived, full of faith, exclaiming (the last words he spoke): "All is well!"

John F. Young, an old and deeply afflicted superannuated preacher, has ceased to suffer within the last few weeks. His sweet-spiritedness while living, his resignation when dying, and his desire to depart and be with Christ but illustrate the power of that religion he professed and taught so long.

David R. Smith, a probationer, sweetly fell asleep in Jesus one month after receiving his first appointment.

Rev. George L. Sexton

was an unusually interesting young man and full of promise. Every thing seemed to be in his favor. The Church looked upon him hopefully and expected much of him. But alas! his hopes were blasted, and the promising fruit was nipped in the bud. Read the sad account of his sufferings and mysterious end:

The subject of this sketch, George L. Sexton, was born in Missouri July 10, 1839. He was married in September, 1860; commenced preaching in his seventeenth year, and from the first gave evidence of no ordinary talent. His preaching attracted the eyes and inspired the hope of the Church to an extent not usual in every "boy preacher."

He was physically small, but possessed of a nervous temperament equal to the vigorous action of the largest brain. Energetic and rapid in all his movements, studious and practical in all his mental habits, accurate and sharp in his perceptions, and with a ready and fluent utterance and deep, earnest piety, he bid fair to make a preacher equal to any work and acceptable to any people. The pledges of extensive usefulness were only equaled by the fields that were white unto the harvest, which in every direction invited his polished sickle.

When the war broke out Mr. Sexton was in charge of the Memphis Circuit, Missouri Conference, M. E. Church, South. The fact that he was a Southern Methodist preacher was sufficient to secure the attention and the threats of the superloyalists of that portion of the State.

Irresponsible parties annoyed him and threatened his life until he thought it best to leave that part of the country and seek safety elsewhere.

He went to Boone County, and for a time supplied the Sturgeon Circuit. But here he was by no means free from molestation. In fact, there was no part of the State of Missouri where a Southern Methodist preacher could feel safe during the whole war, unless it was in St. Louis.

In June, 1862, while on his way to Bishop's School-house, to fill an appointment, he was arrested by a company of "Merrill's Horse," as they were called, commanded by Capt. Stewart, taken to Columbia, and put in prison. Every effort made by his father and others to obtain his release was met by insult. Both Merrill and his officers heaped upon Mr. Sexton every indignity that wicked men could invent. The fact that he was a Southern Methodist preacher was enough in their prejudice and malice to send him to Alton Military Prison for the war. After remaining in prison for some time, he, with others, made his escape and went South, well knowing that he could not remain here in safety.

While in the South, away from home, without employment or means, he accepted a chaplaincy in the army for a time. This, however, he soon resigned, and after an absence of eighteen months started home to see his wife and little ones; but before reaching home he was arrested and sent to Alton, Ill., where he remained for several months in that loathsome pesthouse.

His health was very poor, and his physical constitution was fast giving way under the treatment at that noted military prison. Friends interested themselves in his behalf, and he was finally released and permitted to reach his home. He remained at home with his family several months, trying to follow peace with all men, and prosecute, in a quiet, humble way, his mission of mercy to dying men, avoiding every thing that would seem officious or that would be offensive to the most uncompromising partisan; yet he met only insult, indignity, and denunciation, accompanied by such threats as led him to feel that his life was in imminent peril all the time. Believing that he could not remain at home in Missouri in safety, he again started South. His purpose was to gain a place of personal safety, and not to take up arms against the government. The idea of fighting his fellow-men was so repulsive to his feelings and views of the character and work of a minister of the gospel that he sought only personal safety and religious liberty. While traveling with a friend, and near the Arkansas line, both unarmed and unconscious of danger, they were discovered and shot down by a squad of Federal soldiers. His friend was instantly killed, and Mr. Sexton was severely—perhaps mortally—wounded. The ball took effect in the shoulder. The citizens removed him to a house near by, and kindly cared for him, dressing his wound and ministering unto him. But another squad of Federal soldiers found him, ascertained that he was a Southern Methodist preacher, and, though informed that he could not possibly live, took him away; and *he was never heard of afterward.* Where they carried him nobody knows. When, where, and how he died, and where he was buried—if at all—are known only to the perpetrators of the horrible deed and to the all-seeing eye. One comforting message comes to the sorrowing parents and grief-stricken widow, like "good news from a far country," from the family to whose house he was carried after he was shot. They say he conversed freely while there, and frequently said he was not afraid to die—that all was well.*

Of Rev. Edwin Robinson we have the following notice:

Mr. Robinson was received on trial into the Missouri Annual Conference, M. E. Church, in 1837, with Thomas D. Clanton, Daniel T. Sherman, F. W. Mitchell, and James G. F. Dunlany. His first appointment was junior preacher on the Greenville Circuit, in the Boonville District, with Moses B. Evans his senior, and Jesse Green presiding elder.

He received regular appointments from the Conference every year, and filled them acceptably and usefully to the Church. In 1852 he was made presiding elder of the Richmond District, and for several years filled that high and responsible office to the satisfaction of the Church. He was once honored with a seat in the General Conference, and was always held in high esteem by the ministry and the Church.

Wise and prudent in counsel, and thoroughly Methodistic in all his feelings, sentiments, and practice, he ever conserved the best interests of the Church of his choice. He was not very brilliant in the pulpit, but sound, practical, earnest, and useful. So widely known, he is now as widely lamented.

When the war broke out he saw the necessity of great caution and prudence in all his public services and private ways. He refrained scrupulously from canvassing the exciting events that were so rapidly transpiring. And his very humble, quiet, unobstrusive spirit and manner of life passed him through the troubles of the war about as evenly and safely as any other prominent Southern Methodist minister in the State, out of St. Louis, up to the fatal hour of his cold, cruel murder.

In the fall of 1864 Mr. Robinson was residing about two miles south of Fayette, in Howard County, and traveling the Fayette Circuit. He had formerly lived in Chillicothe, and when the troubles of the fall thickened and darkened around him so alarm-

---

*Dr. Leftwich's book.

ingly he make up his mind to remove his family either back to Chillicothe or into Grundy County, where his wife had some relatives living.

For this purpose he determined to precede his family and provide a home. Before setting out on the journey his wife prevailed on him, in view of the danger of traveling through the country, to go by way of Renick and take the North Missouri railroad. He afterward, however, abandoned that route and set out in company with a colored man who lived in Chillicothe and had a wife at his home, and in whom he had the utmost confidence. Instead of going through Glasgow, they took a nearer and safer route through Monticello and Old Chariton. When they reached the latter place, only two miles from Glasgow, they halted for a few moments in front of Moore's Hotel talking with some gentlemen, when a squad of soldiers, commanded by Capt. Merrideth, rode rapidly up, and the following colloquy was had:

Captain: "Who and what are you?"

"My name is Robinson, and I am a Methodist preacher."

Captain: "A Southern Methodist preacher?"

"Yes, sir."

"That, sir, is enough to damn you," said the valiant captain excitedly, and turning to his men said, "Blow his damned brains out," which was instantly done.

These facts were reported by the negro, to which some ladies who at the time were looking out at the window make the following addition: They say that after the above conversation, and before any order was given to shoot, Mr. Robinson and the negro were permitted to ride on. After they had gone about fifty yards Capt. Merrideth called the negro back and asked him what he knew about Robinson. He replied that he knew nothing about Robinson's politics, but that he had a very bad son who was a bush-whacker, upon which Merrideth dashed up to Robinson and either shot him himself or ordered his men to do it. As to who did the shooting the ladies are not fully agreed, nor is it important. Captain Merrideth was in command, and the public verdict of the people as well as the verdict of history will hold him responsible.

He rode away from his victim after leaving an order that his body should not be removed on pain of death. For some reason the captain did not take the dead man's horse, and the noble animal stood in silence and alone beside the body of his master whom he had so long borne, now pulseless, lifeless.

The ladies, true to the instincts of a finer, purer nature, and the warmer sympathies and loftier courage of humanity, notwithstanding the general terror and panic of the citizens, went out and pulled rails from the fence and make a rude pen around the dead man to prevent the hogs from profaning his body, and then sent a message to Mrs. Thompson, of Glasgow, informing her of the facts. This good lady caused a two-horse wagon to be prepared, and with several other "elect ladies," attended by two gentlemen, went out the following morning, which was the Sabbath, and brought his body into the city. His wife was summoned to look upon and follow to the grave the mangled remains of her beloved companion. Such was the reign of terror that the citizens of Glasgow were afraid to receive the body of the departed minister of God into their house. His body was placed in the Christian Church, and the next day, Monday, followed to the town of Fayette by the disconsolate widow and a few silent mourners and deposited in the cemetery.*

This present writer, who at that time had charge of the Howard College, attended his sad burial. He saw Mr. Robinson when he left Fayette with the negro Saturday morning, on his way to Chillicothe, and remarked at the time that he was making a very perilous trip. He who looked so dignified and manly that morning on his fine horse as he left Fayette in a few hours was dead, shot through the head because he was a Southern Methodist preacher.

Fifty-five preachers were sent out by the Conference to their respective fields of labor, God wonderfully blessed their work during the past year with many and extensive revivals of religion. Al-

---
* Dr. Leftwich's book.

most every number of the *St. Louis Christian Advocate* gave encouraging notices of the great things God was doing for them, in the conviction of sinners, the conversion of believing penitents, and the edification of the Church. Though troubles beset them on all sides, though opposition of various kinds met them almost everywhere they went, God was with them.

Thus encouraged by the experience of the past year, they went forth with renewed consecration and stronger purpose of heart to preach the gospel in its simplicity, purity, and divine power, with greater zeal and earnestness than they had ever done before.

The following paper—sensible, strong, and on the basis of Christian love, truth, and righteousness—will be read with interest:

REPORT OF A COMMITTEE OF THE MISSOURI CONFERENCE ON
THE STATE OF THE CHURCH.

At the late session of the Missouri Annual Conference, held at Hannibal, beginning on the 16th of August, among other interesting proceedings, was the following report of a committee appointed to consider the present state of the country in the bounds of that Conference, which it may be well to say include all that part of the State of Missouri lying north of the Missouri River. The report was presented to the Conference and adopted unanimously. It is difficult to say how the questions considered could have been expressed or discussed in a more clear or satisfactory manner. The report shows the members of the Mission Conference to be *true* men, sensible men of correct feelings and sound views. Read the report carefully and consider it well, especially that part which refers to the word "South," as affixed to the name of the Church. When you have read and considered it then ask yourself: What is the spirit that moves many who call themselves Christians to speak and write and act as they do in regard to the M. E. Church, South, which as a Church is confessedly one of the most evangelical and *unsecularized* Christian denominations in all the land.

The report is as follows :

" In calling attention to this subject, the first thing worthy of note is its imminently perilous condition. Never were the signs of a violent persecution of the Church and the ministry of God more manifest. Never since the days of bloody persecution has opposition to the Church and ministry, and to our common Christianity, been so bold, so defiant, so well organized, and so bitter and determined as now. Never in modern times have combinations against the character, claims, and cause of the Redeemer seemed to be so strong, or wore such a threatening aspect. Truly the kings of the earth have set themselves, and the rulers take counsel against the Lord and against his Christ. (Ps. ii. 2.) Truly the people of God will be called to wrestle with principalities and powers, and with the rulers of the darkness of this world, and with spiritual wickedness in high places ; but the weapons of our warfare are *not carnal*, but mighty through God.

" In the afflictions which have come upon the Church of God in Missouri our denomination has had a double share, and in persecutions yet to come we are singled out for special attention. We have been singled as a ' secession, traitorous, and rebel organization ; ' as unworthy of civil protection ; and, indeed, as only deserving to be suppressed and destroyed by the government.

" This has been done not only by those in low, but also by those in high and commanding positions. Some of our houses of worship have been burned, others dismantled and otherwise injured and destroyed. Of the use of others we have been forcibly deprived for months, and even for years ; and the most painful fact in this bill of complaint is that the latter has frequently been done by men professing to be Christian ministers! These men have come into our own pulpits, and taken possession of our houses of worship, against and in defiance of our wishes, and retain and use them in *open violation of our rights*. Some of our ministers and members have fallen by the hand of violence, while others have had to flee for their lives.

"The principal reason assigned for the bitter persecution with which we have been assailed is the word South affixed to our ecclesiastical name. The charge has been made and repeated until it has grown threadbare, that this word in our name means *secession, treason, and rebellion;* and hence there is nothing more common than for our enemies to call us *the Rebel Church*. And what is more surprising than all is that any man of intelligence or candor should profess to believe, or for a moment be influenced by, an allegation so untrue to history and so mischievous in its design. It seems not to have occurred to some men, of whom we had expected better things, that it is possible for *bad men*, under professed loyalty to the government, to slander those who are *better than themselves*. It has been said by men in high official positions in this State that if these charges are not true we are to blame for not having made *some effort* to set ourselves *right before the community*. Now the fact is simply this: We have made frequent efforts to define our ecclesiastical position, but for the last few years *passion and prejudice* have been so strongly excited against us that our statements and appeals have been disregarded. We wish to say then, distinctly and emphatically, that the word *South*, as it attaches to our ecclesiastical name, *never did, and does not now, have any political significance whatever*. It is simply an affix to the name of our Church indicating the geographical limits of our ecclesiastical jurisdiction.

"In the Plan of Separation of the 'original Methodist Church in America' into 'two General Conference jurisdictions,' adopted in 1844, the word 'South' was applied to that part of the M. E. Church which lay in the South to distinguish it from that part which lay in the North, with the mutual understanding and pledge that neither of these two should invade the territory of the other. It was employed to distinguish a Church existing and operating on the *south side of a line* from one existing and operating on the *north side* of the same line; and, furthermore, this word was attached to our name sixteen or seventeen years before it could have had the political meaning which some seek to give it. The above statement is not only true, but plain enough, certainly, to be understood by the most ordinary mind.

"In this defense of our Church we do not wish to excuse or justify any conduct upon the part of our ministers or members that may have given just cause for complaint, but do disapprove and regret the same. The truth is there is no Christian denomination in Missouri, or in the Southern States, of equal numbers, from whose association fewer persons have gone into the rebellion than have gone from ours. Now, how can this fact be accounted for if this word in our name be the mischievous thing some say it is? It is not of *doctrinal* or *political*, but of *geographical* and *jurisdictional* import. But it may be inquired, if the *doctrine* and *discipline* of the two Churches be the same, why keep up the Southern organization at all? Why not all be one? We answer that the reasons for keeping up our organization are weighty and urgent: 1. More than half a million of souls look to us for the word of light and hold us in honor and duty bound to give it to them. 2. Thousands upon thousands will not only be lost to Methodism, but, what is infinitely worse, will be lost to *Christ* and to *heaven*, if we do not sustain our organization *as the means of promoting their salvation*. 3. There are multiplied thousands in the Southern States, and elsewhere, who will perish in their sins if they are not saved through our instrumentality, for they will hear no *other ministers* and can be reached by no other organization; and in this view of the subject, no Christian, no philanthropist, or lover of his country ought to wish or ask us to give it up.

"We truly regret, as we have ever regretted, that there ever should have been a *necessity* for the organization of the Methodist Episcopal Church, South; but the necessities of the case compelled the organization, and still require its continuance. But others may say sustain the organization, but change the *name* by leaving out the word *South*. To this we reply: (1) That while we devoutly wish it were otherwise, yet a change of our name would not change the *hearts* and *conduct* of our persecutors toward us. (2) A change of name can only be effected by the General Conference, which does not meet until April, 1866. (3) A change of name would involve the loss of all our Church property, or involve a great deal of separate State legislation in order to legalize the transfer. (4) A change of name would now inevitably produce strife and dissatisfaction in our ranks; hence, however desirable such change may be, it cannot now be satisfactorily or legally made. Therefore let us, with meekness of wisdom, Christian prudence, and patient endurance, endeavor to sustain our organization as the means of promoting the interests of the Messiah's kingdom upon earth in the salvation of men. We should be the more encouraged to do this in view of the fact that, notwithstanding the sore trials and persecutions of the last five years, by the blessing of Almighty God our organization still remains intact. This fact itself calls for gratitude to God, and furnishes indubitable proof that the 'Lord of hosts is with us, and that the God of Jacob is our refuge.' When we had no one but God to plead our cause, or vindicate our position, or to support us under the crushing weight of persecution by which we were assailed, he sustained us; for which we thank his holy name and take courage.

"As to the *temporal* condition of the Church, embracing our *educational* and *pecuniary* interests, we refer you to the reports of the respective committees on those subjects. As it respects our *spiritual* state, we regret to say that it is far from what it *ought* to be, and far from what we *wish* it to be. And yet, with gratitude to God, we record the fact that we embrace within our organization in Missouri thousands of those who are among the most intelligent and devoted Christians in the State.

"In conclusion, your committee would offer for your adoption the following resolution:

"*Resolved*, That we still hold on to our ecclesiastical platform —viz.: 1. Obedience to all proper authority, whether human or divine. 2. No ecclesiastical interference with political questions. 3. The observance of all the duties growing out of the established relations of the Society. 4. The preaching of the gospel without any political admixture.

"All of which is respectfully submitted." *

The history of Methodism in Missouri for this Conference year would be incomplete without the names of those preachers who passed through great persecutions and tribulations on account of their unswerving fidelity to the cause of their Lord and Master—men who could not be intimidated

---

* St. Louis *Christian Advocate*, September 21, 1865.

or moved by terrorism, and who would not compromise their divine call to preach the gospel, though refusing to do so might cost them their lives.

REV. W. A. TARWATER.

This name is dear to the hearts of all the preachers in the Missouri Conference—a noble example of a consecrated minister of Jesus Christ—possessed of those natural gifts and Christian qualities that made him beloved and useful wherever he preached. He was a man of sterling worth and considerable ability; had the honor of being a delegate to the General Conference of the M. E. Church, South. This State may well be proud of such preachers, of whom Missouri has furnished a large number. His ministerial labors were greatly blessed of God, and he had many interesting revivals in which scores and hundreds of sinners experienced convicting and converting grace. He was very much disturbed in his ministerial labors during the war, of which he gives the following statement:

> Religious liberty in Missouri has come to an end, at least so far as the M. E. Church, South, in North-east Missouri is concerned. The convention oath of 1861 has been prescribed and administered; but the heaviest blow was struck by the Draconian Constitution, which would make every minister of the land subscribe to an oath as the condition of his continuing in the sacred office. I had made up my mind, on my knees, that I would not take it; for I would not have taken any sort of an oath from any civil authority as the condition of my preaching.
>
> The County Court of Lewis County, Mo., was now in session. I received a message purporting to come from a county official, running about thus: "*Sir:* Change the services of to-

morrow into a prayer-meeting, and thereby secure your liberty another six months."

I thought it would be rash not to comply, as there seemed to be a promise that I would not be interfered with until the following term of the Circuit Court. But such was not the case, as it was soon noised abroad that I should be chastised for not hearing and obeying the voice of men. We had a prayer-meeting. It was a solemn occasion. The congregation never felt the force of civil prohibition as they then felt it. The Holy One was in the hearts of the people. I had already refused to perform the rites of matrimony upon the generally received opinion that it was a civil contract; but feeling most solemnly convinced that no legislative enactment could invade the pulpit, I only refused to quit preaching. I was now waited on by a committee (whether self-constituted or sent by the "Loyal League" I did not know; but so strong was my belief that the latter was true that I did not ask them). They informed me that I must "leave the State, take the oath of loyalty, or quit preaching." I replied, in substance, as follows: "All my interests are in Missouri; my friends are here; it is the State of my nativity, and I feel like remaining, laboring, and suffering with the Church in Missouri. As to the oath, I cannot take it; for if I have any authority to preach, I received it from a higher court than any civil tribunal. I cannot repudiate that authority and claim to be an embassador of Christ, who says: 'Lo, I am with you alway.' Again, I have taken the oath of 1861, which bound me not to take any oath of any Legislature or convention which is in violation of the Constitution of the United States; and, with my present convictions, I cannot take that oath without being a perjured man."

On leaving they informed me that the men who framed and supported that instrument were the men who put down the rebellion, and that they would enforce that law to the end.

I answered: "The Lord being my helper, gentlemen, I shall *attempt* to preach next Sabbath in that church (pointing toward the church-house in Canton)." It should be stated that I afterward stood by the dying bed of one of these men, who asked me to pray for him. I tried as best I could to do so. A short time before his death he expressed a degree of readiness, and said he had some comfort as he passed through the chilly waters of death. Holding me by the hand, and looking me in the face, he said: "To be consistent, I have gone too far."

All the preachers in the county (not Radical) had quit preaching. I stood alone, but enjoyed great peace of mind. Indications of the divine presence were witnessed in almost every congregation. I fully believe the Lord sanctioned my course.

A few Sabbaths came and went, and still I was at liberty. Many threats were made to mob me as a lawless man. I told them that I did not regard myself lawless, while I stood ready to suffer the penalty. Finding that I was not to be moved by threats, they determined upon my arrest. It was Monday morning. I had tried to preach twice in Monticello on the previous day. I felt very much composed. Entering the workshop of a friend, the deputy sheriff came in after me. He read the summons. Placing myself under his protection, I was marched across the street to the court-room of Justice Newland, and was introduced to the court. The deputy who arrested me was one William Cisler, a brother of the sheriff. The court-room was crowded, as it was the first time that a man had been arrested in that county for preaching the gospel, and there was considerable excitement in the village.

When asked if I was ready for trial I replied that I was not, and asked for a change of venue. The justice asked why I wanted a change of venue. I replied that it was upon the ground that he (Justice Newland) was an *ex-rebel* and a *perjured man*, and that I could not hope to get justice in such a court. At this he became exceedingly angry, but when I informed him that some of the best citizens of the county were ready to make good the charge he cooled down and consulted a lawyer as to whether I had a right to take a change of venue.

The court entered into a preliminary examination; called one witness; consulted one Mr. Rollins, who claimed to be a lawyer; went through the farce of an investigation, and bound me over in the sum of one thousand dollars for my appearance at the next term of the Circuit Court, upon which I was dismissed.

Here the question arose: Had I bound myself not to preach? No; I would have gone to jail before giving such a bond. So the following Sabbath I tried as best I could to preach Jesus and the resurrection, morning and evening. I was soon arrested again, held in custody a portion of the day, and acquitted for want of testimony. The man who complained and had me arrested would not appear as a witness in the case. So ashamed was he of the whole thing that he could not be found. A few weeks elapsed, when I was engaged in a very gracious revival of religion in the city of Canton. The sheriff (Cisler) came down to arrest me again. He said: "Sir, I have come to arrest you again, as you will not take the oath of loyalty." I was in a happy frame of mind, and, laying my hand on his shoulder, said: "Sir, I am ready to go with you to Monticello, the stake, or to prison; for the good Lord has done great things for me recently, and I am prepared for the worst; *but I cannot take that oath.* I cannot dare to have my commission renewed by a civil officer." He hesitated a few moments, and said: "I forgot some of my papers, and will not take you to-day."

This was noised abroad in the town of Canton, and some expressed their indignation toward the officer that would not perform his duty; whereupon the city authorities took it in hand, and the following morning Brother James Penn and myself were arrested by Constable Wilson, and brought before Justice Page, who bound each of us in a bond of $500 to appear at the ensuing term of the Circuit Court.

We returned to the church and resumed the meeting, almost under the shadow of the justice's office. The good work went on, and scores of souls were converted at that meeting. It was the most successful year of my ministry. By this time I began to be regarded by that class as a lawless man, a pestilent fellow, and should not be allowed to remain in that part of the country. Two or three unsuccessful attempts had been made to mob me out of the country. Providence so ordered it that there never was a violent hand laid on me. Those persons who seemed to be full of the spirit of mobocracy were encouraged by those who were in honorable positions. It is true that there were some honorable exceptions to this rule who were, though Radicals, opposed to such conduct. At the ensuing term of the Circuit Court a bill was found against me, the result of which has been made known by some of my legal friends.

We call the attention of the reader to the following article taken from the *St. Louis Christian Ad-*

vocate of February 1, 1866, because it gives a concise and general view of things as they were transpiring in different parts of the State:

Persecutions still rage against our preachers in parts of Missouri, and it is hoped and believed that they justly claim the promise: "Blessed are they which are persecuted for righteousness' sake." A Sabbath or two ago one of our most faithful and exemplary men was arrested while in the pulpit; the solemn services of the holy day in the house of God were abruptly broken up; the preacher was hastened off to trial, and there required to give bond, with security, in the sum of $1,500 for his appearance at court.

This thing of serving civil processes on the Sabbath is rather new, but nothing of that kind should be thought *strange* in this country at the present. When hearing of such things how forcibly comes to the mind the words of the holy Psalmist: "Why do the heathen rage, and the people imagine a vain thing? The kings of the earth set themselves, and the rulers take counsel together, against the Lord, and against his Anointed, saying, Let us break their bands asunder, and cast away their cords from us. He that sitteth in the heavens shall laugh: the Lord shall have them in derision."

There, brethren—all of you—read that; ponder it well, and then uncomplainingly, unmurmuringly, patiently, and *joyfully* trust in God. If God will that any or all of us should go to prison or to death, it will be *best* for us; and *in our hearts*, as well as with our lips, we should say: "Thy will be done." Let "the fearful and the unbelieving," the time-serving, the truckling do as they may, be sure that you give not to another the honor that belongs to God alone.

Perhaps there be those in other States who wonder why the preachers of the M. E. Church, South, are so violently persecuted in this State, and ask: "What have they done?" Well, for the information of such be it known: these men are not thieves, to steal Church property or any other property; they are not robbers; they are not seditious persons; they are not stirrers up of strife; they are not even "busybodies in other men's matters;" but they are quiet, orderly, inoffensive men whose only crime (?) is that they will persist in preaching the gospel and exercising the regular functions of their ministry, without first subscribing to and filing an oath which transfers to Cæsar the things which belong to God; or, in other words, an oath which transfers the supreme authority and headship of the Church from Christ, the ever-blessed Saviour, to the State of Missouri, or rather to a faction in the State of Missouri. That is all, and the ministers can well afford to suffer in such a cause.

Rev. J. A. Mumpower wrote to the *St. Louis Christian Advocate* of July 25, 1866, in the following language:

I was solicited by the presiding elder of the Chillicothe District to take charge of the Albany Circuit, which I did. I arrived on my field of labor on the 6th day of April last. Found the brethren glad to see me, as the sight of a Southern Methodist preacher was a desirable one; for the war and its fiery persecutions had driven them from the field of work, and the membership had been peeled and scattered.

I went to work with all my power in my Master's cause to reorganize and get the work in order as soon as possible. I soon found, as it should be, that a pure and unadulterated gospel was what the masses of the people desired, and as our congregations were so very large that it soon attracted the attention of the opposers of our beloved Zion and of religion, and as it was too popular, the officials concluded that they would put a stop to my preaching *Jesus* and *him crucified*. Accordingly, and on the 13th of May, after evening service in Albany (which was one of the old-fashioned meetings in which God was pleased to water the vine with his love, and the shouts of his children went up as an incense of praise), the sheriff came to me and wanted to know if I was preaching without taking the "oath." I told him that I was. He then asked me if I intended to take it; to which I replied that I did not, as a condition upon which I should preach. He then informed me that they would arrest me, which was accordingly done on the 15th inst. I was bound in a bond of one thousand dollars for my appearance before the Circuit Court, which bond was filled by my friends out of the Church.

I have been trying to preach ever since, though often threatened, and at one place (Stark's School-house) was not allowed to preach on account of mob violence.

Never in my life have I seen such interest manifested for the *word of life*. The congregations are so large that the houses are not sufficiently large to contain them.

It has been my happy privilege to enroll over sixty names on the Church book since my arrival on this work. I have just closed a meeting that commenced on the 1st inst., and lasted eight days, at Colvin's School-house. The result was twelve conversions and thirteen accessions to the Church, and still the interest is deepening and widening.

The Church is all alive to her interest, and we are trying to breast the storm as good soldiers for Jesus, knowing that he is our friend, and are looking forward to the time and place where the "wicked cease from troubling, and the weary are at rest." The old ship is safe with King Jesus as her captain; she will proudly mount the waves of sorrow, and breast adverse winds, and safely anchor in the haven of eternal rest. And erelong I expect to see a great harvest gathered on this circuit. Though persecution rages, all must work for good. We are being tried as gold in the fire. May the dross be consumed! O for more of that grace that will enable us to bear the reproach of the world for our Master and count it all joy!

From the pen of Rev. J. D. Vincil in the *St. Louis Christian Advocate* of January 18, 1866:

While in Hannibal spending the holidays with my family I preached two sermons to my former congregation and friends. During the week a complaint was filed before a magistrate and a writ issued for my arrest, which was served. On appearing before his honor, the "'Squire," I was recognized in a bond of five hundred dollars to answer an indictment in the Circuit Court of Marion County, on the fourth Monday in February. The grand jury, at the regular term of the Circuit Court for this county, failed to find indictments against *non-juring* clergymen. But the interests of zealots and heated partisans required our punishment. So a special grand jury was empaneled for the ostensible purpose of indicting a robber, but with the real, as is supposed, purpose of attending to the offending clergyman. Consequently an indictment was found against me.

The *St. Louis Christian Advocate* of March 29, 1866, comes to us in the voice of wise counsel, of justice, of sobriety, and of right doing:

Our Church in the bounds of the Missouri Conference is doing well, taking a deeper and yet deeper hold upon the affections of the people, and gaining rapidly in numbers and in moral influence. The persecutions of the preachers in that and in the bounds of the St. Louis Conference will amount to but little so long as those preachers conduct themselves aright. The *Advocate* still advises them to forbearance and to the cultivation of the spirit of forgiveness; still resorting to and faithfully using all just and proper means to maintain and defend their rights. But be sure they offend not against God, either by doing wrong or neglecting duty. As far as possible they must continue to occupy the field they have so long cultivated, and in no case forsake the people who have so long looked to them for instruction in holy things. This were to prove unfaithful to the trusts committed to their keeping. But while they stand their ground and earnestly maintain by all proper means their rights and privileges, let them see to it that none "render evil for evil unto any," or return "railing for railing." Contrariwise, let them, agreeably to the direction of the Divine Master, bless them by whom they are persecuted, and pray for them by whom they are despitefully used. Then they may confidently expect the presence and help of Him who said: "I will never leave nor forsake you." And if he be with or for them, who are they that can harm them?

At the present time there are difficulties of the most serious kind in the way of our Church and most formidable obstacles before it, which can only be removed and overcome by the help of him who is Almighty; hence a humble and consistent trust in his promises, holy living, fervent prayer, and a faithful performance of all our duties, are the safe road to follow; and just in so far as we travel this road, just so far will we find in the end that "all things work together for good to them that love the Lord." O how earnestly would this paper exhort the brethren in every place to "be sober and vigilant," for truly their "adversary, as a roaring lion, goeth about seeking whom he may devour;" he lurks at every corner, besets every public and private way, assumes every possible garb, urges every possible pretext, resorts to every expedient, tries every art, to seduce and lead us from the path of righteousness; and if he do not succeed, it will not be for lack of energy or perseverance. As a people, therefore, our trust must be in the "Lord, our righteousness," and who faithfully and humbly trust him will never be put to confusion.

Then let us carefully guard against all delusive and deceptive influences, all mere outside show, and seek with all earnestness to maintain the pure spirituality of the gospel of Christ; seek to possess and manifest the meek and quiet spirit of him whose disciples and servants we profess to be, that all may see in us the constant exhibition of a deep, earnest desire to live for God and for his cause—to serve him that we may reign with him hereafter and forever.

PASTORAL ADDRESS.

We direct the attention of the reader to the following Pastoral Address of the Missouri Conference:

Dear Brethren and Sisters in the Lord: First of all we pray that "grace, mercy, and peace from God our Father, and from the Lord Jesus Christ, and the communion and fellowship of the Holy Spirit may be with you all." And may "the peace of God, which passeth all understanding, keep your hearts and minds through Christ Jesus." We, your ministers and servants for Jesus' sake, about seventy in number, have just closed the business of another most peaceful, harmonious, and profitable Annual Conference session, and expect to go to our respective fields of labor to join you in Christian trials and triumphs, and to encourage you in the struggle you are making to gain a home in heaven. And it is with much gratitude to God we record the fact that from all parts of our beloved Zion the cheering intelligence comes to us of a united and determined membership in the maintenance of our ecclesiastical organization as the means of promoting the Redeemer's kingdom upon earth and of saving the souls of men. It is scarcely necessary to remind you of the temporal afflictions and spiritual conflicts of the past year, except for the purpose of exciting renewed gratitude to God for his sustaining grace. In view of the past and present, how pertinent is the language of the Psalmist to your case as it recounts the trials and dangers, proclaims the deliverance, and records the grateful acknowledgments of the people of God. "The Lord is my light and my salvation; whom shall I fear? the Lord is the strength of my life; of whom shall I be afraid? when the wicked, even my enemies and my foes, came upon me to eat up my flesh, they stumbled and fell. Though a host should encamp against me, my heart shall not fear: though war should rise against me, in this will I be confident." For "God is our refuge and strength, a very present help in trouble." And while we would thus "call to remembrance the former days, in which, after ye were illuminated, ye endured a great fight of afflictions; partly, whilst ye were made a gazing-stock both by reproaches and afflictions; and partly, whilst ye became companions of them that were so used. For ye had compassion of us in our bonds, and taking joyfully the spoiling of your goods, knowing in yourselves that ye have in heaven a better and an enduring substance"—we would also remind you that you "have need of *patience*, that, after ye have done the will of God, ye might receive the promise." "Let us hold fast the profession of our faith without wavering; for he is faithful that promised; and let us consider one another to provoke unto love and to good works: not forsaking the assembling of ourselves together, as the manner of some is; but exhorting one another: and so much the more, as ye see the day approaching." The great danger is that under your repeated provocations, persecutions, and trials you should lose your *patience*, your *faith in God*, your *Christian consolation*, and yielding to temptation and discouragement should thus be led into sin. "From whence come wars and fightings among you? come they not hence, even of your lusts that war in your members?" Then "let brotherly love continue," for "love is the fulfilling of the law," and "the end of the commandment is charity out of a pure heart, and of faith unfeigned." Let us remember that although we may give all our goods to feed the poor and our bodies to be burned, if we have not charity it will profit us nothing. *Love is the soul* and good works the *body* of our blessed Christianity. "Be not overcome of evil, but overcome evil with good." Therefore, "love your enemies, bless them that curse you, do good to them that hate you, and pray for them which despitefully use you and persecute you." Dear brethren, if we will but do this, "the gates of hell shall not prevail against us;" for although the storms of persecution in their utmost fury may rage around us, we shall be upheld and defended by the Rock of Ages. As there is a strong probability of your being deprived of the preaching of the gospel for some time to come, we would exhort you to the increased and prayerful study of the Holy Scriptures, to regular, earnest, secret devotion, to daily attention to the family altar, and to prompt and faithful attendance at the weekly prayer and class meetings. And if you do this the flame of piety will be kept alive in your souls and our organization will remain intact till a brighter day shall dawn upon us. And rest assured that we, your ministers, will not forsake you in the hour of adversity; and we hope to rejoice with you in that prosperity which is sure to come if we are faithful to ourselves and to our Divine Master. "Now the God of peace, that brought again from the dead our Lord Jesus, that great Shepherd of the sheep, through the blood of the everlasting covenant, make you perfect in every good work to do his will, working in you that which is well-pleasing in his sight, through Jesus Christ; to whom be glory forever and ever. Amen."

The following is a statement of an effort made to get possession of our church at Lexington:

The suit at Lexington, as you are probably aware, was instituted by certain persons assuming to be the trustees of the M. E. Church against the trustees of the M. E. Church, South. It was an action of ejectment for the recovery of the possession, on the ground of title. The answer set up the action of the General Conference in New York in 1844, embracing the whole Plan of Separation, as also the action of the Southern Conference in convention at Louisville in 1845, as well as the action of the Missouri and St. Louis Conferences in reference to the Plan of Separation; all of which action, it was insisted, was to effect a contract between the parties, and valid and binding as such. I found that the suit had been dismissed, and the M. E. Church, South, left in the undisputed possession of their property.

CHAPTER IX.
St. Louis Conference.

Wise and Judicious Advice of the *St. Louis Christian Advocate*
—No Printed Minutes of the St. Louis Annual Conference—
Statistical Information from Other Reliable Sources—The
Preachers Received Their Appointments Uncomplainingly
and Went Forth to Their Fields of Labor Joyfully—The
Conference Proceedings Were Such as Properly Pertain to a
Purely Christian Organization—The Voice of the *St. Louis
Christian Advocate* in Relation to the Respective Prerogatives
and Duties of Church and State—Statement of Rev. J. S.
Frazier—Trials of Rev. J. C. Williams and Rev. H. M.
Long—Document of Rev. W. S. Woodard—Seizure of Our
Church in Boonville—Notorious Murder of Rev. Samuel S.
Headlee—Pastoral Address of the St. Louis Annual Conference of the M. E. Church, South.

THE reader will no doubt be very much interested in the following appropriate, wise, and judicious remarks of the *St. Louis Christian Advocate*, whose voice has always been on the side of peace and harmony, truth and righteousness:

The preachers and members are more closely and more firmly attached to the Church than ever before. The days of persecution and trial, however, have not ended. Those who have sought its destruction are still active in their efforts to accomplish their unchristian work, and the more bitter, perhaps, because of their past failures. It is painful to witness the bad feeling and bad conduct that characterize their course. Disappointment, mortification, and chagrin have increased their bitterness. They are to be pitied, both for their present condition and future prospects. They will most likely continue to rage, but let none of us return evil for evil. Better suffer wrong then do wrong. "Think it not strange concerning the fiery trial which is to try you, as though some strange thing happened unto you: but rejoice, inasmuch as ye are partakers of Christ's sufferings; that, when his glory shall be revealed, ye may be glad also with exceeding joy. If ye be reproached for the name of Christ, happy are ye." Thus spoke the apostle; and the words are particularly applicable to the ministers and members of the M. E. Church, South, at the present. The persecution will be carried on for some time yet, to come, but will do no real harm in the end except to the persecutors. Upon them, sooner or later, it will recoil with terrible force. Meanwhile, let our preachers and people pursue the "even tenor of their way," giving themselves to works of faith and labors of love, rejoicing in tribulation, "knowing that tribulation worketh patience; and patience, experience; and experience, hope; and hope maketh not ashamed; because the love of God is shed abroad in our hearts by the Holy Ghost which is given unto us." And let all take heed to "the sure word of prophecy, until the day-dawn, and the day-star arise in their hearts." Lift up the hands which hang down. Mark straight paths for their feet, for the "Lord is at hand."

The attachment of our people to the Church of their choice is worthy of all commendation. Rarely, or never, was there more unity of feeling or internal peace in the Church than at present. As soon as the preachers reach their work, they are hailed by the people as the messengers of truth, and welcomed as the servants of the Most High. The scattered flocks are being gathered again—coming together in the fullness of Christian sympathy—and their devotions are characterized by fervent zeal and holy joy; while hundreds are being converted and added to their numbers. And there is every indication that this work will go on increasingly until thousands and tens of thousands, now afar off, will be brought nigh to God by the power of that blood which speaketh better things than the blood of Abel. Truth is mighty and will prevail. Though crushed to earth for a time, it will rise again. This has been the stay and comfort of our people from the first. Now they begin to realize that truth is rising—light begins to beam. The waste places are to be rebuilt; and the Church will come forth from her wilderness state, or from her depression, brighter, better, and more powerful than ever. Let all humbly rejoice in God for his great salvation! With the Psalmist, we may truly say: "If it had not been the Lord who was on our side, when men rose up against us: then they had swallowed us up quick, when their wrath was kindled against us. . . Blessed be the Lord, who hath not given us as a prey to their teeth!"

God has been our Preserver, and to him alone the praise belongs. While, for wise and merciful ends, he permitted our preachers and people to be scattered; many of our houses of worship to be burned or pulled down, or prostituted to unworthy purposes, and others of them to be seized and temporarily occupied by those who were foremost in our persecution, we now realize that, like the Christians of old, though "cast down" we were "not destroyed." "God is his own interpreter;" and after awhile "we shall see as we are seen, and know as we are known;" when this is the case:

> This note above the rest shall swell,
> Our Jesus has done all things well.

Then "let us not cast away our confidence, which has great recompense of reward." Be patient, be steadfast, be humble, watchful, prayerful, cultivating that charity which "beareth all things, believeth all things, hopeth all things, endureth all things, and *never* faileth." Above all, seek the spirit of forbearance and of forgiveness, that "God in all things may be glorified through Jesus Christ, to whom be praise and dominion forever and ever. Amen."*

We find no printed minutes of the session of the St. Louis Annual Conference for this year, 1865–66. There is, however, a report in the *St. Louis Christian Advocate* of said session, from which we get our statistical information. Though not an official document like the other, it is, no doubt, correct and reliable. Though there is monotony in statistics of any kind, yet their importance cannot be overestimated. They furnish the facts and figures

---

* *St. Louis Christian Advocate*, September 21, 1865.

and tell us what we are and what we are doing. They are the solid part and starting-point of our history. In matters of great importance repetition of language is admissible and right, to prevent mistakes, as in law, for instance; and also to a greater or less degree in most statistical reports, giving bare facts and dry figures in which there is no place for the embellishments of rhetoric.

Bishop Kavanaugh opened the eighteenth session of the St. Louis Annual Conference in the city of St. Louis on the 23d day of August, 1865. The religious services were conducted by the presiding bishop.

W. M. Prottsman was elected Secretary; J. W. Lewis, Assistant Secretary; and S. W. Horn, Recording Secretary.

Lewis W. Powell and John Grills were admitted on trial. William Alexander and J. E. Berryman were re-admitted. Received into full connection: L. B. Ellis and G. P. Smith. They were also elected and ordained deacons. The following local preachers were elected and ordained deacons: William Lusk, Clark Brown, J. F. Hogan, and John Grills. The traveling preachers elected and ordained elders were: J. A. Murphy, J. E. Godbey, and John C. Williams. Supernumerary relations were granted to John Whittaker and E. M. Marvin. The following preachers were superannuated: W. B. Quinn, J. F. Truslow, A. Rucker, J. T. Peery, J. T. Davenport, W. R. Babcock, E. W. Chanceaulme, S. S. Colburn, J. N. W.

Springer, Christian Ecker, John Thomas, John McEwin, John Monroe, James McGhee, Alfred Nichols, John W. Bond, and W. H. Mobley.

Having enjoyed a pleasant and profitable session, and having transacted the business of the Conference, the preachers, forty-seven in number, received their appointments and separated with mingled feelings of sorrow and joy—of sorrow at the thought that they in all probability would never all meet again in another Annual Conference, that one or more might not be present at the next roll-call. This thought saddened their hearts and cast a gloom over their feelings, for they love one another as few men love. They are united by the strong tie of Christian love, and for these years past they have been associated in the work of the Christian ministry and in cultivating the Lord's vineyard. Therefore an annual convocation is anticipated by them with great pleasure. It is one of the joyous occasions—an oasis in the desert of life. During the session of the Conference the language of their hearts is: "Behold, how good and pleasant it is for brethren to dwell together in unity." Like Peter on the mount of Transfiguration, they feel it is good for us to be here, and here let us stay. With such an attachment it is easy to see how parting at Conference, with the probability of never meeting again, pains the heart. But as they go forth to their respective fields of labor joy takes the place of sorrow, because the work of preaching the gospel and calling sinners to repentance is to them sweeter than life and stronger than death. The success of the past and the encouraging prospects of the future inspire them with indomitable courage that nothing can daunt.

The attention of the reader is respectfully called to the reports of Conference proceedings as they appear in this number of the *Advocate.* The appointments of the preachers of the Missouri and St. Louis Conferences are given, together with the pastoral addresses of each Conference. The addresses are, at the present, matters of more than ordinary interest. By them it will be learned what views the members of these Conferences entertained in regard to many of those questions now most prominently before the Church. Every true friend of the Church and of pure Christianity will rejoice to witness the calm, dignified, and truly Christian spirit manifested in these Conference proceedings. They remind one of the earlier days in the Church of Christ. In all that was done in the sessions of these Conferences there was nothing that did not legitimately and properly pertain to a purely Christian organization, thus evidencing what is to be hoped will always be the case—that these Conferences represent a *non-secular* Church, a body of *Christian* ministers.

The *St. Louis Christian Advocate* of September 28, 1865, talks wisely to the Church in the following language:

> Let all good and true men combine together—first in opposition to all wrong; especially in opposition to all attempts to sec-

ularize the Church of Christ, no matter by whom or under what pretexts those attempts may be made; in opposition to all intermeddling in State or political affairs by ecclesiastical bodies, no matter what the plea for such intermmeddling may be; in opposition to all prostitution of the pulpit, no matter how great the pressure may be or how plausible the excuse for so doing. If a Church has not apostatized *before* it commences to preach politics and to intermeddle as a Church in State affairs, it will be sure to apostatize soon after. Keep the pulpits and the deliberations of ecclesiastical bodies free from any and every thing other than that which legitimately belongs to them as propagandists of the pure religion of Christ. Against all else than what is thus legitimate let good people set their faces as flints.

In the second place, let all good men combine to oppose, by all proper and honorable means, all unlawful interference on the part of the State in matters purely spiritual. The Church has no business with matters belonging to the State, nor has the State any business with matters purely ecclesiastical. Let each be kept in its proper sphere and in its own appropriate work; let each be respected, reverenced, and obeyed. A non-secular Church and a non-ecclesiastical State should be the motto of all.

In the third place, all good people should combine in honest, persistent efforts to maintain peace and good-will among men; to induce all to do justly, to love mercy, and to walk humbly with God; to fear God and work righteousness; to be gentle, merciful, kind, forbearing, and forgiving; and to live together as rational beings, who have undying souls; and not as ferocious beasts, to bite and devour one another.

The following is from the pen of Rev. J. S. Frazier:

I learn through your columns of occasional arrests of ministers who refuse to take the oath prescribed by the new Constitution of the State of Missouri as a qualification to preach the gospel; and thinking that perhaps it may be interesting to some of your readers to hear from this part of Cæsar's dominion, I submit the following:

There have been two arrests in this county (Madison) since the law took effect—Father Tucker and myself.

I came from the seat of our Annual Conference to this work

last fall, and found by no means a pleasant state of things. Through the advice of some of my friends I desisted from preaching till the 1st of December; for which I am sorry, very sorry, but I hope God will forgive me. Since that time I have been trying to dispense the truths of the gospel to the people of my charge, and I trust that my labors have not been in vain.

I don't think there ever has been a time when our Church had a deeper hold on the minds of the people than now; and I think that, under God, Methodism can be built up again, even here where the horrors of war have been realized to such an alarming extent.

From the time I commenced preaching up to the 11th inst. every thing went on smoothly, and I indulged in the fond hope that I would not be molested; but alas! that hope was blighted. A magistrate and constable came to church on the Sabbath, and demanded by what authority I was preaching; if I "had a certificate." I answered in the negative. They then said: "You are our prisoner." My response was: "I am at your service. What will you have me do?" "Go to my office, and give bond for your appearance at court." I was taken by the constable to the magistrate's office, and put in bond for fifteen hundred dollars for my appearance at the next term of the Circuit Court. I expect to be there, if God permits. While I was thus arraigned before these men I could not but think of the beautiful and appropriate language of the Psalmist: "Why do the heathen rage, and the people imagine a vain thing? The kings of the earth set themselves, and the rulers take counsel together, against the Lord, and against his Anointed."

When the Founder of our holy religion had done all that was necessary by his incarnation and death, and it only remained for him to give directions to his followers, O how unearthly and godlike was his great command, "Go ye into all the world, and preach the gospel to every creature!" He knew that the truths of his word would be rejected and despised; that they would be "a stone of stumbling, a rock of offense;" yet his command was: "Go!" He knew that they would be a "sign that should be spoken against," that the thoughts of many hearts might be revealed. He knew that they would be seen and hated. Still he says to them: "Go and preach." He knew that they would encounter the scoffer's unbelief; that they would be persecuted for righteousness' sake, and some of them be imprisoned, and others put to death; yet his authority must be obeyed. For their encouragement he added this promise: "Lo, I am with you alway, even unto the end of the world." This promise is sufficient; it is full of comfort; it is from the lips of our divine Master; we can claim it as a special promise to us at the present time.

My brethren in the ministry, let us obey our God. Let us "preach the word; be instant in season, out of season; reprove, rebuke, exhort with all long-suffering and doctrine·" let us endure afflictions, do the work of evangelists, make full proof of our ministry. The time may come when they will take us from our churches and incarcerate us in prison for refusing to render to Cæsar the things which belong to God; but "prisons will palaces prove if God be with us." His promise is: "I will not leave you comfortless; I will come to you." Then let us be encouraged; let us be "strong in the grace that is in Christ Jesus," and "endure hardness as good soldiers of Jesus Christ;" "for I reckon that the sufferings of this present time are not worthy to be compared to the glory that shall be revealed in us."*

Rev. H. M. Long.—This faithful minister, also of the M. E. Church, South, was indicted, arrested, and put under bonds for the same offense against the peace and dignity of the State. He was often in imminent danger of mob violence at the hands of those whom he calls "Loyal Leaguers," who made two descents upon the village in which he lived, well armed and with hostile intent. "But soon," says he, "and before our trials came off, the decision of the court was had, which released us from imprisonment. For this we felt very grateful to the Supreme Court of the United States, but more especially to our heavenly Father." †

The reader will find below an interesting document from Rev. W. S. Woodard:

Since your call for material for your forth-coming book, I have been thinking for some time of something to report to you

---

* J. S. Frazier, in *St. Louis Christian Advocate* of March 8, 1866.
† Dr. Leftwich's book.

that might be worthy of a place therein. I have thought of nothing more likely to be of service to you than the following, which I place at your disposal :

It will be remembered that the *St. Louis Conference* met in St. Louis the week preceding the time when the Constitution oath was to take effect. I presume this time was selected to give the preachers an opportunity to consult with each other in reference to what they would do when the Strong-Drake contrivance got between them and their God; and while he said "Go preach," it said, "If you do, you shall be punished."

"In the multitude of counsel there is safety," saith the proverb. Well, we met. The roll was called, the regular business was taken up, the various questions were called, and the interests of the Church were attended to in the usual way. We were nearly through the business—nearly ready to adjourn— and had not yet reached the new Constitution. It did not seem to fall *easily* within the purview of an Annual Conference. What ought to be done ? We wanted to take counsel with one another in reference to our action in the future. But no one seemed inclined to dirty his hands by touching the "unclean thing." No one wanted the journal of the Conference blurred with a resolution that would take cognizance of the fact that the State was making an effort to prevent any one from preaching the gospel except those whom she should choose to license.

Are you going to take the oath ? Will you preach without taking the oath ? These questions were repeatedly asked and answered on the streets, but never on the Conference floor.

Being anxious to know the sense of the Conference, I wrote the above questions in my memorandum-book, and made two columns, over which I wrote "Yes" and "No."

I still have the book. Under the question "Are you going to take the oath?" and in the column headed "No," I find the following names: F. A. Morris, G. W. Horn, W. S. Woodard, Jos. Bond, G. M. Winton, T. W. Mitchell, S. S. Headlee, M. M. Pugh, P. M. Pinckard, J. T. Peery, J. McCary, J. C. Shackleford, D. R. McAnally, T. M. Finney, D. A. Murphy, D. J. Marquis, H. N. Watts, W. M. Williams, S. C. Knowles, John Campbell, L. W. Powell, N. M. Talbot, W. J. Brown, L. B. Ellis, J. P. Barneby, J. S. Frazier H. W. Webster, G. P. Smith, and J. E. Godbey.

Under the question "Will you preach without taking the oath?" and in the column headed "Yes," are the following names: F. A. Morris, G. W. Horn, W. S. Woodard, D. M. Proctor, M. M. Pugh, D. R. McAnally, J. W. Lewis, T. M. Finney, D. A. Murphy, J. T. Peery, N. M. Talbot, W. J. Brown, and J. E. Godbey. The following answered "I think so:" H. N. Watts, D. J. Marquis, G. C. Knowles, John Campbell, L. B. Ellis, and G. P. Smith.

Brother Lewis assisted me in getting the above answers. Some of the preachers did not answer either question. Some answered one who did not answer the other. There may have been some who did not have an opportunity to record their answers.

The oath took effect on Saturday before the first Sunday in September. Some weeks before I had published that I would preach a funeral at the Stone Church, St. Francois County, on the second Sabbath. At the appointed time I was at the appointed place. Some of the friends said: "Don't preach; you will be arrested: the officer is on the ground." I decided not to disappoint my congregation. At the close of the services it was announced that there would be preaching that afternoon.

The hour came, the congregation was there, a number of preachers were present, not one of whom would preach. My health was feeble, yet I was able to read, with some emphasis, the 224th hymn:

> Shall I, for fear of feeble man,
> The Spirit's course in me restrain?
> Or, undismayed in deed and word,
> Be a true witness for my Lord?
>
> Awed by a mortal's frown, shall I
> Conceal the word of God most high?
> How then before thee shall I dare
> To stand, or how thine anger bear?
>
> Shall I, to soothe th' unholy throng,
> Soften thy truth, and smooth my tongue,
> To gain earth's gilded toys, or flee
> The cross endured, my Lord, by thee?
>
> What then is he whose scorn I dread,
> Whose wrath or hate makes me afraid?
> *A man! an heir of death, a slave*
> *To sin! a bubble on the wave.*

Yes, let men rage, since thou wilt spread
Thy shad'wing wings around my head:
Since in all pain thy tender love
Will still my sure refreshment prove.

The sermon that followed was impromptu. Text: "I have not shunned to declare unto you all the counsel of God." (Acts xx. 27.) Brother White preached at night. The meeting continued two weeks, with gracious results.

I preached in nearly every county in South-east Missouri; and was indicted (so I have been informed) in Jefferson, St. Francois, Cape Girardeau, and Crawford Counties, but was never arrested. I witnessed but one arrest—that of Rev. Reuben Watts by the sheriff of Bollinger County.

Church in Boonville.

Boonville, like Lexington, has an early interesting history. Prior to railroads it was one of the leading towns in the State. It flourished most in the days of steam-boats, and was one of the most important shipping points on the Missouri River. It had extensive trade, and supplied the country south of it for hundreds of miles, extending at one time, if we mistake not, as far as the Arkansas line. Wagons might have been seen in South-west Missouri, on the different roads, conveying the produce of the country to Boonville, and returning laden with all kinds of goods to meet the wants and demands of the people.

The citizens of Boonville, like those of Lexington, have always been distinguished for their culture, intelligence, refinement, and sociability.

The history of the Methodist Church is so closely interwoven with that of Boonville that it would be difficult to separate them. They have grown up together; for the pioneer preachers planted the standard of Methodism there at an early period, and for many years it has held a high position among the Churches of Missouri. Its pulpit has been filled by the best talents of the Church—such as Father Light, Joseph Boyle, and others.

When the division of the Methodist Church took place in 1844 the Church at Boonville adhered to the M. E. Church, South. They lived in the undisturbed and peaceable possession of their house of worship until the Civil War. The M. E. Church, in their raid through Missouri, seizing the property of the M. E. Church, South, certainly would not have overlooked the church at Boonville, as they had taken forcible possession of other churches elsewhere of much less value.

The following particulars respecting the seizure of the church were sent to the *St. Louis Christian Advocate* by a citizen of Boonville who, it seems, was not a member of the Church, and who signed himself "An Honest Looker-on:"

It affords the people of this community pleasure to hear from other quarters; perhaps others would be equally interested to hear from us. I write more especially for the Church which I believe your paper represents.

The pastor of the Southern Methodist Church, appointed by the last session of the Annual Conference, took charge of his congregation a few weeks ago. He had not been here more than two or three weeks before he and his congregation were turned out-of-doors by the Methodist Episcopal preacher in this city. First, under pretense of an order from the County Court, he demanded the key, with all the authority usually exhibited by his class on such occasions. Failing in this, he secured the co-operation of a few kindred spirits, and, having secured the services of one skilled in such matters, proceeded to the Church, about the going down of the sun, effected an entrance, removed the locks, replaced them with new ones, and took possession in the name of the Lord. It was not the last of the old year, but it is said that they *kept watch-night* (?), it being as they supposed the last of the old Church. Whether their devotions kept pace with their watchfulness we are not informed. Meanwhile, in strict conformity to the Scriptures, they *watched;* also having their sentries (armed it is supposed) stationed at the door; not knowing what hour the thief might come, they *watched* until the morning. If they expected any interference from the owners or former occupants, they have yet to learn that it will not do in every case to judge others by themselves. For the first time in many years their hearts inclined them to go to the house of prayer.

The eyes of the community have since regarded some of these with peculiar solicitude, looking for further indications of a future religious development; but the old proverb is verified: " The dog is turned to his own vomit again; and, The sow that was washed to her wallowing." Alas for Ephraim! his goodness was transient as the morning cloud and early dew.

The day of their calamity did not overtake the poor Southern Methodists unprepared. They were found with their lamps trimmed and oil in their vessels. There was a good supply of fuel, properly prepared, carpets, Sunday-school library, etc. They found the house itself swept and garnished. The ladies had given it a thorough cleansing only a day or two before. Poor souls! their labor was not in vain in the Lord.

Southern Methodism in this city, though cast down, has not been destroyed. Sister Churches felt and manifested sympathy. The Presbyterians kindly offered the use of their church on the following Sabbath, and a gentleman who makes no pretensions to religion generously tendered the use of a hall, which they are now occupying. The varied character of the seats—chairs, boxes, rough plank, old sofas, etc.—might excite a smile; but, under the circumstances, they are regarded as very comfortable. The attendance on the services of the sanctuary has doubled since this wholesale excommunication. The same is true of the Sabbath-school; and on every hand there are manifestations of increasing interest. The Church is manifesting a very good state of feeling, exhibiting very little of that bitterness and malice which such injuries are apt to engender.

A writ prohibiting the interference of the Methodist Episcopal Church with the property and rights of the Southern Methodists was granted by proper authority, and was sustained by the Circuit Court last week. The former occupants patiently wait for the officers of the law to execute their trusts.

REV. SAMUEL S. HEADLEE.

The news of the unprovoked, deliberate, and cruel murder of this good man, whose righteous life and extensive usefulness were well known throughout South-west Missouri, filled many hearts with sadness and spread gloom all over the country. It produced a lasting sensation, and made a profound impression. But we have not space to enlarge. Read the following thrilling narrative:

> Rev. Samuel S. Headlee was a native of Tennessee. His parents moved to Missouri at an early day, where Mr. Headlee was raised, converted to God, and entered the ministry. He was received on trial in the St. Louis Conference of the M. E. Church, South, at Lexington, in 1852, Bishop Paine presiding, D. R. McAnally, Secretary, and was appointed to Rich Wood Circuit, in the Jefferson City District, with J. K. Lacy as presiding elder. He was returned to the same circuit the next year, only it was put into the St. Louis District, with W. Browning presiding elder. The next year he was admitted into full connection, and appointed to the St. Louis Circuit. The next year he was appointed to the Tremont Circuit, in the Springfield District. Wherever he went he was a faithful and acceptable minister of the Lord Jesus in word and doctrine. It is needless to follow him through all of his appointments and all of his labors. He was humble, pious, and zealous, unobtrusive and diligent; not profound or brilliant, but possessed of a mind deeply imbued with religious principles, and thoroughly sanctified by grace divine, he gained ready access to the hearts and

confidence of the people, and was everywhere "highly esteemed in love for his work's sake."

The most of his life was spent in the counties of South-west Missouri, where few men stood higher in the estimation of the people, and *none* had a purer record or a more spotless character. He loved the Lord Jesus Christ in sincerity—loved his cause, loved the souls of men, and publicly and from house to house ceased not to warn men to flee from the wrath to come. He gained for himself "a good report of them which are without," as well as among his own brethren.

Dr. McAnally says of him: "The love of Christ constrained him, and he preached 'the word, reproved, rebuked, exhorted with all long-suffering and doctrine.' Ardently loving the Church of his choice, and having a good understanding of her doctrines, discipline, and usages, he labored faithfully and constantly to extend the benign influences of Christianity, as developed through that organization, and everywhere sought to build up believers in their most holy faith. He was truly exemplary in the full sense of that word. To his superiors in age, wisdom, and experience he was deferential and respectful; to his equals, courteous and agreeable; and to the weak and erring he was pitiful and kind. For his meek, quiet, inoffensive spirit he was remarkable. Possessed of exceedingly tender and delicate sensibilities, he acted toward others as if they possessed the same, and would not willingly wrong any one, harm any one, or offend any one. His naturally mild and quiet disposition was greatly improved and sweetened by the refining influences of deep, earnest, and consistent piety—a piety consisting in supreme love to God and universal love to man. He was the enemy of none; nor was there an intelligent, honest, upright, or good man or woman in all the land that was an enemy to him. A truer, kindlier, sweeter-spirited, or more heavenly-minded man is rarely found."

His last appointment was presiding elder of the Springfield District, St. Louis Conference, where he labored faithfully and extensively to reclaim the waste places, to reorganize and rebuild the scattered and desolated Church.

So complete and extensive had been the wreck and ruin of the Church in that part of the State that for years after the war closed it was called, by way of distinction, "the burnt district."

In this "burnt district" but few churches remained standing, and but few Societies preserved an organized existence. Mr. Headlee had done as much, if not more, than any other man in that part of the State to save the Church, prevent disintegration and absorption, and defeat the purposes of the Northern Methodist disorganizers and church thieves. He was faithful amid the faithless, but neither officious in the affairs of others nor offensive to any right-minded, honest man. Yet his firmness and fidelity to principle, though quietly and cautiously maintained, encouraged the timid, assured the doubtful, steadied the wavering, inspired hope and courage everywhere, and thus defeated the purposes of designing men, and provoked the malice—even vengeance—of the faithless fanatics who were bent on the destruction of the Southern Methodist Church. To be a faithful, devoted Southern Methodist preacher, in that country at that time, who could neither be scared nor bought, was equal to a man's life. Mr. Headlee had prevented some Churches from breaking up and becoming a prey to the prowling wolves in sheep's clothing, and was extensively useful in gathering the scattered membership and reorganizing the dismembered Societies. The following narrative of his cruel murder will show how much this "work of faith and labor of love" cost him, and how much it was worth to the Church. In the same biographical sketch from which quotations have already been made the following account of his murder is given:

"His death occurred on Saturday, July 28, 1866; and never, perhaps, in all the history of the United States was there a more deliberate, a more unprovoked, or more atrocious murder.

"The killing was done in Webster County, near what has been called Pleasant View Church—a house of worship legally and morally belonging to the denomination of which Mr. Headlee was a minister. As presiding elder of the Springfield District, this Church was in his bounds and regularly under his care.

"Thither he had gone to hold a quarterly meeting and reorganize the Church, which had been greatly scattered, torn, and distressed by the public troubles of the country.

"The appointment of the meeting had been publicly announced and generally circulated for some time previous. At the appointed time Mr. Headlee arrived at the church punctually, and was met by an armed band of some twenty or more men. These men were led (or seemed to be led) by one Henderson McNabb, a man who at the beginning of the late war was a member and once a steward of the M. E. Church, South, but who some'time during the war changed his Church relations by attaching himself to the M. E. Church (North); and, for aught I know or have ever heard, is still a member of that Church. This man acted as spokesman for the armed company, and told Mr. Headlee that he could not and should not preach in that church, and threatened him with violence if he attempted it. Mr. Headlee expostulated, and asked by what authority they threatened him and forbade his preaching to the people then and there assembled at *their own house*. McNabb, waving his hand to the armed band, replied: "There is my authority." The parties being well known to each other, Mr. Headlee proposed a friendly discussion, and stated that he knew that he was preaching without having subscribed to the oath required by the new Constitution, but that he was ready and willing to answer to the law for that, and that he expected to answer. In reply he was told that they cared nothing about the law, but intended to stop his preaching there.

"Finding all his persuasions vain, and being abused and cursed the more mild he was, Mr. Headlee at length proposed to go to the grove, about three-fourths of a mile distant—which grove was on his own land—and there preach, provided they would not interrupt him. To this they agreed. He and a number of the people then prepared to go. As he was going to his horse some of the band placed the muzzles of their guns against him, pushing him forward, all the time using foul and abusive language. His only remark was: "Let me alone; I can walk without help."

He and his company having gone about half a mile toward the designated grove, four of the armed band came galloping up. One rode up to Mr. Headlee's side and began abusing him and asking some impertinent questions. Mr. Headlee replied: "If you talk to me as a gentleman, I will talk to you." At this the man drew a revolver and fired three shots. The first entered Mr. Headlee's right side and passed through the lungs, the second passed through the lapel of his coat on the right side, and the third struck him on the hip, making only a flesh wound. The assassin and his accomplices then galloped back a short distance to McNabb's house, where the rest of the band were waiting.

On being shot Mr. Headlee neither screamed, nor spoke, nor moaned, nor did he change his position in the saddle; but sitting erect as though nothing had happened, he rode some fifty yards to a shade, alighted from his horse, took off his gloves, put them in his pocket, and calmly remarked, "Friends, I am a dead man," and turning his face toward his murderers, who were still in sight, added: "Those bad men have killed me! Lord have mercy upon them! Lord save them!" The men in company with Mr. Headlee were terror-stricken, not knowing but that they would next be shot; but the women acted the part of true Christian heroines, and waited around the dying martyr as faithfully as others of their sex once waited around the cross of the dying Saviour.

The nature of the wound and the intensity of the suffering were such that he had to be kept in a sitting posture. After considerable delay and some trouble a chair was procured on which he was carried to the house of his sister, half a mile distant, where he died at 10 o'clock that night.

His home was twelve or fifteen miles distant. His wife was immediately sent for, and what occurred after she reached him an eye-witness relates as follows:

"He was shot near 12 o'olock, and his wife reached him about 7 o'clock. When she went in he raised his right arm and put it around her, but did not speak for a minute or more. He then said (she was crying and sobbing): 'Ma, you must not grieve for me. I thought I was doing right; I still think I was doing my Master's work. Think of me often, and tell my brethren I fell at my post. All is clear; I have no doubt as to my acceptance with God; my whole trust is in the mercy of God through the mediation of Jesus Christ.' He then told her all that passed between him and McNabb; how they called him names, and one ruffian caught hold of him and pushed him around and jerked him about till a lady interfered; said he did not for a moment lose his balance; that he kept calm and tried to reason with them. He said he knew he had to die as soon as the man 'Drake' rode up. His wife asked him if he did not feel scared. 'No, no,' said he; 'I never felt the least alarmed or excited.' 'How did you feel when he drew his revolver?' asked his wife.

'Well,' said he, 'God had most graciously removed all fear of death by violence. I knew that my time was come, and I felt that I was ready and willing to go.' He told her that she must not let the children forget pa; that she must talk to them of him often, and train them for heaven and glory. His talk with his wife was with much difficulty, as his lungs were all the time bleeding profusely, and he was suffering intensely and sinking rapidly. Just one hour before he died his only brother reached him. He was then wading deep in the cold Jordan of death; but on seeing his brother he held out his hand and said: 'Asbury, I'm almost home; I'm almost home! O that I had strength and time to tell of my prospects of heaven and immortality! O those bad men, those bad men! Lord have mercy upon them! Lord save them!' With but a few words more of endearment to his wife and messages of love to his children he fell asleep, not gently, like the babe on its mother's bosom, but with intense physical agony, like the martyred Stephen amid a volley of stones. Thus he lived and thus he passed away."*

Pastoral Address.

The following interesting and important Pastoral Address of the St. Louis Annual Conference of the M. E. Church, South, which contains so much wise counsel, good advice, and Christian love, will very appropriately close the history of this year:

The preachers of the St. Louis Conference to the brethren still in our bounds and to those who are scattered abroad, greeting: "Grace unto you, and peace be multiplied."

We give glory to the King of kings that the storm of civil war which has rolled over us for four years is ended, and that peace returns with healing wings.

In the general devastation we have suffered greatly in common with other Protestant Churches, and perhaps we have suffered most. "But having obtained help of God, we continue to this day," and are in good hope of recovering soon all that we have lost.

---

*Dr. Leftwich's book.

1. The following brief statement will give you some idea of the present state of the Church in our bounds:

In St. Louis District we have been permitted to hold and occupy all our houses of worship, have kept up the regular work, and have been blessed with revivals of religion in most of the circuits and stations.

In Boonville District the work has been greatly disturbed; nevertheless we have held our churches and have had some success in various places.

In Lexington District the appointments have been generally filled on the Wellington, Saline, Arrow Rock, and Dover Circuits and the Lexington Station, and with revivals of religion. But on the rest of the district the work has been broken up, and some of our churches burned or so mutilated that they are unfit for use. In the city of Independence our church and parsonage are in the hands of the Northern Methodists, which they hold without our consent and to our injury. On this conduct of theirs *comment is unnecessary*. We will only add that we hope soon to regain the possession of our property in that place.

In Steelville District we hold the possession of all our Church property; on five of the circuits the regular work has been kept up; gracious revivals on Fredericktown, De Soto, Richmond, and Caledonia Circuits, and on the last named *three hundred accessions* during the past two years.

In Cape Girardeau District the circuits have been generally without preachers during the war, some of the churches destroyed, and the regular work of preaching for the most part suspended; but at Charleston, Bertrand, Big Lake, and Rush's Ridge the appointments have been filled with success.

In Springfield and Lebanon Districts the country, with here and there an exception, has been desolated by the war, churches burnt up in common with all other things, preachers driven off, and the people scattered.

In looking over the whole field, while we deplore what we have suffered, we are thankful that we have not been destroyed; and with the blessing of God upon our mutual labors we hope soon to see the wilderness and the solitary place made glad and the desert rejoicing as the rose.

2. You have noticed in the newspapers an occasional article

about the *reunion* of the Northern and Southern Methodist Churches. All that we have to say on this subject is that in our judgment the reunion is neither *desirable* nor *practicable*. From all that we can learn about the matter, it seems to be the universal desire and the purpose of our preachers and people to maintain our own ecclesiastical organization.

3. We cannot close this brief address without exhorting you, dear brethren, to be faithful to God in these "perilous times." "Evil men and seducers will wax worse and worse, deceiving and being deceived." "But ye, beloved, building up yourselves on your most holy faith, praying in the Holy Ghost, keep yourselves in the love of God, *looking for the mercy of our Lord Jesus Christ unto eternal life.*" "Be patient, brethren"—patient amid all trials and persecutions, amid the agitations and commotions of the world—"for the coming of the Lord draweth nigh." While the infidel scoffs and sneers, saying, "Where is the promise of his coming?" and while "the evil servant saith in his heart, My Lord delayeth his coming," and is smiting his fellow-servants, eating and drinking with the drunken, "let us consider one another to provoke unto love and to good works: . . . exhorting one another; and so much the more, as ye see the day approaching." Know "the time, that now it is high time to awake out of sleep: for now is our salvation nearer than when we believed. The night is far spent, the day is at hand." The long and dreadful night of the world's curse is far spent, and the day-break of eternity is at hand. And when that glad morning shall break gloriously forth, darkened by no cloud and followed by no night, with what exultation shall the song be sung: "Arise, shine; for thy light is come, and the glory of the Lord is risen upon thee. . . . Thy sun shall no more go down; neither shall thy moon withdraw itself: for the Lord shall be thine everlasting light, and the days of thy mourning shall be ended!" May the Lord hasten it in his time!

Finally, brethren, pray for us that the word of the Lord may have free course and be glorified, even as it is with you, and that we may be delivered from unreasonable and wicked men, for all men have not faith. But the Lord is faithful who shall stablish you and keep you from evil.

CHAPTER X.

St. Louis Conference.

The Sound of the Battle-cry Is no Longer Heard—Session of the Conference at Lexington—Bishop Doggett Presided—Statistical Business—Memoirs of J. T. Davenport, W. H. Mobley, L. Riley, John McEwin, S. S. Headlee—Rev. L. F. Aspley's Trials in Time of the War—Church at Potosi Captured—Rev. J. C. Williams in Trouble—Origin and Early History of Methodism in St. Louis—Revival Notice of Rev. W. L. Powell and Other Ministers—A Description of the Different Charges in St. Louis in Connection with the Introduction of the Church Conference as a New Institution of the Church—Accounts of Revivals by Rev. D. J. Marquis, W. G. Horn, Rev. J. A. Murphy, and Others.

IT is a very gratifying thought that with the history of this year the persecution of the M. E. Church, South, will terminate. There will be no more bloody scenes through which to conduct the reader, no more heart-rending tragedies of cruel murder, of midnight assassinations, no more stricken hearts and desolate homes. How thankful we feel that the chapter of suffering will soon have ended. Then the thoughts of the writer and of the reader will be turned to things more in harmony with their tastes and feelings.

On the 18th of September, 1866, the annual session of the St. Louis Conference was opened at Lexington, Mo., by Bishop Doggett, the President of the Conference, and W. M. Prottsman was elected Secretary.

J. F. Hogan, L. P. Siceloff, T. M. Cobb, and J. D. Wood were admitted on trial; and C. C. Wright, S. A. Blakey, L. W. Powell, and J. S. Frazier remained on trial. L. Pulliam, W. C. Godbey, and P. W. Duncan were admitted into full connection; and A. M. Rader, A. W. Thompson, M. R. Anthony, and A. Peace were re-admitted into full connection. The traveling preachers W. C. Godbey, L. Pulliam, and P. W. Duncan were elected and ordained deacons; and the local preachers J. A. Ross, E. K. Porter, T. M. L. Bedsworth, and J. F. Hogan were elected and ordained deacons. L. F. Aspley, G. C. Knowles, and S. P. Smith, traveling preachers, were elected and ordained elders. J. McCary, J. Godbey, H. S. Watts, and W. B. Quinn were supernumerary; and C. Eaker, A. Rucker, J. T. Peery, J. N. W. Springer, W. R. Babcock, J. McGhee, A. Nichaolds, N. T. Shaler, and J. Thomas were superannuated.

They reported this year 7,912 white members, 43 colored, and 65 local preachers. No report from Springfield District.

The following five ministers died this year: J. T. Davenport, W. H. Mobley, Luther Riley, John McEwin, and S. S. Headlee. No memoir of Davenport and Riley; have already given that of Headlee.

John McEwin.—We cannot say when and where Brother McEwin commenced to preach the gospel. The first mention of his name on our present records is in 1854, when he was superannuated. We believe he sustained that relation to the

Conference till his death. He was always ready and willing to do what he could. He preached faithfully and his labors were blessed. He left his home in Wayne County, Mo., to visit his daughter in Saline County, and on his way, near Versailles, he was taken sick and died August 5, 1866. He was advanced in age, and had been much afflicted for years. He died in peace.

W. H. Mobley was born in Kentucky in the year 1830. In 1852 he removed to Missouri. In 1854 he was licensed to preach and joined the St. Louis Conference. He continued to travel and preached regularly until 1861, when the troubles of the war compelled him to fly to Arkansas, where he remained till 1865. He was taken sick with consumption in this year, and went to Kentucky, that he might die among his friends. He died in Hickman County, Ky., July 27, 1865. A short time before his death he requested his wife to have a letter written to his brethren of the St. Louis Conference, to inform them where and how he died. About the last words he spoke were: "If I know any thing, all is right with me." His submission to God is expressed by him thus: "The will of the Lord be done." Before he died he selected as a text for his funeral sermon: "For me to live is Christ; to die is gain." He was a good man and an efficient preacher. He rests in hope of a resurrection.

Rev. L. F. Aspley, a faithful member of the St. Louis Conference, M. E. Church, South, gives the following brief statement of his trials during the war: "I too was numbered with the sufferers of Missouri. I was a prisoner several times; my life was threatened. I was driven from home; my house was burned, and the last dollar's worth of property I had in the world was taken from me. I was indicted twice by the grand jury of Scott County for preaching without taking the oath prescribed by the new Constitution. I do not wish to complain of the hardships and sufferings through which I have passed, but I thank God that I was counted worthy to suffer for his name's sake."

Church at Potosi.

As has been already indicated, the Northern Methodists put into practical operation a very extensive system of Church seizure in all parts of Missouri—east, west, north, and south—embracing the entire territory of the State. If there was one county that escaped the visitation of church seizers or burners, we have no knowledge of it. The following notice of the attempt to capture the church at Potosi was furnished by the presiding elder of the Potosi District:

I send you statements of an attempt of "our brethren, the enemy," to take, hold, and possess our church at Potosi.

Some time during the year 1865 a Maj. Miller came to Potosi and reported himself a minister of the "old Wesleyan Methodist Church;" that he was neither North nor South, but belonged to the good old Mother Church.

As our people had no pastor, they permitted him to preach in our church, and attended his ministry. He made an earnest effort to proselyte our members, but failed. Rumor said he intended to take possession of our church, but he denied it.

Early in 1866 Mr. Sovin, his presiding elder, announced publicly from the pulpit on the Sabbath that the house belonged to them, and henceforth they intended to hold and possess the same.

That week Brother Wallace, one of the trustees of the Church, who had been a member for twoscore years, locked the door, took possession of the key, and notified Mr. Miller that he could not preach there any more.

Mr. Miller then notified Brother Wallace that he would bring suit for the church. Brother Wallace assured him that *when the law gave him the house* he would give him the key.

In the meantime the Radicals of the town rented a hall for Mr. Miller, in which they put an organ to help him make music.

I held a quarterly meeting in Potosi in January, 1867, and

while there I learned that the Rev. Major had sold his friends' organ, pocketed the money, and gone on a long journey toward the north pole. So Madam Rumor reports.

Our people are in quiet possession of their church-house, have an excellent Sunday-school, an organ to help the children sing, a very gratifying increase in the membership of the Church, have no fears of being disturbed by Messrs. Sovin, Miller & Company, unless they do as their confederates did on Castor—burn the church.

Several of our church-houses at other points have been quietly occupied by them, but I believe they have run their race and are not likely to trouble us much more.   W. S. WOODARD.

And how very short was their race when the authority of military law ended and the civil law was enforced! Then justice had a voice and equity claimed its right. Then church-houses were turned over to the persons who built and paid for them. Yes, when Justice is seated on her throne, how soon do oppression, usurpation, and tyranny disappear! They cannot exist where the civil law is the governing power. Mr. Wallace knew what he was talking about when he told Mr. Miller that he would surrender the key when the *civil law* gave them the church, for he understood full well that the civil law would protect the rightful owners in the possession of their property. So it did, and the key was never surrendered.

REV. J. C. WILLIAMS.

Of Mr. Williams the writer says: "This good and useful minister and member of the St. Louis Conference, M. E. Church, South, was arrested by ruffians, with pistols in their hands, in the midst of his duties as a teacher, dragged from the schoolhouse, and taken to Potosi, in Jefferson County, under an indictment for preaching. After giving bond for his appearance at court, he went on preaching the gospel of the grace of God to dying men, and was again indicted, arrested, and put under bonds." *

We are satisfied that the reader will be deeply interested in the following account of the origin and early history of Methodism in St. Louis:

Editor Advocate: I here dedicate to you, sir, the following lines and items, entitled "The First Days of Methodism in St. Louis," being a detailed account of the same from its birth and progress up to September, 1830:

> As yet I gaze, the vision fades
> Like frost-work touched by Southern gales;
> The altar sinks, the light that's shed
> By glimmering tapers—all are fled.
> Fled are they, with the flight of time,
> Gone down to ruin and decay;
> Now risen again, more grand, sublime,
> They bloom unto a brighter day.

The first meeting of the Methodist persuasion ever held in St. Louis was in the month of December, 1820. In a log cottage, 12 by 16, which then stood on the south-west corner of Third and Spruce Streets, the pioneer preacher of Methodism in St. Louis first unfurled the banner of the cross. This noble and beloved embassador of Christ, known well among religious denominations as old Father Walker, preached here in this humble log cabin to a still humbler congregation his first *sermon* to the citizens of St. Louis. I would merely state here that the congregation entire consisted of Father Walker as pastor, Brother and Sister Finney, and three boys; two of the three boys being myself and a younger brother. The other boy was named Frank Schoto. This was the first congregation which

---

* Dr. Leftwich's book.

met in St. Louis to hear the gospel of the Lord proclaimed by a Methodist minister.

After the sermon had been preached Father Walker called on Brother, then on Sister Finney, to pray, which they did. After the services had been concluded Father Walker shook hands with us boys, and said he was glad to see us come to the house of prayer, and inquired our names. He spoke encouragingly to us and invited us and requested us to invite our friends and our parents and all to come to preaching. He told us there would be preaching on the Sabbath, both morning and evening, and also on Wednesday night; that there would be prayer-meeting every Friday night; hoped he might see us little men often, and hoped also that we would try to get as many to come as we could.

A meeting was held on Wednesday night—and a bitter cold night it was—snow about twelve inches deep—and perhaps this fact may excuse somewhat the smallness of the congregation on that eventful evening—eventful in being the first attempt in this great work. I attended also on the following Sabbath, both morning and evening, and the congregation was increased to about a dozen, among them the venerable pair spoken of above, and a widow lady named Dunlavy, afterward known as Sister Hayden, which name she obtained by a second marriage. The meetings were held regularly, and God continued to add to their numbers. Toward the end of the winter Father Walker was aided in the ministry by Brother Pickett, and occasionally by Brother Glanville and Brother Scripps, who was from Illinois. By the time spring opened up *the little log cabin*, "*the house of prayer*," was found to be too small to accommodate the numbers who now waited upon the word.

On the same lot was also a long, low, frame building which had been fitted up for a theater. At this time it was unoccupied, and Father Walker rented it and converted it into a church, and here he preached with energy and power to a growing congregation. Many were added to the Church of God who are now with him singing praises and hallelujahs to Him who sitteth upon the throne in the eternal world of joy. May I too, who was present at the commencement of the work, be found worthy to join them when my work on earth is done!

The congregation continued to worship in this house for a

year or more, and when they became able to build a house for themselves, at their solicitation Father Walker undertook the project. He erected a church-building on the north-west corner of Fourth and Myrtle Streets, where John H. Gay bought a residence years after that.

At this time there was a small congregation of Episcopalians in St. Louis, who had a small frame church near the south-west corner of Second and Walnut Streets. They had no pastor, and were not able to procure one. They proposed to donate to the Methodist Church their pews and pulpit for the privilege of holding service in the Methodist Church once on Sabbath whenever they could procure a minister. The arrangement was agreed to, and it was a great help toward completing the church. When this was done the congregation left the place where the first standard of Methodism had been planted in this then small city, and removed to their new church on Fourth and Myrtle. The church to which they moved was a two-story frame thirty-six feet long by twenty wide, with galleries on three sides. After the congregation had been worshiping for some months in the new church Father Walker preached a very touching sermon to his people. After the close of the sermon he said it was forcibly impressed upon his mind that his work in St. Louis was about completed; that he was impressed with the belief that God had called him to carry the glorious gospel to the benighted Indian, and that he was going to obey the call; that the Conference would assemble in a few weeks, and that he would remain with them until the Conference met; that Conference would supply them with another pastor and send him on a mission to the red men of the frontier. This announcement was heard by the congregation with regret. Some—"yea," many—shed tears, and they all felt that they were losing in him a father and a friend.

Conference met, and the words of Father Walker were verified. He preached his farewell sermon to a very attentive congregation, of whom I was one. He exhorted us to be faithful to the grace given us, and said: "If I never meet you again on earth, meet me in heaven. I want to see you all there—every one"—closed with the remark that the desire of his heart was to spend a happy eternity with the members of the Methodist Church of St. Louis. Father Walker's wish was to be a pioneer in the cause of Christ, and to be the first to proclaim the gospel to poor, perishing sinners.

I do not remember who was sent by the Conference to the Church in St. Louis as Father Walker's successor. I believe it was Brother McAlister. I know he came among us at that time. He was an able minister, powerful in argument, so clear and so conclusive that he would convince one of the truth of his doctrine contrary to his will.

Besides Brother McAlister there were several local preachers living in St. Louis at that time. Among them were Dr. Heath, of Virginia; Brother Peck, of Tennessee; and Brother Keyte, from England. So we had no lack of ministerial aid. There was regular service, and the word of the Lord was preached to large congregations, sometimes filling the church, audience-room and galleries, to its utmost capacity. Many were added to the Church during the Conference year.

The next Conference appointed Rev. Andrew Monroe to the St. Louis Station. He was a faithful preacher, and many sinners were convicted and converted under his ministry—particularly young men who united with the Church and became co-workers with the older members of the Church in cultivating the Lord's vineyard. Nearly all my old associates united with the Church, and many of them have crossed the river and are now happy and rejoicing in the paradise of God. May I rejoin them when my earthly pilgrimage is ended!

Brother Monroe was so successful that he was returned by the Conference to the same work in St. Louis. His labors the second year were even more successful than the first year had been. As his second year had expired, and as he could not be sent back to the station the third year according to the Discipline, the Conference made him presiding elder of the St. Louis District; consequently we had him with us every quarter for two years more. The result was we had a revival season every time he labored with us.

By this time (1828) the congregation began to think about getting a house of greater capacity to accommodate them, having become too large for the old church. Col. John O'Fallon proposed to give a lot on Fourth Street and Washington Avenue and $500 in money toward building a church on said lot. This generous offer was accepted, and they proceeded at once to build the old "Fourth Street Church," so well known to every person. This church-edifice was completed, and occupied for the first time in the month of September, 1830.

Previous to its being occupied Conference met and began its labors in the frame church on Fourth and Myrtle. On Sunday before the 22d of September they moved from the old to the new house of worship. I suppose very few knew, or even suspected, who was going to preach the opening sermon. The Conference plotted a pleasant surprise to the congregation.

Sabbath morning arrived. The church was filled to its utmost capacity. All were curious to know who would address them. Some thought this preacher, others thought that, but all expectations were soon put to flight as the "founder of the Methodist Church in St. Louis" arose and commenced the service by reading the hymn:

> And are we yet alive
> And see each other's face?

The whole congregation seemed to be greatly excited. Joy and gratitude so filled the souls of the old members, and of the new ones as well, that strangers did not understand it. This was a scene in the early history of Methodism in St. Louis that will never be forgotten. What a striking contrast was this fine superstructure to the little log cabin of 1820! What a contrast between that vast audience and the five persons—two grown and three boys—who first met in the log hut! But Christ verified his promise to them: "Where two or three are gathered together in *my* name, there am I in their midst." Yes, he had been in our midst. He had prospered his work, and old Father Walker's heart rejoiced greatly as he gazed upon the vine which he had planted when but a little thing; which had been transplanted again and again, and now bearing good fruit so abundantly. May the work continue to go on! Of the history of the Church since its establishment at Fourth and Washington Avenue I did not deem it worth while to say anything, as it is so well known.

Yours respectfully.   ROBERT D. SUTTON.*

Success is crowning the labors of the M. E.

---

* *St. Louis Christian Advocate*, May 1, 1867.

Church, South, all over the State, and the kingdom of light is advancing gloriously against the kingdom of darkness. Glad tidings are coming to us from every direction and from all parts of the country of the wonderful displays of divine power in the salvation of the people. Nothing can be more interesting to the writer and to the reader than the progress of the Church in the great work of saving souls. The history along this line is written and read with intense interest.

We find in the *St. Louis Christian Advocate* of September 19, 1866, a letter from Rev. W. L. Powell, giving an account of the general condition of his work on the New Madrid Circuit, as follows:

Mr. Editor: Perhaps the friends of the Church would like to hear what the Lord is doing for us on the New Madrid Circuit. I will first give you a general account of the state of the work when I came here. I found the Church disorganized to a great extent, and much discouraged. Our people seemed to think it impossible to restore and build again the waste places of Zion. Our churches had been pillaged of every thing that could be carried away or appropriated, and in many instances the buildings themselves badly damaged. Our class-books were nearly all taken away or destroyed. It was a long time before I could learn who were the members of the Church.

After having gone round the circuit and learned its condition, I organized classes at all the appointments. Soon the members and friends of the Church came up to the work and repaired most of the churches. We then began to feel a little encouraged. The work advanced gradually, with occasional symptoms of the revival spirit.

About six weeks ago Brother Anthony and myself commenced a series of protracted meetings at various points on the circuit. The fire of primitive and spiritual Christianity immediately broke out and spread through the surrounding country. All of our meetings have been successful, and some of them have been truly seasons of grace to the Church and a great blessing to the country.

I will notice one of these meetings more particularly. Twelve days ago we commenced a meeting in the town of New Madrid. The good work began immediately. The interest has increased daily, until all classes in town and in the surrounding neighborhood have become deeply interested in the cause of religion. Up to this time there have been at this meeting thirty-five conversions and fifty accessions to the Church.

While writing this article I will notice one circumstance which took place within the bounds of the circuit. Brother Jackson commenced a Sunday-school near Guyozo, in which he was assisted by another brother. At this school they commenced a weekly prayer-meeting. All of the scholars and many of the people became deeply penitent. Two weeks ago, at one of these prayer-meetings, thirteen persons were converted and twenty joined the Church. This should encourage Sabbath-school superintendents and teachers.

The total results of the meetings above mentioned are sixty-five conversions and one hundred accessions to the Church. The Lord is truly doing a great work on the New Madrid Circuit.

On September 7, 1866, Rev. J. M. Proctor writes in the *St. Louis Christian Advocate* thus:

My fourth quarterly meeting for Perryville Circuit was held at York Chapel, commencing August 25, and continued five days, resulting in sixty-five accessions to the M. E. Church, South, and nearly the same number were happily converted to God.

The Lord is blessing us in a wonderful manner. I have received one hundred and seventy-two persons in the Church this year. Among them are many noble young men and women, who promise great usefulness to the Church of Christ. Glory be to God!

The following interesting letter needs no explanation:

CALIFORNIA, MONITEAU Co., September 6, 1866.

Dear Advocate: Inasmuch as no tidings are more cheering to the ministers and people of Christ than to hear of the conversion of souls and the building up of Zion, suffer me to report through you the work of God now going on through this region of the country.

The Lord has been pleased to bestow his grace on the people at Bethel, and upward of a hundred souls who were in spiritual darkness are now in the clear light and enjoying the power of God's saving grace. Brother Hogan, our most faithful preacher, tells me that forty or fifty have been added to Bethel. The work has been spreading over Moniteau, Cole, and Cooper Counties, and is yet in progress. Our fourth quarterly meeting continued nine days, resulting in over forty conversions.

Since Brother Hogan took charge last April upward of one hundred and sixty members have been added to the Church as the result of the revival which has been going on and is still in progress. Hundreds are now in love and fellowship with the people of God. The best members of the community are foremost in this great work. The prospects of our Church were never so good for the last ten years as at the present time. The ministers to whom we are indebted for help in this glorious revival are: A. Thompson, of the Cumberland Presbyterian Church; John Maxy and J. Martin, of the Baptist Church; our beloved presiding elder, J. Godbey, and J. M. Hardy; also our faithful Hogan and your humble servant.

JOHN MONROE.

Rev. A. M. Rader gives a very interesting account of his work on Arrow Rock Circuit, Saline County. At different points on his circuit he had several successful meetings. In his protracted efforts he was assisted by Revs. Brown T. Wallace, J. H. B. Wooldridge, and W. M. Pitts. He had about one hundred and twenty conversions and seventy-six accessions to the Church during the last five weeks he was on his work. Such reports of the power of the gospel to save sinners as are given this year by the preachers are very encouraging to the people of God. The cheering thought is that these reports are not few, but numerous, coming from all quarters of the State. So it seems that the revival spirit pervaded the whole State in 1866-67.

In the *St. Louis Christian Advocate* of this year we find a summary given of the religious *status* of the Southern Methodist Churches in the city of St. Louis; also an interesting account of the introduction of the Church Conference among them. Being something new, it attracted no little attention, and the members attended its first meetings, if from no other motive than to see what it meant.

The committee of the General Conference who recommended the plan for the organization of the Church Conference spoke in favor of it in the following language: "It is believed that by this means discipline will be better maintained, and the membership of the Church awakened to new life, and a new energy imparted to them, adding greatly to the aggressive force of the Church."

There can be no doubt that the committee entertained a correct view of the subject. If rightly appreciated and properly observed, it cannot do otherwise than promote all the interests of the Church, material and spiritual, temporal and eternal; for it takes into consideration all these interests and all the institutions and enterprises of the Church, missions, Sunday-schools, education, etc. The intelligent reader cannot fail to see at once that the

Church Conference is of paramount importance. We cannot see how it is possible for the members to attend its meetings regularly and transact all its business as it should be done without feeling a deep and abiding interest in the success and welfare of the Church. It is such a good place for every member of the Church to find something to do in the Lord's vineyard. In the multifarious work of the Church certainly every person can find some place he can fill successfully. But, unappreciated and unobserved, like the neglected class-meeting, prayer-meeting, and love-feast, the Church Conference will avail nothing:

Church Conference at Centenary Church—Dr. W. A. Smith, Pastor.

The first feature that we observed here indicative of an awakening to new life in the membership was the *immense gathering* of the members. If they were not all present, perhaps it were well, for certainly the lecture-room would hold no more. It was full and crowded, and when those hundreds of voices united in lifting up their hearts—

> In praise to our redeeming Lord,
> Who saves us by his grace,
> And bids us, each to each restored,
> Together seek his face—

we began to think there was a strong probability of a "force" being awakened that had not been anticipated. We often hear *old-fashioned Methodism* spoken of as something that has passed away with those who practiced it, and the fact of its having passed away seems much to be regretted. Well, we are too young to know by experience much of old-fashioned Methodism; but when we all knelt in prayer, and the clear, loud voice of the pastor led our supplicating hearts and appeals at the throne of grace, and as the warm desires of the pastor's full heart came gushing up, and his utterance seemed the very flow of inspiration, and "Amen! amen!" was heard in all parts of the house, we thought of old-fashioned Methodism and said: "*Here it is.*"

Then came T. Childs, the Secretary, with the volume of the records and the long roll of membership. These records make the history of individual society, and these will give us authentic Church history. A good feature this in Church economy; an important office this position of Secretary, and right faithfully and efficiently is it filled by the young brother who holds it. What attention there was to the calling of the roll! Each one seemed to listen and wait to hear his own name, as though there might have been a renewing and righting up of the books, and perhaps his name "dropped." But none had been dropped, and all who were absent were accounted for. We began to listen for the end of that long roll; for we had heard of a falling off in the membership of the Southern Methodist Churches in St. Louis, in the days which tried men's religion by party politics, and their qualifications for business by their Church relations, and we listened attentively to the report on numbers as revealed by the roll. It may be possible that there were some who could not stand the test of persecution; for there be some Christians who do the fighting, and some who do the running. But we cannot infer this from the numbers; for at the close of the Conference year 1860 the membership in this Church numbered *two hundred and fifty-two*, and at the present writing it is *four hundred*.

The "order of business," as given in the Discipline, was called over by the chairman, and every item of business pertaining to the interest of the Church was properly attended to. And even more than this, for on this occasion an opportunity was afforded for an evidence of the liberality in financial matters for which this Church is so justly celebrated.

At the last session of the St. Louis Annual Conference the bishop found the demand upon him for preachers greater than his supply, and, consequently he had to leave several places "to be supplied." Among these are Wesley Chapel and Stoddart's Addition. Rev. T. M. Finney, presiding elder of this district, by correspondence with the bishop and others, and by much fervent prayer to the great Head of the Church for help, had found able and desirable men for these vacant places, and nothing was now lacking to place them in regular working order but the *necessary means* for the support of their pastors. No

Church in St. Louis suffered half as much from the war as Wesley Chapel; but this was not from disaffection in the membership, nor from any intentional harm from the military authorities, but from its location. As it regards its relation to the city, its location—corner of Eighth and Chouteau Avenue—is as good as any in the city; yet it was situated in the very midst of Schofield Barracks. It was literally invested and surrounded by soldiers. This was a blessing to the soldiers, for many of them worshiped there, and several of them experienced the converting grace of God; but the military parade on Sunday morning had the tendency of keeping many persons from church who had been in the habit of attending there.

And now that at least *two thousand dollars* is necessary for the support of a pastor there, the presiding elder, who neglects no preacher but himself in financial matters, not seeing the ability at Wesley Chapel to support a pastor, called on the Centenary Church to assist in the matter. And noble indeed was the response. Dr. Smith presented the subject in plain, but very meaning, words, and then in a few strains of his peculiar and soul-stirring eloquence spoke of sacrifice and self-denial for the salvation of souls; and then the vote was taken, and the presiding elder was authorized to look to them for means to support Methodism at Wesley Chapel until it is able to take its place again with its sister Churches as self-sustaining. And while this was being done at Centenary an equally generous and noble work was going on at First Church for another needy Church. But of this we will speak hereafter.

The most interesting feature just now at Centenary is the *revival spirit* that is manifested, and the daily increase in religious activity. LOCAL.

The foregoing is certainly a very interesting presentation of the Centenary Church; and as we feel satisfied that the reader would like to hear from the other Churches in the city by the same writer, we will give him that pleasure.

CHURCH CONFERENCE, FIRST CHURCH—DR. J. BOYLE, PASTOR.

On the first Sabbath of the month we dropped in on Brother Boyle to observe the working of the *new feature* in Methodist economy in the Church of which he has charge. And here, indeed, were seen the promised "new life, new energy, and increased aggressive force of the Church" in the *immense gathering* of the membership. And none were idle spectators; none seemed to have come simply as lookers-on; but all, every one, of the vast congregation of the Church appeared to feel the burden of souls. It is the Christian's privilege not only to be *alive*, but to be *lively;* and here they seem to appreciate this truth, and to practice it too, for here is Christianity in earnest. Talk of old-fashioned Methodism; here it is, not in some of the modern style of fixtures, but *around her altars*, where mourners are called, and fervent, warm, heart-feeling, heart-gushing prayers are made, and hearty amens are heard responding; and better than all, *souls are converted.* Now if this is not old-fashioned Methodism, pray tell us where will you find it? It is, in fact, the Methodism that spreads scriptural holiness over these lands—the Methodism of Wesley, by which the Church more than a century ago was awakened to a sense of its fallen condition, and restored to righteousness and usefulness.

The reports of the different departments of this Church—that is, pastor's, class-leader's, Sunday-school superintendent's, stewards', etc.—were listened to with an attention that manifested great interest in these matters. In all these departments of the Church all was life and activity. But the most interesting feature of this meeting, and that which stamped the labors of the pastor and the faith and prayers of the membership with the seal of the divine approbation, was the large number who presented themselves at the altar for membership, as the fruits of the past month. Thirty-one responded to the call, and circled around the pastor to take upon themselves the vows of their holy espousals to Christ.

During the administration of the ordinance of baptism the solemn silence of the congregation was of that spiritual gathering together of all hearts in one prayer, that only the moistened eye spoke as it went up to God. And when the fervent voice of the pastor, in all the earnestness of his burdened heart with immortal souls, was heard to pray, "Grant that they may have strength and power to have victory and triumph against 'the devil, the world, and the flesh,'" an involuntary "Amen!" seemed to come from the entire congregation.

On the reception of these applicants into the Church, when, in his warm and fervent manner, Dr. Doyle put the searching question, "Wilt thou, then, obediently keep God's holy will and commandments, and walk in the same all the days of thy life?" there went up a united prayer of many voices for grace to enable them "so to do." But it was in the prayer consecrating these souls to God, and asking in the name of the Redeemer that they might endure patiently to the end, that all their hearts seemed to melt into one petition that the whole Church might be filled with heaven, and baptized with power from on high.

The First Church in St. Louis was enjoying a remarkable visitation of the divine presence and power at the time of this writing. The Church was lifted to a high plane of Christian experience, and was characterized by great spirituality. For a long time they realized that "the tabernacle of God is with men." It was their privilege to have a perpetual revival—sinners converted every day at their daily prayer-meeting, which was continued indefinitely. It was in these meetings that Sister Boyle, that consecrated woman of God, accomplished an incalculable amount of good. Bright will be her crown, and hundreds will rise up in that day and pronounce her blessed. Dr. Doyle and his wife will no doubt occupy high seats in heaven, near by the throne of God.

An account of St. Paul's Church will now claim the attention of the reader:

CHURCH CONFERENCE, ST. PAUL'S—REV. W. M. PROTTSMAN, PASTOR.

In the operation of the "new feature" in Methodist economy in this Church we observed on the part of the pastor a close attention to the "observance of every point, great or small, in the Methodist Discipline;" and the strict observance of the order of business by the pastor seemed to be nothing new to the membership, and altogether in accordance with their views of Methodist discipline. The reports from the several departments of the work were listened to with interest, and indicated a determination on the part of the membership to bring this old "Mound Charge" back again to its former prosperity.

At the close of the last Conference year Brother Prottsman recommended the sale of Mound Church, and the building of another and better house of worship in a more eligible location. This recommendation was very heartily concurred in by the entire membership. Accordingly the old church was sold for $6,500, and a lot purchased on Jackson Square, Twelfth and North Market Streets. This lot is certainly suitaole for Church purposes, and is the most desirable in North St. Louis.

It is the intention of the congregation to build on this lot during the present year (if at all practicable) a substantial but plain church, with ample capacity to meet the wants of this part of the city.

At present this congregation worships in a comfortable and well-finished hall on the north-east corner of Jefferson and Fourteenth Streets.

There are members in this charge who have the ring of sound metal—members who have been tried by the allurements of the world, under the demoralizing influence of the war, when *pecuniary interest* became the line of Church latitude; and who have been triea by the fires of persecution also; and yet were ever true to the Church.

Such a people must and will prosper; and they are every day increasing in spirituality and numbers. We pray that their new church-edifice may soon be finished, and the labors of their worthy pastor be abundantly blessed.

The reader's attention is directed in the next place to the notice given of one of the Southern Methodist Churches in another part of the city:

WESLEY CHAPEL.—REV. S. S. BRYANT, PASTOR.

Owing to a want of supply of preachers at the last session of the St. Louis Annual Conference, Wesley Chapel was left to be supplied. As long as it was at all practicable for him to do so, Brother Prottsman supplied the pulpit here on Sunday nights, and since Dr. Smith's arrival at Centenary he has preached regularly here on Sabbath afternoons. The Sunday-school, under the superintending care of that faithful young man, Samuel Gaddis, has been kept in good working order, and although without a pastor, is in a prosperous condition.

Rev. S. S. Bryant, late of Virginia, has been sent on by Bishop Doggett to take charge of this Church. He has met with a very welcome reception, and has entered upon his duties cheerfully, prayerfully, and hopefully. He and the members of his charge are expecting much fruit unto the Lord from their labors, and the other Churches in the city are praying for their success.

Wesley Chapel needed at this time such a man and preacher as Brother Bryant. Its location, on Chouteau Avenue and Eighth Street, the center of a most respectable community, gave it prominence as a place where there should be a large congregation. Such was the case in years past; but an army of soldiers came and made their barracks around this church, and then many of the congregation sought other houses of worship; but a few faithful ones stood by the Church in all her vicissitudes, and now they rejoice in the prospect of great future prosperity.

"Local" has, in the opinion of this writer, given a very interesting survey of the M. E. Church, South, in St. Louis at the time of his writing. It will no doubt be read with a great deal of pleasure, at least by those immediately interested. Indeed, all the Methodists in Missouri feel an anxious concern about the success of Methodism in St. Louis; for its influence must be felt more or less throughout the State. Yes, St. Louis being the metropolis should give type and tone to the Methodism of Missouri.

Rev. D. J. Marquis gives in the *St. Louis Chris-*

tian *Advocate* of September 26, 1866, a very encouraging account of his work in Jefferson, Ste. Genevieve, and St. Francois Counties—a number of revivals at different points on his circuit. He was assisted in his special meetings by Rev. John C. Williams and Dr. T. M. Finney, the presiding elder. The quickening and purifying grace of Christ was experienced in the Church, reclaiming backsliders and reviving the people of God; while the convicting and converting power of the Holy Spirit was manifested among sinners. At the time of his writing there had been seventy-five conversions, among whom were a number of very promising young men. It seems that there was a forward movement all along the line of his work. Also a very interesting report given by Rev. S. M. Winton of his work on the Springfield Circuit. He says: "The meeting at Ross's Chapel continued two weeks with glorious success: about fifty conversions and thirty-two accessions to the Church, and others will join at other places, so that the Church will gain about fifty members. The conversions were clear and powerful. Quite a number of young men of great promise were brought into the Church. The old members were thoroughly revived." This is only a report of one of his meetings, while he speaks of others in very encouraging language.

The Lord is graciously and extensively blessing the labors of his servants, and we record with a great deal of pleasure the wonderful displays of divine power in the salvation of so many precious souls. The M. E. Church, South, is certainly coming up out of the wilderness of persecution as clear "as the sun, as fair as the moon, and terrible as an army with banners" against all sin and unrighteousness. She is nobly fulfilling her mission of spreading holiness over all these ends of the earth.

Rev. G. W. Horn, pastor of the Church at Jefferson City, writes of his charge in the *St. Louis Christian Advocate* of February 6, 1867, in the following language:

News from the Churches is always welcome and read with interest by the lovers of Zion. As others from all quarters are giving in their reports, I also will add mine—not as good as some others, but good after its kind.

When I came to this charge I found the Church in a low and lowly state. There had been no regular pastor here for five years past, and of course the congregation had well-nigh gone down. A few had remained firm, watchful, and hopeful, but many had fallen off by death, removal, and otherwise, and only twenty-eight members could be found. Brother Long, under many difficulties, had striven to keep up the Sunday-school of ten or fifteen scholars.

Such was the condition of the Church here when I commenced four years ago. In addition to this, the house of worship was much dilapidated, having been used and abused by the soldiery. We went to work, however, planning, talking, preaching, praying, "exhorting, reproving, rebuking," etc. All worked together; for, be it said, we have some willing hands here, especially among the ladies. The stewards made a very liberal allowance for the pastor, and he, grateful, felt at least no less willing to do all in his power to benefit them.

The result of the work thus far may be expressed about thus: A good congregation, a promising Sabbath-school, and a thoroughly renovated house, with a prospect of precious spiritual achievements. We have expended over four hundred dollars in repairs and improvements on the house. "A great door and effectual is opened unto us," and we are waiting before the Lord for a "time of refreshing from his presence."

Rev. J. A. Murphy, presiding elder of the Boonville District, thus writes in the *St. Louis Christian Advocate* of January 30:

The interests of Christianity are common interests. Her successes or reverses, her joys or her sorrows need only to be made known to be shared by her numerous votaries. If the conversion of a single soul is an event that stirs anew the joy of heaven, it remains among Christians a common privilege to send up a jubilant shout "to him that cometh in the name of the Lord," when Zion's ark is advancing; or to hang their harps upon the willows in the days of her calamity, praying: "Turn again our captivity, O Lord, as the streams in the south."

Impressed with this view, I count myself happy to sketch, in short, a field of extensive bounds, "white already to the harvest. Of the fourteen preachers employed in the district all abound in the choice gift of Providence—health—except Brothers J. Godbey and S. S. Colburn, both of whom do what they can in the service of the Church. According to the understanding of Bishop Doggett, Brother W. M. Pitts will be fully given to his work by the opening of spring. He has already begun the labor of reorganizing the Church in the devastated region. He finds that our people, with an astonishing unanimity and true fidelity, have adhered to our Church, though it has cost them much suffering and loss. The first quarter has closed showing an increase in membership, some gracious revival interest, and indications of coming good.

From the same source we get important information respecting the condition of the M. E. Church, South, in the south-western part of this State, by a local preacher as follows:

I have been looking and waiting ever since Conference for a preacher to make his appearance, but so far in vain. I would like to know why the presiding elder and circuit preacher appointed here have not come on. Are they coming at all? If so, when? If not, why? I have been laboring incessantly for twelve months past to hold the influence here for Southern Methodism. I shall not attempt to describe the toil and privation which I have undergone, and the difficulties I have encountered—thankful that I have succeeded so far. I have under my care here, at this time, about two hundred and fifty living Southern Methodists, while our Northern brethren have in the same bounds five or six preachers and less than fifty members. Our Church is now twice as strong here as ever before, and, should I attend every call, I would have to preach twice every day, and then could not do it. Meanwhile, a school to attend to of seventy-five scholars; so you may reasonably conclude that I do not eat much idle bread. If I were so situated that I could spend my whole time in preaching, I could, by divine help, revolutionize this south-western country. But the people are generally poor, were broken up during the war, are hard run to make a living, and are not able to pay much to support a minister, and I have to meet the expenses of my family by some other means. Hence I can only devote a small portion of my time to the work. No man is, perhaps, more devoted to the Southern Methodist Church than myself, and I would be more than willing to sacrifice luxury and ease for her interests. But the facts are before you. Cannot something be done to meet the wants of our Church in this part of the State? There is certainly a wide and open field before us, which should be entered and occupied at the earliest period practicable. All honor to the Church-members who remained steadfast amid the terrible trials through which they had to pass!

Rev. W. S. Woodard, presiding elder of Cape Girardeau District, gives the following interesting account of their District Conference: "The meeting was a splendid success. We had a very good attendance; eight circuits were represented. Bishop Doggett presided over our deliberations with great profit to the Conference. He preached Sabbath morning and evening to large and delighted audiences. The Holy Spirit attended the word. Sinners were convicted and penitents were converted, while Christians felt an unusual glow of divine love. The reports of the preachers show a majority of the circuits to be in a prosperous condition. The future is promising and hopeful."

CHAPTER XI.

Missouri Conference.

The Fiftieth Annual Session of the Missouri Conference—Statistical Business—The Blessings of Peace in Contrast with the Evils of War—United as One People, the United States the Greatest Nation on Earth—Would Give a High Christian Civilization to the World—Is not That the Divine Purpose?—Rev. J. A. Mumpower Speaks of His Work—Also Rev. Thos. Hurst and Rev. W. E. Dockery—His Usefulness and Persecution—Revival Notices by Other Preachers—Revival in a Sunday-school—Rev. Jesse Bird's Work—Church at Glasgow—Work of Rev. A. Munroe, Presiding Elder of Fayette District—Chillicothe Station, Rev. S. W. Cope, Pastor—Revival Notice by Rev. John D. Vincil—Work on St. Joseph District by Rev. W. M. Rush, Presiding Elder—Trials of Rev. Jesse Faubion during the Internecine War—Also of Rev. S. J. Burgin—Revivals Reported from All Parts of the Conference—Also a Revival of Building Many Houses of Worship in Different Portions of the Country.

WE have been giving the minute business of the Conferences to some extent because it perpetuates the names of the preachers who are spending and who have spent their useful lives in the service of the M. E. Church, South, and to whom the Church owes her great success and prosperity under the blessing of heaven. It will be very gratifying to their relatives and friends, after these faithful, consecrated ministers shall have gone to their future reward of mansions in heaven, to find their names in the history of the

Church—names that should be embalmed in our memory and transmitted from generation to generation as the ages roll on.

The fiftieth annual session of the Missouri Conference was opened by Bishop Doggett September 5th, 1866, John D. Vincil acting as Secretary by the appointment of the Conference.

H. W. James was admitted on trial, and J. A. Mumpower, T. Penn, J. Metcalf, and B. F. Zumwalt remained on trial. Joseph King was admitted into full connection, and Jesse Bird, H. A. Davis, and M. McIlhany were re-admitted. The traveling preachers, Joseph King and J. Smith, were elected and ordained deacons; also the following local preachers: J. Rickman, T. R. Hedgpeth, and M. McIlhany. The traveling preachers who were elected and ordained were: S. J. Huffaker, J. O. Swinney, J. Smith, S. Alexander, J. W. Adkisson, S. J. Catlin, and J. O. Foresman. Also the following local preachers: J. Craft, L. S. Cornell, G. S. Huffaker, and L. W. Cooper. R. H. Jordan was supernumerary, and M. L. Eads, D. C. Blackwell, and Tyson Dines were superannuated. Reported at the Conference 11,551 white members, 346 colored, 57 Indian, and 82 local preachers.

As we leave the war behind us and as we advance in the history of "Methodism in Missouri" the glimmering light which has cheered us on through the darkness of the past grows brighter and brighter and the horizon is becoming luminous with the golden beams of the rising Sun of Peace.

Yes, the war cloud has risen, lifted, and is gone, and the clear, calm, blue sky is smiling upon the earth. The gentle, balmy zephyrs are wafting sweet peace on their soft wings, to every heart and home in the land. How much better is peace than war, is harmony than strife, is love than hate, is happiness than misery, is union than division! Could we as a nation but rise above all sectionalism and partyism, and be governed by the advice of the immortal Webster, that noble patriot and great statesman, who said, "Know no east, no west, no north, no south, but be one," what a mighty nation would the American people become—a model nation of virtue, intelligence, and Christian civilization, whose influence and power would be known and felt all over the world!

It is clear to the mind of this writer that God designed to make our nation his own peculiar people for the evangelization and Christianization of all the heathen nations of the earth. He has given them the finest country in the world, the best civil government in the world, founded on the solid principles of the Bible. In its organic structure the supreme claims of God and the equitable rights of man are its chief corner-stones. He has made them the greatest nation on earth—exalted to heaven in point of privileges and blessings. In all these things the purpose of God is manifestly indicated. But like the Israelites or Jewish nation, we may frustrate that purpose. Notice the parallelism. The Jews had the choice country of the old world, the best government in the world, were the greatest people in the world when loyal to their divine government, were raised to heaven in privileges and blessings. The Bible teaches that it was the design of God to save the world through the Jewish nation, his own chosen people. But in this he was defeated by their willful rebellion and stubborn wickedness, culminating in the rejection and crucifixion of the Son of God. Let us not follow their example of disobedience and rebellion against the authority and righteous government of Heaven.

The following is from the pen of Rev. J. A. Mumpower to the *St. Louis Christian Advocate* of January, 1867:

Having been appointed to Bucklin Circuit, Linn County, I came on to my work as soon as my health would permit, and found it at some points in a tolerably good condition, but at others in a very deplorable state; the membership scattered and almost broken up during the war, which worked like some foul fiend against the interests of Southern Methodism.

Viewing the wreck, I went to work collecting the fragments together, and by the blessing of God have seen the good work progress. I appointed a protracted meeting to commence at Yellow Creek Church December 29, which lasted fourteen days, and resulted in nineteen conversions and eleven accessions to the Church, and the membership greatly revived.

I commenced a meeting at King's School-house on the 12th of January, which lasted one week, resulting in eighteen accessions to the Church and the same number of conversions.

Since my arrival on the work I have taken into the Church about sixty persons, forty of whom are new converts. So you see that Southern Methodism is not dead here yet.

17

The interest manifested by the people for a pure gospel is such that we are forced to say: "The harvest is great, but the laborers are few." O that God would send laborers 'nto the field, such as will glory in nothing but the cross.

Rev. Thomas Hurst reports a good work on the Maysville Circuit. He says: "We protracted our first quarterly meeting with good results. I then commenced a protracted meeting at the Parrott school-house, which was continued through the holidays. There were seventy-two accessions to the M. E. Church, South. I am glad to say that nearly all who joined the Church were converted. I have received one hundred and twenty persons into the Church since October."

Rev. W. E. Dockery speaks thus of his district: "I make my first report of Chillicothe District. I was able to attend all my quarterly meetings. We have had about fifty additions to the Church. The quarterage is almost double what it was on my first round last year. I do not think the Church will starve her preachers in the bounds of the Chillicothe District this year. Our new churches at Richmond and Chillicothe are finished, and but little debt on either. The preachers are well and at their work, except Brother Proctor. His health having failed, I employed Brother T. B. King to take charge of the work. He is the son of Governor King."

It is very remarkable how rapidly and extensively the revival spirit in the M. E. Church, South, spread over the State of Missouri so soon after the war. The same spirit was in the Church all the time, and the cessation of hostilities only gave it an opportunity to manifest itself.

REV. WILLIS E. DOCKERY.

How dry, how dull and tame would the annual session of the Missouri Conference be without the presence of the good-humored, hilarious, laughter-making, soul-exhilarating, veritable Dockery! When the proceedings of the session are becoming prosy and monotonous let Brother Dockery arise to his feet and address the Chair, and instantly the whole Conference realizes the inspiration of new life, and business moves forward more briskly and with greater interest. He is indeed the life of the Conference, and his absence would be sadly felt by all the preachers. He was for a long time the leading chorister of the Conference, and is yet to a considerable extent. Whenever his clear, sonorous voice starts out upon one of Zion's favorite hymns, with the whole Conference joining in the song, you may expect to hear soul-enrapturing music that will lift you above the sublunary cares of this fading, dying world into the blissful scenes of paradise.

Not only is he useful in these directions, but he is competent to perform successfully any work the Conference may think proper to give him on the circuit, in the station, or on the district, all of which places he has filled in a manner that reflects credit upon him. This present writer cannot call to mind any member of the Missouri Conference who has done more for Southern Methodism in North-west Missouri than Willis E. Dockery. Yet he had his trials during the war in common with other Southern Methodist preachers, as the reader may see in the following statement given by another:

> This faithful servant of God and prominent member of the Missouri Conference, M. E. Church, South, did not escape the hand of the persecutors. He was traveling the Chillicothe District, and was in various places in his district threatened with mob violence by the self-constituted executors of the law. But he faltered not nor hesitated in the presence of duty or danger. In the fall of 1866 he was indicted by the grand jury for Lewis County and arrested by James A. Neal, sheriff of the county, and required to give bond in the sum of $1,000 for his appearance at court. At the following spring term of the same court he was again indicted. Judge R. E. Debolt presided in the court, and continued the cases from time to time until the decision of the United States Supreme Court, when they were dismissed.*

Rev. Jesse Sutton gives a brief report of a good meeting at Wesley Chapel, Lincoln County, as follows: "My first quarterly meeting was held at Wesley Chapel October 27th. Brother Horace Brown, the presiding elder, was with us, and preached in his usual powerful and convincing manner for three days, and then had to leave for other work. But we determined to protract the meeting. It was continued two weeks, the result of which was fifty-eight accessions to the Church and about forty-five conversions, and the membership greatly revived. During the meeting I baptized thirty-eight adults and two infants."

---

*Dr. Leftwich's book.

In the *St. Louis Christian Advocate* of November 21st the Rev. George Fenton, of the New Bloomfield Circuit, Callaway County, writes in the following manner: "We are receiving some gracious blessings on the New Bloomfield Circuit. At the fourth quarterly meeting of last Conference year, held at Shiloh in August, we had a gracious revival, resulting in a number of conversions and thirteen additions to the Church. We also held a protracted meeting at Rocky Branch, embracing the fifth Sabbath in September, resulting in many happy conversions and seventeen additions to the Church. We are now busy repairing our house of worship, and we are still looking forward for greater displays of God's saving power."

The following interesting statement is found in the *Advocate* of November 14:

At what is known as "Spring Garden School-house," about two miles from St. Joseph, in the neighborhood of Col. Thomas Ashton's, a few friends started a Sabbath-school last spring. I was invited to visit them occasionally and encourage the enterprise. I did so, both with pleasure and profit. The people seemed to give such good attention to the word preached that encouragement was given to a little extra effort which was made, and I have just suspended a meeting of ten nights' continuance, which resulted in thirty-seven accessions to the Church, and about forty-five professing conversion.

They were organized into a soicety, with a class-leader and a steward, and attached to the St. Joseph Station. The meeting suspended for the time, that the religious interest might be transferred to an adjacent neighborhood where Brother Barrett is holding a meeting. He has just closed one at Rushville with good results, and we may expect to hear a good report from Hyde's School-house, where the meeting is now in progress. Our blessed Lord has not "forgotten to be gracious," nor will we forget to make this record to his praise.

The reader will take considerable interest in the forth-coming letter from Jesse Bird in the *Advocate* of February 10, 1867:

Indulge me in saying a few things concerning affairs on the Plattsburg Circuit. I cannot report large accessions to the Church. A few have united with us since Conference. Our first quarterly meeting at Haynesville was continued for ten days, resulting in the addition of six to the Church, with a good degree of interest among the outsiders. At Gosneyville we had a good meeting about the 1st of January.

On Friday, the 4th of January, we commenced a meeting at Plattsburg and continued one week, during which we held a regular Church meeting. I was there, and then resolved to hold a prayer-meeting, when there was no preaching until a better state of things should be realized. The meeting continued until the first Sabbath in February. On that day we administered the holy sacrament to the people and had a general class-meeting in the afternoon, and a more interesting time I have never seen among the members of the Church. The prayer-meetings are still kept up.

Now you may call this a revival notice or what you please. If a great outpouring of the spirit upon the Church is a revival, then we are having a revival at Plattsburg. If to see men and women earnestly struggling for a *clean heart* and for higher attainments in the Christian life is a revival of religion, then there is a revival on Plattsburg Circuit. We are trying to get our people up to a higher standard of religion, and we have been greatly encouraged in the effort. To God be all the glory! At the close of the meeting on Sunday night two men joined the Church; two others had joined during the meeting. They promise to be an advantage to the cause of Christ. Earnest, faithful, and persevering prayer always results in blessing to the people.

We are furnished with an interesting historic sketch of the

CHURCH AT GLASGOW,

which we give in the following pages:

A short summary of events transpiring in Glasgow just preceding the Conference of 1865 is necessary to the proper understanding of the situation there at that time:

Our brick church had been occupied for several months as a hospital by the Federal troops, and was so used until June of that year. A Society of the M. E. Church (North) had also been organized the preceding spring. The pastor of this Society was the Rev. D. A. McReady, who had been transferred from the Pittsburg Conference by request, made through Gen. C. B. Fisk.

This organization, in its initial, was conceived by a few persons who, under stress of danger in war times, had abandoned our Church. They doubtless supposed, as did many others then, that the M. E. Church, South, would never again have an existence in this country. Two of our ministers had tried to supply the pastorate here made vacant by the death of Brother Caples, but were compelled to leave in a very short time—one, the venerable Andrew Monroe; the other, H. A. Bourland. The membership were therefore deprived of both their houses of worship and their pastor, and were living daily in constant apprehension of greater evils yet to come. It was currently talked that the Southern Methodist Church would, in the main, be absorbed by the Northern Methodist Church, and the remnant be dispersed among other denominations.

To begin such a work here then seemed, therefore, to be but anticipating the inevitable tendency of events. The movement was also commenced by shrewd calculations of prudence and safety. It would relieve all who entered into it from the odium of being in fellowship with what was stigmatized as the "rebel Church," and at the same time put them under the sheltering wing of that Church which had so industriously earned the appellation of the "Union Church."

These opinions and calculations very naturally suggested another line of policy. In order to demonstrate their loyalty and insure the confidence of the army, the State, and the Church, this new Society was induced, through specious arguments, and by well-timed threats from their imported pastor, to seize all the property of the Southern Methodist Church in Glasgow. This consisted of an old frame building, used as a church before the separation of 1845; a brick church, built in 1846; and a parsonage, bought a few years later. They claimed legal title to the old frame, under cover of the original deed made to the M. E. Church in 1840, before the division. The new brick and the parsonage were simply taken under the protection of the military power.

In August, 1865, Mr. McReady was preaching in the brick church and occupying the brick parsonage, while their negro members had possession of the old frame. The character of this McReady was now being fully revealed. The bold, unscrupulous advantage which he had taken of men, because of the circumstances then around them and the lengths to which he had driven them, clearly exposed his *animus* and caliber. It was known that the liberty, life, and property of any individual man in this community was suspended upon the capricious will of that petty tyrant, Col. Kutzner, and his gang of drunken, murderous freebooters, who had been so long fastened upon this people. Soon after their removal in June, 1865, just after our Palmyra meeting, one of our preachers, visiting Glasgow, was introduced to McReady, and said to him: "I hope that when our pastor comes this fall you and he can work together cordially, and bring about a better state of religious feeling among the people." He replied: "I do not know about that. I have no terms to make with rebels. If I am attacked, I shall know how to defend myself." On another occasion, when told that the civil law would compel him to give up the property of our Church, he angrily asked: "Do you suppose that there is a court in Missouri that would dare to decide against the *military?*" It was this very fanatical audacity of the man which enabled him to dominate men, and precipitate them into acts then which, under other circumstances and in cooler moments, they would have condemned and spurned. He played upon their ignorance and their fears.

In members, character, piety, and wealth, our Church here, before the war, was a very strong one. It enrolled many names conspicuous throughout the State for morality, liberality, intelligence, and enterprise. Among these may be mentioned the Lewis families, of whom Judge Henry Lewis was truly a patriarch of Methodism in Missouri; the Bartons, the Birches, the Earicksons, the Harrisons, and the Swinneys, of whom William D. Swinney was a life-long steward and the financier of the

Church, who died in 1863. We can give an instance in testimony of Brother Swinney's liberality to the Church. At the close of a Conference year we told him there was a deficiency. He asked how much. We told him nearly one hundred dollars. Without saying another word, he handed us the amount.

All shades of political opinion prevailed among the members, especially after the first reverses of the South, and after Gov. Jackson was driven from the State, opinions ranging from ultra unionism to the extremist secession proclivities. Some fled, some were banished, and some were killed. Among the outspoken Radicals were Benjamin W. Lewis and his brother, James W., who were large slave-holders and property owners. Thereafter they took quite an active part in public affairs during the war, and were the prime movers in organizing the society of the M. E. Church here.

James O. Swinney was sent to Glasgow Station by the Conference of 1865. Being fully informed of the situation, he went directly to St. Louis, and laid the facts before Gen. Pope, the commander of the department, and asked for an order to restore the property of the Church, South, in Glasgow to its lawful owners. The order was forwarded to him by mail in a few days, at Glasgow. In a pleasant conversation with B. W. Lewis, who was also in St. Louis, that gentleman was evidently disposed, now that the war was over, and the military withdrawn, and every thing quiet, to act with that prompt, shrewd, determined judgment which had always characterized him. To sum it up, he said: "I want nothing, and will do nothing that is not lawful and right." When the order of Gen. Pope was received at Glasgow the pastor and trustees got the key of the brick church from the negro sexton employed by McReady, and, going in, elected two new trustees to fill the vacancy in the Board.

Upon coming out they were met by McReady and Noah Swacker, who peremptorily demanded the key, declaring that they had an order from the Governor authorizing them to hold the building.

They were greatly surprised when shown the order of Gen. Pope, and retired for a consultation with their friends. A few hours later they said the matter would be settled when Col. B. W. Lewis came home, but that if there was any trouble the Kutzner militia would be recalled. Such a threat created quite a panic in town. In a day or two Col. Lewis arrived, and sent word that it would be better to surrender the key than to get into more trouble.

Telegraphing to Col. Denny, commander of this district at Huntsville, he replied: "Surrender the key." Accompanied by Maj. H. C. Cockerill, the pastor went to the house of Mr. Lewis and handed him the key, saying: "We obey military order, and hand you the key, Col. Lewis, as a member of the Governor's staff." He took it and handed it to McReady, and the interview soon ended. In a few days, being convinced that there was no renewal of martial law as had been asserted, but on the contrary that civil law was in full force, Mr. T. Shackelford, the most prominent lawyer here, and a member of the M. E. Church, South, was asked what legal process was necessary to get possession of our property. He declined to advise, saying: "It is too dangerous to attempt any thing now." Judge William A. Hall and Capt. Reid, of Huntsville, being called upon, gave the necessary instructions and drew up the form of demand to be signed by the trustees and presented to McReady, saying that if he refused to comply they could bring suit against him before any magistrate and put him out in five days.

B. W. Lewis was still a trustee of our Church property. After all the other trustees had signed the demand it was taken to him, and the disciplinary law governing trustees was shown to him. He was then asked as an avowed law-abiding man to sign the paper. After a few moments' earnest thought, he asked: "Will it be necessary for me to sign this if the key is given up?" Being answered that it would not, he said: "Then meet me here to-morrow morning at 9 o'clock."

The next morning he brought McReady with him, who gave up the key quietly. In doing this Mr. Lewis stipulated that in restoring the brick church and the parsonage, the trustees should refund what it had cost him to repair the houses, but that he would assume his proportion of the amount. This was readily agreed to, and thus ended the matter.

McReady still asserted legal claim to the old frame church. No contention was made over it until after our General Conference in 1866. In pursuance of fraternal resolutions adopted by that Conference, a well-accredited minister of the African M. E. Church, traveling through the State organizing Societies, came to Glasgow and succeeded in gathering about twenty members into his Church, most of whom had previously been members of the M. E. Church, South, here. This fact being made known, our trustees made a deed to them for the old frame, because it had been used by our colored members for nearly nineteen years already.

The deed was delivered and recorded, and then a formal demand was made by the A. M. E. Church trustees upon McReady for the delivery of the property to them. He refused, and suit was begun in Circuit Court at once. Before the day of trial arrived, however, better counsels prevailed, and the M. E. Church purchased the property from its owners for two thousand five hundred dollars, which was a very fair valuation.

The membership of the M. E. Church, South, here has varied from one hundred and forty to one hundred and sixty since the war. Deaths, removals, and business failures have greatly diminished its financial strength. The sad train of evils brought in by the war have impaired its spiritual tone and weakened its social power. But it is nevertheless the leading Church in Glasgow to-day.*

Rev. A. Monroe, presiding elder of the Fayette District, gives a very interesting communication in the *St. Louis Christian Advocate* of February 22, as follows:

I am always glad to hear from the other districts through your columns, so perhaps others would be pleased to hear from my field of labor.

I commenced my year's work the 12th of October, and, with the divine blessing, have met my appointments in regular order. Found the preachers at work doing battle for God. Several of our meetings were seasons of refreshing. The quarterly meetings at Rocheport and Glasgow were continued with protracted efforts by their pastors, whose labors were not in vain. At both meetings souls were converted and the Church revived.

The labors of the present quarter were commenced at Sturgeon, in the Middle Grove Circuit. Our house of worship at

---

* Rev. J. O. Swinney, MS.

that place was greatly damaged during the war, but through the untiring efforts of Rev. W. T. Ellington, has been thoroughly repaired and furnished for public service, and seats a large congregation. This is creditable to the community. We are also indebted to our friend in St. Louis who generously gave material aid in time of need. No doubt he will rejoice with those concerned when he hears that the labor and liberality have already been rewarded a thousand-fold by the conversion of souls. A glorious revival of God's work commenced at my quarterly meeting. Great seriousness prevailed from the beginning; the interest increased until Monday, when the power of the Lord was present "to wound and to heal." There were several clear and powerful conversions, and the happy subjects did not wait for the preachers first to publish the good news, but virtually cried with a loud voice: "Come unto me, and I will tell you what he has done for my soul!" I remained over Wednesday night; left the meeting in the hands of Brothers Ellington and Taylor. It was continued many days, as I learn, with great success: eighteen conversions, twenty-three additions to the M. E. Church, South. This is the Lord's doing, and marvelous in our eyes, considering that we were a few months ago no people. We have now forty or fifty members and a comfortable house of worship.

I left Sturgeon, and after a ride of thirteen miles reached the town of Benick, where I had a night appointment. When at the appointed time we repaired to the house of God through mud and water I thought the congregation would be quite small, but was agreeably surprised to find the large church pretty well filled with attentive hearers. This is also a new building—a great achievement for that community. What they need now is a powerful revival of true religion. When we retired the weather was still mild; but, alas for the poor itinerant! morning came, and with it a severe snow-storm from the northwest; ground hard frozen. Friends said: "You must not go; can't make the trip; road as rough as one can imagine; the storm direct in your face; four miles of prairie." But I was responsible for the meeting to commence that night in Huntsville, twelve miles distant, so I said it was useless to confer with flesh and blood. I had breasted many wintery blasts in the last years, and with God's blessing would try it again. So, all things ready, I mounted my old companion in tribulation, and turned my face to the storm. It was a severe trip for man and beast; none more so during my intinerant life; but I was well fortified, and reached Huntsville in less than four hours, without serious injury. Owing to the severity of the weather, the congregations were small. Brothers Swinney and Root were present, and by Saturday night others came: Brothers Richardson, Warren, James, and Broddis. There being so few preachers present, we did but little as a District Conference; but adjourned to meet at Roanoke. All agreed to unite and labor for a good meeting. Up to Tuesday, when I had to leave, there were manifestations of the divine presence and strong indications of good.

From the same source we find a very interesting account given of Chillicothe Station by the pastor, Rev. S. W. Cope. He says: "We have had a precious meeting of three weeks' continuance; had the efficient ministerial aid of Brothers Dockery, Shores, and Metcalf. The results of this somewhat protracted effort are very cheering. The members of the Church are greatly revived, backsliders reclaimed, and sinners awakened and converted to God. During the meeting twenty-nine joined the Church, making in all since Conference forty-seven additions to the membership of our little station. We feel assured that the Lord of hosts has been with us, and will be with us to the end. All agree that it was indeed the work of God. The standard of piety among us has been raised many degrees. Many of us, in our Christian experience, live much nearer heaven than ever before. We breathe a purer, healthier spiritual atmosphere, enjoy a sweeter, holier communion with God, and have a livelier hope and brighter prospect of heaven. Our path is 'as a shining light that shineth more and more unto the perfect day.' Thus we are happy and rejoicing, and expect, beyond the rolling river, in a 'nobler, sweeter song to sing God's power to save.'"

Also, from the same source, Rev. J. D. Vincil, writing from Callao, says: "I wrote you a few days since concerning the opening of a very encouraging revival at this point. The work has been spreading and deepening during the progress of our meeting, embracing every age from the youthful Sabbath-school scholar to the old man. It is, in every view, one of the most remarkable and powerful revivals I have witnessed in my life. I have rarely ever seen so deep and telling a work at so early stage of the meeting. Only six days, and there have been quite a large number of clear, deep, and powerful conversions—over twenty, with twenty valuable accessions to our Church; and it really seems as if the work had just commenced. The community is trembling while the ark of the Lord is moving forward gloriously. Every coming together is crowned with success and blessed results. The work goes on, and the meeting will continue."

The *St. Louis Christian Advocate* contains an important communication from Rev. W. M. Rush, the presiding elder of St. Joseph District, in which he gives an interesting account of his entire field of labor, tells what every preacher is doing, and the condition of every station and circuit in his district. It is indeed *multum in parvo*, "much in little" that is, much history in a nutshell. We give it below, and feel satisfied that it will interest the reader who takes pleasure in our Church history:

I have just completed my second round on the St. Joseph District. I am glad to be able to report a very encouraging progress during the first half of the year. The preachers are all at their respective work; and a more earnest, diligent, and faithful set of men it has never been my privilege to be associated with. Each seems determined to make the most of his opportunities for usefulness, and the Great Head of the Church is crowning their labors with encouraging success.

St. Joseph Station.—Brother Leftwich is emphatically a working man, and his labors have rendered a blessing to the people, not only in his own immediate congregation in the city, where he has had encouraging success, but in the neighborhood where he has conducted a gracious revival of religion, and in other places where he has preached the gospel in its divine power.

Rushville Circuit.—Here Brother Barnett is endearing himself more and more to the people, by his diligence and faithfulness and zeal in the work of the ministry. He goes in and out as a "father among the people," and God makes him a blessing to them, and they love him. He has recently enjoyed a gracious revival at old Sparta.

New Market Circuit.—Here Brother Collet is doing a good work. The first quarterly meeting at Union School-house was protracted with blessed results: about thirty conversions and accessions. Some success also at other points.

Platte City and Weston Circuit.—Brother Austin is, under the blessing of God, doing a good work on this circuit. A gracious revival influence is pervading almost every part of the work. Sinners have been convicted and many have been converted and added to the Church.

Liberty Circuit.—This circuit was left to be supplied at the last Conference. Near the close of the first quarter I appointed Brother Joseph Y. Blakey to take charge of this circuit. Already the prospects are very encouraging. At Parkville we have had a blessed revival, and, the circumstances considered, it may be regarded as a triumph for the Church. I believe that Brother Blakey will be a blessing to that circuit.

Plattsburg Circuit.—This circuit is favored with the labors of Brother Bird, who is literally warning the people day and night with tears. Happy are the people who have so faithful a pastor, a minister so able to dispense to them the word of life. A goodly number have been converted and added to the Church. Brother Bird is doing a very good work in the Church.

Maysville Mission.—A most glorious revival has prevailed on a portion of this charge. My heart was made glad at the second quarterly meeting to witness the fruits of this gracious work. Brother Hurst has been doing a faithful work, and well may he be encouraged.

Savannah Circuit.—This circuit was left to be supplied at our last Conference. We had no supply the first quarter. It was supplied the second quarter by Brother Thomas R. Hedgpeth, who did faithful and acceptable service, but could give to the circuit only a portion of his time. I have now appointed Rev. J. W. Ellis to take charge until next Annual Conference. Some valuable accessions on this circuit this year.

Maysville Circuit.—Here, I think, we have the right man in the right place. Brother Davis is in favor with all the people. No great revival, but a steady onward movement. Success is certain if we are faithful.

Albany Circuit.—Brother Zumwalt has here a wide field for usefulness, and although there is much to discourage, yet the prospects are growing brighter. In Albany particularly our Church has a strong hold. We have had a good number of conversions and some very valuable accessions.

Oregon and Rockfort Circuit.—This circuit, like the last two mentioned, lies in that section where, during the war, our Church was greatly persecuted and desolated. Brother McEwen is doing a good work, and the Church is steadily gaining favor with the people. A number of conversions and accessions since Conference.

The presiding elder reports that he is putting in his time and strength as best he can. Since Conference he has traveled fifteen hundred miles, held twenty-two quarterly meetings, performing at each his official duties, preached one hundred and fifteen times—being an average of between five and six sermons at each quarterly meeting. He has witnessed the gracious manifestations of the divine presence in the salvation of many souls.

The same person gives a summary report of his labors at the close of the year in the following language: "I have just completed my work for the present year on the St. Joseph District, Missouri Conference, and will say it has been to us a year of encouraging success. About one thousand persons have been added to the Church. The tide of public sentiment is greatly in our favor. In Graham, Nodaway County, where last year Brother Hedgpeth was compelled by mob violence to close his quarterly meeting, we held a quarterly meeting two weeks ago. Congregations were large and orderly. Had a good meeting, and nineteen were added to the Church."

Though the war has ended, and the roar of the cannon is no longer heard in the land, persecution is still rife in some sections of the State under the operations of the "test oath," the last instrument of persecution during those troublous times. Indicting, imprisoning, punishing in many ways, and even putting to death persons for not taking an oath—which oath was itself in direct violation of the Constitution and laws of our Federal government.

REV. JESSE FAUBION.

This loyal citizen, this worthy minister of the

gospel and honorable member of the Missouri Conference, M. E. Church, South, met with trying and sore persecution during the war and the prevalence of the "test oath." He has given a plain and straightforward statement of his troubles and sufferings in his own language, as follows:

In the year 1860 I was appointed to the Princeton Mission, Missouri Conference, and settled my family at Lineville, where I remained till the 2d of July, 1861. From the very outbreak of the war persecution commenced against the M. E. Church, South, in that region, and increased in violence until by the first of June of that year it was scarcely possible to hold a meeting without disturbance. These disturbances became so common, and the spirit of lawlessness so fierce against the M. E. Church, South, and especially against me as a minister of that denomination, that for purposes of safety my brethren advised and urged me to abandon that field of labor and seek a home elsewhere, which I did on the 2d of July, 1861. The *pretext* for all this persecution was the allegation that the M. E. Church, South, "*was the cause of the war;*" in connection with which the assertion was often and bitterly made, accompanied with horrid oaths, that as a Church and as ministers of that Church we should not be allowed to remain in the country; that they intended "*to wipe us out*," etc.

From Lineville I went to Callaway County, Mo., and by the advice of the presiding elder of that district I took a supernumerary relation to the Conference, rented a farm and commenced trying to make a living for my family. In September, 1862, about *forty* armed men under the command of Col. Brunce, stationed at Jefferson City, came to my house in my absence, and robbed us of our blankets and all my wearing clothes except what I had on, and took also my saddle-bags, pocket-knife, and even my spectacles. They also took my horse, and when my wife was pleading for him one of the company told her she only wanted him for her husband to ride "*in order to preach d—n lies;*" but they afterward left my horse at the house of a neighbor, where I subsequently got him. After this, in the year 1864, a band of men came under cover of night and took the only horse I had, and which I was never able to recover. In 1865 I moved to Shelby County, Mo., and settled at Shelbyville. On my arrival I found that there had been no preaching there since the inauguration of the "test oath," and it was not considered safe for any man to preach in that community without taking it. The members of the Church were being scattered, and the young members were being led off to dancing parties and other bad places. After surveying the ground I thought that I might just as well be sacrificed as any one else, and in order to get the people out I made an appointment to lecture, which I did two or three times before the people came out in sufficient numbers to encourage me to make an appointment for preaching.

I then preached several days during Christmas week, when the people came out in such great numbers that the friends of the new law compelling a minister to swear fealty to human government before he could be allowed to obey his divine Master were greatly exasperated, and on February 6, 1866, I was arrested upon a charge of preaching without taking the oath of loyalty. The County Court being in session, I was brought for trial before *one of that body*—viz., Mr. Robert Lair. The arrest was made by the deputy sheriff (Mr. James Collier), and the prosecution conducted by Attorney M. J. Mandeville, who insisted that it was *an aggravated case*. He said that the prisoner had not only *preached*, but had also *lectured*—the whole lecture being used to cover up the *infamy of the crime*—and said that the bond should be made *strong*, to prevent the prisoner from making his escape.

The trial being ended—if that may be called a trial where both the spirit and letter of the law are disregarded, for this county justice had no jurisdiction of the case—I was compelled to give bond in the sum of one thousand dollars for my appearance at the next term of the Circuit Court, or go to prison.

From the best testimony I could get, Lieut. William Holliday, County Clerk and a member of the M. E. Church, was the main mover in that act of persecution, for he was both plaintiff and witness in the case. The 14th and 15th of February, 1866, was the time appointed for holding the quarterly meeting for Shelbyville Circuit. Between the time of my arrest and the time for holding the meeting a man, who is a prominent member of the

M. E. Church, told our members that they had better use their influence to prevent us from holding the meeting, for if we did not cease preaching without taking the oath blood would be shed. But, notwithstanding the threats of mob violence and the prevailing excitement in the community, Brother Newland, presiding elder of the district, came and held the meeting without any material disturbance.

On Saturday night of this meeting, and on Monday morning and night after it closed, circumstances took place which are very significant; and I merely mention them and leave them to speak for themselves. I was living in a house which had four distinct tenements, divided by partitions, all of which were occupied at that time. Ou Saturday night, *after we were gone to bed, one of these families moved out.* On Monday morning another moved out; and on that night, some time before day, this building, with all its tenements, was consumed by fire, the fire originating in a part of the building where there had been no fire during the winter. In this fire we lost every thing, and very narrowly escaped with our lives.

At the sitting of the May term of the Circuit Court, 1866, I appeared, and answered to my name when called, in connection with the names of other alleged criminals, when my securities were released, and my case was referred to the grand jury in and for Shelby County, Mo., who, being strictly charged by his honor, Judge Harrison, in regard to ministers of the gospel guilty of the crime of preaching without taking the oath, found me guilty in three separate cases, to answer to which I was held to bail in the sum of *three thousand dollars.* Messrs. C. R. Cotton, J. R. Taylor, William Cotton, H. Montgomery, J. Muldrow, W. Gouch, T. Swearingen, Mr. Vaughn, and J. M. Ennis were the noble men who went on my bond, for which act of kindness to me Mr. Gouch was disfranchised. I wish to mention in this connection that Hon. Mr. Hawkins, of Canton, Mo., and H. S. Lipscomb, of Palmyra, volunteered their professional services, and saw me through this persecution in the courts until my case was dismissed. But notwithstanding threats of violence—such as the shedding of blood, riding on a rail, etc.—I continued to preach until the November term of the court, when my case was continued, I being required to give bond with new securities for my appearance at the next term of court, when it was finally dismissed because the Supreme Court of the United States had pronounced the test oath null and void.

REV. S. W. BERGIN,
a faithful and useful minister of the M. E. Church, South, gives the following plain and unvarnished narrative of his persecution during the war and under the test oath:

Only for the sake of our beloved Church, in her just and reasonable request for incidents relating to the persecution of her ministers, would I write this brief sketch of our wrongs in Harrison County. You will please accept this as a true history of our persecutions here during the time of our late troubles, and pardon me for referring to myself as the chief sufferer in this portion of our Lord's vineyard.

Soon as the war commenced I seemed to be an object marked for destruction. Our preachers (W. C. Martin, G. C. Brown, and George N. Newton) sent to this work all retired from the post of danger, leaving me to stem the torrent as best I could. Our people still desired preaching, and, yielding to their wishes, I kept up regular appointments at various places on our circuit. Meanwhile I was shunned, slandered, insulted, and threatened.

The rope, the bullet, confiscation, etc., were all nothing more than my due! I often looked for death or ill treatment by the roadside or at the place of public worship. Flags waved over me while preaching, and many took pleasure in reproaching me.

A public school-house was burned to prevent my ministrations in that quarter. The Union League at Eagleville decreed my banishment, and an armed band brought me the unwelcome tidings, giving me only ten days to escape. The provost-marshal (H. T. Combs) refused to give me a hearing, and favored my exile. I trusted in God, and was delivered from the destroyer. But the new Constitution came, crowned with the terrible oath of loyalty, and, as I could neither bow the knee to Baal nor render him honor, I must no longer preach Jesus and the resurrection. I resorted to prayer and class meetings. But *this* was too much, for the law forbade teaching; and, gathering strength and boldness from public mandate, an attempt was made for my indictment before the grand jury.

Failing in this, effectual means were to be used in seizing and binding me, at Snellsville, and beating me with rods. I moved my appointment to another place. About this time I was reorganizing two classes of my torn and scattered members, and a prominent member of the M. E. Church told me that *this* was the occasion of the threatened treatment.

But my cup of sorrow was not yet full. In May, 1867, a time ever dark in memory's history, we attempted to hold a quarterly meeting in Snellsville, at a home reared by voluntary subscription from our members and others for school and other public services. A night or two preceding its commencement a party met there and decided that we should not hold the meeting at that place, which becoming known, we moved to Brother Woodard's, in the immediate neighborhood. In this assembly were members of other denominations. Whereupon a plan was originated, doubtless, to break up by mobbing the meeting, which had progressed finely on Saturday. Under the disguise of keeping order, a constable was employed with a writ, who arrested my son on Saturday night or Sunday morning before day, and was proceeding on his way to Snellsville to bind him to keep the peace, when an armed mob arose out of ambush, seized the prisoner, dragged him through the brush and swollen creek, tore off his clothes, beat and mangled him miserably, stamped him in the face, tarred him, then left him lying on the ground. He had been a regular Confederate soldier, but was then a peaceable man, a member of the Church, and was quietly attending the meeting. They also struck my eldest son, a local preacher, across the face with a club, inflicting a deep scar, and producing indistinctness of vision for life.

I will here record another incident relating to that eminent servant of God, William Ketron. By request he came up to give us a quarterly meeting at McCollum's School-house. But services had hardly commenced when an armed band came rushing up, took the old man out of the house, and *disregarding his loyal papers*, hurried him off to Eagleville, where he was subjected to the form of a sham trial. Finding no fault in him, they released him, but compelled him to leave immediately for home. It was late in the evening. He came by my house, depressed in spirit and suffering from heat and fatigue.

All these things and many others occurred here, doubtless,

for the manifest design of breaking up our Church in this place. But she still lives; and now a traveling preacher and his family live peaceably in my house, flushed with the success that attends his labors, and rejoicing in the prospect of a bright future. The Lord be praised for our happy and wonderful deliverance!

This year is characterized by a general visitation of the Holy Spirit to the M. E. Church, South— glorious "times of refreshing from the presence of the Lord." The *St. Louis Christian Advocate* is teeming with revival news from all parts of the State. Hundreds and thousands of conversions and additions to the Church are reported by the faithful embassadors of Christ. The work of grace in the Church is no less wonderful: backsliders called home from their wanderings, the standard of Christian experience greatly elevated, and a more complete consecration to the service of God.

Rev. W. A. Tarwater speaks encouragingly of his work on the Flint Hill Circuit. Had revivals at several of his appointments, assisted in his protracted meetings by Rev. J. Allen, whose ministrations were blessed of God in the conversion of souls and the edification of believers—fifty-eight accessions to the Church during the year.

Rev. T. B. King gives a good account of his work at Richmond. A new and excellent house of worship was dedicated to the service of God. Dr. W. M. Leftwich, of St. Joseph, officiated in the dedicatory service. The meeting was continued, and God filled the new church with the majesty, power, and glory of his presence, signifying thereby his recognition of the dedication. The hearts of God's people were filled to overflowing and were turned like "streams in the south," and they were heard to say: "The Lord has done great things for us, whereof we are glad." Brothers Devlin and Proctor assisted in the meeting, preaching the gospel in its simplicity, purity, and power. Thirty-eight persons united with the Church.

The labors of Rev. R. A. Austin on the Weston and Platte City Circuit are being crowned with great success. He had an unusually interesting revival at Platte City, in which sixty persons experienced the converting grace of God and were made to rejoice in his great salvation from the power of Satan and the dominion of sin, fifty-five of whom enlisted in the service of Christ and avouched themselves to be on the Lord's side by joining the Church. A large proportion of the converts were old men and heads of families, who proved the genuineness of their religion by erecting domestic altars around which they gathered their families for morning and evening sacrifice of prayer and praise to the Father of Lights, from whom cometh every good and perfect gift. About twenty promising young men were made to feel the joy of pardoned sin, two or three of whom it is thought will become preachers. The influence of the revival pervaded the entire community, and religion became the all-absorbing theme. It also reached the colored people, a number of whom embraced religion and united with our Church. They have obtained permission to build a gallery in our church for their accommodation, and are now raising the money for that purpose. The revival has visited every appointment on the circuit except one, and Brother Austin was making arrangements and rallying his forces to besiege it as early as practicable. Dr. Leftwich and Rev. Catlin constituted his help in the meetings. To the present time the membership of the Church has been increased by one hundred and twenty-five persons.

Liberty Circuit, under the pastoral care of Rev. J. Y. Blakey, is also being visited with the convicting and converting power of the Holy Spirit. At several different points they have been favored with gracious revivals. Had a joyous time at Faubion Chapel, where God gloriously manifested his great power in the salvation of immortal souls. They also had an interesting time at Missouri City. The members there manifested their zeal for the Lord by building a neat and convenient house of worship. The accomplishment of this enterprise was very creditable to them in view of their small membership and financial weakness. The house is not only built, but all indebtedness has been liquidated. They demonstrated the truthfulness of the old familiar adage: "Where there is a will there is a way." At the preacher's last report seventy-five persons had their names enrolled in the Church register. Revs. S. H. Newton and L. W. Cooper rendered ministerial help in the meetings.

Rev. W. E. Dockery, presiding elder of Chillicothe District, speaks words full of cheer concerning his field of labor. They are having revivals in almost every charge in his district—one in full blast at Carrollton attracting public attention and bringing the community under its sacred power. When last reported forty-one had joined the army of the Lord and were fighting the good fight of faith under the banner of Prince Immanuel. It is a good sign to see persons working for their Master immediately after they are converted. It is one of the satisfactory evidences of their spiritual regeneration—that they have passed from the death of sin into the life of Christ. "I must go and tell it to others" is one of the first feelings of him who is "born again." Indeed, is not the interest we feel for the salvation of sinners a very good criterion by which to judge our religion?

"Two new churches completed and paid for this year—one at Richmond, the other at Chillicothe; two others commenced—one at Carrollton, the other at Breckenridge, Gallatin Circuit; also working on the old churches and putting them in good repair. Now, as the war is over, they are in possession of all their churches in the district. Five hundred persons have united with the Church, and peace prevails in all their borders. The presiding elder rejoices in the personal realization of the fact that Chillicothe District is not dead, but alive and working earnestly in the Lord's vineyard, while their labors are crowned with glorious success. We are not at all surprised at his rejoicing, for such a blessed state of things was enough to make him jubilant."

CHAPTER XII.

MISSOURI CONFERENCE.

Statistical Business—Increase of Membership—Eighty-seven Preachers Receive Their Appointments—Biography of Rev. W. G. Caples—Incident in the Early History of Bishop Marvin—A Good Report of Chillicothe District by Rev. W. E. Dockery—Sketch of Rev. E. R. Miller's Life and Work by Himself—Rev. T. B. King Gives a Good Report of His Field of Labor—Other Interesting Accounts of Revivals by Revs. D. C. Blackwell, J. R. Taylor, and Other Preachers.

ON September 4, 1867, the fifty-first session of the Missouri Conference was opened by Bishop Marvin at Macon City, Mo., John D. Vincil elected Secretary.

The following preachers were admitted on trial: W. McK. Gilliam, S. L. Woody, P. D. Vandeventer, W. L. Blackwell, E. Carlyle, H. W. Currin, J. Y. Blakey, G. Tanquery, W. F. Thrasher, H. P. Bond, J. W. Jordan. Admitted into full connection: T. Penn, J. A. Mumpower, B. F. Zumwalt, J. Metcalf, and T. B. King; and were also elected and ordained elders. Local preachers elected and ordained deacons: J. S. Hardgrove, S. L. Woody, E. Carlyle, W. D. Fortune, J. Y. Blakey, and G. Tanquery. The following traveling preachers were elected and ordained elders: J. King, N. P. Halsey, and H. A. Davis. Located this year: F. A. Savage, H. S. McEwin, S. K. Fowler, and J. F. Riggs. Supernumerary: J. O.

(284)

Swinney, T. Hurst, and A. Albright. G. Fenton and M. L. Eads, superannuated.

Reported this year: White members, 13,778; colored members, 324; local preachers, 105. Increase in membership over last year, 2,250.

Having enjoyed the pleasant associations of another Annual Conference, and being greatly encouraged by the success of the previous year, the preachers, eighty-seven in number, received their appointments and went out "quickly" on their way rejoicing in hope of another successful year in preaching the gospel and in the great work of saving immortal souls. Nothing delights them so much and makes them so happy as to see sinners converted and prodigals returning to their heavenly Father's house.

WILLIAM G. CAPLES.

The biography of this eminently great and good man should have appeared in the Conference year of his death, but we had written the history of that year before we received a suitable historic sketch of his ministerial life and character. We feel satisfied, however, that it will be read with no less interest let it appear in whatever part of this history it may. The biography of one so extensively known and so universally admired will itself attract attention and elicit interest regardless of every thing else. It has been furnished by one who was long and intimately acquainted with him, and reads as follows:

William Goff Caples was a man of such commanding abilities, and so naturally a leader, that his personal impress will long abide with the M. E. Church, South. His very name is a household word to-day in the older Methodist families throughout all North Missouri. His memory therefore deserves more than a passing mention. A short sketch of his ministerial character ought to have a place in this history. As we recall him, how vividly he stands before us! Above the medium height, and of somewhat angular form, he comes with a slouching gait, but with a firm tread; while he carries his head slightly advanced, and looks altogether like a man moving forward with a purpose. Upon a nearer view his swarthy complexion and furrowed lines about his brow and mouth become visible.

It is only when he speaks, however, that his wonderfully expressive and mobile countenance lights up, and the real man begins to appear. Power and gentleness, intelligence and sagacity all seem blended in the glance of that large, clear, black eye, while firmness and courage are unmistakably written on his massive lower jaw, and his mouth is formed to express all human emotions at will.

You would say he was a homely man at first sight, but never after you knew him well. There was a mysterious power within that somehow completely transformed the outer man.

He was one who seemed to hold life as a happy treasure, which he had found in Jesus Christ. He was evermore the glad immortal grasping two worlds as verily his own. It was a common form of greeting with him to say to a brother: "God bless your immortality!" Yet he was no sentimental fanatic. His was a stalwart faith, working on the Pauline model of true manliness, ever ready to face all the facts of this life with a cheerful and unfaltering spirit. If there was any excess of enthusiasm in him, it was in that he sometimes fancied that he could discern the hand of God working in the affairs of men so as to forecast his future providences. Upon some occasions he almost claimed prophetic visions. Perhaps it was this high degree of impressibility and exalted fervor which gave him such extraordinary supremacy over men. While thus lifted up in spirit almost to the third heavens, the grandeur of his conceptions and the great boldness of his utterances attracted and entranced all who heard him. Many now living can testify to the spiritual power which sometimes seemed to be given him in the pulpit. If so many, among the thousands converted under his ministry, have remained steadfast in the faith, it was not from any thing like a logical conviction of the truth as presented by him. His sermons were not constructed that way. But it was because his direct vehement deliverance of the truth so penetrated their consciousness as to awaken a compulsory answer from them to the felt claims of God upon their souls.

So deep, so pungent, so all-pervading was the experience wrought in them that no after experiences could ever expunge the records of consciousness made in that hour. He was what has been not inaptly termed a "Holy Ghost preacher." He was not a student of books. He *studied* the Bible, and the Bible alone—studied it on his knees, and from it he drew his inspiration, and by it sought to be "thoroughly furnished unto every good word and work."

He loved to preach, because he loved men with all the constraints of Christly love. He was eminently social. Magnanimous, generous, with lively sensibilities and tender sympathies, he could say what he would and you felt that he loved you. Few could withstand the spell of his personal magnetism. His marvelous powers of wit, humor, and mimicry sometimes led him beyond the limits of propriety—sometimes wounded the feelings of the oversensitive; sometimes called down upon him the censure of his sober friends. But his joyous, loving spirit was irrepressible. Nothing could daunt him, nothing could dry up the fountains of immortal joy and hope which were constantly welling up from the depths of his heart. As occasion required, his versatility to make a quick and complete transition from one state of mind to another was simply marvelous. His unbent bow could in a moment be strung again, and the arrow directed to the intended mark.

He has had many imitators, but for the most part their humor has been simple frivolity, and their wit a mere play upon words. They lacked that deep under-current of brotherly love which was the well-spring that gave coloring to all his witticisms. If he lashed the lazy idler, or berated and shamed the sluggish soul; if he transfixed the scoffer with pitiless ridicule, or played the pretentious hypocrite, he did it with the same intent that he wept with the mourner, or whispered words of the tenderest sympathy and comfort to the disconsolate soul; it was that he might do them good for the love of Christ.

Having once counted the cost, his purpose never flagged to be true to the Master and to be ready to answer to every call as a minister of the gospel. In what he conceived to be duty, or in defense of that which he deemed to be right, he was ever bold, sometimes even rash. No work was too hard for him; for he was a model itinerant, and accepted his appointment as having been assigned to him by the great Head of the Church. If the charge he served would not support his family, he could and did do it, even if he had to cut cord-wood and haul it to market.

Next to God he loved the Church and studied to direct her resources and spiritual energies into the widest fields of usefulness. To him the Church in Missouri is largely indebted for that system of education that is now in successful operation. Central College, supplemented and supported by district high schools, was his plan for which he labored with unremitting zeal. He insisted upon and eloquently advocated at every Conference a thorough course of theological study for the young preachers. Uneducated himself, he was not blind to the demand for that ability and skill which critical book knowledge alone can give to combat successfully the errors of the times.

But for highest spiritual education, for greatest development of the heart, and for the thorough knowledge of human nature which can make a man wise to win souls, he magnified what he loved to call the "Methodist college on horseback"—an *untrammeled itinerancy.*

What a man he was at Conference! His spirit seemed to pervade the whole body. He knew by heart what it was to be on the circuit, in the station, around the district. He knew the people everywhere, and, quick to discern character, he soon sized the preachers, and he loved to look over the whole field as the workers stood before him. Sometimes with admirable sagacity and tact he could say, or do, or look just the right things to tone up or to tone down, to encourage or restrain every single preacher there. A very notable effect of his personal bearing at these annual reunions was the contagiousness of his brotherly love. It tended to inspire and unify the Conference to such a degree that the Missouri Conference became noted among the Conferences for the good-will and kindly consideration which each member habitually entertained for every other member.

What fervency, what pathos there was in his Conference prayers! While he talked with Jesus, entreating his constant leadership and care the coming year for that devoted band of consecrated heralds, the very lowliest one there felt himself borne upward into a clearer, purer atmosphere of faith, hope, and love. The Holy Ghost would come down and baptize every soul with renewed unction, until each heart burned with a more ardent devotion to Jesus and his word. So it was at the Conference in 1863. Surely God was preparing his messengers in that hour for the baptism of persecution and blood so soon to overtake them.

Brother Caples came to Glasgow that year with the most anxious solicitude. This was one of the oldest Churches in the State. It was a large slave-holding community, and the center of extensive trade and great wealth. Being a point of so much importance, he was selected as the one perhaps best qualified to meet the peculiar demands upon the ministry during those troublous times. With a few exceptions, to be mentioned hereafter, the membership of the Church at that time were all, in a greater or less degree, what were known as Southern sympathizers. The opinions and position of Brother Caples were well understood. He had at one time started out as chaplain of a company recruited in Chariton County for Price's army, but was captured at Blackwater and kept prisoner in McDowell's College, St. Louis, for several months.

Being released at last on parole, he had resumed pastoral work in the summer of 1863. But this incident had made him a marked man in military circles. The personal difficulties and dangers which such a position involved at that time he never seemed to realize. He had unbounded confidence in the ultimate success of the South, for he was an ardent adherent of the State's rights doctrine. So strong were his convictions that among supposed friends privately he did not restrain the free expression of his views and feelings. It was this confidence in future results, in professed friends around him, that led to all the trials and indignities to which he was subsequently subjected.

No counsels of caution were heeded. Even those who loved

19

him and coincided in view with him were often alarmed for him as they listened to his rash utterances. But such was the man. He believed that he was right and that God was on his side, and he knew no fear, and disdained policy. The rift in the Church here had already begun. It was born in the spirit of purely political policy, and took definite shape and action in the fall and winter of 1864. As the months passed by the Federal authorities become more and more watchful and exacting. Spies were set to watch Brother Caples. Betrayed by some whom he trusted, he soon became extremely obnoxious to the military commander here. Gen. C. B. Fisk said: "That man Caples is doing us more harm than could a whole regiment of rebels." In vain was Brother Caples steadfastly consistent in all his ministrations. In vain were all his sermons and his prayers of a purely religious character, for *his private talk spread more rapidly and had greater effect than did all his pastoral labors.* From that hour he was "spotted." He was ordered, under forfeit of his life, to keep open the telegraph line coming into Glasgow. He did the work daily, and reported at head-quarters in true military style. Troops were made to quarter on him frequently. Threats were made against him, only to call forth a smile of confident safety. Being under parole in a garrisoned town among life-long friends, he laughed at the thought of danger.

No doubt his cheerfulness and courage were largely due to the fixed purpose he had formed. It was his cherished belief that he had a mission to fulfill *after* the war. The conflict over, peace restored, and the South victorious, he believed that his work would be to allay all smoldering animosities in Northwest Missouri, to comfort the sick, the wounded, the crippled, the widows and orphans—in short, to be a minister of consolation everywhere. To do this successfully he said it was better that he should suffer all that might befall him, for so only could he be effectually brought into full sympathy with the suffering. Such was his faith and his consecrated purpose on the day when that strangely directed shell struck him the fatal blow. Had he lived a little longer, he would most probably—indeed, most certainly—have been tortured to death by the same man who wantonly murdered Robinson, Price, Haston, and others in this vicinity.

May we not suppose that this firm believer in special providences was watched over and taken from the evil to come just at the time when his faith, fortitude, and consecrated purpose were all in full tide of earnest activity? So we estimate him now. The great judgment-day alone can perfectly reveal the character of this wondrously gifted man.*

The following is a short, thrilling incident given in a secular paper by Rev. S. W. Cope. Referring to the time of the incident, the writer says:

The Church is being sorely tried, her faith is being put to the severest test, the wheels of Zion are clogged, and the powers of darkness are seemingly too great for the forces of the Church. In their discouragement some waver and others give up in despair. At this juncture of the meeting there is a large audience seated, waiting to hear preaching. Comparatively a young-looking man is in the pulpit. His personal appearance is not at all commanding or prepossessing. He is known to the Church, however, as one worthy of her confidence. Like Barnabas, "he is a good man, and full of the Holy Ghost and of faith." The Church is in sympathy with him, and while he preaches she is engaged in earnest and agonizing prayer. The preacher, comprehending the situation, casts himself on God for help. The help came, mighty to save. Divine and human agencies are combined, and victory through our Lord Jesus Christ is the glorious result.

In the midst of the sermon the preacher seemed to be brought face to face with the devil. Now it is a hand-to-hand fight. With a sudden stamp of his foot, the preacher exclaimed: "Begone! Get ye out and away from here, Satan!" The powers of darkness gave way, and the enemy disappeared. These were words of all-conquering faith, and with their utterance came the turning point, followed by a succession of victories the most grand and glorious. The preacher was none other than our beloved E. M. Marvin, subsequently one of the bishops of the M. E. Church, South, than whom no one ever stood higher in the confidence of the Church and in favor with the people.

---

*Rev. J. O. Swinney, MS.

Rev. W. E. Dockery gives a good report of the Chillicothe District, in the *St. Louis Christian Advocate* of February 12, 1868:

I make the following as my first report from Chillicothe District: The preachers are all well, and doing good work in the service of their Master. The spiritual condition of our people is improving; family religion is becoming more common; prayer-meetings are well attended, and other means of grace are not neglected; but the best of all, God is with us.

The power of God is gloriously manifested at our quarterly meetings in the salvation of sinners. Four hundred accessions to the Church, and about the same number of conversions since Conference! Spring Hill has been blessed with a glorious revival of religion. Our quarterly meeting for that circuit resulted in thirty-two accessions. They were in debt five hundred dollars for their church, which we had the good fortune to raise, Brother James Wynn giving one hundred dollars, the debt being due him. Brother Cope, the preacher in charge, is the right man in the right place.

Brother Shores, of Gallatin Circuit, will soon have our new church in Breckenridge completed. His charge is in a good condition. Brother Penny, of Kingston Mission, is laboring earnestly and looking anxiously for the fruit of his labors. The Church at Millville, under the judicious care of Brother Alexander, is advancing. Brother Dines, of Richmond Station, is preaching to large and attentive congregations; and Sister Dines is visiting and praying with the membership. Brother Blakey, of Camden Circuit, is working faithfully in the Lord's vineyard. May God bless him and his good people!

Carrollton Circuit is doing well. Brother Devlin labors earnestly and faithfully, day and night, all the time, and his labors are rewarded with a revival almost at every appointment. The energetic Carlyle, of Milan Circuit, is not idle, but is extending his borders along the Iowa line. More than one hundred persons have been added to the Church in the bounds of his work since Conference.

Brother S. S. Hardin will take charge of Lineville Circuit. This new field of labor promises well. Chillicothe Mission is moving forward successfully under the efficient labors of the pastor, Brother Jordan. Brother Warren is addressing himself to the work of Linneus Circuit with a hearty good-will.

Chillicothe Station, with Brother Miller as pastor, is prospering. His congregations are large and appreciative, and he is working and praying for a gracious revival.

REV. E. K. MILLER.

The reader will no doubt be highly interested in the following sketch of the ministerial life and work of one whose career has been characterized by great success and usefulness, and whose genial nature and noble character have given him a high and influential position in the Church. Yes, one, among others, of whom Missouri may well be proud —ay, proud of being the country in which such men were born and raised. But read the sketch, written by himself:

I was licensed to preach by the Quarterly Conference of Paris Circuit, at Spencer Chapel, May, 1851, Rev. Jacob Lannius, presiding elder. Preached my first sermon one week later, at the old town of Clinton, Monroe County. By the same Conference I was recommended to the traveling connection, and was admitted on trial in the Missouri Conference of 1851, at Fayette, Bishop Capers presiding. The last official act of my presiding elder, Rev. J. Lannius, was the presentation of my recommendation. He was taken sick soon after, and died within a week from the adjournment of Conference. He was a great and good man, but was cut down in the prime of life and in the midst of great usefulness, at the age of 37 years.

I was appointed junior preacher on the Columbia Circuit. Rev. R. P. Holt was preacher in charge. He still lives, though in "age and feebleness extreme." My association with him and his kind family was interruptedly pleasant and profitable to me. It was most fortunate for the young preacher that he was placed under the care of so good and true a man. After the death of Brother Lannius, Brother A. Monroe was appointed to the Columbia District. This was my first acquaintance with this great and good man. It was the beginning of an acquaintance which ripened, notwithstanding our great disparity in age, into great affection and intimacy. I learned to love him greatly, and to reverence him as I did no other man. He was indeed a true father in Israel to me to the end of his life. More than to any other man Missouri Methodism is indebted to Rev. A. Monroe for laying the foundations of our Church, deep and strong, all over this great State. A great preacher, for those early times—indeed for any period—sound in doctrine, eminently wise in counsel, indefatigable in labor, he did what should be done to build up and establish Methodism in Missouri.

The Columbia Circuit at that time embraced the whole of Boone County, except Rocheport, which is now Columbia Station. Ashland Circuit, Mount Zion Circuit, and the country embraced by Sturgeon and Centralia were all included in that first circuit. There were no railroads then, and no towns except Columbia. I preached regularly at old Brother Roberts's, on whose farm the present town of Ashland was located. I had appointments in the country, near where the towns of Sturgeon and Centralia are now located.

The year, on the whole, was a very pleasant and profitable one to me. The people, except a few at the beginning, were very kind to the young preacher. They encouraged and helped him in his weakness and unworthiness. Many precious names come up before me while I write. I cannot forbear to mention a few of them—some still living, others have passed on before. There is Brother McAlister, at whose home I found shelter and encouragement when I first came to the circuit. He still lives, the patriarch of Methodism in Columbia. His faithful wife went to heaven only a year ago, full of years and ripe in Christian character and experience. It was my privilege, after thirty years, to be pastor again at Columbia, where I found these and a few others of the old members to greet me, now among the old men of the Conference. Then there was D. B. Cunningham, near Nashville, still living, and his children all living and in the Church. Then there was J. H. McNeill's, the home of the young preacher, and his precious wife, then an invalid. I owe much to that consecrated woman—to her prayers, her counsels, and her words of encouragement, when I was ready to give up in despair and yield to the temptation to give up the ministry. She still lives in Davies County with her children—the same holy, Christian woman. Moses U. Payne lived in the bounds of this circuit. He was a great help in many ways to the young preacher. No truer man to the Church! He still lives, and is known throughout the Church for his devotion to Southern Methodism—famous for his large liberality and sterling Christian character. One other name I must mention—that of Brother John Reed, who was a member of Mount Zion, and is still a member at that place. He is now nearly ninety years of age. A grand old Roman, he has always been true, and for scores of years has been a tower of strength in the Church. Many others I could mention, but space forbids. Their names are in the book of life.

In the fall of 1852 the Conference met at St. Joseph. The journey from Columbia to the seat of the Conference, a distance of two hundred miles, was made on horseback. Bishop Paine presided over the session of the Conference. It was here I first saw the now venerable Dr. McAnally, and heard him preach. It was his first visit to our Conference. Dr. Sehon, the Missionary Secretary, was present. At this Conference I was sent to Edina Circuit, Rev. A. Monroe, presiding elder. This circuit then embraced the whole of Knox County, with appointments in every adjoining county, extending from Emerson, Marion County, to Sandhill, Scotland County, and from Lewis to Macon Counties east and west. It was a three-weeks circuit, with appointments for every day in the week except Monday; and from two to three appointments every Sabbath. These appointments were from six to ten miles apart. This was a grand field. The country was new, the people hospitable and kind, and generally disposed to hear the word preached, and we had some very gracious revivals. At Newark there were a great many Universalists. Rev. W. M. Rush assisted me at the meeting, preached a series of sermons against universalism with telling effect. Six leading Universalists of the town and vicinity came to the altar of prayer at one time; were converted, and became members of the Church. At Sandhill we had a glorious meeting. One of the converts of this meeting was George Primrose, who subsequently joined the Missouri Conference and afterward distinguished himself as chaplain in the Southern army, by his labors in the hospitals and looking after the sick and wounded and dying, until his name throughout his division was the synonym for self-sacrifice and tender, loving care for the suffering soldiers. He and his good wife have long since entered into rest.

After a delightful pastorate of two years on the Edina Circuit, I was sent to Canton. This was a new station, organized perhaps the year before. Rev. R. H. Jordan was my presiding elder. Rev. A. Monroe had been sent to take charge of our new mission field in Kansas. Canton at this time was a flourishing young town, a place of considerable importance. La Grange, seven miles below, was also a station, and at that time was one of the most flourishing towns on the river. A place of great wealth, where our Church was strong at that time. Rev. H. M. Turner was appointed to this charge. Two months afterward he died, and I was with him during most of his sickness, heard his last testimony, and closed his eyes and laid him away to rest. He was a good man and died in great peace. After the death of Brother Turner the two charges, La Grange and Canton, were united and I was put in charge of both. It seemed the best that could be done, but the demands of each place were too great to be met by such a division of labor. The result was not very satisfactory, though the year passed very pleasantly and with some success.

In the fall of 1855 the Conference met at Richmond, Bishop Early presiding. This was his first visit to the West. He was a rigid parliamentarian, and to our free and easy Western men he was almost a terror for the first day or two of the Conference. The drill was needed, however, and we soon learned to admire the courtly man and love him for his earnest Christian spirit. Bishop Early was a great man, and unique as great. He was born to rule. In political life he would have taken a high position, and been a leader in the State, as he was for so long a period in the Church.

At the close of this Conference I was sent to Shelbyville Circuit. This circuit then embraced most of Shelby County, with two appointments in Marion, Andrew Chapel, and Philadelphia. The Hannibal and St. Joseph railroad had not been built. Shelbina, Clarence, and Hunnewell were not in existence. But the entire county was traveled over by the preachers of the Shelbyville Circuit, and in every neighborhood we had an appointment and class-meeting. Shelbina, Clarence,

Novelty, Hunnewell, and Philadelphia Circuits are now composed largely of the territory, with many of the surviving members, of that old circuit. Rev. Joab Spencer was my junior preacher this year—his first year in the ministry. He was an admirable young man, and our association was of the most pleasant character—the beginning of an affectionate friendship, that has continued to this day, growing and strengthening with the passing years. This year was one of the happiest and most successful of my ministry. Many hundreds were converted and added to the Church. Had many gracious revivals at many points on the circuit, notably at Shelbyville, Philadelphia, B. Chapel, North River Camp, and a point not very far from the present town of Hunnewell. Many of the converts of this meeting are still living, and many have fallen asleep. Quite a number now on the roll of the itinerancy were members of my charge at that time—E. M. Bounds, W. W. McMurry, J. R. Taylor, and the young brothers, Frank and James Taylor, little boys then, were practicing for the itinerancy, by looking after the preacher's horse and running down the yellow-legged chickens when the preacher came to the hospitable home of their father, one of the stanchest Methodists and best of men, with a Christian wife, his equal in goodness and devotion to the Church. There too was J. B. Short, the companion of McMurry, who entered the ministry and went as a preacher to Oregon, and died soon after in the triumphs of faith. He was a young man of great promise. His short ministry in Oregon made a profound impression, and the brilliant young Missourian is remembered in that far off land by many to this day. There were so many names of good and true men and women of that circuit at that time of whom I would gladly speak: the Marmadukes, the Cottons, Dines, Ralphs, the saintly Sigler, for many years a traveling preacher, until failing health compelled him to retire; Dr. Irwin, good and true, and his Christian wife; the Shackelfords, the Hollidays, the Vandivers, the Lyells, and a host of others, all good and true, whose names are in the book of life. Indeed, our Church was composed of the best material of the country, and as the result, then as now, Methodism dominated that entire country. My brief pastorate of the Shelbyville Circuit was one of the brighest years of my itinerant life.

In the fall of 1856 the Conference met at Louisiana. Bishop Pierce presided. This was his first visit to the Missouri Conference. He was at the height of his fame, and he more than met the expectation of the people and the members of the Conference. His sermon on the Sabbath of the Conference was absolutely overwhelming, literally swept every thing before it. Saint and sinner mingled in one promiscuous shout of praise to God. Never before, nor since, have I witnessed such an effect upon an audience.

At this Conference I was sent to St. Joseph, very unexpectedly to me and the good people of Shelbyville. Bishop Pierce was then, and continued to be as long as he lived, a one-year man, and believed in frequent changes. For that early time, it was perhaps wise and generally for the best; but times and circumstances have greatly changed, and what was then wise policy would, as a general rule, be unwise policy now.

I went to my new and responsible charge with fear and trembling. The entire distance of two hundred miles across the State, with wife and little one, was made by private conveyance. What a change since then! I was cordially received, and had two very prosperous and happy years. The Lord was with me in blessings upon my own soul and my unworthy ministry. We then occupied the old brick church at the corner of Felix and Third Streets. The first year we had a glorious revival in the old house. There were, as well as I remember, about sixty conversions and additions to the Church. Some of the converts of that meeting are still members, good and true: some in Francis Street Church and some in Tenth Street charge. One is in the ministry, Rev. Henry Kay, of the Missouri Conference, the son of James Kay, who is now a member of Francis Street Church, and who has been for forty years a strong pillar of our cause in St. Joseph. Also a young man whose name escapes me, but who, as I learn, became a Presbyterian minister.

In 1857 the old church was sold and the site of Francis Street Church was selected. The ground was donated by Rev. J. T. Hoagland for that purpose, and in the fall and winter of 1857–58 the present church was erected. We moved into the basement the first Sabbath in March, 1858, and continued to occupy it during the rest of the year. The audience-room was finished on the inside the following year, under the ministry of Rev. N. G. Berryman, and was dedicated in the summer of 1858 by Rev. R. A. Young, now and for many years at Nashville, Tenn. Even at that early date the Church was strong in membership and piety. It was then, and has always been, a very spiritual Church. Many of the best and most solid and intelligent men and women of the city constitute the membership. It was then the leading Church of the city, and to this day Southern Methodism is the prominent Protestant Church of St. Joseph, in the spirituality and number of its members and the size of its congregations. This is to be attributed largely to the character of its membership in that early period. With such men as G. T. Hoagland, Kay, Kemper, Vories, Heaton, Brittain, Jennings, and a host of others just as true and good, it is no wonder that the Church commanded the confidence of the community and was firmly established and grew to be a mighty power for good. At the close of my delightful pastorate in St. Joseph I was sent by the Conference at Chillicothe to the Savannah District. This was not to my liking. I always shrunk from that responsibility. But I accepted the situation and went cheerfully to my appointment. This district embraced what are now eleven counties—from the Hannibal and St. Joseph railroad, and considerably south of it, up north to the Iowa line, and from east of the Grand River to the western boundary of the State—with appointments ranging from forty to fifty miles apart. As I had no family, I lived mostly on the district, traveling and holding meetings. I traveled on horseback, reaching my appointments usually on Thursday or Friday night; then preaching continuously until time to leave for my next quarterly meeting, to begin the same routine of labor. Not unfrequently I would leave appointments at school and private houses by the way.

This was continued, with only a little respite now and then, during the year, with several camp-meetings during the summer, which required extra labor and responsibility. The result was, though possessed of a strong constitution, my health gave way, and I went to Conference quite broken down. The year, however, was a glorious one. The preachers in the main were faithful, and the Lord greatly blessed the year's work in all parts of the district. At the close of this year a new district

—the Gallatin—was formed, composed of the eastern portion of the old Savannah District and a portion of the district lying to the east. I would be glad to mention the names of the faithful preachers, my co-laborers during that year. Of the entire number, I believe I am the only one now in the Conference. Rev. B. R. Baxter, a local preacher, is in Oregon, Dr. W. G. Miller, now pastor of First Church, Memphis, Tenn. His junior colleague, R. R. Baldwin, is a member of the South Indiana Conference, M. E. Church. How sweet the memory of my association with those brethren! How I loved them, and it is pleasant to think that it was mutual. Then there was the saintly and true "Father Ketron," as we loved to call him. Early in the war he went to heaven. It is a joyous thought that I shall meet all those faithful co-laborers of that year of toil in the general assembly and Church of the First-born in heaven.

The Conference of 1859 was held in St. Joseph. Bishop Paine was again with us. I was relieved from the district and sent to Hannibal, where I succeeded that faithful man of God, Rev. C. I. Van Deventer, who had been in charge two years. These two years were very fruitful. My faithful predecessor had labored earnestly, sown good seed, and watered it with his tears, and secured heaven's blessings upon it with his prayers. I found the harvest ready for the reaper. I never felt more sensibly the truth and force of the words: "one soweth and another reapeth." And while I entered into his labors he rejoiced with me in the gracious harvest of souls. I had in him, as my presiding elder, every help and encouragement in his power to give. He will let me thank God and him after all these years in this way for his timely courtesy and kindness and the great help he gave me during my pastorate, and above all for our sweet, Christian fellowship and that mutual affection then enkindled, and which has not lessened by the lapse of years.

The work of grace during the first six months of my pastorate at Hannibal was the most wonderful that I have ever witnessed. The entire city was under a deep religious awakening. Every Protestant Church caught the sacred fire and large numbers were converted—many in the houses of worship, many on the streets, some in their counting-rooms and places of business, and a great many in their homes. Between four and five hundred souls were converted and added to the different Churches. To our Church about one hundred and sixty were added. It was one of the most genuine revivals of religion that I have ever known, and the results were largely permanent.

It would seem that the Lord was specially blessing his people to prepare them for the fiery ordeal through which they were so soon to pass. The results of that meeting, the full measure of good accomplished, eternity alone can reveal.

It was soon after the close of this meeting that the question of a new church was agitated, and but for the war which soon followed it would most likely have been built. The result of this, could it have been done at that time, or immediately after the war, would have been to secure a much more satisfactory future for our Church at Hannibal. We doubtless lost much by failing to build a commodious and attractive house of worship at the proper time. If the present beautiful church had been erected twenty years sooner, we would to-day doubtless be far in advance of what we are. We have a good church and congregation still, but it is scarcely as strong as it was twenty-five years ago. In many places in our Connection we have fallen behind and lost prestige from the same cause.

The last year of my pastorate in Hannibal was interrupted by the war. Hannibal became a military camp, and a reign of terror was inaugurated which put a stop to all active Church operations. I was, however, permitted to pursue my labors unmolested in any direct way, until the close of the year. For some reason all Southern Methodist preachers were regarded with suspicion, and as in some sort and in some way connected with secession and the Southern side of the war. This grew out of ignorance in a large measure, in regard to the history of the M. E. Church, South, and the distinctive features and economy of that Church. Even Gen. Rosecrans, when approached by a committee to know why he exacted of the ministers assembled as a Conference at St. Louis to take the oath of allegiance, when no other religious body was required to do so, replied: "Because the Southern Methodist Church was organized in the interest of the rebellion." The venerable Dr. Boyle, one of the committee, said to him; "That cannot be, general, because the Southern Methodist Church has been in existence since 1845—

organized sixteen years before the war." The general was astonished, confessed his ignorance in relation to the matter, and that he understood that the Southern Methodist Church was organized after the war began in the direct interest of the rebellion. "Certainly," he said, "the order shall be revoked, and you will be protected so long as you obey the authorities of the government." How many intelligent men like Gen. Rosecrans are to this day ignorant of the true *status* and history of the M. E. Church, South!

In the fall of 1861 the Conference met at Glasgow. Having no bishop, Rev. W. G. Caples was made President. The whole country was in confusion and in a state of great excitement. The Conference held its session, however, without hinderance or interruption, and adjourned on Monday night.

I was read out for Chillicothe. Within a week I was at my new field of labor, and found the town a vast military encampment. Every church closed and without a pastor, except my own. On my first Sabbath and subsequently my own church was mostly filled with soldiers. I did the best I could to look after and gather my scattered flock and hold the Church together. Though a Southern man with Southern sympathies, I felt that I had a mission to all and a message from God to the soldiers. I preached to them, went among them in their camps, held prayer-meetings, visited their sick in the hospitals, and did what I could for their spiritual good. I was greatly blessed in my own soul, and I trust was made a humble instrument of some good to them. I made friends with them, and the Lord inclined them kindly to my ministry. They were regular troops, made up of the better elements of other States. From them I never received other than the kindest courtesy and deference to my calling and character as a minister. Toward the latter part of the winter, however, the Missouri militia took the place of the regular troops. As generally throughout the State, so in Chillicothe, the greatest trouble, persecution, and cruelty experienced by the people were from these State militia. As the regular troops from other States were of the best element, these militia, on the contrary, were of the very lowest and worst elements of this State. I have reason to know that they were held in utter contempt by the regular soldiers.

On the first Sabbath in March, 1862, on going to church, I

found a great mob of militia about the door, and as I entered the church they followed me in a most disorderly manner; while I was kneeling in prayer they nailed the flag to the pulpit, swearing at the same time that I should preach under the flag or I should not preach at all. What did they care for the flag or for the country? The Lord was with me most graciously that day. I had no fear and unusual liberty in trying to preach from the text: "Seek first the kingdom of God." He who restrained the lions from harm to Daniel restrained these men. The service was undisturbed, and we returned to our homes in peace.

About this time I received a letter from Brother A. Monroe urging me to attend the General Conference, which was to meet in New Orleans in May, 1862. Of all the delegates, seven in number, not one could attend. I was only an alternate, but I was alone—my two children provided for; and he thought I could be absent indefinitely without too great a sacrifice. He urged that it was absolutely essential to the safety of the Church in Missouri that we have one representative at the General Conference. He feared that in the heat of excitement, as the Church was largely within the bounds of the Confederacy, they might possibly take some hasty action that would commit the Church as such to the Southern Confederacy, which would have effectually destroyed our Church in Missouri. Coming from such a man, his strong arguments and earnest solicitation produced the conviction in my mind that it was perhaps my duty to go. I was entirely averse to going under the circumstances. However pleasant it might be to attend General Conference in time of peace, it was any thing else than pleasant in time of civil war. But I felt that duty called and the safety of the Church demanded the sacrifice. After earnest prayer, I replied that I would go. I put the Church at Chillicothe in charge of Rev. W. T. Ellington, who was teaching there at that time. I quietly left Chillicothe and went to the house of my father near Hannibal to make preparation for the perilous trip. Application was made to the military authorities for permission to pass the Federal lines, the object of my trip being clearly stated. They not only refused to let me pass, but positively forbade my going. I determined to obey God, to serve him and his Church, rather than man. My father gave me a fine mule for the trip, and equipped as well as circumstances would permit, armed only with a small pocket Bible, I set out all alone on my dangerous journey. I believed that it was God's will and that he would take care of me, and most wonderfully was his protecting hand seen and felt all the way through. After a continous journey, muleback, of fifteen days —a journey of hair-breadth escapes and most striking exhibitions of God's special providence—I reached Batesville, Ark. I there learned that the General Conference had been postponed indefinitely. My special mission was at an end. What next to do was the question. I could but wait and let God direct. I was offered a chaplaincy in the army and urged to take it. I tried to pray over the matter, but could not feel that my line of duty led in that direction. I may have been mistaken in this, but I honestly tried to follow the leadings of Providence. After two or three weeks in Batesville and some other points preaching and waiting, I finally decided to return to Missouri; and did so under the belief—which seems unreasonable to me now in the light of subsequent experience—that I would be permitted to resume my work as a minister of the gospel of peace, unmolested. On my return I was arrested in Boone County, by the militia, on the 20th of May; was taken to Jefferson City, where I remained for over two months in a most loathsome prison—a room sixteen by eighteen feet, into which from twenty-five to thirty-five prisoners were crowded. You may imagine our condition during the hot weather of June and July. I was tried by a military commission, charged with having run the blockade, and being in hostility to the United States government. What the verdict of that commission was I never knew. On the first of August I, with many others, was sent to Gratiot Street Prison, in St. Louis, the old McDowell College, and on the 7th we were sent to Alton, where I remained until toward the last of January, 1863.

Of my prison experience I will not write in detail. No tongue can tell, no pen can describe or give an adequate expression to the suffering and misery that I endured. In the inclosure of the old penitentiary grounds at Alton there are perhaps two or three acres not occupied by buildings. There were in this inclosure from fifteen hundred to twenty-five hundred prisoners. The fare was meager and miserable, the water was deadly, and the poor prisoners died by the hundred. I addressed myself, as far as I was able, to the work of caring for the sick. I sought and obtained a position in the hospital for this purpose, and as best I could administered to the spiritual wants of the sick and dying. I never felt more of the presence and sustaining power of God than during these months. My very prison was made a palace by the presence and comfort of Jesus. It seemed clear to me that God was in it all, that my very imprisonment was of his ordering, that I might minister the consolations of the gospel to these suffering thousands. No part of my life, as I look back upon it now, has yielded me such sweet satisfaction as those months of prison life and suffering. I realized too that, terrible as was the experience, it was my personal safety, and that I was thereby no doubt preserved from the deadly assassin, by whom so many were cruelly murdered during that dark time. Certainly God was in it all.

After three months of labor in the hospital, and great personal suffering, I too was brought down by a lingering chronic disease. My life was despaired of. Through the efforts of friends I was paroled to the city, and taken to a quiet boarding-house to die, as it was thought. But God ordered it otherwise. I began after a time slowly to recover, and after some two months was in a measure restored to health. Through the intervention of some influential friends I was at last released by a special order from President Lincoln, and was once more a free man. I returned to the home of my father near Hannibal, and as I had opportunity preached at different points in the surrounding country during the spring and summer of 1863. On my return home a friend, who was a member of the Union League, had said to me: "Be quiet and careful and make yourself easy. If any danger threatens you, I will know it and give you warning." I was the subject of constant, very unpleasant, and annoying surveillance from the militia, but I spent the spring and summer without any special trouble. Toward the latter part of August my friend of the "League" warned me that I was in danger of losing not only my liberty, but my life, and advised me to get away as quietly and as quickly as possible. I lost no time, and in thirty-six hours I had crossed the Missouri River, in company with a younger brother, and was on board the stage-coach bound for the West. I had no definite plan, only to get to a place of safety

20

and await developments. I had no thought of remaining away longer than the war made it necessary. I spent thirteen months at Austin, containing a population of about six thousand, mostly men; preached the first sermon ever preached in the town, married the first couple; organized a Christian Association—the best I could. I continued to preach to them during thirteen months, while I supported myself with my own hands. I was still a member of the Missouri Conference. At the session of the Conference held at Mexico in 1863 my name was announced to work in Nevada. I was the only appointee from the Conference ever *sent* to that field. In the fall of 1864, at the solicitation of brethren in California, I consented to transfer to the Pacific Conference; and was so transferred by Bishop Kavanaugh, and stationed at Sacramento, where I remained two years; then to San Francisco, two years; to San Francisco District, three years; Colusa Station, four years; Santa Clara Circuit, one year; San Jose, two years. In August, 1878, I was transferred back to my old Conference; reached the Conference during its session, and was again with my brethren of other years, after a painful absence of seventeen years.

It will be seen from the foregoing that my leaving Missouri was not from choice or inclination. Necessity was laid upon me. I had left my charge at Chillicothe in obedience to the call of the Church. After my return I had no pastoral charge; indeed, could not obtain one; was cut off absolutely from the pastoral work; was hunted down by the militia until I had to seek safety as best I could.

I have thus given a brief account of my ministerial life, and especially my experience during the war. It is but the experience of many, indeed hundreds of others of our ministers and members. It is an essential part of the history of Southern Methodism in Missouri. I have set down nothing in malice. I have long since learned to love even my enemies, and to forgive all the wrongs of the past as I hope to be forgiven and accepted in that day. As life's sun hastens to its setting I catch, more and more, glimpses and sometimes brighter visions of that better country where the former things have passed away, where only are joy and gladness, and sorrow and sighing are fled away.*

---

* Rev. E. K. Miller, MS.

Rev. T. B. King writes from Platte City in the following language:

I will report progress. My first protracted meeting of a week's continuance was held at Farley, resulting in six conversions and as many additions to the Church—all of mature years. During Christmas I went into Bethel Church neighborhood, where the war had left the claws of a few members of the Church, who had been exercising their powers in a "Kilkenny" cat fight. Our good and substantial church-building had been abused, and not used for some years. This we had repaired, and collected and reorganized a class of ten persons. We left the Church and community in a hundred-fold better condition.

We next held a meeting of one week at Brink's School-house, during which meeting there were forty-five conversions and forty-nine additions. It was an extraordinary good and profitable meeting. The entire membershp was revived, and the old members joined the new converts in shouting the praises of God. The members of other denominations cordially participated in the religious exercises of the meeting, and received a common blessing with ourselves.

The next appointment was a quarterly meeting at Parkville, conducted by our presiding elder, Rev. W. M. Rush. Here we had some twenty conversions and twenty-three additions. On Sunday we had the largest congregations ever assembled in Parkville—enough to fill two such houses. Brother Rush is loved for his Christian spirit and admired for his ministerial power and learning by all the people. The love-feast on Monday morning was a most delightful occasion.

During this quarter the accessions to the Church have been ninety-two. O that each one may be found "like a tree planted by the rivers of water, that bringeth forth his fruit in his season; his leaf also shall not wither; and whatsoever he doeth shall prosper." Yet it is sad to think that so many members are in the Church as barren fig-trees, who when they attend divine service are nothing else than idle spectators, like those who go to the opera, the theater, and the circus. "They are hearers only, but not doers of the word." But, thank God, the picture has a bright side as well as a dark one; for there are the faithful ones who bring forth some thirty, some sixty, and some a hundred fold in the vineyard of the Lord.*

Rev. J. R. Taylor, in charge of the High Hill Circuit, writes thus:

We held a protracted meeting at Cottonwood of one week's duration. As the Church had experienced a gradual and healthy growth during the year, the members were ready for the good work, and the revival commenced with the meeting. Many Christian hearts were made happy, many wandering prodigals were called back, and sinners were powerfully convicted and converted, and twenty-one persons avouched themselves to be on the Lord's side by uniting with the Church. The Society has increased this year from nineteen to fifty-five. They intend to build a new church, and are going about it in good, hard earnestness. The Church is materially and spiritually coming up out of the wilderness.

Before we could close the meeting at Cottonwood our sacramental meeting commenced at New Providence; fortunately, however, Father Eads was present to conduct the meeting. Brothers Nichols and Slavens, local preachers, were also there to assist him. Brother S. W. Cope preached for us and worked with us in the meeting a week. Then came Father Monroe, who was with us one day and night and preached twice. The meeting was characterized by considerable spiritual interest and saving power, in quickening the Church and convicting and converting sinners. One hundred persons have been received into the Church on this circuit since the Conference.*

Rev. D. C. Blackwell gives an encouraging account of Bloomington Circuit:

We have been engaged in protracted meetings for nearly three weeks. The first of the series commenced on the 8th of August at Liberty. Brother Vincil was with us most of the time, and preached with power and great acceptability. But better than all, the good Lord was with us to kill and make alive. Thirty-two were added to the Church, and about the same number converted. Convictions were pungent and the con-

---

* *St. Louis Christian Advocate.*

versions clear. The revival was general. Brethren who had been at variance were brought together in bonds of renewed Christian fellowship, and were made to realize that "love thinketh no evil."

The meeting continued twelve days, Brother Vincil remaining two days after I was compelled to leave. I was to have commenced a series of meetings on Saturday, the 19th, at Griffin's School-house, four miles north-west of Bloomington; but was detained at Liberty, and did not get there until Monday evening; but the brethren kept up prayer-meetings. They were determined not to be disappointed, and when I arrived there was a good congregation. At the close of the first sermon penitents came to the altar of prayer. The meeting continued to increase in interest until Friday evening, when I was compelled to leave in order to attend another appointment at Bethlehem. At the time of my leaving twelve had united with the Church.

We are now in the midst of a glorious revival at Bethlehem. We have had ten conversions and accessions, and at the three meetings mentioned there have been fifty-four additions to the Church.*

In reporting his work on the Millville Circuit, Rev. S. Alexander, among other things, says:

There has been a conflict going on in the Church between a "form of godliness and the power thereof," but it seems after so long a time that the victory has turned decidedly in favor of the "power thereof." Spiritual influence on the sinner's heart, and the necessity of being "born of the Spirit," are generally acknowledged. These powerful revivals show how *empty* a mere form of Christianity is. May the good Lord multiply such revivals until formality is driven out of the Church!*

This writer would with all his heart say amen to the petition with which Mr. Alexander closes his remarks. Will not all the preachers unite in the prayer for that kind of revival that will forever exclude all formality from the Church?

St. Louis Christian Advocate.

CHAPTER XIII.

St. Louis Conference.

The Ministers Addressing Themselves Earnestly to the Work of Rebuilding the "Waste Places of Zion" in Missouri—Session of the St. Louis Conference Held by Bishop Marvin at Kansas City—W. M. Prottsman, Secretary—Usual Statistics—Memoir of Rev. H. E. Smith—Rev. J. S. Frazier Speaks Interestingly of the Church—Rev. J. W. Cunningham Visits the Southern Methodist Charges in St. Louis—South-west Missouri, by Rev. H. W. Webster—*Multum in Parvo*—Origin, in this Country, of the Different Christian Denominations, and Their Respective Status—What the Character of the Ministers of the Gospel Should Be.

THE Civil War having ended and order being restored, the Church, with renewed consecration and divine strength, has gone to work in earnest to rebuild the waste places of Zion. She does not look upon the wreck and ruin of her organizations and institutions with a faint and faltering heart, but, like the faithful Jews on their return from the Babylonian captivity, she is addressing herself with a persistent purpose that knows no failure, and with an indomitable resolution that surmounts all difficulties, to rebuild the temple. This she is doing, not in her own strength, nor looking to her own resources, but in the strength of Him who says "Not by might, nor by power, but by my Spirit" shall success crown her efforts. Under the guidance, protection, and blessings of God, the Church is moving forward, grandly filling her mission of salvation to a lost world. It will be the pleasure of this writer to record, from time to time, her successes, her victories, and triumphs over the world, the flesh, and the devil, and in spreading scriptural holiness over these ends of the earth.

The session of the St. Louis Conference was opened by Bishop Marvin in Kansas City on the 18th of September, 1867. W. M. Prottsman was elected Secretary.

The following preachers were admitted on trial: W. M. Bewley, C. C. Woods, W. F. Graves, E. S. Frazier, W. P. Hulse, and T. Ament. The following remained on trial: J. F. Hogan, L. P. Siceloff, T. M. Cobb, and J. D. Wood. Admitted into full connection: L. W. Powell, J. S. Frazier, and S. A. Blakey. Re-admitted: S. S. Bryant, J. W. Maddox, R. Minshall, J. Tillery, T. Wallace, and J. T. Gibson. The following traveling preachers were elected and ordained deacons: S. A. Blakey, T. M. Cobb, and L. P. Siceloff. Local preachers elected and ordained deacons: C. C. Woods, C. Bluejacket, and H. Stanley. The following traveling preachers were elected and ordained elders: W. C. Godbey, T. G. Atchison, D. A. McNight, L. W. Powell, and J. S. Frazier. Local preachers elected and ordained to the same order: L. M. Carter, D. Dofflemyer, and J. Tillery. Supernumerary: J. Boyle, J. McCary, W. B. McFarland, and N. Scarritt. Superannuated: M. R. Anthony, E. W. Chanceaulme, C. Eaker, A. Rucker, J. T. Peery, J. N. W. Springer, W. R. Babcock, and N. T. Shaler. Total members this year, 12,362; local preachers, 84; colored members, 159; showing an increase over last year of 4,450 members, 19 local preachers, 116 colored members.

The following is the memoir of Rev. H. E. Smith, who died during the year:

Howard E. Smith has recently departed this life, and we have but few facts in connection with his life and death. But the meagerness of facts cannot prevent the expression of our regard for one who has been for twelve years a laborer with us in the ministry. Brother Smith was admitted on trial in the year 1855, from Neosho Circuit. He was ordained deacon in 1857, and elder in 1859. He continued to labor in the itinerant work till the late war, when, the foundation being broken up, he did what work he could. His last illness is said to have been caused by overlabor in his vocation. He lingered for some length of time, exhibiting much patience and resignation during his suffering. He died about the 1st of July, 1867, triumphing in the faith of Christ. Those who knew Brother Smith best testify that he was not only a good man, but an excellent man—humble, devout, kind, spiritual, and was loved by all who knew him. His only regret in death was that he left his family destitute of the necessaries of life.

The following from the pen of Rev. J. S. Frazier, appertaining to the condition of things in South-west Missouri, will, if we mistake not, be read with interest:

It is well known that the Southern Methodist Church was, prior to the war, the most influential denomination in this portion of Missouri. To one acquainted with it eight or ten years ago, to compare its condition then with its condition now is painfully sad; but to compare its promising condition with what some of its truest and best friends thought two or three years ago to be its hopeless condition is truly gratifying.

I heard when I was far away in the most favored parts of the State of the ordeal through which our people were passing in the South-west, but confess that I did not fully appreciate the character, variety, and magnitude of their afflictions until I came among them and heard from their own lips their severe suffering. There are hundreds in this country to-day rejoicing in the prospect, and hopeful of the triumphant success of that which with sorrowing hearts they once regarded lost. During those dark days, the like of which I hope may never return, the lovers of our holy religion had, no doubt, feelings similar to those of the captive Israelites when they sat down by the river of Babylon and "wept, when they remembered Zion." Their love for the cause of God constrained them to say: "If I forget thee, let my right hand forget her cunning. If I do not remember thee, let my tongue cleave to the roof of my mouth." And thanks to Him who doeth all things well, his people did and do still remember Zion. They remember her in their tears, for they have the noble sentiment expressed in one of our beautiful hymns, "For her my tears shall fall;" and for her their prayers ascend to heaven's throne. They remember her in their labor of love. "To her their toils and cares are given." God remembered her in that he has not "forgotten to be gracious." He has been and is still with his afflicted people. They have "consolation in Christ, comfort of love, and fellowship in the spirit." They are "like minded, having the same love, being of one accord, of the same mind."

At various places in this district there have been interesting revivals of religion. Brother McGehee, of Greenville Circuit, in his characteristic way is doing a good work: has had a number of conversions and accessions to the Church. Brother Ross, who is an able defender of the doctrines of the Bible, is accomplishing much good on Bolivar Circuit. On that circuit, at Hickory Grove, a revival has been in progress four months. Thirty persons have united with the Church, and the meeting is still going on. The members are so much encouraged that they have undertaken to build a new house of worship. Having twelve hundred dollars subscribed, they are collecting the materials for the erection of the house, which they expect to have completed by next spring.

I will now give the reader all the information I have concerning Springfield Station. This work was left to be supplied in consequence of the M. E. Church (North) having possession of our church-edifice and parsonage, to which they have no more right than I have, and I have none. Some people may think, or pretend to think, that I have no grounds for making the above statement. I think we ought to give publicity to such conduct. I would be glad if every man, woman, and child in Missouri knew all about this and all similar cases of which the members and ministers of the M. E. Church (North) were guilty. They are shamefully guilty of great wrongs in the view of all right-minded people. May they "*cease to do evil and learn to do well!*"

We have no house in which to preach regularly in Springfield, but the pastor and members of the Presbyterian Church, to whom we are under obligations, have been so kind as to give us theirs when they are not occupying it themselves. Brother Winton preached there last Sabbath to a respectable and appreciative audience with gratifying results. He is greatly encouraged with present prospects, and sanguine as to the success of our cause in the bounds of his district. He is doing the "work of an evangelist."

According to the best information, Brother Hill, who is in charge of the Marshfield Circuit, is giving satisfaction.

About Springfield Mission I know more, of course, than about any other part of the district. On this work, till this Conference year, there has not been a preacher since 1862, during which time our members were scattered as "sheep without a shepherd." On coming here I expected to find the Church in a very deplorable condition. In this I was not mistaken. On account of sickness I could not commence operations in this field for a month. But I recovered and went to work, as I thought, in the strength of the Lord. There were from the beginning large congregations, and much interest manifested by some of them. Up to the present time there have been fifty accessions to the Church on this work, many of whom are among the best citizens of Green County. The work of "reconstruction" is about complete, and I think there will soon be a victorious army in the field.

The people here are poor, rendered so by the war. But they are talking about trying to build churches in two different neighborhoods on this circuit. I believe they will succeed. They say also, notwithstanding they are poor, that they are going to pay fifty dollars to the cause of Missions—the amount appropriated to them as a mission.

Our second quarterly meeting will be held at Ebenezer, in connection with which there will be a District Conference, which will be the first one ever held in this district.

There is much that should be done by this body. For instance, to resuscitate the school at Ebenezer. We need a good school in this county more than any thing else at this time. There are several young men here who wish to go to school with a view of preparing themselves for the Christian ministry; but there being no good school in this section of the country and being limited in means, they are deprived of educational advantages.*

Rev. J. W. Cunningham, editor of the Kentucky Department of the *St. Louis Christian Advocate*, gives a very interesting description of his visit to the different Southern Methodist churches in the city of St. Louis, and we will give to those into whose hands our history may fall the privilege of reading it as furnished below:

Sabbath morning was spent at Carondelet with the Sabbath-school and congregation of Dr. McAnally's Church.

Carondelet is a suburb of St. Louis, about seven miles from the center of the city, yet connected with it by a continuous chain of houses. We, however, avoided the dust and din of street travel by going back and forth on the Iron Mountain railroad, six miles of the distance along the river bank under the bluff and out of sight of the inhabited region. Many persons doing business in the city live in Carondelet and have cheap transportation every hour in the day. Among the denizens of Carondelet are the editor of the *Advocate* and our old Kentucky friend, J. C. Bull, both of whose hospitalities we enjoyed. The former is pastor of the Church and the latter superintendent of the Sunday-school.

---

*St. Louis Christian Advocate.

The church is a cosy little edifice embowered in trees; a young forest flourishes on an adjoining lot; many homes around have ample grounds about them and are adorned with trees, shrubbery, blooming flowers, and vegetable gardens—all conspire to give the neighborhood a rural appearance and make it a delightful place of residence to those who have homes there. The church is very neat and pleasing in its interior appearance. A nice Sunday-school throngs its seats in early morn, and a full house cheers the minister in the pulpit at 11 o'clock. A great improvement has occurred of late years in the Carondelet church. For some time after its erection the attendance was discouragingly small; now it is encouraging in a high degree.

A pleasant interview with the Sabbath-school and a sermon to the congregation occupied the forenoon of the Sabbath.

DEDICATION OF ST. PAUL'S TABERNACLE.

Rev. W. M. Prottsman is pastor of a congregation in the northern part of the city. The war operated disastrously upon the old Mound Church in that region, and furnished our Northern brethren a number of proselytes. The old church has been sold, and a lot secured in a more eligible locality, where it is expected to erect a handsome church-edifice after awhile, to bear the name of "St. Paul's." For the present the Sunday-school and congregation occupy a neat and commodious brick edifice just completed and dedicated on another lot. It is called the "Tabernacle," and is to be to the new church in contemplation, what the "tabernacle" in the wilderness was to the temple in Jerusalem. Not that the coming temple will equal that which Solomon built, but that the present edifice is to prepare the way for the other.

Under the guidance of Rev. P. M. Pinckard we left Carondelet at half-past 2 o'clock P.M., and at half-past 3 o'clock by the aid of steam and horse cars had left nine miles of the city and its suburbs in our rear, and were at the door of the Tabernacle, at the corner of Tenth and Benton Streets. The house was full, but we found a place on the pulpit platform, in company with several of the city pastors, and heard a practical and appropriate dedicatory discourse from Bishop Marvin.

His text was: " Go up to the mountain, and bring wood, and

build the house; and I will take pleasure in it, and I will be glorified, saith the Lord."

We shall make no effort to report even a synopsis of the discourse, only saying that one point he made was that God is glorified by his people in the erection of suitable houses of worship, but some church-houses are neither creditable to the people who build them, nor do they glorify Him to whom they are consecrated. Not that God may not be profitably worshiped in a log cabin or other rude structure, where people are poor and can do no better, but when the people are able to honor God with an elegant temple of worship it is their duty to do so, and if they fail to do it God is not glorified, nor his cause properly promoted. In great cities, where architectural beauties are visible all around in human habitations, houses of business, and places of amusement, God must not be dishonored by the erection of poor and rude structures for his worship, but must be glorified by the consecration to him of temples in keeping with their surroundings. Rude church-edifices and elegant surroundings are repulsive to strangers; elegant ones are inviting, and the multitude will pass the former and be lured by the attractions of the latter. He had witnessed several efforts to inaugurate new Church enterprises in that city, but they had been on a scale not equal to the demand, and they had been failures, as all such efforts will be in the future.

The tabernacle then to be dedicated was a harbinger of the more stately and elegant temple to come. It cost only three thousand and one hundred dollars; yet there was a debt of fifteen hundred dollars upon it that must be liquidated. In a short time about sixteen hundred dollars was subscribed, and after a dedicatory hymn, announced by the writer and sung by the choir and congregation, the prayer of consecration was made by Rev. W. A. Smith, D.D. After the doxology, sung by the entire congregation, the benediction was pronounced by Rev. P. M. Pinckard. We omitted to say that the introductory services consisted of appropriate Scripture lessons read by Rev. Dr. Camp, and singing and prayer led by Rev. R. A. Jordan.

The tabernacle is a comely edifice for the purpose, of sufficient capacity to meet the present demands, and as a mere forerunner of the church to be erected hereafter does great credit to the congregation, and speaks most favorably of the energy and industry of the pastor. It was a happy day for pastor and people. The tones of a large cabinet organ filled the edifice, and a number of well-trained voices in the choir and congregation added in the sacred songs that were sung to the interest of the occasion.

CENTENARY CHURCH,

of which Rev. W. A. Smith, D.D., is pastor, is located on the corner of Fifth and Pine in the center of trade and fashionable display. Hotels and business houses are all around, and the noise and confusion incident to such a locality on the Sabbath somewhat disturb the preacher and congregation and detract from the pleasures of divine worship. Very few of the large membership live near the church. Most of them live remote, and many of them miles away. As in Louisville, so in St. Louis, residences yield to the inexorable demands of business; human habitations give place to houses of commerce and palaces of trade, and population retires to the more quiet suburban regions. Thus the Centenary Church has been left by a retiring membership far inside the circle of business, though it is as far from the river as Walnut Street Church in Louisville is from the Ohio.

The Centenary Church yields to necessity. On its door appears the words: "For sale." It will be sold soon, will command more than one hundred thousand dollars, and with the proceeds thereof a new church will be built on the corner of Pine and Sixteenth Streets, about a mile farther out, where a beautiful lot in a desirable locality has been secured for a church and parsonage at a cost of thirty-five thousand dollars.

The new house to be built for the Lord will doubtless be an ornament to that portion of the city; will be equal to the demands of the times and the taste of the age in its architecture and adornings, a credit to the congregation, an honor to the denomination; and, as in the "house" to which reference is made in the late dedication text of Bishop Marvin, it is hoped that God "will take pleasure in it" and be glorified therein.

THE PARSONAGE

to be erected in connection with the new church will be a valuable addition to the Centenary congregation and preacher. Rents are so enormously high that a hired house for the pastor of a St. Louis Church is a heavy annual tax. Twenty-seven squares from the river a home for the present incumbent of Centenary costs eleven hundred dollars per annum.

The Roman Catholics of St. Louis have been wiser in their generation in one respect than the Protestants. The Catholic Church has become the proprietor of a vast amount of valuable property. Very much of this was secured at an early date from the old French Catholics as donations while in health, or bequests when they came to die. The supposed possession by papal priests of the "keys of the kingdom," and an imagined possession of the power to grant absolution to papal penitents, have been a source of great revenue to the Church. Many valuable lots and large sums of money have been consecrated to the Church by devout Papists or imperiled penitents in that solemn hour when death appears in view and all earthly possessions lose the value previously attached to them by the dying one. The Church becomes the inheritor, and uses the inheritance to enlarge her borders.

Lots purchased by "the Church" in years agone at small rates have, with the lapse of time and the growth of the city, become immensely valuable, so that the wealth of the Church of Rome is beyond computation, and one is amazed at the number of Catholic churches, asylums, schools, and convents in St. Louis. It is devoutly to be hoped that Protestant preachers will never claim nor attain the power over human consciences that is exercised by Roman priests over the laity of their Church; but it would be wise in Protestant denominations to secure the possession of property in these young and growing Western States, both in country, town, and city, which will, after awhile, be valuable and remunerative to the Church.

The Centenary Church owns the ground on which it stands, and that occupied by the buildings in which the *Advocate* is printed, and in the vast increase in value since it was purchased, and the high price recently paid for a lot for the new church, has been taught a lesson of wisdom. If Centenary and First Church, in each of their existence, had bought only a single lot, at a small price, and the wealthier members who have died had made a reasonable bequest for the purchase of Church property, the increase in the value thereof would have enabled Methodism ere this to have a fine church in every desirable locality in the city.

First Church.

The old Methodist Church in St. Louis originally stood on Fourth Street, but the encroachments years ago induced the congregation to abandon the old locality and retire with the retreating population four squares farther out, where a new and elegant church-edifice was erected and where the congregation now worship. The First Church is a handsome building without, with corresponding appearance and appointments within, and a commodious and handsome parsonage on the same lot, in which the family of the present pastor, Rev. Dr. Camp, is installed. Under his guidance we explored the various apartments of his church, and learned of enlargements and other improvements to be made very soon to the already large and handsome Sunday-school room.

The First Church contains a membership of six or seven hundred, entirely too large and scattered a body of Christians to be congregated in one church. Impressed with that idea, they have determined to build a new church and divide the congregation.

St. John's Church.

St. John's is to be the name of the new church now being erected by the membership of the First Church. The policy of the First Church in this matter is to be highly commended. It is most commonly the case that when a new church is to be erected in city suburbs, the expense falls chiefly upon those who happen to reside in that particular region, and in many instances upon comparatively poor men. Such being the fact, the new congregation is forced to erect a very plain and cheap edifice, without any exterior architectural beauties or interior adornings. Its homeliness within and without renders it uninviting to people of a refined taste, and they seek more attractive places of worship. If we understand it correctly, the membership of First Church make the erection of St. John's Church a common cause, and when it is completed all will be at liberty to take membership where it suits them best.

Under the guidance of Dr. Smith we took a survey of St. John's. It is located on the corner of Locust Street and Ewing Avenue, about thirty squares from the river. The walls are complete and the roof is in process of construction, and the building is to be completed this summer. The entrance into the main audience-room is from Locust Street. Its floor is only a few feet from the ground, avoiding the ascent necessary in two-story churches. In the rear, but connected with it, is a two-story building with a lower front entrance on Ewing Avenue. The lower story is divided into a spacious lecture-room and class-rooms, including pastor's office, and the upper room is large and is for the Sunday-school. The entire building will be very commodious and very handsome, and be the chief ornament of that part of the city, which is the abode of wealth, and where fine residences abound. St. John's will be a church of which St. Louis Methodism may justly be proud; and we trust the Lord will take pleasure in it and be glorified therein by a faithful ministry, a prosperous Sabbath-school, a multitude of conversions, and a devoted people.

Remarks of the presiding elder, Rev. H. W. Webster, concerning matters in South-west Missouri:

The interests of the Southern Methodist Church in the bounds of the Granby District are evidently on the advance. The preachers seem to be in fine spirits and are doing good work. There may be found in almost all portions of this country the best of families, good and true, whose shoulders are at the wheel, and although torn and shattered by the storms of the war, they have the industry and the energy, and they still live, and under the blessing of a merciful Providence they will live, and they cannot be kept down; and last, but not least, they are willing that others should live also.

This class is not confined entirely to the old settlers; but those from other States, and from the Northern States, as they have learned the true position of the M. E. Church, South, and find it to correspond with their views of right, make it the Church of their choice, and cast in their lot with us, and prove their sincerity by their works. And there are a goodly number of us out here in this backwoods country that really think they have made a wise choice.

Our preachers have generally large congregations, and at many places fine revivals. One on the Nevada City Circuit of extensive interest, and resulting in about forty accessions to the Church.*

---

* *St. Louis Christian Advocate.*

MULTUM IN PARVO.

We give the following document a place in our history because of its intrinsic value to the Church. Commencing with their origin in this country, it gives a condensed statistical history of the different Protestant denominations, furnishing facts and figures all the way through. It is a summary concisely given of much solid information, and we know not where the same amount of useful knowledge can be obtained in so small a compass.

It contains the mature thoughts and sound opinions of one who has been a profound thinker and writer for more than half a century. It would be difficult to find a person who has served the Church longer—over sixty years—more faithfully, more successfully, and who has made a cleaner, better record than Dr. D. R. McAnally? As it was said of the lexicographer, Dr. Johnson, that he was a walking dictionary, so it may be said of Dr. McAnally that he is a walking library, an encyclopedia of general knowledge. To him hundreds have gone and obtained the desired information and the solution of difficult and intricate questions.

The utterances of this good man should be regarded as the results of his long and large experience, and should certainly have weight in the Church to which he has devoted all the years of his useful life. It cannot fail to interest the religious, thinking class of readers. He makes the following passage of Scripture, in Deuteronomy i. 11, the basis of his thoughts and remarks: "The

Lord God of your fathers make you a thousand times so many more as ye are, and bless you, as he hath promised you!"

As the generation which heard the law of God at Mount Sinai had with a few individual exceptions passed away, it was deemed proper that, before the death of Moses, he should repeat in substance, or give to the then living generation a second edition of the law, and this forms the matter of the book of Deuteronomy, as the word itself signifies. Under God, Moses had been the leader and instructor of that people during forty years. His deep and abiding anxiety for their welfare was intense, and perhaps the more so now, that he was soon to close his earthly career—go hence and leave them to the care of others. He begins by referring to the past—recounting mercies, blessings, protection, defense, supply of all needs, and wondrous works in their behalf—alludes to their numerical increase and parenthetically throws in the above passage: "The Lord God of your fathers make you a thousand times so many more as ye are, and bless you, as he has promised you!"

This was doubtless the sincere and honest prayer of his heart; and it is the prayer of every true Christian man and woman on the face of the earth, in regard to the numerical increase of the Christian people. Moreover it is the prayer of every denominationalist in regard to the particular denomination with which he is connected. Each denomination honestly believes it has some peculiarities better calculated to accomplish the great work of saving souls than are found elsewhere; and while as Christians they pray for all, they specially pray for the success of the denomination which they represent. Considering human nature as it is, no reasonable objection can be used against this.

It is, however, not to be supposed that any sane man in these days expects the desired end to be unconditionally attained. Moses did not expect it, nor do we. Hence it becomes us to inquire into the conditions—ascertain what they are, and how they are to be complied with. But before undertaking this—that is, undertaking to ascertain how we, as a denomination of Christians, may increase—it may be well to take a hasty view, both positively and relatively, as to what we have been and are now.

The introduction of Christianity in this country was first by the Catholics. At its discovery possession was taken in the name of the Holy Catholic Church, and before the end of the sixteenth century they had planted stations all along the coasts from Florida to California, and from the mouth of the St. Lawrence to the head of the valley of the Mississippi, thence down to the Gulf, and this from forty to fifty years before a Protestant, as such, had set foot on American soil.

Protestantism was introduced by Virginia colonists in 1607. These were connected with the Church of England, and nominally remained in that connection for 180 years, till the Protestant Episcopal Church was organized in 1787.

The leading denominations of the country are (1) the Protestant Episcopal Church, whose date is just given; (2) the Congregationalist, whose entrance here was in 1620; (3) the Baptist, whose first church here dates in 1662; (4) the Presbyterian was first organized in 1684; (5) the Methodist, in 1766. These five are still the leading denominations. I have named them in the order of their dates. I might include the Lutheran as a leading denomination, but the date is not at hand.

From the dates given you may see that the Methodists as a people in this couutry are 159 years younger than the Episcopalians, 146 years younger than the Congregationalists, 104 years younger than the Baptists, and 82 years younger than the Presbyterians. So these denominations had the start by the number of years given—that is to say, they had labored these many years before the Methodists began.

Now, let us inquire as to their success. At their first Conference, in 1773, the Methodists had 10 preachers and 1,160 members. I have not the statistics of the other denominations for that year, but for 1775 the Episcopalians reported 300 churches and 250 ministers; the Congregationalists, 700 churches and 575 ministers; the Baptists, 380 churches and 350 ministers; the Presbyterians, 300 churches and 140 ministers; the Methodists reported 19 ministers and 3,146 members. Nothing was said about churches, nor have I any statement as to the number of members in the other denominations at that date; but the statistics of 1800 give the number of communicants of the Congregational Church at 75,000; Baptist (regular and Free-will), 103,000; Presbyterian, 40,000; Protestant Episcopal, 12,000; Methodists, 65,181.

Let us now look at the statistics of 1880, and see how these Churches stand after eighty years' labor. The statistics of 1880 give the number of communicants of the Congregational Church at 384,332; Baptist (all kinds), 2,452,878; Presbyterian, 937,640; Protestant Episcopal, 347,781; Methodist, 3,574,485.

Now let us deal fairly, and add an increase of 25 per cent. of members for the time since 1880, which will give an additional increase to the Congregational Church of 96,083; Baptist, 613,219; Presbyterian, 234,410; Protestant Episcopal, 86,945; Methodist, 893,621.

This increase of 25 per cent., added to the statistics of 1880, gives the following membership for 1888: Congregational Church, 480,415; Baptist, 3,066,097; Presbyterian, 1,172,050; Protestant Episcopal, 434,726; Methodist, 4,468,106.

This may or may not be strictly correct, but it is as fair for one as for another. In regard to the Methodists, I am satisfied that it is not correct. They make their reports not by the calendar, but by the ecclesiastical year, which includes parts of two calendar years; and for the ecclesiastical year 1886-87 the net increase of the Methodist Church was over 200,000; and the probabilities are that the increase during the ecclesiastical year 1887-88 will be as great, or 400,000 in the two years. So the increase since 1880 must have been more than 25 per cent. My own convictions are that the aggregate membership of the Methodist Churches to-day is nearly or quite 5,000,000. And here let me make a remark: The Catholic Church has been operating in this country 250 or more years longer than the Methodists. They estimate their population—that is, all baptized persons, adults and children—in this country at about 7,000,000.

The Methodists have nearly 5,000,000 communicants, not counting the baptized children. But suppose there be one baptized child for every adult member, then they would outnumber the Catholics by at least 3,000,000. Comment is unnecessary.

The total number of communicants in the several Protestant Churches in this country is about 12,000,000, and if we allow two adherents for each communicant there are 36,000,000—more than half the entire population of our country—members of or close adherents to the Protestant Churches. The Methodists alone form one-twelfth of the population of 60,000,000, and, allowing them one adherent for each member, they form one-sixth.

But to make the nearest approximation to the real state of the case that the latest official figures will allow, I give in detail the figures as made at the latest reports on hand, all of which are from 6 or 8 to 18 or 20 months old. First, Episcopal Methodists: M. E. Church, 2,020,511; M. E. Church, South, 1,107,456; African M. E. Church, 475,000; African M. E. Zion, 350,000; Colored M. E. Church, 166,729; Union M. E. Church, 21,000. Total, 4,140,696. Second, Non-episcopal Churches: Protestant Methodists, 144,559; Congregational Methodists, 3,000; Independent Methodists, 5,000; Free Methodists, 16,826; Wesleyans, 18,260; Primitive Methodists, 5,002; Reformed Methodists, 2,500; kindred bodies, 335,561. Total, 530,708. Grand total of all, 4,671,404.

It may now be of interest to take a hasty view of our own Church, separately from the other branches of Methodism. At the end of the Conference year 1845-46—the first year after the division of 1844 was effected—our total membership was 455,217, of whom 124,961 were colored people, and 2,972 were Indians, with 1,433 traveling and 2,830 local preachers.

Fifteen years after that—or in 1860—there were 2,615 traveling and 5,353 local preachers; total number of members, 757,605, of whom 171,857 were colored, and 3,395 Indians. So you see that in those fifteen years we gained over 300,000 members, an average of 100,000 every five years, or 20,000 annually.

But the next six years tell a sad tale. In 1866 our total membership amounted to 505,101, a loss of over 250,000 in six years, a loss that covered five-sixths of the gain of the preceding fifteen years. Of this loss nearly 100,000 were colored people, and of the 3,395 Indian members in 1860 only 701 were found in 1866.

The colored members, numbering 174,857 in 1860, were reduced to 78,742 in 1866; and these were soon after separated, and at their own request were organized into a different body. So that in about six years our entire loss was about 300,000, fully equaling, if not exceeding, the gain of the preceding fifteen years; while those who remained were dispirited, sick at heart. Their church-houses to a large extent had been alienated or destroyed; in many places their organizations were broken up, their country laid waste, and themselves reduced from affluence or competency to penury and want Other Christian people predicted that most assuredly we never could or would reorganize, and kindly opened wide their arms to take us in. Some went so far as to pledge their word and honor that no organization would ever occur, and entreated aud implored our people to come out of the wilderness waste into their fold, and find peace. Others there were who resorted to other more forcible and more objectionable means to reach the same end. But enough of that for the present.

When I think over the past (for, as some who read this know, without dodging, flinching, or wavering, I was there and went through it all), when I call to mind I feel in my consciousness that if the Lord God of our fathers had not been with us and blessed us we never would or could have reorganized and recuperated as we have done.

After twenty-two years from 1866, we stand, and, as stated, can see a Church with 1,107,456 members, with 4,530 traveling and 6,192 local preachers, by whose faithful ministry about 100,000 persons are baptized and brought into the Church every year, with 11,724 Sunday-schools, 82,205 teachers, and 649,104 scholars, 11,304 church-houses, estimated at $15,242,538; 2,199 parsonages, estimated to be worth $2,487,936, with Missionary Societies among the men and women, and Church Extension Societies pay from $300,000 to $400,000, and increasing year by year, with missionaries at home and abroad, and others steadily going forth—all endeavoring to keep the unity of the Spirit in the bond of peace. At the same time there are institutions of learning, colleges, seminaries, and high schools in nearly every Conference in the Connection for the education of the youth of both sexes. All this and much more may we behold, and gratefully contemplate.

It is not said nor intimated that we have done all we could and should have done, but that much has been done is undeniable.

Let us direct the reader to the passage of Scripture selected as the basis of these remarks: "The Lord God of your fathers make you a thousand times so many more as ye are, and bless you, as he has promised!" Now is it to be supposed that this prayer will be unconditionally granted? Surely not. Then what are the requisite conditions? We reply:

First, the preaching of a pure gospel by men of clean hands and pure hearts, who in their inner consciousness know the gospel is true, know it is the power of God unto salvation, who have imbibed its spirit and live by its precepts, and feel " Woe is me if I preach not the gospel "—no Pelagianism, no Antinomianism, no mere sensationalism, but the plain truth as it is in Jesus—set forth in its plainness, pointedness, purity, and entirety. We must have preachers, not pulpit actors, nor mere pulpit elocutionists; not men to make mere oratorical displays, pouring forth their thoughts in circumlocutory sentences and studied periods—not the dealer in vapid frothiness, nor the scientist to analyze matter and tell us of its component parts, of the relation of one part to another, then give the history of the whole; nor the philosopher to expatiate upon the wonders of physical nature, the correlation of forces, and all that sort of thing; nor yet the dealer in abstruse metaphysics ranging through spiritual worlds, of which neither he nor his hearers can know but little; nor least of all do we want the mere sensationalist with his songs that are mere twaddle music, which for aught I know may be suited to the circus, but certainly not to religious devotion, and his stand up, sit down, marching, counter-marching, hand-shaking sort of conversions, when perhaps not more than one-fourth of these converts make good Church-members, while the rest fall back to be pointed and sneered at as the fruits of the great revival. No, none of these, but preachers of the gospel, expounders of the divine word, offering repentance and remission of sins to all people in the name of Christ.

Give us men after God's own heart, that will not hold their peace day or night, but cry aloud and spare not. Paul did not go forth with enticing words of man's wisdom, but in the power and demonstration of the Spirit; and so should we. He determined to know nothing in his preaching but Jesus Christ and him crucified; so should we. He counted all things but loss for the excellency of the knowledge of Jesus Christ; so should we. Science, philosophy, and the wisdom of this world have their appropriate places. They are not to be despised. Rightly employed they are extensively and variously useful; but the pulpit is the place for the cross of Christ, whence should be discussed those spiritual interests so vital and important in the present, and which extend through the roll and sweep of eternal ages

To have the needed preachers, great care must be taken by all on whom the duty of licensing, ordaining, and continuing in the ministry is devolved. Let us begin at the beginning. Churches must be very particular as to whom they recommend for license to preach. Here is the starting-point where great care is necessary. It is a work in which personal friendship or sympathy have little or nothing to do. No one should be recommended simply because he is a good, kind brother, well beloved, and we shrink from wounding his feelings. Has he the intelligence, the gifts and graces suited to the ministry? Let the Church hear him and act intelligently, as well as cautiously in the recommendation, taking the responsibility on themselves, and not turning it over to the Quarterly Conference.

Then, when before the Quarterly Conference, let the examination be careful, close, and thorough; so that no unworthy or incompetent person be licensed. Let the members of the Quarterly Conference keenly realize their responsibility, and not ask, "How shall we save the brother's feelings?" but, "How shall we save the Church?" And when they recommend men for admission into the traveling connection or for deacon's or elder's orders, let them be, if possible, still more careful. First, license no man whom they are not willing to hear preach as occasion might require, and whose preaching would do them no good. Secondly, recommend no man for admission into the traveling connection whom they would be unwilling, under ordinary circumstances, to receive as their pastor; and recommend no preacher for orders from whose hands they hesitate to receive the sacraments of the Church. What right has a Quarterly Conference to turn over to others what they themselves would be unwilling to take? There may possibly be exceptional cases or mitigating circumstances, but as a general rule there is no such right at all.

Close and continued observation has forced upon me the conviction that a large proportion—the greater part, indeed—of our difficulties in regard to incompetent and consequently inefficient preachers, are directly traceable to either the incompetence or unfaithfulness of the Churches and Quarterly Conferences as the recommending powers. The Churches feel kindly toward the applicant, desire to avoid wounding his feelings, and throw the responsibility upon the Quarterly Conference; and the members of that body, with the same class of feelings, refer the case to the Annual Conference, and the Annual Conference receives or ordains the applicant on the faith of these recommending bodies; when in point of fact, if either the Church or the Quarterly Conference had been required to take final action, the man might not have been licensed at all. You may think this an extreme case. I reply: Extreme cases do sometimes occur.

As to the Annual Conference, it is by no means clear, at least to the mind of this writer, that there is that closeness and rigidity in the annual examination of the moral ministerial character of the members there once was, and perhaps ought still to be, and I am strongly inclined to the opinion that there has been greater or less decline in efficiency and success since the practice of carrying on examinations with closed doors, excluding all except actual members, was abandoned. I do not advocate any practice or action because it is old, but, if it be proved to be good as well as old, I see no reason for its abandonment. If there be any of you who remember the close and critical, yet kind and tender manner in which every preacher was examined concerning his manner of preaching and of conducting public service generally, his deportment in public and in families, his personal religious experience, and indeed all that pertained to his life as a man and as a minister, they will not, I think, hesitate to give that practice the preference over that which now too generally prevails. Of course this examination was in the presence of his ministerial brethren alone, by whom he was reproved, exhorted, or advised, as occasion seemed to require, and, unless in case of moral delinquencies, the whole matter was prudently kept from the public. If Methodist preachers expect to secure the success of the Church, among their first objects should be that of preserving the purity and effectiveness of the ministry. They should desire this far more than the friendship of any man, far more than their own comfort and peace, and very far beyond their own personal popularity, or to be well spoken of by others. When they do really and sincerely desire this purity and efficiency they will need no promptings to inquire into the rumors that affect any one of their body. There will be no particular favorites, no pets among them. There will be the same moral standard for all, and by that standard all will be judged. It is not sufficient that preachers think themselves pious—others must think so as well, for the very life of our system depends upon the confidence of the people in the unadulterated piety of their ministers. They expect from them much more than ordinary piety, and if their confidence becomes shaken their co-operation becomes faithless and weak. If the Conference annually "pass the character" of the preachers, and the verdict upon their purity leaves them still liable to suspicion, or even charged, though informally, with departures from rectitude, if passage of character means no more than not openly condemning, and the people come to believe that justice has not been done in the matter, then I do not see how decline and ultimate ruin is to be avoided. The people can judge of the purity of life and effectiveness of a minister, and if they see, as I am compelled to believe they sometimes see, inefficient and comparatively useless men shifted from circuit to circuit and station to station until they have burdened the whole Church; or if they see men kept year after year near the same place because of their real or supposed social qualities, or because they are favorites or tools of some wealthy and influential people—influential only on account of their wealth, or, more correctly, the wealth which owns them, the Church all the while not improving but rather declining in piety—now can they feel that respect and confidence necessary to the hearty and effective co-operation in the work of the Church?

Conferences are trustees solemnly pledged before God to preserve the purity and effectiveness of the ministry. As such they may not act toward delinquents as individuals against individuals, nor try experiments on the Church by closing their eyes to manifest incapacity or moral obliquity on the part of any of their members, and continuing useless members from year to year in hope they will amend. That is sickly sort of sympathy which under such circumstances asks, "How shall we save the man?" and it deserves and should have no place in the proceedings of Annual Conferences. If there ever was a body of men bound by the fearful responsibilities of spiritual guardianship, and by that sense of honor which even in godless men is stronger than life itself, that body is a Methodist Conference when it sits in judgment on its members. If they abuse a trust so solemn and so important to others, to what then can we look for evidence of ministerial integrity?

Let me refer to another matter of importance. In order to the success of a Church, sound doctrinal preaching must be accompanied by healthful Church discipline. Of this there can be no reasonable doubt, nor can it be questioned that in this respect there is great laxity among us. Our General Rules are not observed as they should be, and must be if the Church have real and permanent prosperity. The duties of fasting, family prayer, regular reading and study of the Scriptures, and many others are not faithfully performed, while a worldly spirit largely prevails not only in regard to the acquisition of worldly goods, but in regard to those pleasures, entertainments, and amusements of the world looked upon by evangelical Christians as opposed to the letter and spirit of the gospel. If this spirit has not been encouraged, it certainly has not been rebuked by the numerous entertainments, public rehearsals, recitations, suppers, sociables, fairs, festivals, and the like—all carried on in the name of the Church, and professedly for its benefit. But baptizing them in the name of the Church is like the baptism of Simon the Sorcerer, leaving them the same as before, with the same worldly spirit and worldly effect.

Now let young ministers and Church-members who may live and bear a part in the activities of religious life long after I shall have passed away, hear me: If the Methodist Churches ever decline and cease to prosecute their mission to the learned and unlearned, to the rich and to the poor—especially the latter—and to all classes and conditions of society, the cause will be found not in our cardinal doctrines, they are of God; not in our Discipline, it is in accord with the Bible; not in our modes and instrumentalities of operation, nor yet in the deficiency of means. It will be in the ministry, and no where else. No other cause can be found. If the ministry be what it should, and no insurmountable obstruction prevents their access to the people, the Church must prosper. Keep the doctrines and Discipline of the Church pure and in full force. Keep the ministers full up to the gospel, and the disciplinary standard up to their ordination vows. Let the general superintendents discharge the functions of their office fearlessly, fully, impartially, and completely; then no man, nor devils, nor earth, nor hell shall or can prevent the success of the mission of Methodism to all classes of society and to all conditions of men.

CHAPTER XIV.

Missouri Conference.

Fifty-second Session of the Missouri Conference Held by Bishop Kavanaugh at Weston; J. D. Vincil, Secretary — Our Church-house a Large and Splendid Edifice—Weston Is Full of Good Houses of Worship—Institution of Learning Founded by Rev. W. G. Caples, but Now Belongs to Rev. W. H. Lewis—The Conference Full to Overflowing—Influence and Popularity of the Bishop—Good Statistical Report—Increase of Members Nearly Thirty-five Hundred—Great Improvement in Sunday-school Work—Should Be As Many Scholars in Sunday-school As Members in the Church—Dr. W. G. Miller Reports Favorably of Weston Female College—Rev. D. A. Leeper's Funeral Preached during Conference by Bishop Kavanaugh—His Memoir—Rev. J. Devlin's Work on Carrollton Circuit—Rev. C. I. Van Deventer's Life and Work, by Himself—Our Church and Moberly—Rev. J. A. Mumpower's Life and Work, by Himself—Rev. George C. Light, D.D.

THE fifty-second session of the Missouri Annual Conference was opened by Bishop Kavnaugh at Weston, Mo., September 9, 1868; John D. Vincil, Secretary.

We find in the *St. Louis Christian Advocate* a notice of this Conference, which we substitute in the place of the statistics given in the published Minutes:

It was the privilege and pleasure of the writer to attend the late session of the Missouri Annual Conference, which was held at Weston, Mo.

The town of Weston has improved very considerably since last we visited it. Many new and some rather elegant buildings have been erected, and there are now evident signs of thrift and prosperity. It is backed by one of the most wealthy and fertile portions of the State of Missouri, and a population which, for intelligence, industry, and enterprise, equals any other.

Our Church in the town or city, which it may be called, is reported to be in a very healthy and prosperous condition. For two years last past Rev. R. A. Austin has been in charge, and under his faithful ministrations the Church has prospered well. Very recently there has been completed a magnificent house of worship, one that is alike an honor to the builders and an ornament to the town; a more convenient and beautiful house we rarely find in the Western country. May it ever remain as a house of prayer and praise! and when "God righteth up the people, may he count that this and that man," and thousands of others, "were born there!"

Indeed, this town has more and better church-houses proportioned to the whole population than any other town or city in the State. The population is about two thousand and five hundred, and they have *nine* substantial and neat church-houses belonging to the following denominations, and costing, as we learned, the sums annexed: M. E. Church, South, $18,000; Baptist, $7,500; Catholic, $8,000; Christian or Campbellite, $6,000; Episcopal, $4,000; Lutheran, $4,500; German Methodist, $4,000; Presbyterian, $4,000; Colored Methodist, $500.

With a taxable property estimated at not more than half a million the people of this town raised for Church purposes during the last twelve months *forty-one thousand and five hundred dollars*, exclusive of the salaries of their preachers. We doubt if such another instance of liberality can be found in any part of the Western country, if, indeed, anywhere else.

The high school founded and carried forward for a time by the labors of the late Rev. W. G. Caples has come again under the control of our Church, Rev. W. H. Lewis having purchased the buildings and organized a school. The buildings are very good, capacious, and elegant. The location for a school is an excellent one, Mr. Lewis is an experienced and successful educator, and there are good reasons to expect a large and prosperous school, at which many of the youth of the land may receive a sound and useful education.

The Conference, taken as a whole, is in a gratifying condition. The members of the Conference are a set of most excellent men—at peace among themselves, love one another, and all united in purpose and effort to do what they can to promote the spiritual welfare of the people by advancing among them the principles of a pure and holy Christianity. Nor are they behind other Conferences in talent and experience.

In Methodist parlance, this Conference is full, full to overflowing—that is, there is an abundant supply of preachers for the work within its bounds. The supply was good before, but at this session the number has been increased by the addition of ten promising young men, and also six preachers, who had once been in the traveling connection, and were re-admitted from the local ranks, making the total increase of traveling preachers in the Conference this year *sixteen*.

The bishop who presided during the session was that faithful servant of God and of the Church, H. H. Kavanaugh. He was in excellent health and spirits. The first Conference over which he presided after his election to the episcopacy was the Missouri Conference in 1854. He is greatly beloved by this Conference, and he deserves to be; presides with calmness, patience, and great urbanity. His influence for good among the preachers is great, while his pulpit efforts are highly appreciated. On Monday evening of the Conference he preached the funeral of the Rev. D. A. Leeper, a member of this Conference who had died during the past year. After the sermon the holy communion was administered. It was a solemn, impressive, and profitable occasion.

The Committee on Statistics kindly furnished us with the following abstract of part of the regular Conference statistics: Whole number of members in the bounds of the Conference, 17,313; number of increase this year, 3,430; number of Sunday-schools, 167; number of officers and teachers, 1,466; number of scholars, 8,413; number of volumes in libraries, 24,210; amount raised for the support of the bishops, $864.85; for Domestic Missions, $3,475.36; for Foreign Missions, $1,774.72; for Conference Fund, $1,746.73; for Sunday-school purposes, $2,939.50; for Church Extension, $1,006.05.

These statistics exhibit a gratifying state of the Church in the bounds of this Conference. But a large field white unto the harvest is still before the preachers. Heavy responsibilities rest upon them. May grace sustain and glory crown them!

It is pleasing to learn of the improvement there has been in reference to the Sunday-school work. The reports show from one-third to one-half more schools, teachers, scholars, etc., than were reported last year. And yet, in the sober judgment of the present writer, the numbers reported are not more than one-half what they might have been, and, perhaps, ought to have been. We think that the number of children under Sunday-school instruction ought to be at least equal to the number of Church-members there may be in any Conference, or district, or circuit, or station, or any individual Church.

Few well-informed persons will doubt but that this might be the case, and would be were the proper attention given and the proper efforts made. Let any minister look around him and see if there are not more children connected with his congregation than there are members of his Church. In a great majority of cases it will be found that there are, and we think that the effort of every preacher should be to have as many children under regular Sabbath-school instruction as there are members of his Church or under his pastoral care. Let no one stop short of that point. It can be attained and ought to be attained, and *when* attained it will greatly advance the interests of the Church.

Of the Weston Female College, to which the above writer directs the attention of the reader, Dr. Wesley G. Miller, pastor of the M. E. Church, South, at Weston, speaks thus:

It affords me much pleasure to inform the friends of the Church that our educational enterprise in this locality promises to be a complete success.

The preachers of this district, in their third District Conference last year, resolved to establish a District Conference school, to be located at Weston. They appointed a committee to make suitable arrangements for carrying their resolution into practicable operation. For the accomplishment of this important object the committee procured the services of Rev. W. H. Lewis, A.M., known throughout the State as an old and successful educator.

In September last Brother Lewis and his corps of excellent

teachers organized the school in the old "Weston High School" buildings, which buildings were erected under the direction of the lamented Caples, and the object of his highest ambition, and which buildings Brother Lewis had purchased. The school is now known as the Weston Female College, and matriculated 140 pupils this year. The school was opened under disadvantages and embarrassments; for it had been sorely mismanaged while from under the care of our Church, and commanded no patronage and no confidence. But it is an encouraging feature under the present organization that the number of scholars is continually increasing. The interesting literary entertainment given by the students on last Wednesday evening, to a large and intelligent audience, has tended greatly to increase its popularity and confirm the confidence of its friends and the public generally.

As I and my family board in the College, I have unrestricted privilege of visiting the recitations at all times. Therefore I am prepared to speak understandingly on the subject, and I give it as my conviction that no school in the State affords greater facilities for obtaining a solid and thorough education than does Weston Female College.

It is evident that our Church needs in this part of the State just such a school as we have at Weston. Nothing tends more to give to the Church position, influence, and power in a community. The location is an admirable one, easy of access by railroads and river. The college buildings are ample in their arrangements for the boarding department as well as the literary. The school is now in successful operation. The teachers have given satisfactory evidence of their competency and adaptation to the responsible work in which they are engaged, which fact is fully acknowledged in this community.*

One death has occurred during the Conference year: Rev. D. A. Leeper, whose funeral, as has been stated, was preached by Bishop Kavanaugh during the session of the Conference. We were personally and intimately acquainted with Brother

---

* *St. Louis Christian Advocate*, December, 1868.

Leeper, and a better man and a more consecrated man to the Christian ministry we never saw—a man of remarkable affability—gentle, kind, agreeable, social, always pleasant, and never failed to meet you with a gracious smile. But, without further comment, we call the attention of the reader to his memoir as read before the Conference:

D. A. Leeper was born in Hopkins County, Ky., March 15, 1819 (his father came to Missouri the following fall); and died in Chillicothe, Mo., at his residence, in the twenty-seventh year of his ministry. We have seen many men die, and have heard the last words of many departing Christians, but seldom one like this good man. After a long and painful illness of forty-two days, endured without a murmur or complaint, he came down at last to the river and looked across without a fear or a shudder. He always expressed a most perfect readiness for the final hour—that resignation which nothing but a life of piety and an habitual exercise of faith in God can give.

Brother Leeper began the ministry in 1841, and since that time he has been a man of one work. Through privations and hardships he has gone, preaching the gospel to many thousands, and seeing scores and hundreds brought to Christ through his faithful ministry. He was presiding elder for sixteen years consecutively. How he performed that office the preachers who shared his trials and rejoiced with him in their successes are still living to testify. He has often been honored with a seat in the councils of his Church, being a member of the General Conference in 1854 and 1858, and was also elected to the General Conference in 1862, which was to meet in New Orleans.

When first taken ill he said to his wife that on preaching his last sermon he was greatly blessed. His text was, "On this rock I will build my Church, and the gates of hell shall not prevail against it;" but he said a voice had been saying to him ever since: "Come home; your work is done; you have suffered enough." He said to Brother Dockery ten hours before his death: "I am so happy!" And when told that he was dying, he said: "I am falling asleep in Jesus!" Brother Cope asked him if he had any message for the preachers? He said: "Tell them to raise the gospel standard high." He took hold of his brother James's hand and said: "Bless God! I see the heaven of heavens above me, and I will soon be there!" He said also: "My calling as a preacher of the gospel is a glorious mission. I have suffered greatly, but I now begin to see my reward and my crown." To his faithful physician, Dr. Poindexter, he said: "I thank you for your kindness, but all we can do now is to meet in heaven." He then exclaimed: "O my dear wife and children!"

It was wonderful as we stood around his bed, expecting to see him breathe his last, to behold a calm, beautiful smile lighting up his pallid countenance. I asked him if he felt that God was with him. He answered in the strongest affirmative, and added: "This is the sweetest moment of my life." I asked him if the heavenly hosts were coming to meet him. He said, "They are already here—father, mother, Alice, Martha," and others he named. He said also: "Such revelations I never could have conceived of." After awhile he roused up a little, and said: "Why, I thought I would have been in heaven before now. I thought once I was there. Heaven, my friends, is no fiction, but as real as the soul and body. While it was only the twilight, I could see ahead, and I saw the great white throne of God, and the redeemed around God's throne. I heard the music of their songs and saw a hand beckoning me to come." He said he recognized many friends there he once knew on earth. He told his wife he knew it was hard on her, but God would take care of her and the children. He told her to trust in God and not be afraid, and it would be right. He said to a relative who stood at the foot of the bed: "Sam Law, I always loved you; meet me in heaven." All the time he talked a most beautiful smile played over his countenance. When his brother came he said: "John, I am glad to see you again; we shall meet under the tree of life." To another he said: "I am about to be off." Being asked, "Are you ready?" his answer was, "Yes, I am ready;" and then fell asleep in Jesus.

We find in the *St. Louis Christian Advocate* an encouraging account given by Rev. J. Devlin, that holy man of God, of his work on the Carrollton

Circuit. He "has been holding a series of protracted meetings in different parts of the circuit with success. Has received into the Church, since Conference, two hundred and eighty-eight persons. Three young men have been licensed to preach, with a view of joining the Annual Conference this fall. Much has been done in the way of repairing and building church-houses—now, at the time of this writing, they are laying the foundation of a good, substantial, and commodious brick church at Carrollton."

In the brief notice given above we see the true elements of successful work in the Church of God —many souls brought into the fold of Christ, young men called to preach the gospel, old, dilapidated houses of worship repaired and put in order, and new church-houses built. If that is not the right kind of work and in the right direction, we do not know what is. We regard it as unmistakable evidence of a Holy Ghost revival, when young men are made to feel that they are called of God to preach, with the conviction fastened in their consciousness that "woe is unto me, if I preach not the gospel."

It is a sad feature of the subject that in so many and so extensive revivals all over the country, in which scores and hundreds and thousands are converted, so comparatively few young men enter the Christian ministry. The world is now ready for the gospel. Every door has been unlocked, every gate unbolted, and every barrier removed, and Ethiopia is stretching out her hands unto God. But how very few respond to the commission of the Lord Jesus Christ: "Go ye into all the world, and preach the gospel to every creature!" The whole Church should send up a united prayer to God to send forth more laborers into the field, which is already white to the harvest.

REV. C. I. VAN DEVENTER.

The moral excellency and high Christian character of this eminently good man are so well known to all persons who are living within the bounds of the Missouri Conference that any word of commendation from us would be regarded as superfluous and unnecessary. He has furnished us with an historic sketch of his ministerial life which will no doubt be read with intense interest by his numerous friends:

I was admitted on trial in the Missouri Conference, September, A.D. 1844, and was appointed with Rev. George W. Love, junior preacher on the Liberty Circuit. The following two years I was on the Bowling Green Circuit, the first year as an assistant with Rev. J. Lannius, and part of the second year with Rev. George Smith, and the latter part of the same year was in charge of the circuit, on account of the failing health of Brother Smith. The next two years I was in charge of the Danville Circuit; the next two in charge of the Fulton Circuit. The next year I was sent to Glasgow. The next two years I was appointed in charge of the St. Joseph Station. The next year I was at Weston; the next two years I was stationed at Louisiana, and the next two at Hannibal. I was ordained deacon in 1846 by Bishop Paine, and elder in 1848 by Bishop Andrew.

The events and persons connected with the history of those years of sunshine and shade, of toil and struggle are not without much interest, at least to the writer. But as I am limited in space, and have much before me, I will not make mention of said persons and events.

At the Conference held in St. Joseph September 15, 1859, Bishop Paine presiding, I was appointed presiding elder of the Hannibal District, including the following charges and preachers: Hannibal Station, E. K. Miller; Palmyra Station, W. M. Newland; Canton, to be supplied; La Grange Station, A. P. Linn; Waterloo, Louis Baldwin; Alexandria, J. R. Taylor; Monticello, M. R. Jones; Fabius, J. W. Penn; Hydesburg, D. Mason; Frankford, T. D. Clanton; Canton Station, to be supplied by J. W. Barrett, who was also in charge of the Canton high school. T. D. Clanton was transfered early in the year to Oregon, and J. W. Markley, a local preacher, was employed in his place on the Frankford Mission. This was my first appointment as presiding elder. The district embraced the north-eastern part of Missouri, reaching over in two different places into Iowa. My first quarterly meeting was held at Alexandria, in Clarke County—considered rather a hard place, but I did not find it specially so. During this year Brother E. M. Bounds, then a young attorney at law living at Hannibal, Mo., yielding to a previously unsettled conviction of duty, was licensed to preach, and employed the last six months of the Conference year to travel with Rev. M. R. Jones on the Monticello Circuit.

In my new relation to the Church I was of course much from home, always to me a very great privation. But the society of the preachers and their families, with the added kindness of many friends, brethren, and sisters, ministered much to my comfort and the pleasure of my work, now so varied and enlarged. The memory of their sympathy and co-operation with the young presiding elder is still lingering in his heart. Several of these dear brethren, co-laborers in the work of the ministry, have been called to their reward; while many others of the laity also have finished their course. May we each and all who remained be ready for our change when it shall come! During this Conference year gracious revivals of religion were enjoyed by most of the charges.

At the Conference held at St. Charles September 12, 1860, Bishop Kavanaugh presiding, I was re-appointed to the Hannibal District. During the early part of the Conference year the pastors were generally favored with encouraging success. But the cloud of civil war was already hovering over the land, and the first and bitter fruits of the times which followed were being gathered. Having a large family, as a matter of economy, we moved to our large, unoccupied house in Louisiana, Pike County. The change added considerable to the amount and inconvenience of my travel. But with God's blessing I continued in my appointed work.

The Conference of this year was held at Glasgow September 11, 1861. In the absence of the bishop, Rev. W. G. Caples presided. It had been appointed to meet at Hannibal, and was changed to Glasgow. I was returned to the Hannibal District. Nothing of very special importance is remembered in connection with this year. "Wars and rumors of wars" prevailed. Christians and Churches were sorely tried, and hearts and homes were made sad and desolate.

Amid the gathering gloom the Lord was with his people. The venerable Martin L. Eads, who was in charge of the Emerson work, had in 1842, as preacher in charge, signed the exhorting license of his present presiding elder.

The Conference for this year was appointed to meet at Fulton in September, 1862; but did not convene, for the reasons assigned in the following historic order of Bishop Kavanaugh:

"*Postponement of Conferences.*—For the preachers of the St. Louis, Missouri, and Kansas Conferences. In view of the war excitement now raging in Missouri, the perils of travel on your rivers and railroads, and the serious embarrassment to which your preachers would be subjected by removal from one field of labor to another, I have deemed it expedient to postpone the sessions of your Conferences until such time as tranquillity shall be restored to the territory embraced within your bounds."

A few changes were made by the presiding elders in their districts, but the appointments remained principally as they had been during the previous year.

At the Conference held at Fulton October 14, 1863, Rev. Andrew Monroe presiding in the absence of a bishop, I was appointed in charge of the Louisiana Circuit, with Rev. A. P. Linn, supernumerary. My Sabbath appointments were Louisiana, Clarksville, Paynesville, and Prairieville—territory included in my second circuit. My work was prosecuted in this charge with some success and without obstruction, except at Louisiana, where our house of worship by the *forms* of law (but unlawfully) had been put in possession of the M. E. Church; while we were under the necessity of making the best arrangement we could, itinerating from one unsuitable place to another, until one good brother, J. Zumwalt, purchased a large and comfortable school-house, and put our little congregation in possession of it. Here we worshiped until we were restored to the possession of our church by the Supreme Court of the State. These were times and experiences which it is unpleasant to remember, and such as God grant may never return.

At the Conference held at Mexico September 14, 1864, Rev. A. Monroe presiding, as there was no bishop present, I was re-appointed to the Louisiana Circuit, with Rev. L. R. Downing supernumerary. On account of the dangerous illness of our son, Olin, I was not present at this session of the Conference. My appointments were the same as the year before. The Civil War had ended, but peace and quiet were far from being restored. Amid many discouragements and gloomy predictions of the future of our Church, I tried to walk by faith, to trust in God, and do right, hoping and praying for a better and brighter day.

At the Conference at Hannibal in September, 1865, Bishop Kavanaugh presiding, I was appointed to the Hannibal Station. I was not a stranger here. It was at this place, then a small town, that our family landed when we first came to Missouri in the fall of 1836. And here I had, in my past ministry, spent two years as pastor and four years as presiding elder. During the last year of my former pastorate in this city a good parsonage was built, but not in time for me to occupy it, but now it was to be our home for the three following years.

At the Conference held in Macon City in September, 1866, Bishop Marvin presiding, I was re-appointed to the same charge, and also at the Conference of 1867, held at Richmond, Bishop Doggett presiding. This old, historic charge, on account of some *pleasant* and some *sad* memories, is sacred ground. Here, with many of the *usual* and some of the *unusual* trials incident to ministerial life, I toiled to win souls to Christ, and to build up the Church of God; and while my life and labors were very imperfect, I trust and believe they were not in vain in the Lord.

At the Conference held in Weston September 9, 1868, Bishop Kavanaugh presiding, I was appointed pastor of the St. Francis Street Church, St. Joseph, which charge I served the four years following, closing with September, 1872. These years were years of much labor and care, but years of much happiness in my home and in my work; and I trust they were not unfruitful in the accomplishment of good. In this already large and growing Church, the only organization of our denomination in the city at that time, the pastor's head and heart and hands and feet were brought into requisition. The Church of this period had greatly advanced beyond its proportions in 1852, when I was its young pastor; and now at the present writing (January, 1890) its progress is still more manifest, with five resident pastors and the presiding elder living within the city limits, while there are other prosperous charges contiguous. "What hath God wrought!"

At the Conference held at Mexico September 11, 1872, Bishop Pierce presiding, I was appointed presiding elder of the St. Joseph District, with the following charges and preachers: St. Joseph Station, Francis Street, E. R. Hendrix; Tenth Street, S. W. Atteberry; St. Joseph Circuit, Cyrus Doggett; Forest City, J. W. Huffaker; Rockport, T. R. Hedgpeth; Hamburg, J. F. Muroe; Graham, H. A. Davis; Maryville, William Barnett; Alanthus Grove, P. P. Doak; Savannah Station, M. M. Hawkins; Flagg Spring, A. P. Parker; Rushville, C. Babcock; New Market, J. C. C. Davis; Agent for Central College, W. M. Rush. The territory of this district embraced a part of Platte County, with Buchanan, Andrew, Holt, Atchison, and Nodaway Counties, in North-west Missouri; and one charge principally in South-west Iowa. This field of labor was comparatively large, and to reach some of the appointments at this time, before railroads, required considerable travel over large prairies. The presiding elder was busy and happy in his work, and he has had a growing interest in this important region as the years have gone by. The Conference year was favored with revivals in most of the charges. One special need was suitable houses of worship, and ways and means were being considered looking to the erection of several church-houses that year.

At the Conference held at Carrollton in September, 1873, Bishop Wightman presiding, I was re-appointed to the St. Joseph

District. The labors and results of this year were not different materially from those of the preceding year.

The Conference held in St. Joseph September 22, 1874, Bishop Keener presiding, re-appointed me to the St. Joseph District. Additional interest and pleasure were experienced at this Conference by the presence and preaching of Bishop Marvin. Who that was present will ever forget when, on Thursday night at the close of his sermon, he sung

> My latest sun is sinking fast·
> My race is nearly run, etc.,

while his enraptured spirit seemed almost ready to break away from the prison of his feeble body and be borne on angels' wings to his heavenly home?

At the Conference held in Glasgow October 6, 1875, I was re-appointed to the St. Joseph District. At this Conference Rev. A. P. Parker was appointed a missionary to China. For several years he was chiefly supported by the contributions of the Sunday-schools of our Conference. He had been four years in the Christian ministry from the time of his admission on trial, his first appointment being to the Maryville Circuit, and all of them in the St. Joseph District. From St. Joseph, in company with Mrs. Lambuth and her son, this youthful preacher started to his distant mission field. There God has honored him with an open door and a successful ministry.

At the Conference held in Hannibal in September, 1876, Bishop McTyeire presiding, I was appointed to the Plattsburg District, with the following charges and preachers: Plattsburg and Mount Moriah, W. H. Lewis; Osborn, G. Tanquary; Weston Circuit, W. S. Conner (supply); Platte City Circuit, D. F. Bone; Parkville, A. T. Lewis; Liberty, J. A. Beagle; Camden, W. C. Campbell; Richmond, G. N. Keener; Millville, C. Babcock; Maryville, T. E. Rose; Palo, J. W. Perry; Gosneyville, T. R. Hedgpeth; Haynesville, J. A. Hyder. Within the bounds of this district was the field of my first circuit, which included all of Clay County and all of Platte County east of Platte River, now organized into four or five pastoral charges. It was pleasant occasionally to meet a friend, or the son or daughter of a friend of other years; but many had passed away. Brother Conner's health failing, Brother J. W. Ellis—at the time a local preacher

—was employed to supply the Weston charge. This year was one of much labor, with some encouraging success.

At the Conference held in Fulton in September, 1877, Bishop Marvin presiding, I was appointed presiding elder of the St. Joseph District, with the following charges and preachers: St. Joseph—Francis Street, T. J. Gooch (M. B. Chapman, supernumerary); Tenth Street, W. E. Dockery; St. Joseph Circuit, D. R. Shackelford; Forest City, William Barnett; Craig, J. W. Bain; Hamburg, S. H. Milam; Wayneville, D. C. O'Howell (L. F. Linn, supernumerary); Lamar, W. McKendree Gillum; Savannah, D. K. Tindall; New Market, C. A. Davis; Davis Chapel and Mount Moriah, D. F. Bone; Hopkins Mission, McGinnis Jeffries. This was an unexpected appointment, having so recently been in charge of this district. But the year was filled with busy labors among old and new friends. This was the last session of the Missouri Conference at which Bishop Marvin presided. During the Conference his only brother died at Louisiana, Mo. They were greatly endeared to each other, and the bishop was deeply bereaved by the death of his brother. They have no doubt met in paradise, where loved ones part no more.

At the Conference which convened in Macon City in September, 1878, Bishop Doggett presiding, I was appointed to the Osborn Circuit, in the Plattsburg District. My Sabbath appointments were Osborn, Turney, Morrow Chapel, and Stewardsville. The pastoral work was heavy for me, the members being scattered over a large territory, and my health not being very good. During the following winter and spring my general prostration was such that I was not able to preach for several months, most of that time being confined to my room, and much of the time to my bed. Brothers John Stone and James Potter, local preachers, kindly supplied my lack of service on the Sabbath; and under this arrangement the charges got along the best they could until Conference. It looked as though my active service was about at an end; but I believe, in answer to prayer, with the blessing of God upon the treatment of skillful physicians and wife's good nursing, that the good Lord raised me up again, and in a measure restored my health.

At the Conference held at Louisiana in September, 1879, Bishop Wightman presiding, I was appointed to the St. Joseph District, with the following charges and preachers: St. Francis Street Church, E. K. Miller (M. B. Chapman, supernumerary); Tenth Street, W. E. Dockery; F—— Avenue, to be supplied; St. Joseph Circuit, D. F. Bone; Forest City, J. Bird; Craig, A. Spencer; Hamburg, A. S. Doak; Waynesville, H. C. Bolen; Lamar, D. K. Tindall; Savannah, W. T. Conwell; New Market, William Barnett; Gower, J. A. Hyder; Fillmore, J. W. Bain; A. P. Parker, missionary to China. During this year, in the midst of abundant and useful labors, Brother W. T. Conwell was called, while yet young in years and in the ministry, to his eternal reward. He lived and died well. May we all meet him in the land of everlasting rest!

I was continued on the district the three following years, and was then appointed to Hundley Chapel, in St. Joseph, in which charge I continued three years, when failing health assigned me to the superannuated relation for one year. This year I was Senate chaplain to the Thirty-fourth General Assembly of Missouri; after which I was appointed to the Centenary charge, St. Joseph, and continued one year. The next year I was appointed to the Conference Trust Fund agency, and was re-appointed to the same work this Conference year, 1889-90.

God has permitted me to live not only in an eventful period, including more than half of the nineteenth century—a period marvelous in the history of our country, and distinguished for many wonderful and useful inventions, with which the civilized world is blessed. And perhaps that part of the time between the years of 1860 and 1880 furnish the most interesting and important *data* in the history of the M. E. Church, South. During these years lay representation, Church Conferences, District Conferences, the organization of the Woman's Missionary Society, and the Church Extension Board (including the Woman's Department) have, with other important branches, been incorporated into our ecclesiastical economy.

God grant that our Church may be not only in Missouri, but throughout its entire connection, true to the letter and to the spirit of the gospel, and to the doctrines and polity of our fathers, and continue on this line as long as time endures! Within these twenty years—1860 to 1880—more than a score of itinerant preachers have failed to answer to the Conference roll-call; many useful local preachers have also ended their labors, while hosts of religious laymen and godly women have been transferred from the Church militant to the Church triumphant in heaven.

The names of many dear brethren and sisters who lived, labored, and suffered within the bounds of the several charges mentioned in this paper, and some of whom have crossed the last river, whilst others remain to work in the Master's vineyard, are remembered and will never be forgotten by him who is now writing these lines. We have not the space to enroll all their names on these pages, but when the last great day shall come, and the "books shall be opened," may we all, with our families and with our charges, find our names written in the Lamb's book of life, and be forever with the Lord!*

Our Church and Moberly.

One of the important factors of the successful progress of Methodism is its power of adaptation to the circumstances by which it is surrounded. This remarkable adaptability enables it to adjust itself to the existing condition of things, and thereby gives it success almost everywhere its standard is planted. Defeat is a thing of rare occurrence, when its ministers will resolutely, patiently, and perseveringly do their whole duty. We see the marvelous results of this wonderful adaptation in its growth and development with the people of this vast Western country. The history of its success and progress is interwoven with the history of the country. It permeates society wherever it goes, and elevates the moral tone of the people. This is known to be true in every place where Methodism prevails.

Take the history of Methodism and of Moberly

---

*Rev. C. I. Van Deventer, MS.

as an illustration that Methodism adapts itself to its environment. The mixed, heterogeneous, and transient character of the population of Moberly— a railroad town and, like all railroad towns, notorious for its wickedness—is very unfavorable to religion, and makes success in the cause of Christ very difficult—indeed, impossible—without divine co-operation. Yet Methodism, though small at first, has gradually advanced, in spite of all antagonistic elements, with the growth of the town. When their house of worship became too small the Methodists sold it and built another of larger capacity. When that became too small they sold it, and are now building a magnificent edifice of larger proportions, which will be an ornament to their growing city, and will reflect great credit upon the Church and their indefatigable pastor, Rev. T. G. Whitten.

We find a piece of history in the *St. Louis Christian Advocate*, from the pen of Dr. Vincil, written about two decades ago, which will give the reader a very good idea of what Methodism in Moberly was at that time; and by comparison he cannot fail to see the progress of the Church to the present time. He says:

As an item of Church news, I take pleasure in announcing to your readers that the Southern Methodist people have erected a good and tasteful house of worship in the town of Moberly. This is a great achievement, in view of all the circumstances. The importance of the locality gives character to this most successful enterprise. Moberly is a young and thriving town of several hundred inhabitants. It is located on the North Missouri railroad, nearly 150 miles from St. Louis, and about 20 miles from Macon City. From Moberly starts out the west branch of the North Missouri railroad, which runs through Huntsville, Salisbury, Keytesville, Brunswick, and up the Missouri River bottom to Kansas City.

Moberly is destined to grow into a city of no ordinary consequence as a railroad center. The Hannibal and Moberly railroad is to find its connection here with the great western thoroughfares. Looking to the future of the place, and desirous of providing for the present wants of the rapidly increasing population, a few earnest men resolved to build the Lord a house. Every thing considered, the undertaking was a heavy one; but there was a *heavy* man in the harness. The preacher in charge of Huntsville Circuit determined to make himself felt in that community, and during the past Conference year went to work with commendable zeal to push forward the glorious cause of "church extension." Who that knows Rev. D. H. Root will doubt his *ability* to *push* any movement uphill? Being warmly aided by a band of co-workers, "tried, true, and trusty," the building of the Lord's house went forward. Though many prophesied evil concerning the work, and said, "What do these feeble Southern Methodists?" still the house was undertaken, carried forward to completion, and declared ready for dedication in a surprisingly short time. In truth I was not aware of the existence of the enterprise until informed that it was about ready for presentation to the Lord of hosts. Being honored with an invitation to attend, and lead in the dedicatory services, I visited Moberly, and found a neat and substantial wooden structure ready for use. The house is a one-story frame, 30 feet wide and 50 feet long, most eligibly situated. It is neatly plastered and very well seated, though the painting is not quite finished. Upon the whole, it is a good and pleasant house of worship, where the people may meet and serve the God of Israel in simplicity of mind and sincerity of heart, unaffected by the presence and influence of style and gorgeous display.

On the Sabbath a large concourse of people assembled in the new church to witness and participate in the interesting services. After the sermon was over five hundred dollars was raised and the house of worship, being now free from debt, was declared to be the property of the Lord and was solemnly dedicated to his service. Thus another house of prayer has been erected as a resort for the people, whither they may go up to wait on the Lord and renew their strength.

Let the reader compare the frame building dedicated by Dr. John D. Vincil on the above occasion with the church-edifice now in process of erection, and he will have some correct idea of the progress of Methodism in Moberly the last two decades.

Rev. J. A. Mumpower.

The M. E. Church, South, in Missouri has no cause to be ashamed of her own preachers. They are not few, but many, and as noble a set of men as ever entered the Christian ministry—"tried, true, and trusty." They will suffer nothing in comparison with the ministers of other Conferences, other States, or other denominations. They have filled every position and office in our Church, from the lowest to the highest, from the circuit preacher to the bishop, with efficiency and success. While they may not be distinguished for their brilliant talents and great oratorical powers, they are characterized by something of more importance—deep piety, unswerving fidelity to God, moral courage and activity, zealous, indefatigable work in the Lord's vineyard. Their religious integrity was thoroughly tested during the Civil War, and while many suffered martyrdom for the truth as it is in Jesus, not one betrayed his Lord and Master by compromising his faith or by yielding one single Christian principle. This fact is demonstrated in the life of him whose name appears

23

above and who has given a brief account of his labors and trials in the Christian ministry as follows:

In April, 1862, I was licensed to exhort by the Quarterly Conference of Chillicothe Station, and in August (the 9th) I was licensed to preach by the same Quarterly Conference; Brother W. T. Ellington being employed by the presiding elder, Rev. W. G. Caples, as pastor. Brother Caples was not at either Quarterly Conference. Hence my license bears the signature of W. T. Ellington, preacher in charge.

These were days of trouble to all people, and especially to Southern Methodists. Brother Ellington was teaching school in Chillicothe, and after our regular preachers had left he was employed to do what he could for the Church at Chillicothe and in the country round about.

The fall of 1862 I was employed to take charge of the Chillicothe Circuit by the presiding elder, W. G. Caples. I did what I could in that charge for one year—kept up the appointments, had some good meetings, and organized a class at Brother William Wallace's (since called Zion). The cause of our Church did well, and they kept together on the circuit. The Church never did disband. So much for what a local preacher can do. After my time expired Brother E. Carlyle, a local preacher, kept the work going.

In the winter of 1863 I was employed by the presiding elder, Brother William Ketron, to take charge of Milan Circuit. I went to work, remained during the winter and spring, when the war troubles became so great that my friends prevailed on me to leave. Brother J. L. Wood had been killed, and I was in divers ways threatened and annoyed, was closely pursued and dogged all the time, so I was compelled to give up my charge. At Scottsville I was followed out of town by a drunken fellow who tried to make me go back with him. I refused because the town was full of men just like himself. He then drew a revolver on me, but I was so close to him that he did not dare to use it. By presence of mind I was able to overcome him, and after giving him a good talk he left me and went back, but threatened me as he left.

There were some local preachers on Milan Circuit who did

not leave; among whom were S. S. Hardin, J. Wattenburger, John and Alex. Harmon, John W. Duskey, and William Jones, who kept the work going and our Church intact as best they could. Brother Ketron, the presiding elder, sent me to Spring Hill Circuit in 1864. He was soon after taken sick, and was not able to preach any more. He lived near Edinburg, and was much beloved by all the people. I went to see him frequently, and he was a great help to me.

The whole of the responsibility fell upon me, but I had good counselors in such men as Brothers Smith, Conklin, Ray, Devorse, Bowen, and a host of others who gave me help in many ways. This was a glorious half-year's work. The Lord was with us at almost every appointment, in reviving his work and saving souls, at Edinburg, Antioch, Gus Creek, Lillie's Chapel, and Ketron's Chapel. At the latter place we had a revival in August, resulting in more than one hundred conversions and about the same number of accessions to the Church. This revival was far-reaching in its influence. There were converts all over Davies County; also Grundy, Livingston, and Gentry Counties. Another characteristic of this revival was the power of God manifested in the meetings. Men and women would fall prostrate as by some unseen power. Some of them remained in that condition until they were converted. Even members of the Church would become helpless and remain so for hours, and some all day. I have never witnessed anything like it since. Brother Samuel Alexander came to my help toward the close of the meeting, but most of the work was done by the lay brethren of whom I have spoken. Truly God was with us in very great power.

We had war troubles here too. During so much of God's presence, and while great good was being accomplished, the adversary was busy, had his emissaries at work, tormenting us by wicked soldiers and others, but the Lord of hosts was with us and gave us the victory. This was another stronghold of Southern Methodism, and they never disbanded on the Spring Hill Circuit. It was from this circuit that I was recommended to the Missouri Annual Conference at Mexico in 1864.

That fall Brother Joseph Devlin was put in charge of Spring Hill and Gallatin Circuits. I was sent to Marysville Circuit, but could not do any thing on account of war troubles. I crossed the plains next spring, spent the summer, and returned to Missouri in the fall. I assisted Brother Devlin in his extensive work under Brother W. E. Dockery, the presiding elder.

In the following spring Brother Dockery sent me to the Albany Circuit. When ready to start, Brothers John D. Vincil, who was stationed at Chillicothe, and William M. Leftwich, who happened to be there, told me to cut down the bridge behind me so that retreat would be impossible. I found the work disorganized and our people not knowing what to do. But the Lord went with me and manifested his presence. I went to work, organizing and holding meetings. It was one continual triumph from early spring until time for the Annual Conference to meet. Every appointment on the circuit was blessed with a revival of religion. Many precious souls were converted, and the Church strengthened and put into good running order.

Here also we had trouble from those in authority and power. I was arrested for preaching without taking the oath. They tried to incarcerate me and put me in jail, but for fear of the people they did not succeed. I preached frequently when I was told that if I did so I would not get out of the pulpit alive. I never was happier in all my life. Brother Dockery stood by me in all these trials; so did my many friends, and I started to Conference in a happy state of mind. It met at Richmond, but I was taken sick at Gallatin, and did not get there.

By the Conference which met at Richmond in the fall of 1866 I was sent to Yellow Creek (now Bucklin) Circuit. Here I had over two hundred and fifty conversions and about the same number of additions to the Church—a year of great success and prosperity. From here I went back to Albany, in the spring, to answer to the indictment of the grand jury for preaching without taking the oath. I came out all right. and finished up a prosperous and happy year.

The next fall I was sent to Savannah Circuit, in which charge I remained three years. I found the Church here in a badly disorganized condition, but the good Lord did help me, and in the three years of my pastorate I had the satisfaction of seeing the Church grow and increase in influence for good. I organized two new Societies—Platte Chapel and Bedford's Chapel—though the houses of worship were not finished until after I left. Here I found friends of the Church who stood by her in all times of trial; such as Dr. M. F. Wakefield, N. Farrow, Rev. Alexander Bedford, J. P. Shoemaker, N. Bird, P. Richardson, and others, of whom honorable mention might be made. Some of them have gone to the better country, their heavenly home for which they lived and died.

In the fall of 1870 I was appointed to Weston Station. Here I had a pleasant year—was married April 27, 1871. This fall I was appointed to the Gallatin District; served it two years as best I could.

In the fall of 1873 I was sent to Carrollton Station for one year; in 1874, to Gallatin Station, where I remained four years; then to Macon City, four years; Fayette District, four years; and this year (1890) is my fourth year on the Mexico District. The Lord be praised for his wonderful goodness to me through all the past years of my ministerial life, and for owning and blessing my unworthy labors in the salvation of sinners, and in the accomplishment of good! By and by, when my work is done, and the toilsome strife of life is ended, I shall meet those dear loved ones with whom I have been so delightfully associated in the service of God on earth—shall meet them beyond the rolling river in that bright world whose sky is always clear and cloudless, whose sun never sets, and whose inhabitants are supremely blessed and perfectly happy in serving and praising the God of their salvation.

REV. GEORGE C. LIGHT, D.D.

In writing the history of "Methodism in Missouri," we cannot pass over in silence this great and good man, this gifted minister of the gospel, this able defender of "the faith once delivered unto the saints." In view of the high estimation in which he is held by the Methodists of Missouri we feel satisfied that the following information of the closing scenes of his life will be read with no little interest:

In many respects Dr. Light was a remarkable man. Possessing naturally a fine mind, with a wide grasp of thought, he used his mental capital to the very best advantage. Those who heard him in his palmy days will remember how completely error and false doctrine were routed when he brought to bear his well-mounted battery of reason, truth, and eloquence. Perhaps no man in his day wielded a wider and more decided influence for good than did Dr. Light.

In person he was commanding, possessing a vigorous constitution and an affable and courteous address, which made him a welcome guest wherever he went. Taking him all in all, we shall not soon look upon his like again. But he is gone; his work is done; and calmly and peacefully he laid aside his shield and sword, and, delivering up his parchment to the Shepherd and Bishop of souls, he exchanged the cross for the crown. The reader would, no doubt, like to know how he spent his last days and ended his life.

At the Conference of 1859, held in Jackson, Miss., he reluctantly took a superannuated relation, but, as before mentioned, his age and increasing infirmities compelled him to retire from the ranks of the active ministry, but his active mind and zeal for the cause of his divine Master would not let him remain idle. He filled one appointment every month on the plantation of Mr. William Love, and had also offered to fill the pulpit of the writer as occasion might demand. The Sabbath before his death it was my privilege to hear him deliver a cogent and earnest discourse to the servants in the Church at Canton, from the text: "Say ye to the righteous it shall be well with him." He had little thought that in two short days he would go to reap the reward of the righteous, which he knew so well how to describe. The day following I went to Vicksburg in company with Dr. Light, and enjoyed the privilege of holding converse with him while on the way. During the conversation he commented beautifully on three passages of scripture: "Hearken unto me, ye that follow after righteousness;" "I have seen an end of all perfection, but thy commandment is exceeding broad;" "And thou, Solomon, my son, know thou the God of thy father, and serve him with a perfect heart." He remarked, after he had commented on these passages some time, that if he lived to see the next day he would be seventy-five years of age, and, so far as he was concerned, if the world was put up at auction, he would not be a high bidder. His conversation seemed to be peculiarly in heaven. He repeated several beautiful couplets of poetry; one on procrastination, the other on man's free will and God's prescience, and also the hymn commencing, "Vain man, thy fond pursuit forbear," expressing a regret that this hymn had been left out of the new Hymn Book.

On reaching Vicksburg he complained greatly of a pain in his shoulder, and, taking him to the hotel, I procured some liniment with which I laved his shoulder. He then expressed himself better, and on taking my Bible to read, he requested me to read to him the first chapter of Colossians, upon which he commented most beautifully for more than an hour, greatly to my edification.

He slept quietly, and seemed as well as usual next morning, arose, dressed himself, and, after kneeling in prayer, desired me to read the fifth chapter of Second Corinthians, saying that it gave him comfort. He dwelt upon the passage: "For we know that, if our earthly house of this tabernacle were dissolved, we have a building of God, a house not made with hands, eternal in the heavens;" and also with evident delight on the seventh verse: "For we walk by faith, not by sight." Also on: "Willing rather to be absent from the body, and to be present with the Lord;" "the love of Christ constraineth us;" "therefore if any man be in Christ, he is a new creature;" and so on to the end of the chapter. He spoke of the kind of bodies we shall have in the resurrection, and the locality of heaven, remarking that although it is true that where God is there is heaven, yet, inasmuch as God has made us social beings, he believed that there is a special place where the redeemed will be reunited and dwell together forever. Speaking of the body as the tabernacle, he said that when the body dies the *man* does not die, and when we look upon the body we do not see the *man*—only the outer vestment—remarking that in reality it is a very little matter for the Christian to die; it is only to be absent from the body, and to be present with the Lord.

After breakfast we went to the Book Depository, where he met and conversed cheerfully with some of his old friends. We parted at 12 o'clock, agreeing to meet in the evening at Brother Clinton's. After dinner with Brother Howe, he started to call on Dr. Marshall, about 4 o'clock in the afternoon, but before reaching there was taken with violent pain about the region of the heart, which proved to be a metastasis of rheumatism from the shoulder. With great difficulty he reached Brother Marshall's, remarking when he met him at his door that he was "almost dead." He was assisted in, and after being seated and given a stimulant, he was somewhat revived and commenced conversation with Brother Marshall in his usual cheerful manner, but in a few moments his head fell back on the chair and, without a groan or a struggle, his spirit passed away to that God who gave it. Thus departed from earth one of God's faithful ministers, whose name for years was a tower of strength on the walls of Zion.*

---

* Dr. Camp, in *St. Louis Christian Advocate*.

CHAPTER XV.

St. Louis Conference.

At Jefferson City, Bishop Kavanaugh Presiding; W. M. Prottsman, Secretary—Preaching at the Capitol on the Sabbath by the Bishop—An Occasion of Unusual Interest—Statistical Reports Favorable—Increase of Membership 2,000—Missionary Anniversary a Success—Missionary Cause Growing in Interest—Also an Advance Movement in the Sunday-school Interests—One Hundred and Forty-six Church-houses—Dr. W. A. Smith Delivered an Address on Education in the Interest of Central College—Education on Upward Grade—South-east Missouri—Also South-western Missouri—Same Country Spoken of by Alonzo Dante—Rev. J. A. Murphy on Revival Interests—Future Prospects of Kansas City, by "S."—A Voice from South-west Missouri Again—New Madrid Circuit—Marvin Camp-ground, Near St. Louis.

THE annual session of the St. Louis Conference was opened by Bishop Kavanaugh at Jefferson City, September 23, 1868. W. M. Prottsman was elected Secretary.

As the *St. Louis Christian Advocate* furnishes an interesting notice of this Conference, including important statistical information, we shall give it a place here for the benefit of the reader:

On Sabbath during the Conference there was more than an ordinary degree of religious interest manifested in this city and in the country round about. The central point of attraction was the Capitol, where, in the forenoon, the bishop preached one of his best and most effective sermons, at the close of which he ordained six licentiates to the office and work of deacons in the Church of God. In the afternoon Rev. S. S. Bryant preached at the same place, after which six deacons were ordained to the office of elder. Two other ministers were received into our Church as being in orders. One of these was from the Protestant Episcopal Church and the other from the Northern Methodist Church. Sunday night Dr. Smith delivered an able and instructive sermon at the Capitol. At the Methodist Church the present writer preached as best he could in the forenoon, and at night Dr. W. M. Leftwich, of the Missouri Conference, delivered an excellent discourse. There was also preaching by members of the Conference in the Baptist Churches, of which there are two in the city, one for white, the other for colored people. Then, the churches, school-houses, etc., for several miles around were similarly occupied. In the afternoon the writer had the pleasure of preaching to a large, intelligent, and well-behaved congregation in Calloway County at a church opposite to this city. It was indeed a privilege and a pleasure to be with them.

Conference statistics are not as yet complete, but as far as ascertained the following may be regarded as correct. The aggregate of members of the Church in the bounds of the Conference is *sixteen thousand one hundred and fifteen*, being an increase of a little more than *two thousand* during the past year. Adding these numbers to those reported to the Missouri Conference, it will be seen that the aggregate number of Southern Methodists in the State of Missouri is, in round numbers, *thirty-four thousand*, a little over *five thousand* of whom joined the Church during the past year. That is, the *increase* of the aggregate number during the year was more than *five thousand*. This, too, in a Church that four years ago was solemnly pronounced dead—certainly and surely dead—and those so pronouncing proceeded to minister on its effects. "There is life in the old Church yet."

The Conference Missionary Society held its anniversary meeting last night at the Capitol. Addresses were delivered by R. A. Hatcher, Esq., and Bishop Kavanaugh. They were to the point, not sensational, but argumentative, and characterized by a deep vein of true piety. The collection taken up at the close of the addresses amounted to a little over *nine hundred dollars*, a large sum for the time and place, a place where only a few years ago this Conference would not have been allowed to hold a session at all. The aggregate of collections for missionary purposes in the bounds of the Conference was a little more than *four thousand five hundred dollars.*

The interests of the Sunday-schools have been advanced considerably, although they are by no means what they ought to be. The number of schools, teachers, and scholars was increased during the year, and the reports at this Conference show an increase over the reports made at the last Conference. This year the aggregate number of Sunday-schools is reported at *one hundred and fifty-nine.* The number of officers, *four hundred and thirty;* teachers, *nine hundred and eighty;* scholars, *nine thousand and seventy-one;* volumes in library, *sixty-seven thousand and ninety-eight.*

This is, in some aspects, a gratifying report. Still I must insist the numbers in each case are about one-half of what they should be. I must insist that the number of children under Sabbath-school instruction among us ought in every Conference to equal the number of Church-members in that Conference.

It must be remembered, however, that many, very many of our people and their children are connected with Union Sunday-schools, organized and carried on under the agency of the American Sunday-school Union. So that many more of our children are under Sabbath-school instruction than is indicated in the reports made to Conference, as these reports refer only to such schools as are exclusively under the control of our Church; no reference at all to schools of any other kind.

There are in the bounds of this Conference *one hundred and fifty local preachers,* many of whom are men of strength and extensive usefulness.

There are *one hundred and forty-six* church-houses—few, it is true, when compared with the number needed, but *many* when compared with what there were at the close of the war. There are eighteen parsonages—very few, indeed, in proportion to the number of preachers to be accommodated. The number of adult baptisms during the past year was *nine hundred and eighty,* and the number of infant baptisms was *six hundred and forty-two.*

This morning six preachers, men who came well recommended, were admitted on trial in the traveling connection. Two of these were from the M. E. Church (North). So it seems that we are advancing a little in almost every respect.

In writing the other day I referred to a few of the older members of the Conference by the names then given. There may be added the names of Andrew Peace, John T. Peery, John R. Bennett, H. N. Watts, J. C. Godbey, and a few others who have long gone in and out before the people endeavoring to teach them "the good and right way," "to fear God and keep his commandments;" men whose record is on high, and the full fruits of whose labors eternity will make known.

Next to these in point of age in the Conference—that is, in the order of time during which they have been members of this Conference—are such as W. M. Prottsman, T. M. Finney, J. M. Proctor, W. S. Woodard, S. M. Winton, and others, who are now perhaps the most active members of the body. The first two named are very efficient and active members. Then there are other men here, such as Dr. W. A. Smith and S. S. Bryant, who, though not long members of this Conference, have been for many years active, able, and successful ministers elsewhere. On Tuesday evening Dr. Smith delivered an address on the subject of education generally and the interests of Central College particularly. At the close of his address about *two thousand dollars* was subscribed to the endowment fund of that college.

South-east Missouri.

The design of the following article is to give the reader some knowledge of the condition of things in certain portions of South-east Missouri within the bounds of the St. Louis Conference. The writer uses highly figurative language and striking illustrations, no doubt for the purpose of arresting the attention and impressing the minds of the reader. He commences thus:

Did you ever see a heavy sleet in winter, whose weight was such as to bend the flexible trees, and make their branches pendent? Did you ever see the freeze continue until one broad sheet of ice overspread all the country round? I presume you have. Well, then, you have seen an ice-clad country that can be used to illustrate the condition of things in former days, in relation to the M. E. Church, South, in this section of the country. But I suppose you witnessed a great thaw as this vast sheet of ice melted away. So likewise the Sun of righteousness, with his radiant beams, has raised the temperature of our religious atmosphere until the great sleet has almost wholly disappeared.

Doctrines adverse to Methodism and very baneful to society obtained footing in past years in these parts, and chilled the feelings of the people into a frozen state. This condition of things during the reign of terror was indeed most appalling, but, thank God! a better state of things has come about. Our Church is now doing a work in this country that is manifestly deep and broad and changing the whole phase of things. The sentiments of some men have undergone a wonderful transmutation, and in some cases their hearts and lives have been entirely changed by the preaching of the pure word of God. Other men have been awed into respectfulness toward us, and are yielding to the religious influence of the M. E. Church, South, though some of them are doing so very reluctantly, and would perhaps gladly have it otherwise if they could.

It is a little amusing to hear a few men talk about our Church being erelong lost in and swallowed by the M. E. Church (North). But at the very time such observations are made, with some there is no doubt a secret wish that they were in the Southern Methodist Church. Just as the fortunes of Joseph in Egypt were succeeded by a sequel whose power and dignity put him in close proximity to King Pharaoh, so in like manner will the depressions, persecutions, and struggles through which our Church has passed tend to her elevation in moral purity and increasing usefulness. There was a time when the life of Joseph was despaired of, when they sought to take his life and destroy his influence, when they persecuted him and confined him in a dungeon, a military prison, and he was neglected and forgotten. Mourning and tears were spent over Jacob's lost son. But blessed be God that the dispensations of divine Providence were such in Egypt and the surrounding country as to bring the lost Joseph to light. This Heaven-favored child under the safe protection of God, who has plucked princes from their thrones, and elevated the despised and neglected till at last he reached a place of honor and power that secured to him the " ring, vestments of fine linen, and the use of the second chariot in the kingdom, together with the management of all the important affairs of the land." The day of famine and trial came on, and the identical Joseph who was supposed to be among the dead and forgotten was the dispenser of the substance of Egypt. Inasmuch as our people have passed through similar scenes of persecutions and trials, is not the time at hand when the M. E. Church, South, will be promoted, as was Joseph? Will not the period come when similar promotions and honors will crown our Church? Will not the providence of God so change the times and transform the circumstances as to place a non-political Church as high in public esteem and in honor as Joseph was promoted in Egypt.

Will not God dash in pieces like a "potter's vessel," the systematic and legalized opposition to our innocent and non-secular Church? Will not the unfolding events of the future bring us to the position which will attract as many eyes as gazed upon Joseph when clothed in linen and decorated with gold in his chariot of State?

How strange are the events of the past! Equally singular has been the movements of that cloud whose emblem hung in momentous import over a people as mysteriously led through hardships and dangers as he has conducted our Church through perilous times in these latter days. Yet it may be in the near future when it shall be said of us: "Beautiful for situation, the joy of the whole earth, is Mount Zion." May "the eternal God be her refuge while the everlasting arms shall be underneath her!" May her triumphant course be successful to the confusion of enemies and in the salvation of millions of our race—all to the glory of God!

Pemiscot County is the south-eastern county of our once free and happy Missouri. Before the inauguration of that unchristian Civil War Pemiscot County, for the intelligence of her citizens, for the spirit of morality and religion manifested by her people of all ages and sexes, for her schools and system of internal improvements, in proportion to her population and advantages, stood behind no sister county in the State. Her people then were happy. Then there was no political proscription, no iron code to insult and crush the spirit of free Americans. Then it was an honor to be an American citizen. Then we had a county second to none on earth. But alas! our hopes of a glorious future sickened and died within us. The dark pall of anarchy and woe was spread over our country, and a reign of terror was inaugurated,

During the four years' war, Pemiscot County was the theater on which were enacted scenes over which angels might weep and devils rejoice. Freebooters and banditti, taking advantage of the helplessness of the people, plundered without let or hinderance; and a soldiery with no guiding star but blood and booty laid their unhallowed hands on goods and property not theirs by gift or purchase; and oftentimes the death-cry of the helpless and defenseless would ring out upon the air, while the soldiers and murderers cursed the spirit as it left its tenement of clay. Thus our people were robbed and cruelly put to death, and when the clarion blast of war was hushed and the welcome sound of peace was heard, what a scene to behold! Our people demoralized; our plantations desolated and laid waste; the rank weed, the rugged brier, and the thistle taking possession of our fields; our school-houses harbors for owls and bats; our court-house the rendezvous for sheep and cattle; our records burned except those that were hidden; our levee, which at the commencement of the war was nearly completed on the river side of our county at an immense expense, a complete ruin. In short, devastation, desolation, and ruin were written in burning letters everywhere and on every thing.

But we are not a people to lie down and die in despair. Under the promise that was made us, that the government of our fathers should protect us once more, we went to work in good faith and in earnest to repair our wasted fortunes and forget the bloody past. And nothing but the high-handed proscription and bad faith of corrupt men in power prevented Pemiscot County from taking its stand in the front rank with its sister counties.

Notwithstanding all its drawbacks, the people are at work, religiously, morally, and physically. Once more our thoroughfares are being cleared, and our plantations are turning into the garner a bountiful supply of cereals. Our school-houses, courthouse, and churches have been repaired, and are now used for the purposes they were intended.

We will now give a brief statement of what our Church is doing and has been doing in this section within a short time past. Rev. Madison Adams, the preacher in charge of this circuit, and a faithful old soldier of the cross, held a meeting in the southern part of this county, during which there were thirty-five accessions to the Church. In this neighborhood there had been no preaching since the commencement of the war. This fact alone is sufficient to show that there is a Christian principle in these people, which only needs to be called forth by preaching the unadulterated gospel.

Again, not over two months since Rev. C. D. Davis, from Kentucky, came among us. Rev. Adams requested him to hold a series of meetings at New Salem Church, in the northern part of this county. He did so, assisted by Rev. S. Jackson (Methodist) and Rev. Tilford Hogan (Baptist). His work was arduous, but the reward will fully repay him. He has the honor of reporting thirty-six conversions and twenty-eight accessions to the Church. Mr. Davis is a man of good talent, and is a bright and shining light in the world. At Concord Church, near the central part of the county, preaching was continued during a week, with good results, Rev. S. Jackson conducting the meeting.

With a fair chance our county will show as good a record as any county in the State, any libelous newspaper report to the contrary notwithstanding. We have been slandered by newspapers, and consigned to infamy and oppression by designing men, without benefit of clergy; but, in spite of all this, we intend to travel the right road, and console ourselves with the belief that when we close our eyes in that sleep that knows no waking we shall have done our duty. God will bless the right and sustain the good, though his people may meet with sad reverses, and pass through fiery trials and sore persecutions.*

Further interesting information is given respecting the M. E. Church, South, in south-western, as well as south-eastern portions of the St. Louis Conference:

The Conference year of 1867-68 is closed, and the ministers of our Church, those faithful servants of their divine Master, have gone to their Annual Conferences, there to give a report of their labors during the past year, and to devise plans for the future success of the Church. I think that we of this south-

---

* Meiosis and G. W. Carleton, in *St. Louis Christian Advocate*.

western portion of the State have reason to be very thankful for the condition in which we find our Church at the close of the year. Our prospects are very flattering. The spirituality of the people is more alive than it has been for a long time.

But a short time ago the moral sky of this portion of the country was overcast with dark and angry clouds; the passions of the people were lashing about with wild and savage fury, like the waves of a troubled sea. The prospect for bringing order out of the general confusion was indeed gloomy; but those faithful ministers of God whose duty it was to labor in this part of the country took a survey of the field, and no doubt their hearts shrunk within them as they viewed the desolation of the Church and country. But the Spirit said "Go;" and, like the prophet who was commanded to prophesy to the valley of dry bones, they went, trusting in God; and although some of them fell on the way, those who were spared pushed forward in humble obedience to the divine command, proclaiming the gospel of salvation.

It is now about two years since the work commenced, and the change has been great indeed. The dark clouds have disappeared, and the invigorating influence of the warm and genial rays of the Sun of peace is felt. Hence Churches are being reorganized and built up, and great revivals of religion are taking place in various parts of the country. We have just closed one at Elm Spring, that consecrated spot where our lamented S. S. Headlee loved to labor and worship, and where his body is now peacefully resting. The meeting was commenced on Saturday, August 28, by our preacher in charge, and continued several days before he left for Conference. It was still continued, under the labors of some local preachers, aided by some brethren of the Baptist and Presbyterian Churches. Denominational and political prejudice was laid aside, and those who had been widely separated in feeling and sentiment during the last few eventful years met around the same altar, and joined hands in brotherly love and true Christian fellowship. I do not know the number of conversions and accessions to the Church; but they were quite numerous, and mostly young men and women who may do much good in the neighborhoods in which they live.

I don't claim that the great change which has taken place in this part of the country is attributable altogether to the work of our ministers. There are many good and true men—ministers of other denominations—that have labored much and efficiently for the good of the people, and they should share in the credit of the good done.*

Alonzo Dante says in the *St. Louis Christian Advocate:*

I must be excused for alluding to some unpleasant facts which came into my possession while I was at Benton. The minister who had been sent to this work in a very short time became dissatisfied, and abruptly gathered up his effects and went elsewhere. The presiding elder was not consulted, nor any one else. No one knew of his intentions in this direction until he had gone. Imagine, therefore, the mingled surprise and mortification of all when it was understood that he had taken " French leave." Thus for nearly twelve months the charge was without a pastor. It is to be hoped that, yet, mature reflection may bring him down to the stern duties of a Methodist itinerant, and cause him in the future to respect Church authority. He had been sent to a worthy people—none more so, I am assured, in the bounds of the Conference—and a people, too, who always take great pride in treating their pastors kindly, and who never fail to meet promptly their financial obligations.

From this point I hastened on to Charleston, the county seat of Mississippi County, and the location of the work of Mr. Pitts. How much was I delighted with this place! The finest land, I think, I have ever seen is around this town. It is a vast alluvial prairie. But, not being a real estate agent, I will leave the land subject. The Methodist church arrested my attention. Truly a splendid structure! It is made of brick, and is very commodious and handsomely finished. We have no finer church south of St. Louis, Arcadia not excepted, nor even Caledonia. All praise to the Methodists there, who indeed are a noble people. They are intelligent, wealthy, and intensely devoted to their Church. I do not blame Mr. Pitts, their excellent pastor, for being proud of his charge. He has the best reasons in the world for it. Meantime I have every reason to know that this regard is mutual. Mr. Pitts is highly esteemed by his people,

---

* W. H. Pipkin, in *St. Louis Christian Aavocate.*

on account of his excellent qualities as a Christian gentleman, his solid and efficient abilities as a preacher, and his earnest devotion to his calling. He is a whole-souled man, full of generous impulses, genial and kind, and wonderfully social in his disposition. He is a near kinsman of the gifted Fountain E. Pitts, of the Tennessee Conference, whose fame as a pulpit orator is so justly celebrated throughout Tennessee and Alabama. He has done a great work this past Conference year; revivals almost everywhere within the bounds of his work, and Sunday-schools all over his circuit! Considering his aldermanic proportions, it is curious to know with what vigor and persistence he prosecutes his laborious duties; and, although from the bleak prairies of the North, he seems to defy the swamps and lowlands of the South. Ah me! if the ague should have the temerity to assault him, what a time it would have with that vigorous constitution and that robust frame!

When I tell you that Methodism is the prevailing religious element of this section you will concur with me when I say that we should strive, by all laudable means, to foster and build up our great interests there. We must recognize the inexorable fact that the growing wealth and expanding intelligence of this prosperous region demand ministerial ability of no ordinary grade. No common man can possibly meet the wants of such a community. At present we have, fortunately, a strong man whose services are properly appreciated. Our people know how to estimate intellect and good preaching. Next year they should have a stationed minister. They deserve one, and they are amply able to support him. They have a splendid brick church, an excellent organ, and a good and comfortable parsonage; and, altogether, I do not know a more desirable field of labor than this. None of your D.D.s need consider themselves humiliated by being sent there, and let me assure you that they would have to take with them something more than their imposing titles to command respect.

Rev. J. A. Murphy, in the *St. Louis Advocate*, gives a thrilling note of revival interest in the following lines:

We are passing through a remarkable season of converting

grace. A deep religious awakening is prevailing in this part of our Conference. Nowhere does failure succeed to a faithful effort. Scores, and even hundreds, are bowing at the altar of God, and taking their places among the lovers of the "Crucified." Hoary age, behding upon the staff, treads tottering beneath the cross; while the voice of the children is heard in the temple, crying: "Hosannah!" This glorious work is free from undue excitement; yet the joy of the believing heart often breaks forth into an audible "Hallelujah!"

Our second quarterly meeting for Columbus Circuit was held a week ago at White Chapel. This church-house has been in an unfinished state for half a score of years or more, and is situated near Basin Knob, Johnson County, by which name it has been formerly known. It is now creditably completed, and was solemnly dedicated on Tuesday at 11 o'clock. The Church and community there owe much to Brother James Sanders for this honor to their neighborhood. Brother R. Minshall, the pastor, is doing his work nobly, zealous for the glory of God and the honor of the Church. The last act of the meeting was the baptism of two interesting young ladies.

Brother W. R. Litsinger, the preacher in charge of Wellington Circuit, is now assisting in a meeting at Fairview, where a score or more precious souls have found peace, "being justified by faith."

In Lexington, where I now write, there is a growing desire among our people to be wholly consecrated to the service of God. I think many are seeking and finding full redemption in the blood of the Lamb. At this date upward of fifty have united with the Church, and more than sixty have been hopefully converted to God. On Sabbath afternoon of the quarterly meeting Brother Camp received into full fellowship about forty persons, whom we trust have received the witness of the Spirit. The communion followed. Rev. J. A. Quarles, of the Presbyterian Church, assisted in the distribution of the elements, while many of his Church surrounded the table. What a sight! The more we love the blessed Jesus the more we love each other. Loved ones whom sin had hitherto separated now knelt for the first time together to receive the emblems of the body and blood of Christ. Brothers Camp and Shackelford are untiring, faithful, and full of the Holy Spirit. Bring a tribute of gratitude to the feet of Jesus, make mention of his love to us in your thanksgiving, until the ascending strain of gladness below unites with the swelling volume of "joy in the presence of the angels of God."

A traveler signed " S." talks through the *Advocate* in an interesting manner, thus:

Though Kansas City is in Missouri, it borders on the State of Kansas, and may some day cross over the line into Kansas. The town of Westport is four miles south. Kansas City, a few years ago, was not Kansas City, but "Westport Landing," on the Missouri River.

Soon after our arrival we found our excellent friend, Rev. J. W. Lewis, the pastor of the M. E. Church, South, in this city, and occupying a fine brick parsonage, which has been erected through his instrumentality. We felt greatly at home. Brother Lewis and other members of the family seemed to vie with each other in trying to make us comfortable and happy. We enjoyed the contest, as Milburn would say, hugely.

It was Saturday, and the first thing Brother Lewis did was to act the presiding elder in making out the appointments for preaching on Sunday, very generously leaving himself out of the ring. Now enjoying something of an immunity from "firstly," " secondly," and "thirdly," he is ready to show us the city. What shall be said of this young " Queen of the West?" At the close of the war Kansas City had about six thousand inhabitants; the number is now estimated at about thirty-five thousand. The principal street is about a mile in length, and is well built up, many of the houses being four stories high. It will soon be rivaled by other streets west of it, and in every direction we see wonderful displays of thrift and energy. At every point of the compass we hear the sound of the saw·and the hammer, and see the brick masons diligently applying their trowel. It really seems as if thousands of people had gathered in from the surrounding country, as well as from more distant localities, to build up a great city.

We ride through and around the town, and on the farther side of the hill from the river and where we expected to find only a few suburban residences we see, to our surprise, what looks like a town of several thousand inhabitants, with good sidewalks and paved streets, and built up with substantial brick houses. Patches of a city are to be found on all sides, and we predict that in less than ten years these detached portions will blend all harmoniously together in a city of one hundred thousand inhabitants.

Kansas City has perhaps twenty or thirty large wholesale establishments. The property of the city doubles itself in value every year or two, and capital is coming in rapidly from various places. The M. E. Church, South, has an influential position in the city. The members propose to sell, erelong, their present house of worship and lot, preparatory to the erection of a church-edifice adequate to the wants of the large and increasing congregation. It is evident, too, that another Southern Methodist Church might be established in the city without taking any thing from the existing organization. Now is the time to push the enterprise.

On Monday we were introduced to Brother Cobb, of Westport, and also met with Brother Murphy, the presiding elder of Kansas City District. Brother Murphy is a North Carolinian, and the longer you remain in his company the more loath you are to part with him. Sight-seeing at Kansas City is about at an end, only in so far as we look over upon the hills of Kansas and survey the little town of Wyandotte, not forgetting to notice minutely the great bridge recently erected over the Missouri River.

Think, too, of the Shawnee Indian Mission, for many years superintended by that excellent man, Rev. Thomas Johnson, who was murdered during the war. When we used to read of this "Indian Mission" in the "Minutes" it seemed to be beyond the borders of civilization in the "Western wilderness." That mission was only four or five miles from the present Kansas City. We are here now in the heart of the civilized world. Rev. J. T. Peery, the pastor of the Kanas City Circuit, lives a few miles east of the city. At this delightful sylvan retreat we spent one night in company with Brother Murphy. We learn much from Brother Peery of former times, and of the present condition of the Church and the country.

The next day was spent at Independence, a place of about six thousand inhabitants, one of the prettiest and pleasantest towns in Missouri. We are here at the parsonage with Brother Bryant, the pastor, a North Carolinian. The Church suffered much during the war, but through the labors of Brothers Pugh and Bryant, the pastors successively, and the well-directed efforts of the presiding elder, it has recuperated rapidly, and its present prospects are encouraging. The spacious brick church-edifice is a credit to Methodism, and the parsonage as well.

Having now seen something of Missouri, we have a sublime idea of her resources and destiny. Lands how rich! minerals, how valuable and inexhaustible! commercial and manufacturing facilities how grand and inviting! It is estimated that five hundred persons per day come to Missouri seeking homes. What a field for Christian enterprise! How every phase of society seems to invite the influence and operations of the M. E. Church, South! May her achievements accord with the purity of her doctrines, with the excellency of her discipline, and with the glorious fame of her departed heroes!*

A voice from South-west Missouri makes an earnest appeal through the *Advocate* for help. Read what he says:

It is now time for the St. Louis Annual Conference to meet, and of all the questions and interests they have to consider I think none is so important as the claims of South-west Missouri. A rich and beautiful country, none more inviting. Taking Vernon County as a stand-point, we find a vast territory that is being thickly settled by an intelligent and industrious people, and the services of no Church are so much desired and needed as ours. Two good ministers are needed in Vernon County, and can be comfortably supported. A more liberal people cannot be found in Missouri. Methodism can be made the prevailing religion of all this country, if only the proper effort is put forth. It has the ascendency now in many parts of this region, yet the Conference has treated this and adjoining counties as undeserving notice. It is to be hoped that this country will be districted, and the interest of all parties so considered as to make it more equal among the preachers and just among the people. The question may well be asked: "Are the districts arranged and manned now more to accomplish the glory of

---

* *St. Louis Christian Advocate.*

God and to promote the kingdom of Christ or to suit the conveniences of men?"

As to health, where can you find two healthier counties than Bates and Vernon? That chills may prevail this fall over all South Missouri, if not through all the West, need astonish no one after such a rainy year. But we would like for you to name a healthier county in the State of Missouri than Vernon. The whole country should not be condemned because it is sickly in some parts of South-west Missouri.

As to a good support, there is no question about that, provided a preacher goes who is imbued with the spirit of the Master and has the work at heart. They need an intelligent, working ministry. The intelligence of the people between Fort Scott and Nevada City, Vernon County, is equal to that of any part of Missouri with which I am acquainted. Before the war such men as Revs. J. R. Bennett, Ashby, Prottsman, the Headlees, operated there. Such men as Senators Peyton, Waldo P. Johnson, and other eminent lawyers lived there and further south.

We earnestly hope that the interests of that country will not be overlooked by the Conference this year. Such men as Dr. White, J. Beard, Judge Weyand, and J. Shackelford have offered to board, without remuneration, the Methodist preacher and family all the year, and to furnish him means of conveyance, horse and all necessary equipment; and they are men who mean what they say and never go back on their word. As to accommodations generally, none are better anywhere in the State. Rev. J. Duren, Judge Weyand, Mr. Rider, Dr. Blevens, and others can testify to these facts. Is not the idea widespreading that most of our preachers have gotten to a point that raises them above their divine commission to "go into all the world." Nowadays don't most of them choose their fields of labor and manipulate their own appointments? or they will kick out of the harness and won't go at all. Have the preachers of the present day the same self-sacrificing spirit of those earnest ministers of God who planted Methodism in this great country of ours? Let them read the self-denying life of Bishop Asbury, and then answer this question.

The remarks of W. M. Williams, the preacher in charge of the New Madrid Circuit, as given in our Church paper cannot fail to entertain those who are interested in the cause of Christ:

I am just now recovering from a spell of the fever, brought on, I have no doubt, by constant preaching and labor during the past five weeks of hot, dry weather. My physical health could not stand the strain and fatigue incident to the position I was placed in. I have no local help, and the traveling preachers in this section have all they can do to cultivate their own fields. The fact is, there are not preachers enough in this portion of our Conference. My work is sufficient to keep two able men constantly employed, and then all the work would not be done. I am saying nothing now of the country beyond. I am constantly applied to for preaching in places where the sound of the gospel is seldom ever heard, and the Macedonian cry is still heard saying: "Come and help us."

We cannot close our eyes to the significant fact that something should be done for a better supply of the preached word of God in this section. This country has been in the bounds of the Conference for years, and yet it is only here and there that you will find any thing has been accomplished toward bringing the mass of the people to the knowledge of the truth as it is in Christ Jesus. This is not the fault of the men who have so faithfully labored here in days gone by; no, for a more self-sacrificing, unflinching, and devoted class of men cannot be found than those who have labored in this field. But it is because they had more to do than could be done without more laborers. They have been too few in numbers, and they have simply worn themselves out in trying to do what was beyond human endurance. I am aware that South-east Missouri is not an inviting field, that there are sickness, heat, and floods with which to contend; yet shall it be given up on that account? Are not these hundreds and thousands of starving souls here, now perishing for the bread of life as precious in the sight of God as those who are living in a higher latitude and in a more healthy country? Does not the divine commission, "Go ye into all the world, and preach the gospel to every creature," embrace those living in low, wet, and sickly lands as well as people living in healthy country? How I have wept when I have looked out upon this people perishing for the bread of life!

Previous to my sickness I preached every day. My first meeting at Reedle's Point was truly a season of refreshing from the presence of the Lord. Twenty-five professed religion, and the same number united with the Church. My next meeting was at Caruthersville, where I preached seven days. This meeting was one of great power, such as I have never seen before. Eighty-five were soundly converted to God and joined the Church. The day before the meeting closed I baptized thirty-five adults and sixteen children. When the meeting closed there were between thirty and forty penitents at the altar. I was compelled to close in order to meet another appointment. In all my meetings the old and the young were alike the subjects of saving grace. Men, women, and children experienced the converting power of God.

MARVIN CAMP-GROUND.

The following is an interesting account of the origin and establishment of the enterprise indicated by the above heading:

Some months ago, when the question of the practicability of holding a camp-meeting in St. Louis County was first mooted, very few anticipated that it would be held; or if held, that it would be a success. The idea first received form and unity in the monthly Conference of the official members of the Church in St. Louis District, who determined to make an attempt to revive that agency, which, in the earlier history of the country had been so signally owned and blessed of God in the conversion of souls. Some doubted the propriety of holding such a meeting near so large a city as St. Louis, fearing that good order could not be preserved; while a few were positively opposed to it on the ground that all who had a desire to hear the gospel had abundant opportunity by attending the various churches scattered all over the city and country. But, under the inspiration of an earnest zeal to carry the gospel into the regions beyond, it was determined to make the attempt, humbly trusting in God for his blessing.

The grounds selected are on the farm of Brother L. H. Baker, and are situated near Bonfil's Station, on the N. M. R. R. Nature seemed to have adapted the place to the purpose, and, with some assistance from art, it will be one of the most admirable camp-grounds we have ever seen.

Brother Baker has generously dedicated these grounds to this holy purpose, and has given them to the Church to be used as such as long as may be desired, besides contributing largely to their improvement.

We trust that through many years yet to come he may live to witness the annual gatherings of anxious crowds of earnest listeners, and hear the happy songs of praise to God welling up from thousands of consecrated hearts. There were on the ground seven comfortable board tents, and between forty and fifty large cloth tents. The pulpit was placed at one end of the inclosure, with pleasant seats in front of it capable of accommodating about three thousand people.

The religious services began on the evening of the 11th of August, and continued until the morning of the 20th. During the early part of the meeting the inclemency of the weather prevented many from attending, in consequence of which the congregations were not large. Those who were present, however, were not seriously interfered with in their religious exercises and enjoyments. A large tent had been prepared, affording ample protection from the rains when the congregations assembled. When the Sabbath came the clouds dispersed and the bright rays of the sun cheered the hearts of many already rejoicing in the inspiring beams of the "Sun of righteousness." The congregations on the Sabbath were very large—estimated at several thousand—and serious and solemn attention to the word of God pervaded the entire assembly. Indeed, most excellent order prevailed during the entire meeting.

There were the following ministers present: Rev. Joseph Boye, D.D., presiding elder of the St. Louis District; George H. Clinton, D.D., First Church; Rev. C. D. N. Campbell, D.D., pastor of Centenary Church; Rev. C. P. Jones, D.D., St. Paul's Church; Rev. F. A. Morris, D.D., St. John's Church; Rev. J. W. Robinson, of Wesley Chapel; Rev. J. W. Springer, of St. Louis; Rev. Wesley Browning and Rev. W. C. Godbey, of the circuit; Rev. W. D. Shumate, of Mount Olivet, St. Louis County; Rev. Ditzler, Illinois; Rev. M. Doggett, St. Charles; Rev. Talbot, of Fenton; Rev. Lewis, of Galveston, Texas; Rev. Ellington, St. Charles County; Rev. P. M. Pinckard; Rev. J. H.

Pritchett, presiding elder of the St. Charles District; and Rev. Parks, of the Presbyterian Church.

The ministers seemed baptized with the spirit of the Master, and labored with unabated zeal for the conversion of sinners. Indeed, the whole Church seemed alive to her responsibilities and privileges, and on every side might be heard the voice of prayer and praise.

The results of the meeting will be revealed in eternity, but we know the record will be glorious. Many of the children of those having tents were happily converted, and, indeed, every tenter realized the truth of the promise: "They that wait upon the Lord shall renew their strength."

More than one hundred professed conversion, and very many had their first love rekindled. We felt, all felt, that it was good to be there. May we all meet there again, and yet again, till we meet in heaven!

The occasion has its lessons, which are of peculiar interest— one of which we desire to indicate as of special local application: It orginated in the idea of closer fellowship between the different charges of the district, particularly those of the city. The meeting developed the spirit of that idea and afforded constant and signal demonstrations of its blessedness. The undertaking and the results of this meeting are the fruits of united counsel and confederate zeal. Such a sense of community of feeling and interest pervaded the entire membership of the Church in the district, and associating its resources and energies is felt as a palpable and urgent need among us. If fostered, it will contribute to an unprecedented growth and power of our beloved Methodism. It demands the serious consideration of those especially who hold official station and direct its affairs, whether the results of our Church work in this city during a period of nearly half a century are not utterly disproportionate to the measure of our opportunity and the possibilities of our resources. Does not the sad and discreditable fact continue from year to year, and still exist? If we shall inquire for the causes, may it not be in fact and largely because the very genius of Methodism is overlooked? It is the peculiarity of Methodist organism that it is connectional and not congregational. The spirit of pre-eminent fellowship is, therefore, a necessity to its very conservation. It is the bond of cohesion and at the same time the motive power of the efficiency of the system. A due recognition and appreciation of this radical principle of Methodist economy would put Methodism here and everywhere in the foreground of evangelical power and success. Our church-houses would multiply and our missionary operations ramify the entire city and surrounding country. The pulpit would augment its power, and the assemblies of our Israel, at stated services, as well as on special occasions, would constantly illustrate the blessedness and good fruits of the "unity of the Spirit in the bonds of peace." *

---

* *St. Louis Christian Advocate.*

CHAPTER XVI.

MISSOURI CONFERENCE.

Bishop Pierce, President; J. D. Vincil, Secretary—Schools and Colleges Doing Well—Interest in Missionary Cause—Sunday-schools Improving—Church Literature Circulated—Death of Rev. Henry H. Hedgpeth—His Memoir—District Reports of Presiding Elders Contain Historic Information—Report of Plattsburg District, by Rev. S. W. Cope—Report of St. Charles District, by Rev. A. Monroe—An Autobiographical Sketch of the Life and Labors of J. H. Ledbetter—His Position in the Ministry—A Biographical Sketch of Rev. George J. Warren, Given by Himself—The Life and Character of Rev. John Thatcher, by Rev. G. W. Hughes.

BISHOP PIERCE opened the fifty-third session of the Missouri Conference at Chillicothe, Mo., September 15, 1869; John D. Vincil, Secretary.

We learn from the reports of the different committees that the M. E. Church, South, is moving successfully in all the departments of her important work. The various schools and colleges of the Church are represented as doing well. It is very gratifying to see the growing interest of the Church in relation to this vital question. A Christian education elevates the Church to an influential position, and gives her durability and permanence. Additional attention is also given to the missionary enterprise, manifesting some appreciation of its commanding importance as the great work to which the Church of God is divinely called. Likewise, more active efforts are being made to advance the interests of the Sunday-school cause, which is second only to the divine commission to preach the gospel; for what is preaching the gospel but teaching the gospel, which is the legitimate work of the Sunday-school? They seem also convinced of the duty of patronizing our own Church literature. The perpetuation of Methodism in its simplicity, purity, and power depends greatly on our people circulating and reading the newspapers, periodicals, and books of our Church, whose literature compares favorably with that of any other Church, or with the secular literature of the country. Years ago it was customary for the preachers to carry these publications around with them on their circuits and sell them to persons whom they visited. As the result you might see our books in almost all the Methodist houses on the circuit. Hence our people were well-instructed and intelligent Methodists, and were not easily carried away by false teaching and the vain and foolish philosophy of this godless and sin-loving world. But has not this custom passed away to a large extent, like many other good things with which our Church was once blessed?

The increase in membership was nearly two thousand, and the future prospect hopeful.

One death this year, and we give below his memoir as read before the Conference:

Henry H. Hedgpeth was born in Green County, Ky., June

5, 1832. In 1837 he removed with his parents to Buchanan County, Mo., and in 1841 to Nodaway, an adjoining county.

Brother Hedgpeth enjoyed the advantages of an early religious education, and at the age of seventeen years he became deeply and thoroughly awakened to the sense of his guilt and danger as a sinner. With penitence and tears he sought and obtained the forgiveness of his sins by faith in Jesus Christ. His conversion was clear and satisfactory, and its genuineness was well attested by a subsequent life remarkable for its devotion to God and his cause. Soon after his conversion he became deeply and solemnly impressed that it was his duty to preach the gospel of the grace of God. This feeling of duty was not a mere sense of obligation to do good in a general way, but the line of duty was made plain before his face, and a clear conviction was wrought upon his heart, "Woe is unto me, if I preach not the gospel."

Having received license to preach and being properly recommended, he was admitted on trial into the traveling connection by the Missouri Conference at its session in the city of St. Joseph, in the year 1852. Thus before he had reached his majority he entered that work which for more than sixteen years commanded the energies of his whole being. In 1852 he was appointed to the Weston Circuit. He traveled this circuit two years. In 1854 he was appointed to Yellow Creek Mission; in 1855, to Paris Circuit; in 1856, to Oregon Mission, where he continued two years. In 1858 he was transferred to the Kansas Conference, where he continued to perform important service for the Church until late in the year 1861, when the cloud of war having fully burst upon our country, he found it altogether impracticable to continue the work in Kansas; and so he returned to Missouri to remain until the storm should be overpast. In 1863 he was appointed to St. Joseph Station. Here he did much valuable service, and will long live in the memories of the people of that charge. In 1864 he was appointed presiding elder of the St. Joseph District. He continued two years on this district, discharging with great acceptability the duties appertaining to his office. The General Conference having dissolved the Kansas Conference, and having attached all that portion of it lying north of the Kansas River to the Missouri Conference he was, in 1866, appointed to the Leavenworth District. This was a large and important field of labor. In 1867 he was appointed to the Savannah District, composed of a part of his former district and the northern end of the St. Joseph District. To this district he was returned in 1868, but before he had quite completed the first round he was stricken down by disease. He was taken sick about the 22d day of November. By a persistent effort he succeeded in reaching the house of Sister Wilson, near Grantville, Kan., the widow of the late Rev. Mr. Wilson, formerly a member of the Kansas Conference. His heart was filled with thankfulness to God when he found himself at the house of Sister Wilson. Soon the symptoms of typhoid fever became clearly marked, and for more than twelve long weeks (eighty-five days) he languished under that disease until wasted to a mere skeleton. On the evening of the 15th of February, 1869, having ruptured a blood-vessel by a slight cough, he passed away from earth to join the general assembly and Church of the First-born whose names are written in heaven.

During his long and painful illness he received from his brother, Rev. T. B. Hedgpeth, and the excellent family with whom he was sick every attention that love and tenderness could suggest. With him patience had a perfect work. No word of complaint fell from his lips. He suffered as seeing Him that is invisible. He was entirely resigned to the will of God, ready to depart and be with Christ, but willing to remain a little while longer that he might accomplish some more good in the world. During his sickness his faith in God was unshaken, and he was filled with comfort in the Holy Ghost. He was at times unspeakably happy; tears of joy would flow down his wasted cheeks, and at times when visions of heaven would break upon him he would shout aloud for joy.

As a Christian Brother Hedgpeth presented a life of most beautiful consistency. He gave evidence of his love for the Master by keeping his commandments. He cultivated diligently his own heart, and those who knew him most intimately saw richly developed in him the fruits and virtues of our holy religion.

As a preacher he was a man of one work. With his convictions of duty he was ready for any field of labor to which he might be assigned. During more than sixteen years of his itinerant labor he was never heard to complain of an appointment, although he filled some of the most difficult and laborious in the Conference. His early educational advantages were meager, but having given himself to the ministry, he studied to make himself a workman that needed not to be ashamed, and the writer of this believes that he has known but few men who at the age of thirty-six knew so much as did Henry H. Hedgpeth. As an expositor of the word of life he might well be ranked among the first men of the Church. To the intelligent, thinking, and attentive listener it was a great privilege to hear him preach. Nor was his usefulness as a preacher confined to a few; his method of presenting the great truths of the gospel was so simple and clear that all the people heard him gladly and were edified. Long will he live in the memories of the people whom he so faithfully served.

In 1853 he was married to Miss India A. Kenion, an amiable and excellent Christian woman, who had preceded him several years to the better country. They now sleep side by side in the cemetery at Fillmore, in Anderson County, Mo. There remains to them a little daughter, whom we commend to the sympathy and prayers of the Church. W. M. RUSH, *Chairman*.

There is much that is historic in the reports of the presiding elders, who give a faithful representation of their respective districts. By so doing they furnish the desired information respecting all the preachers who are laboring in their districts as well as what they are accomplishing in the work of the ministry, also respecting the spiritual state and religious condition of the Church. While the reports of the pastors are generally short, detached, and separate, the presiding elders give a connected and comprehensive view of the whole field.

PLATTSBURG DISTRICT.

S. W. Cope, presiding elder, thus writes of his work on this district:

I commenced my first round and year's labor on the Cameron Mission; Rev. J. B. Jewell, preacher in charge. I found him at his post ready to devote his whole time and talent to the work and interest of the mission. The Lord graciously blessed us with his presence and divine power in the revival of his work, convicting and converting sinners, and in the sanctification of his people to a holier and higher Christian life. It was a timely effort and a precious meeting for the Society at Parrott's School-house, inspiring both preacher and poople with confidence and the hope of abundant success this year. Seventeen sorrowing penitents found peace in believing, and were happily translated into the kingdom of light and life and of great power.

Next I went to the Stewartsville Circuit, where I met the pastor, Rev. C. W. Sanford, who had preached the night before and was already anticipating a good meeting. His expectations were realized and prayers answered in two happy conversions, seven additions to the Church, and a general and hopeful revival of the membership. I received a letter from Brother Sanford a short time since. He says: "The condition of the charge is tolerably good. Not so much vital godliness as I could wish, yet I am hopeful as to the future."

Rev. W. L. Blackwell is pastor of the Breckenridge Circuit. He had been sick for weeks, consequently had not been round his circuit. He joined me on my way to my quarterly meeting. Few were present at the commencement of the meeting, and the financial report meager. As the meetings progressed the congregations continued to increase, with increasing spiritual interest. We gained something over the enemy, but the victory was not complete. Two pledged themselves to the service of God, and promised that they would meet us in heaven. The preacher is entering upon his work with a zeal and fixedness of purpose that generally insure success and inspire confidence in the members of the Church.

This is the second year of Rev. D. F. Bone on the Camden Circuit. As his labors have been crowned with success in the past, we hope it will be the same, only more abundant, in the future. The quarterly meeting was attended with some interest. Two persons joined by letter and one adult baptized. We hope the bread cast upon the waters may be gathered after many days, and the good seed sown produce abundant fruit.

One young lady asked an interest in the prayers, which we hope may be answered in her salvation.

The quarterly meeting for the Liberty Circuit was held at Missouri City. The people of this circuit may consider themselves fortunate in having for their preacher this year Rev. Jesse Bird. He is equally fortunate in serving a people so kind and generous, so worthy and appreciative, so able and willing to support the ministry and the benevolent institutions of the Church. Financial claims nearly full. The religious services were a success. A revival would no doubt have been the immediate result could the meeting have been protracted.

Rev. W. P. Wilson is pastor of Haynesville Circuit. The quarterly meeting was at Haynesville. There seemed to be a revival influence from the first. The prospects were more and more encouraging until Monday afternoon, when a snow-storm came, which continued through the night and most of the next day, breaking up the meeting. Brother Wilson is well received, and will no doubt be well supported. He is laboring faithfully for the salvation of souls, and is anxious to have a revival. May he not be disappointed in his most sanguine expectations!

Lathrop is a flourishing little town on the line of the Cameron and Kansas City railroad. The Lathrop Mission is in charge of Rev. Joseph Metcalf, who begins the labors of the year under encouraging auspices. There are only eighty members on the mission, and yet, with the very limited assistance from the Board of Domestic Missions, he will be, I think, financially sustained. The love-feast and sacramental service were particularly encouraging. Up to the time I left one had joined the Church, and two persons had requested the prayers of God's people.

Bethany Mission is supplied this year by Rev. J. W. Duskey. It extends northward, up into the State of Iowa. The quarterly meeting for this mission was held six miles north of Bethany. It was a good meeting. Brother Duskey is well received, and is vigorously laboring to push forward all the interests, temporal and spiritual, of the mission.

The Albany Circuit is under the pastoral care of Rev. James A. Hyder. This is a good work. Here, as elsewhere, I met noble-hearted men and women doing battle for the Lord. The meeting, which was held at Albany, was one of more than usual interest and power. Two joined the Church, and one was baptized. I learned from Brother Hyder that the prayer and class meetings are well attended, and that the spiritual condition of the circuit is good. Peace and harmony prevail generally. The members are striving for higher attainment in the divine life. From Albany I went to Pattonsburg. This is a new and comparatively small field of labor, but one which will yield, if properly cultivated, a rich and abundant harvest. Rev. R. H. G. Herann, preacher in charge, is a Virginian, a young man, and a young preacher. His parishioners are chiefly from the same State. Their new church, "Bethel," was dedicated on the Sabbath of the quarterly meeting by Brother Jesse Bird. I remained here five days, and left the meeting still in progress. Up to my leaving three had united with the Church on profession of faith, and two by letter. Six or eight were at the altar for prayers who have since, with others, been converted.

My next appointment was Gallatin Station; Rev. C. Babcock, pastor. It is perhaps proper to say that the Church and people are pleased with him, and he with them. A gradual revival interest is being awakened. Almost every Sabbath one or more persons join the Church. There were four additions on Sabbath night of the quarterly meeting, and several penitents came forward for the prayers of the Church. I left the meeting in progress, with pastor and people hopeful of an extensive revival.

The quarterly meeting for the Plattsburg Circuit, held at Mount Moriah, closed my round of twelve weeks' labor, with great satisfaction. This is Rev. D. R. Shackelford's second year on this circuit. He reports ten converts and twenty-two accessions to the Church since Conference, with the organization of a new society. The financial report was the best made on the round, the stewards bringing and sending up an overplus of greenbacks. I left the meeting in progress, with encouraging prospects for a revival. Several had joined the Church, and it was expected that others would follow their example.

As already indicated, we get a condensed and comprehensive view of the workmen and work of the Church, in the reports made by the presiding elders of their respective districts. .The following report of the

St. Charles District

is given by the Rev. A. Monroe, presiding elder:

St. Charles District embraces twelve charges, and its territorial lines include St. Charles, Lincoln, Pike, Montgomery, and Warren Counties entire, with portions of Calloway and Audrain. I entered upon my work conscious of my responsibility and that my help must come from God. Thus far he has helped me and given me favor with preachers and people, so that I have met with a cordial welcome and hearty co-operation in every charge. My worthy predecessor was greatly beloved, and it was not strange that some disappointment and regret should have been felt on account of his being changed to another field of labor; but our people in St. Charles are thorough Methodists, and as such they love the itinerant system—indeed, the entire polity of the Church—and readily acquiesce in its legitimate operations; so that whoever is appointed by the Conference is *their* preacher, and if faithful in every department of his important work will be loved for his work's sake—not in word only, but in deed and in truth.

Jonesburg Circuit.—I commenced my round on the Jonesburg Circuit in a new church not quite finished, at a place called Cottonwood. The appointment was so soon after Conference that the attendance was small, and the circumstances being against continuance we closed Sunday night. The Society at this place will have a neat chapel, well adapted to the wants of the community. It speaks well for the zeal and liberality of the community. Brother Joseph Allen, preacher in charge, is most cordially received, and with his consecration to God and his work we feel encouraged to look for and expect a prosperous year.

New Florence Circuit.—Next comes New Florence Circuit quarterly meeting, at Loutre Island. Here also we had a slim attendance, owing to intervening circumstances. On Sabbath we preached the funeral of that good and useful brother, Thomas Talbott, who never was absent from a quarterly meeting unless providentially hindered. At the funeral the large house of worship was well filled. The colored people also manifested their respect for the deceased by their presence. He has been taken from labor and affliction to rest, but who will fill his place? ah, who? Brother Smith, the preacher in charge, is cordially received, and the omens are favorable for a prosperous year.

Montgomery City Circuit.—My next meeting was at Martinsburg, in the Montgomery City Circuit. On my way I preached at High Hill, Montgomery City, and Wellsville. The congregations were not large, owing to the inclement weather. Two severe snow-storms this week, but the appointments had been previously published. The meeting at Martinsburg was thinly attended, owing to bad weather, but I trust good was done. Brother Craig has been cordially received for the second year on this work, and every thing is in favor for a year of success and prosperity.

Portland Circuit.—My next quarterly meeting was on this circuit, at Ham's Prairie; Brother G. Penn, pastor. This meeting was well attended by the official members. The congregations were large and appreciative—an old-fashioned love-feast with closed doors—a time of refreshing with the Church; a large congregation and a good sacramental occasion. Brother Penn is more than ever consecrated and very kindly received. Both preacher and people are praying and laboring for a successful year. I stopped with Brother Penn at his house in Fulton, where I preached to a good congregation according to a previous appointment. After a pleasant night with Brother Penn and his family and having an early breakfast, I left in the stage, and on Wednesday met my wife and daughter at O'Fallon, where we spent a day and night very pleasantly with my old friend, Dr. Williams, and his kind family, who spared no pains to make our visit enjoyable. Thursday after a tedious delay we took the train for St. Charles, but found ourselves stopped at the suburbs of the city by obstructions in the road. By the aid of a friend to pilot us and, after walking about a mile, we reached the home of our good friend, Dr. Overall, somewhat fatigued, but the kind reception and cordial Christian greeting of the doctor and family soon made us forget the trials of the past. I suppose if we traveled by telegraph a moment's delay would make us impatient.

St. Charles Station.—On Christmas-day we commenced our quarterly meeting exercises in St. Charles. The congregations were good both in quality and quantity. The presiding elder preached Saturday morning and night, also Sabbath morning, and the pastor preached at night. The sacrament on the Sabbath and the love-feast Monday night were both profitable occasions. All things considered, the meeting was pretty fair, but the bad weather and the holiday amusements interfered very much with the meeting. I learn that the congregation has largely increased since Dr. Leftwich has taken the charge. He is laboring, praying, and hoping for a gracious visitation of spiritual power. He has the co-operation of his Church and people, and we may reasonably look for gracious results.

Paynesville Circuit.—After two days' rest at home, I left on horseback for Paynesville, a distance of sixty miles. The roads were bad and the weather unpleasant, but no time for parley. The work was before me, and I must go. A ride of twenty-six miles, through snow and rain, brought me to comfortable quarters in Middletown; where, after a little rest and refreshment, I preached as best I could to a considerable congregation. Next morning after breakfast I left upon a hard-frozen and rough road, and with all the patience I was master of rode thirty miles to Brother G. Turner's, five miles from Paynesville. Here, in this preacher's home, every want was quickly anticipated, and man and beast so kindly cared for that the toils of the day were soon forgotten, and a night's rest in a warm room and a comfortable bed, with God's blessing, prepared me for the duties of the quarterly meeting. Thank God, we had a good time. There were a few happy conversions and six additions to the Church. I was glad to meet many old friends, and especially Sister Forgey, who, after a tedious and protracted illness and great suffering, had so far recovered as to preside at her table and unite with the congregation in public worship. I mention this fact because many other preachers and friends will rejoice to know that she is still spared to her family and the Church. Thursday night I preached at Clarksville, and talked to our members on the importance of sustaining the institutions of the Church.

Louisiana and Prairieville Station.—Friday I left with Brother King for Prairieville, the place of the quarterly meeting. By going several miles around, we visited Father and Mother Tinsley, living with Mr. Smith, their son-in-law. The old people are worthy members of our Church, but now too infirm to attend meeting. On being apprised of our coming, they gathered in a few of their neighbors that I might preach to them, which I did, and we had a refreshing season of religious worship, very much to the comfort of these dear old people. They belong to Brother King's charge, who is a faithful shepherd and cares for all his flock, old and young. He is in favor with his people, and is laboring with zeal to save souls and build up the Church. Saturday morning we rode seven miles to Prairieville, and commenced the work of the quarterly meeting in company with the pastor, Brother Tarwater, who is for the first year on this work, more of a stranger than the elder; so we took it turn about in preaching. Our meeting was continued till Monday night. Congregations large and serious, and the Church much revived. Brother Tarwater is cordially loved, and will have the support and co-operation of the membership.

Auburn Circuit.—Friday night I attended at Oak Grove, the place of the quarterly meeting for this circuit. Here Brother Jesse Sutton preached to the gratification of an attentive congregation. On Saturday we commenced the labors of the meeting. The preachers of the circuit, Brothers Spencer and Gillum, with several local preachers, all took part in the exercises of the meeting, which was continued until Thursday night. One bright conversion and the Church powerfully blessed. This is a large and important circuit, of which the preachers seem sensible, and are prosecuting their work with much zeal and great faithfulness. God will no doubt own and bless their earnest labors.

Ashley Circuit.—I rode to Ashley on Friday to hold my quarterly meeting on the following Saturday and Sunday. Here our Society is small, and the roads bad, and the attendance meager; yet a few faithful ones were present from the different parts of the circuit, and our meeting was not without profit. Sunday morning and night the house was well filled. Brother Sutton is greatly beloved by his people. He cares for them, and they in turn care for him. I trust that much good will be done and many souls saved.

Cottleville Circuit.—I left on the cars Friday for Mount Zion, on the Cottleville charge. We commenced our meeting on Saturday, and closed Tuesday night. God favored us with a gracious revival. The Church was greatly blessed, and about sixteen persons converted, with an addition to the Church of about the same number. A majority were students of Fairview Seminary. Brother Loving is greatly encouraged and is working and praying for a general revival, while he is sustained and assisted by a faithful membership.

Wright City Circuit.—The quarterly meeting for this circuit was at Warrenton. By appointment I met the district stewards at Jonesburg, and preached at night. Commenced the quarterly meeting Friday night at Warrenton, and staid until Monday, when I went home, leaving the meeting in charge of their pastor, Brother Van Deventer, who has found an open door and a hearty welcome among his people. He is working faithfully in his Lord's vineyard.

Wentzville Circuit.—My next meeting was at Flint Hill, for the Wentzville Circuit. I found Brother Doggett in the parsonage and in tolerably good spirits, with a determination to do all in his power for the circuit, and the brethren promise their hearty co-operation and support. The congregation was not large, but Sunday morning quite fine at 11 o'clock and better still at night, when we felt that the meeting could have been continued with profit; but other imperative engagements prevented, so with some reluctance we closed Sabbath night. One incident is noteworthy: After all else had communed, Capt. Harnett, now in the ninety-second year of his earthly pilgrimage, arose from his chair in the aisle, and for the first time in his long life presented himself at the altar to receive the emblems of Christ's body and blood. The reader can easily imagine the great sensation produced in the congregation.

As the time had come, I took the cars for "home, sweet home," where I arrived at 3 o'clock P.M., and found all well, and a gracious revival of religion in progress in our little city of Mexico, under the leadership of Brother Bourland, whose earnest efforts in the pulpit and godly visits from house to house have been owned of God in a wonderful manner.. Had he relied altogether upon his pulpit efforts, I verily believe there would have been no revival; but connect the pulpit with fervent, earnest, believing prayers, and the power will come and the work will go forward.

An Autobiographical Sketch of the Life and Labors of Rev. J. H. Ledbetter.

We need not state that Brother Ledbetter is an

active, efficient, and useful minister of the gospel and member of the Missouri Conference. His successful ministerial career since he came to Missouri has gained the esteem and confidence of all with whom he has been associated, and the following autobiographical sketch of his ministerial life will be read with interest by his many friends, clerical and lay:

Joseph Herndon Ledbetter was born in the old town of Cokesbury, S. C. It was near this town, in the old "Tabernacle" Church, that Dr. Olin, "the Great," first taught school in the South; and there under the ministry of a local preacher, James Glen, he was converted.

The present writer came of Methodist parentage. My father was Rev. W. H. Ledbetter, at one time a member of the South Carolina Conference. My mother was Miss B. D. Herndon, of Cokesbury, S. C. The Ledbetter family came from England before the great Revolution. One member of the family settled in Virginia. From Virginia they have scattered throughout the South and South-west. In Virginia, about the beginning of the Revolution, Henry Ledbetter was born. He was my grandfather. This Henry Ledbetter was converted under the preaching of Bishop Asbury, and was one of Asbury's preachers during the last years of the eighteenth century. After his marriage he settled on a large plantation in North Carolina. That home was one of Asbury's stopping-places while on that part of his vast diocese.

There on the beautiful Pee Dee he reared a large and highly influential family. One of his sons, Henry W. Ledbetter, was my father, and was born in June, 1800. He was converted in 1812, began to preach in 1820, and was a member of the South Carolina Conference about seventeen years. He married in 1837 and located the same year. He settled near Cokesbury, S. C., and became a planter. Of this marriage came twelve children, three of whom are Methodist preachers. I was the sixth child, and had a well-defined Christian experience at the age of eight years, but was not received into full membership until I was eleven. About that time my father removed with his family to Russell County, Ala. There he became a cotton planter. The plantation was near the old Methodist town of Glenville, where the State had located a military institute. There were about one hundred and twenty-five cadets, ranging from thirteen to twenty years of age. In the fall of 1861 I was registered a State cadet, one of the youngest of the corps. There I remained until 1863, when the school was broken up by the Civil War. I entered the Confederate Army at Dalton, Ga., in 1864, and was with the army at Greensboro, N. C., when the war closed in 1865. Then back to Alabama, working and going to college through those dark and perilous times from 1865 to 1868. In 1868 I did mission work in Montgomery, Ala. In 1869 and part of 1870 I taught in a high school and had charge of the Church at Montevallo, Shelby County, Ala. It was at Montevallo that the great event of my maturer life occurred. I met, loved, sought, won, and married the lovely and accomplished daughter of Rev. W. H. Meredith, D.D., President of the Montevallo Female College, in which Miss Sue was teaching at the time of her marriage.

In the fall of 1870 I attended the first session of the North Alabama Conference as one of its under-graduates. Bishop McTyeire was there, hunting recruits for the West. At his request I came to Missouri. I was appointed to Louisiana Station, Missouri Conference. When I reached St. Louis, December 14, 1870, I learned that Rev. A. Monroe, presiding elder of the St. Charles District, had already supplied the place. At the request of Rev. J. W. Lewis, presiding elder of the St. Louis District, I took charge of the Labadie Circuit for the rest of the year.

In September, 1871, I reported to the Missouri Conference, then in session at Palmyra, Mo., and was entered among the under-graduates of the Missouri Conference.

At the close of the Palmyra Conference Bishop Doggett announced me stationed at Fayette. I was the first regularly appointed stationed preacher at Fayette. The membership was at that time very small, but full of zeal and pluck. No one ever had a more pleasant Board of Stewards to deal with. Adam Hendrix, Thomas Swinney, Dr. J. J. Watts, William Nipper, James Hicks, J. J. Watts, Jr., and others. The old church under the hill, dedicated by Bishop Pierce before the war, had been sold to the negroes, and our people were using the chapel of Central College Library Hall. No young man ever had better friends than Dr. Wills, F. X. Foster, W. G. Miller, and O. H. P. Corprew, the teachers in Central College.

During the year there was a very gracious revival of religion in the Church. Brother E. R. Hendrix (now bishop), then stationed at Macon City, helped me for a week. Between fifty and sixty were added to the Church. There are two or three incidents connected with the year's work which may be worth recording. One night during the meeting E. R. Hendrix preached a sermon of great clearness and force on the work of the Holy Spirit in conversion. There was in the congregation a young lady of much intelligence and of fine culture, a member of the Campbellite Church. This young lady came under deep conviction, and went to her room to think and to pray. The next morning about 10 o'clock, while she was in her room praying, she was happily converted. On the following Monday night she was received into the Methodist Church.

The other incident illustrates how a small thing may become the pivot on which turns the destiny of a soul. One Sunday morning in February, 1872, I was in the pulpit, and just as I was about to commence the service two ladies entered the chapel—one a married lady and member of the Church, the other a girl of eighteen summers and a stranger to us. They walked up the aisle to the second pew in front of the pulpit. The young lady fixed her eyes on the face of the preacher and did not remove them during the services. On the following day I was called to the house where the young lady was visiting. I was introduced to Miss B., the young stranger of my congregation. I found her in deep distress on account of her sins, being under deep conviction. After reading the Bible to her, instructing her, and praying with her, I departed. The next day when I met her she was as happy as she could be, having been gloriously converted. She was baptized and received into the Church the next Sabbath. Here is her story: "I was born of Campbellite parents and raised in that faith. Have been attending Church since early childhood, but never heard an entire sermon until last Sunday; because I never listened, but passed the time in gazing around, whispering, and giggling. But on last Sabbath I went to the Methodist Church with Mrs. P., and she took me up to the front, and when Mr. Ledbetter arose to open the service I looked at him. He so closely resembled my brother who was killed in the war that I looked at him all the time and listened to the sermon, and was convinced of my need of the Saviour."

During the summer of 1872 I became a beggar to raise fifteen hundred dollars for a parsonage at Fayette, which has sheltered every station preacher since its completion. When I started to Mexico in September to attend the Missouri Conference the parsonage was not quite finished. But that did not make any difference with me, so far as my personal convenience was concerned, for I had my order from Bishop Pierce to go to Wright City. Without abusing the appointing power, or asking for a transfer, or crying, or any thing of the kind, I went, and it was ten years before I had the pleasure of living in that nice parsonage.

The Mexico Conference was an interesting one to me, for I was there ordained an elder by Bishop Pierce, the pulpit orator, and one of the truest Methodist preachers that ever lived. At the close of the Conference Bishop Pierce read me out for Wright City, and W. E. Dockery, presiding elder. This was a great surprise to me—was a long, hard move, and my family not in a condition to be moved. However, we went cheerfully and had a good year. It was the first real circuit I ever had. It was thirty miles wide and had nine preaching-places. The four principal appointments were Wright City, Warrenton, Troy, and Marthasville. There were some good meetings, quite a number added to the Church. Some of the converts of that year are now leaders in their Churches. Had fine congregations and good times.

At one of the school-houses where I preached on Sunday afternoon I closed the year without seeing any special fruits of my labor, but some years after found that one soul had been saved. I will give the incident. The convert was a woman. She lived some distance from the school-house, which was the nearest preaching-place to her. One Sunday afternoon she came to preaching, riding on horseback and carrying a child in her lap. Under the sermon that day (1873) she experienced the saving grace of God. Thank God, that year's preaching at the old school-house was not in vain. I hope to meet her in heaven.

That year was full of experiences—some amusing, some sad. I would not be able to tell them in a short article like this. January, 1873, was very cold—at one time twenty-two degrees below zero. I attempted to go from Troy to Wright City. I rode about four miles, and found I could not stand it. Hence I turned into a narrow lane and started for the hospitable farm-house of one of our members. The lane was rough, full of gullies—some deep cuts that had been bridged. The snow was badly drifted, and I could not always find the bridge—sometimes found myself in a gully full of snow. The horse and the driver would wallow around awhile and then scramble out as best we could. By the time I reached the house I was stiff with cold. The brother had to lift me from my saddle. But a hearty welcome, a big fire, and an old Missouri supper made it all right and put me in good shape to continue my trip next day, reaching Wright City without any difficulty.

At Troy the cholera prevailed in the summer of 1873. It was a fearful scourge—many persons died. All the resident pastors left. When the time came for my monthly appointment at Troy some of my friends advised me not to go. But I felt that it was my duty to go; so I said good-by to my wife and two little ones. Reached Troy on Saturday. The town looked lonely and deserted. I preached twice on Sunday. While preaching I saw two processions go by on their way to the cemetery. The last camp-meeting ever held at the Monroe Camp-ground was held at the close of this year.

This year, September, 1873, the Missouri Conference met at Carrollton, Bishop Wightman presiding. This Conference gave me another surprise. I was appointed to the Jonesburg Circuit. But the move was short and the circuit was not large. Only three appointments, and they not far apart. Our Church at Jonesburg was at that time in good condition for work. There was a nice parsonage, and this was our first house-keeping.

As I walked up the principal street on my way to the parsonage an old citizen, a member of another Church, saw me, and noticing my youthful appearance he became alarmed for the Church. With great solicitude he asked one of the members this significant question: "What are you folks going to do with that boy?" Our member replied: "Well, we had a man last year, and could not get along with him, so we thought we would try a boy." We had a pleasant year. One grand revival at Jonesburg—some of the Jones family converted, and Aunt Julia Deering did some of her best shouting.

In September, 1874, the Missouri Conference was held at St. Joseph, Bishop Keener presiding. Here the great fight over the *St. Louis Christian Advocate* began. I was returned to the same work, the Jonesburg Circuit. The people gave us a hearty welcome, and we had another good year. I had two young men in my circuit, members of the High Hill Church, who assisted me in public services this year, as they were looking to the ministry—one of them Rev. Jacob Snarr, now an honored member of the Missouri Conference. Dr. Pittman, one of the prominent citizens of Jonesburg, united with our Church this year.

Rev. W. W. Jones was presiding elder of the St. Charles District, and under his judicious management we had at Flint Hill, in St. Charles County, some glorious camp-meetings. Hundreds were converted at these meetings. The camp-meeting of August, 1874, was the most remarkable meeting of the kind I ever attended. Many persons came forward for prayer—in some instances whole families, all of whom were converted. Some young men had, by mutual consent, organized into a band to pray, to meet on a hill adjacent to the camp-ground just before sunset—especially to pray for the descent of the Holy Ghost. As well as I remember there were in the band the following persons, who were then boys in the ministry: M. M. Hawkins, Henry Kay, J. M. O'Brien, Rufus Gamble, William M. Gillum, and J. H. Ledbetter, and also quite a number of young laymen. Day after day the band of these young men met on that hill beneath the grand old shade-trees overlooking the encampment, and prayed for the revelation of divine power. The meeting was going on successfully, with some conversions, but still the fullness of the Spirit had not come. But on the fourth afternoon the power did come upon that band as none of them had ever experienced before. We had been together about one hour when the first bell rang for evening preaching, so we adjourned. The young men started down the hill to join the great congregation. M. M. Hawkins and myself remained standing by the old log which was used as pew and pulpit. I said to Hawkins: "I don't feel satisfied to leave yet. I feel persuaded there is a blessing for me that I have not yet received." Hawkins replied: "That is just my view of my own case." I said: "Then let us kneel down here and have one more prayer." We dropped on our knees. "You lead the prayer, Hawkins," said I. "No, no;" said Hawkins, "I can't pray. You pray, Brother Ledbetter." Then I began to pray, but I never got beyond the first agonizing cry of my heart, "O God!" for the Holy Ghost came upon us with such power and glory as we had never felt before. We were carried beyond ourselves and cried aloud, and our hallelujahs reached the ears of the others, who returned, and as they came to that consecrated old log they received a similar baptism of power. What a scene! About twenty young men, all under the power of the Spirit and praising God aloud! The second bell rang and we marched down that hill in a file of couples, and into the altar place of that tabernacle, singing the old hymn, "Am I a soldier of the cross?" The vast congregation seemed electrified and joined in the song with enthusiastic joy. The only person who seemed not to be enthused was the preacher. He gave the congregation one of the most inappropriate and juiceless sermons you ever heard. All the time he was belaboring his congregation with his jargon about market-places, there sat those young men so full of joy that they could not hold in. The scene was one never to be forgotten. The preacher, with his little, old, dry sermon and those young men praising God every few minutes during the entire sermon, for the wonderful blessing of God they had just received; while the vast congregation had utterly forgotten the preacher, and their attention turned altogether to those joyful and happy young men. The scene beggars description—sometimes serious, sometimes comic, wonderfully sublime, yet supremely ludicrous. Just two illustrations will show: The preacher was describing the scene in a city market-place. An old pauper woman had stolen a beefsteak. A policeman arrested her. This the preacher acted out, striding across the platform and clutching an imaginary victim as he related the circumstances. Just then one of the young men shouted aloud, followed by a chorus of amens, "Glory be to God!" That was too much for the gravity of that serious and well-behaved congregation. They could not keep back the laugh in spite of them. The only person undisturbed was the preacher. On he went, without spiritual point or design. After some time he reached Chicago in his discourse on markets. He told us how they buy wheat in the "exchange." Just as he was going over the bids and sold his wheat at one dollar and thirty-five cents per bushel, one of the young men who had been for some time on the point of explosion, cried out, thinking no doubt of the blessing of salvation: "Glory be to God! We got it cheaper than that on the hill." This touched off the congregation again, but the preacher, undismayed, kept on his way to the end. He would have preached the funeral of that camp-meeting if God had not forestalled him by pouring out his Spirit on those young men. After the sermon they went out into the congregation and took it for Christ. Every person who came up that night was converted, and every conversion was clear and bright.

At the Conference of 1875, which met at Glasgow, I was read out for the Clarksville Circuit. This was then one of the most pleasant fields of labor in the bounds of the Missouri Conference. Three of the most delightful years of my life were spent at Clarksville. Yet my first great sorrow came then in the death of my father in 1876, and of my little boy, Harry, in March, 1878.

In 1876 we held a series of meetings which continued till the last of March, resulting in about one hundred conversions. These meetings were held by the pastor and his people—no foreign help. The first meeting was held at Clarksville. L. R. Downing, W. L. Terry, Guile, Smith, Jamison, and Ballanger were my right-hand supporters. Some of the members told me it was useless to try to hold a meeting without sending off for a distinguished preacher or evangelist, as the other Churches always did. I thought that the pastor, his people, and God would be enough. Our next meeting was at Paynesville. The principal workers there were Judge Forgey, J. E. Forgey, Rev. T. Pryor, and W. H. Henderson. We owe everything there to Judge Andrew Forgey. He was a grand man, a thorough-going Methodist from Kentucky. His house was always the welcome home of the Methodist preachers. But he has long since entered upon his rich reward in the paradise of God.

Rev. George J. Warren

has furnished us with a brief sketch of his ministerial life, the perusal of which will not fail to entertain his numerous friends in Missouri:

I was born at Salisbury, Wiltshire, England, February 16, 1847. The names of my parents are William and Maria Warren. I moved with my parents to the United States in 1849, and settled in Ray County, Mo.; moved from place to place with my father, who was an itinerant Methodist preacher, until 1856, when the family were finally located in Bloomington, Macon County, Mo.

I was educated in the common schools until 1857, when I entered Macon High School at Bloomington, under the instruction of Rev. O. R. Boughton, and later, Rev. J. P. Nolan. I joined the M. E. Church, South, at Bloomington, in 1860; was "born again" near New Hope Church, in Ray County, at a grove meeting conducted by Revs. A. S. Alexander, W. E. Dockery, and M. Rainwater, in August, 1867; was licensed to preach at the same place, W. E. Dockery being presiding elder.

I taught school during the winter of 1867 and the summer of 1868; was recommended to the Annual Conference for admission on trial by the Quarterly Conference of the Millville Circuit, in August, 1868; was received on trial by the Missouri Conference, at its session at Weston, Platte County, Mo., in September, 1868; Bishop H. H. Kavanaugh, President, and J. D. Vincil, Secretary.

I was appointed to Oskaloosa Circuit, Kansas, Savannah District; was sent the following year to Irvin and Junction City Mission, with Rev. E. J. Stanley, now of the Montana Conference; was appointed the following year to Shawnee Circuit, and remained there two years. Here occurred the second most important event of my life. I was married to Miss S. E. McCuiston, of Ray County, Mo., and began a *new* life, growing better and happier to this blessed hour.

My next appointment was to Nebraska City Station, Neb., remaining there two years. In 1874 I was sent to Holton, Kan.; in 1875, to Wyandotte Circuit, Kan.; in 1876, to Atchison Station, Kan. In 1877 I was transferred to the Missouri Conference by

Bishop Marvin, and sent to Norborne Circuit; in 1889 was stationed at Brunswick (four years); in 1883 was sent to Carrollton Station; in 1884, to Gallatin District (four years); in 1888, to Fulton Station.

This completes the outline of my ministerial life and appointments to date. Nine years of my ministry were spent in the Western Conference. If there is aught heroic in my life, it belongs to those nine years in Kansas. God only knows what I endured mentally and physically during that time, the effects of which are now upon me and making me an old man prematurely.

I was ordained deacon in August, 1870, by Bishop Marvin; and elder in 1871, by Bishop Pierce, at Nebraska City.

My work in Missouri has always been pleasant, and God has honored my ministry in the conversion and addition to the Church of nearly eight hundred persons, leaving out four years' work on the district as presiding elder. I built the new church at Brunswick, which cost $7,000.

At Richmond, in September, 1880, I was elected Treasurer of the Conference Board of Missions. I have seen the contribution for Missions more than double itself within the last decade. During the thirteen years since my return to the Missouri Conference no special or notable events have transpired that would be worthy of historic record.

A SKETCH OF THE LIFE AND CHARACTER OF REV. JOHN THATCHER.

Rev. John Thatcher was born in the State of Connecticut March 17, 1806. While he was quite young his father moved to Pennsylvania, where he grew to manhood.

His father was a farmer, and he worked on the farm until he was twenty-one years of age. His early educational advantages were of the most meager character—only such as were afforded in that early day in a country school. His thirst for knowledge was intense from boyhood, and during the years of toil on the farm he seized every spare moment he could get to improve his mind. After he was of age he attended one term of the Academy at Syracuse, N. Y. This completed his education so far as the school and college were concerned.

After this he spent several years in teaching, in the meantime pursuing his studies with all the ardor of his nature, endeavoring to satisfy his undying thirst for knowledge.

During these earlier years of his life, though deprived of the advantages of a collegiate education, he formed those habits of systematic study which he carried with him through life, and which made him one of the most thorough Biblical scholars of the West. He was not content with reading the Bible simply in its English translation; he mastered the Greek and Hebrew, and the text in the original was almost as familiar to him as the King James translation. Not content with the acquisition of the original tongue of the Bible, as a very large part of the history and literature of the Church and a great portion of its theology were written in the Latin language, he mastered it, that he might be able to go to the original documents themselves whenever he desired to consult them. But not content with these acquisitions, as very much of the highest grade of the theological literature of our day comes to us from Germany, he studied German, so that he could read and speak the German language almost as readily as any one. His constant custom for many years was to daily read the Holy Scriptures in all of these languages.

In regard to scholarship, his motto was thoroughness. He was not brilliant, but solid. He was emphatically a hard student. He reduced every thing to system, and studied how to economize time. Throughout his entire life he was an early riser—generally at 4, and never later than 5 o'clock. While others were asleep he was poring over his books, and acquiring that ripe and thorough scholarship which many of his brethren, much more brilliant than he, and who had far greater advantages, never attained, because they were unwilling to pay the price which wisdom demands. Notwithstanding his thorough knowledge of the original tongues of the Holy Scriptures, he was so modest and unobtrusive that his most intimate friends were unaware of his extraordinary attainments unless something special would call him out. I remember that over thirty years ago Rev. J C. Kimber, who was at that time presiding elder of Springfield District, Illinois, told me an incident showing his profound knowledge of Hebrew, which astonished him and the Faculty of McKendree College.

Mr. Thatcher was on an examining committee at Commencement, and a question was raised in the Hebrew language. The members of the Faculty took one side of the question and Mr. Thatcher the other. Mr. Kimber said he expected to see Mr. Thatcher speedily silenced, but, to his utter astonishment, he silenced the Faculty and convinced them that they were wrong and he was right.

In regard to education, Mr. Thatcher is an illustration of what may be accomplished, under the greatest difficulties, by systematic and persistent application. He was in love with knowledge, and the years of his servitude, to obtain the object of the idol of his heart, were like the years of Jacob's servitude for the lovely and beautiful Rachel—"they were sweet, and seemed but a few days."

He studied on horseback while traveling large frontier circuits, or by the light of the fire, or of the old greasy lamp, or of the old tallow candle in the cabins of his parishioners in the wilderness; but his proficiency was greater than many who had all the advantages of the university. What a *stimulus* to young men entering the ministry, who have not had the advantage of the college and theological seminary, is the example of such men as Mr. Thatcher! And what a reproof it is to those who have had all the advantages and have failed to improve them!

His labors as an itinerant preacher in the Methodist Episcopal Church began in 1834, when he was twenty-eight years of age. Leaving Pennsylvania at the call of Rev. A. Monroe and Rev. Jesse Green, he started westward, but halted one year in Ohio, and traveled a circuit under the presiding elder. The next year, 1835, he came to Missouri and entered the Missouri Conference. He traveled the following circuits in succession: Union, in Franklin County; Keytesville, Macon, Monticello, Bowling Green, Danville, Paris, Boonville, and Arrow Rock. In 1845 he was appointed presiding elder of Lynn District. At all of these appointments he was successful in building up the Church and having revivals, some very extensive ones.

On September 25, 1839, in Pike County, Mo., he was married to Miss Virginia B. Wells, who still survives him. In 1845 he joined the Illinois Conference, in which he traveled until 1869. He died in Mount Eric, in Wayne County, leaving such a record as none but a good man can.*

---

* G. W. Hughes, MS.

CHAPTER XVII.
MISSOURI CONFERENCE.

Rev. Abraham Millice, the Oddity, Known to This Present Writer as the Most Eccentric Person He Ever Saw—Humorous Incidents When Holding Meetings with Him—An Account of His Ministerial Life, by J. B. Landreth—Millice Forced His Landlord to Let Him Have Prayer with Him and His Family—His Cave Church—His Overshot Mill, etc. —M. E. Church, South, in Callaway County, Mo., by Rev. George W. Penn—Fulton Station—Pleasant Grove Church —Prairie Chapel—Miller's Creek Church—Prospect Church —Shiloh Church— Mount Pleasant Church—Williamsburg Church—Reedsville Church.

WE have in our possession a manuscript containing a biographical sketch of Rev. Abraham Millice, from the pen of J. B. Landreth, full of spicy incidents and entertaining narratives. Those of you who were acquainted with the peculiarities and eccentricities of Rev. Millice will not be surprised when you find that a sketch of his life contains things curious and funny and risible.

We had the pleasure of a personal acquaintance with him. When we were stationed at Jefferson City many years ago he was on the Jefferson City Circuit. Being very singular and peculiar, there were some young persons at one of his appointments who were in the habit of laughing and making fun of him. So, on one occasion, he was unusually animated and pathetic, and brought his whole congregation, these young people with the rest, to tears and weeping. When they became overwhelmed with feeling he stopped suddenly and said to those young persons: "Now laugh if you can."

I assisted him in one of his protracted meetings. Some of the friends said to me, "There are two things operating against the success of the meeting: Brother Millice preaches too long and tells too many anecdotes;" requesting me to inform him. So I performed this delicate duty as delicately as I could. He simply said, "I will try to do better;" and requested me when he had preached long enough, to jerk the skirt of his coat, which I did faithfully, and he would immediately take his seat. I was compelled to return to Jefferson City, and when the hour for preaching arrived, they say, he went into the pulpit, and the first thing which he did was to hold up the skirt of his coat before the congregation, and said, "Brother Lewis is not here to pull my coat-tail to-day, and I will preach as long as I please," which was from 11 o'clock A.M. to 1:30 P.M. As it was a little town, quite a number went home to dinner and returned while he was still preaching. It also troubled him not to tell his usual number of anecdotes. When he announced his text he would sometimes introduce the subject with an anecdote, and whenever he got into the brush he would get out by telling an anecdote. But he tried to preach without anecdotes, only to find out that he could not preach at all; then he turned around and looked at me and said:

"If you don't let Millice preach, he can't preach at all." Of course the anecdotes came thick and fast. Here, however, we remark that notwithstanding his great eccentricities, he was a good, sound, orthodox preacher, and quite a revivalist. We now direct the attention of the reader to what his biographer says about him:

In 1846 I became acquainted with Rev. Abraham Millice. He was a Southern Methodist preacher, born and raised in Germany, could not speak English until he was twenty years of age, was one of the most peculiar men I ever saw. He once traveled and preached in Ozark County. I was told that he stopped with a man near the mouth of Upper Spring Creek to stay all night. When it was time to retire the landlord told him where he was to sleep. "Pesure," said Millice, "can't we have prayer before we go to bed?" "No," replied the landlord, "I don't have such d—d foolishness about me." "Vell," said Millice, we will have it here to-night." "Well," replied the man, "this is my house, and I expect to control it." Millice said: "I will pray with you and your family even if I have to whip you. I'll show you what a Dutchman can do. You are a pretty fellow raising a family without prayer. Kneel down and pray or I'll thrash you." So he made the landlord and family kneel down with him while he prayed. Next morning, after a similar altercation, he prayed with the family and then went on his way rejoicing.

That year he held a protracted meeting in a large cave on Bryant's Fork, and that cave was for many years called Millice's Cave. During the meeting there were five or six brothers, by the name of Koontz, who were very wild, wicked, dissipated fellows, and who gave Brother Millice a great deal of trouble. One day his patience gave way, and he told them that they were too mean to live and that God would kill them in less than twelve months, and I was told by a reliable person that some disease got among them, and they all died except one in less than a year. From that circumstance he was regarded by many in that region as a prophet.

He held a meeting at Mount Store, in the corner of Texas County. On Sunday a Campbellite preacher was present, and Brother Millice called on him to conclude the services. But he broke out with a tirade of abuse of Millice's interpretation of the Scriptures, and among other things said: "The Scriptures need no interpretation; they mean what they say and say what they mean, and must be taken literally." When he took his seat Brother Millice then arose and said to the preacher: "Brother, do you claim to be a good man?" He replied: "Yes." Millice then said, "The Scriptures say that out of the good man's belly shall flow rivers of living water. So if the brother is right, if you will put him on one of these high hills you may have a good overshot mill," announced his next appointment, and pronounced the benediction.

When preaching Brother Millice loved to tell his experience, and while Rev. J. Dines was stationed in Springfield he preached for him, and during his sermon he came to a pause and said: "What! me tell mine experience here in Springfield among all these Campbellites? Yes, if the Campbellites were as thick as the dog fennel around this house, and the devil was standing at the door, I would tell it." Notwithstanding his oddities, he was regarded as a good and useful man and a safe expounder of the Scriptures.

OUR CHURCH IN CALLAWAY COUNTY, Mo.

The information contained in the following sketch concerning the M. E. Church, South, in Callaway County has been kindly furnished by Rev. George W. Penn, whose long acquaintance in that section enables him to give a correct representation of our Church organizations in said county from the year 1860. He proceeds as follows:

Fulton Station was occupied by Rev. W. A. Mayhew as pastor in 1860, and was in a prosperous condition, the congregation having just completed the present building at a cost of eight thousand dollars. This year the auditorium was finished, while the basement was left unfinished. The church was dedicated by Rev. W. G. Caples, the entire amount of cost having been secured by subscription. But now comes the dark days of the war, and the subscription, which was then considered good, was rendered worthless. Hence the trustees failed to secure the amount subscribed. The congregation was greatly reduced in numbers. In 1861 H. A. Bourland was sent to this charge. Being a single man and full of zeal for the cause of God, he undertood to raise the amount necessary to relieve the Church of debt, which amounted at that time to four thousand dollars. He continued his work in 1862, but the war being in full blast he was compelled to stop. He succeeded, however, in reducing the debt about one thousand dollars. Thus matters remained until the war was over. The station was placed upon the circuit, and only one Sabbath was given to Fulton by the preacher in charge of the circuit. Revs. Charles Babcock and F. A. Savage served the Fulton Circuit the following years of 1863-64. In the fall of 1866 George W. Penn was appointed to the Fulton Circuit, which then embraced the following appointments: Fulton, Miller's Creek, Prairie Chapel, Pleasant Grove, and Ham's Prairie. The trustees of our Church at Fulton had arranged to let the house go for the debt, but the pastor persuaded them to let him try his hand as Bourland had done—the debt now amounting to about thirty-five hundred dollars. He commenced his work and, by perseverance, at the end of the second year the trustees announced the Church free from all financial embarrassment. From this time (1868) Fulton Church has gone forward. She has been much favored in earnest and faithful pastors—Chapman, Allen, Blakey, Groves, Beagle, Whitten, and others have led her membership in successful battle against the powers of darkness. Among the laymen composing the Church in 1860 were the names of Dr. Veach, J. H. Jamerson, N. C. Coons, Sydney Royster, Joseph Fisher, Martin Key, and others, all of whom have passed to their reward except Coons and Jamerson. In all these past years there were some Christian women, excellent *sisters*, who aided much in the work of the Church. Fannie Worthington was an excellent member, in whom the preachers found a good and faithful counselor. Mother Watkins was another one of these faithful helpers in the work of the Church; also Mrs. Veach and others. They assisted in many ways, and were faithful Marthas and Marys to whom the world is greatly indebted.

Pleasant Grove Church.—This charge is located in the northern part of Callaway County. In 1860 the congregation worshiped in a small frame building which was occupied once a month by the pastor. The Church was composed of some of the best families in Callaway County. The Pattersons, McClintocks, Edmondsons, Brites, Sipples, Hanna, Tinchers, Fishes, and others. In 1862 H. A. Bourland held a series of meetings at the church, which resulted in a large increase of membership. At this meeting Rev. W. A. Hanna, a prominent member of the Missouri Conference, was converted. This Church has furnished four excellent men for the Methodist ministry: James O. Edmondson, B. D. Sipple, W. A. Hanna, and William Fish. The first three are in the traveling connection and the last one is local. This Church was favored with the labors of three local preachers, N. L. Fish, W. Sipple, and George Hatcher, who did much to build up and develop the membership—three men who were always ready to help the pastor, and to stand firmly by the Church in the day of her sore trials. Many of the pastors who served the Church during these years will bear their testimony that these men loved the Church and demonstrated their *love* by their *works*.

In 1869-70 the old house was removed, and in its place a new building was erected. It is an excellent house, a large and commodious edifice, and stands there to-day a memorial of the enterprise and liberality of that community. This building was solemnly dedicated to the worship of Almighty God by Rev. D. R. McAnally, editor of the *St. Louis Christian Advocate*.

Many of the members who worshiped in this church in 1860 have passed over the river, and are now safely housed in heaven. The historian will please allow us to record their names here: A. McClintock, William Sipple, W. Brite, Mrs. Winfield Edmondson, William Sharpe, and others that might be mentioned.

Pleasant Grove has an appropriate name, for it was and still is a delightful place. Of the ministers who have served this Church as pastor we may speak of the following: A. P. Linn, C. Babcock, F. A. Savage, W. W. Jones, William Warren, R. G. Loving, J. R. Taylor, S. L. Woody, P. D. Vandeventer, and J.

Y. Blakey, all of whom were faithful in the proclamation of God's word, and grand results are being manifested as the years roll on, and will continue until time shall be no more. Some of them have been called from the field of labor to rest, and are now reaping the rich harvest of their faithful sowing.

Prairie Chapel is a church-house located about eight miles north-west of the city of Fulton. This house of worship was erected about the year 1854, under the direction of Rev. D. C. Blackwell, the pastor. It was dedicated to the service of God by Rev. N. S. Berryman. It was a frame building, and was almost always filled with devoted worshipers at the regular appointments. Many revivals have been in this church, and many will rejoice in eternity that they found the Saviour precious to their hearts in Prairie Chapel. The families composing this Church were the Givenses, Selbys, McClanahans, Halls, and Loyds. William Givens and his son David and James K. Selby were killed by the Missouri militia at their homes, as were many other good men in Missouri during those dark days of the Civil War. Their loss to this Church was keenly felt, but there came into this community a year or two later, as refugees from the South-west, B. Barrow and Wiley Vinson, with their families, who, being men of deep piety, aided much in rallying the scattered forces of the Church at this point; but they have completed their work, and their bodies sleep in the consecrated grounds of Prairie Chapel.

It was this Church that gave to Missouri Methodism Rev. William Sarter. He first appeared in this community as a poor German boy, under the employ of Brother William Givens, and under the ministry of Rev. A. P. Linn he was converted, and in a few years afterward entered the ministry. He became an earnest preacher, and gave promise of great usefulness; but, being led astray by extreme views on the subject of holiness, he left the Methodist ministry, and finally left the Church.

Prairie Chapel did much in planting and establishing the doctrines of Methodism in that region. William Selby was a man of no ordinary ability. His father was a local minister in the Methodist Church. This circumstance led his son to investigate and defend, with much ability, the peculiar doctrines and usages of Methodism. B. Barrow was a man well informed on all subjects, and especially on the doctrines and usages of our

Church. Rev. F. A. Savage spent several years of his life in this community, and often occupied the pulpit as a local preacher. He was a man of talents, and those who heard him preach can testify that his work was *well done*.

The old church-house having served its time, they have gone to work recently, and have built a structure, neat and tasty, large and commodious, and it reflects no little credit upon the citizens of that neighborhood. It was dedicated in the fall of 1889 by Rev. George J. Warren, of Fulton. Thus we have at this point a strong Church, whose future promises much in the great and important work of saving souls.

Miller's Creek Church.—This was in 1860 a log house, situated near a stream of the same name. It was in this house that such men as Redman, Monroe, Smith, Fenton, Hatton, Spencer, Jordan, Blackwell, and others used to preach. Many happy meetings have been held here, and many souls born into the kingdom of heaven. Here the writer first saw A. P. Linn, who was conducting a meeting at this church. At this meeting we saw for the first time J. Fisher, William Givens, and S. Miller, the Rev. W. G. Miller, William and Josiah Selby. How these brethren sung and prayed, and how they worked with the penitents at the altar! They were field hands indeed. They did whatever was necessary to be done. While the ministers did the preaching, they did the singing and the praying, and there were great manifestations of divine power in the salvation of sinners. Where do you find such worshipers nowadays?

Miller's Creek Church was situated about ten miles west of Fulton, on the western border of Callaway County. The principal families of this Church were the Selbys, Ellises, Millers, Sampsons, Bedworths, and McClures. In 1860 this Church numbered about forty members, and was one of the principal points on the Fulton Circuit. The dark days of the war made a sad impression upon this Church. The house of God was neglected, and the membership was greatly depleted. Regular service could not be maintained. But in 1865 peace was restored, and the membership was rallied. The Church moved forward successfully, and was blessed with gracious revivals, so that in about two years she numbered over one hundred members.

In 1872-73 the congregation built a new house of worship at a cost of about two thousand dollars, Rev. S. L. Woody serving

them as pastor. This new house was dedicated by Rev. John D.
Vincil, who was then stationed at Columbia, Mo. The building
is large, and seats about four hundred persons. In the grave-
yard near by sleep those who have crossed the river, and are
waiting on the other shore. We must not fail to mention Mrs.
Polly Miller, the mother of Rev. W. G. Miller. Her life was
full of good works—a warm friend of the preacher, and a wise
counselor to those who needed it. She took pleasure in hospitality; was a woman of superior ability; very gifted in prayer;
often at the altar laboring with penitents, and pointing them to
the Lamb of God that taketh away the sin of the world. Her
maiden name was Hatton, the aunt of Robert Hatton of precious
memory, who died a member of the Missouri Conference in 1861
or 1862.

Here in this neighborhood Wesley G. Miller was born and
reared by his excellent mother, who now sleeps so quietly in the
grave-yard here. Yes, from her he received those lessons of instruction and wisdom that have placed him in the front ranks
of Israel's hosts doing mighty battle for Israel's God. Eternity
alone can reveal what this excellent lady has accomplished.

Prospect Church.—This house of worship was situated about
three and a half miles due west of the town of New Bloomfield,
and was originally a log building. In 1860 the congregation
constituting the Prospect Church met in this house. John
Hall, G. Emmons, Mrs. Longley, and their families composed
largely the membership. Here the old style of Methodism
could be easily recognized—class-meeting and prayer-meeting
on every Sabbath, with a general rally when the preacher came
round to fill his appointment. The church was often filled to
its utmost capacity. Many souls have been happy in this old
church. Many have heard the word preached from that rude
pulpit by such men as E. B. Marvin, Redman, Monroe, and
other such like able ministers. It was here E. M. Marvin
preached a very remarkable sermon on the language of the
jailer. It was at this point a debate was held between B. H.
Spencer and Noah Flood, of the Baptist Church.

In 1868–69 the congregation vacated the old log house and
built about half a mile east of it a new, large, and pleasant house
of modern style of architecture. Here they have grown into a
membership of about fifty, who are doing good and substantial

work in our Master's vineyard. This Church furnishes a minister, Rev. A. E. Emmons, of the South-west Missouri Conference.

Shiloh Church was situated on the Missouri river bottom opposite Jefferson City. In 1860 it was a small frame house, and was the only church in that community. The people came quite a distance from above and below this point to meeting. The house was always filled, for in those days almost everybody went to church. Here we find the Taltons, Moores, Smiths, Furgusons, Younts, Carltons, and many others composing the membership of this Church. In 1860 George Fenton was the pastor, and he continued another year, and the influence of his work still remains.

In 1870 a new church was planted, and a different location was sought and obtained at Cedar City, a small town about half a mile above the church, and the name was changed from Shiloh to Cedar City. The old house and the grounds upon which it was located were returned to their former owner according to the provisions of the deed. Many precious souls have been saved through the instrumentality of this Church. The new church-building was planned by Rev. J. P. Nolan, the presiding elder of that district, at a cost of twenty-five hundred dollars. It is a good house of worship, and stands there as a monument of the liberality of the people of that community.

Abigail Yount was one of the oldest members, and a true and devout woman she was. Her house was the preacher's welcome home. Here he found food and shelter for himself and horse, and he could remain as long as he pleased, spending days of rest from his weary toil.

Mount Pleasant was situated about ten miles below Shiloh, near the Missouri River. In 1860 the membership here was small. The church was a log structure, and after the war fell into disuse. But in the earlier days of Methodism in Callaway County it was a strong Church. They owned forty acres, upon which was a camp-ground, and here at their annual gatherings very many souls have tasted of the good word of God. It was at this camp-ground, in 1860, that this writer heard a very able sermon delivered by Rev. Horace Brown, of the Missouri Conference, on the text: "All are yours; and ye are Christ's; and Christ is God's." It is near this place that Rev. George Fenton and his wife sleep side by side in a grave-yard, awaiting the resurrection morn.

Two small Churches were formed out of the Mount Pleasant Church—namely, Rocky Branch and Barkersville. At these points the people gladly heard the proclamation of the gospel which saluted the ears of sinners with the joyous tidings of salvation. No place is too obscure to preach the word of God. "Go ye into all the world, and preach the gospel to every creature" is the divine commission under which the Methodist preacher proclaims salvation to lost sinners.

A new church has just been erected (May, 1890) half a mile from the old site of Mount Pleasant, and has been dedicated by Dr. Hammond, of Central College, Fayette, Mo.

Williamsburg Church is one of the oldest Churches in Callaway County. When first organized it was a Church of note and wealth. The house of worship was a frame building located in the town of Williamsburg. The Church was composed of good families, such as the Hobsons, Kidwells, Andersons, Dysons, Paytons, and others. Capt. Anderson was a noted Methodist. He was a man of wealth and great religious zeal, and was a recognized leader in the community. But these excellent families have almost entirely disappeared from the neighborhood, and a different class of people have taken their places. The Church still exists, and they worship in the same frame building in Williamsburg. They have not, however, had any prosperity since the war, and have been gradually declining. It requires quite a struggle to maintain regular service.

Williamsburg Church is situated in one of the most beautiful sections in Callaway County, and possesses peculiar material advantages, and should be a live and influential Church. Nine Mile Prairie, of which Williamsburg is the center, is the garden spot of Callaway County. Since the war the emigration has been from the Northern States. They have their prejudices against the M. E. Church, South; and while many who have come into this community are Methodists, under the influence of the prejudice they bring with them from the East they unite with the Presbyterians.

Bethel Church is situated about one-fourth of a mile from the town of Reedsville, in Callaway County, Mo. This Church was organized in an early day, and was originally called Union.

The congregation worshiped at first in a log house, which was located about one mile east of Reedsville. The principal families composing the Church in 1860 were the Offetts, Garnetts, Scotts, and Gills—families who came from Virginia in an early day. They possessed more than ordinary culture and enterprise. At Old Union, as it was often called, many precious souls were converted. Many great and grand sermons were preached there, and the doctrines of Methodism were firmly planted.

In 1870-71 the congregation sold the old house to the colored people, and erected a new church about one mile west and nearer to Reedsville. It is a good, substantial building, with a capacity to accommodate a good-sized congregation. The people of Reedsville Circuit have erected one of the best parsonages in the Mexico Circuit.

It was in the neighborhood of this church that Dr. Bond came to his untimely death by the accidental discharge of a gun. This accident occurred in 1844 or 1845. He was presiding elder of the district, and was at the time of his death one of the leading ministers of the Church in Missouri.

Bluford Hutts belonged to this Church. He was a plain, unassuming farmer—a man of excellent character. William B. Garnett was very much devoted to the Church, and did much good. Brother Offett is the father of Prof. Eli Offett, of St. Louis, and is a man of great enterprise and earnest piety. We now (1890) have in this community a large and wealthy membership. This church is the center of a large and most excellent circuit, known as the Reedsville Circuit.

CHAPTER XVIII.
St. Louis Conference.

The Minute Business and Statistical Reports—Bishop Marvin's Travels in South-west Missouri—Pleasant Hill—Church Dedication—Harrisonville—Nevada City—Red Oak Campground—Granby District Conference—Reason for no More Missions on the District—The Editor of the *Advocate* Doctored—Reorganization in the South-west—The Strength of the Church in That Part of the State—Report of Lexington District, by Rev. J. R. Bennett—Warrensburg Circuit, Rev. W. J. Brown, Pastor—Warrensburg Station,' Rev. C. C. Woods in Charge—Warsaw Circuit, Rev. R. C. Meek, Pastor—Clinton Circuit, Rev. J. B. Wooldridge, Pastor—Dover Circuit, Rev. N. M. Talbott in Charge—Saline Circuit, Rev. W. S. Woodard, Pastor—Waverly Station, W. F. Mister, Pastor—Lexington Station, Rev. W. F. Camp, Pastor—St. Louis District, Rev. Joseph Boyle, Presiding Elder—First Church, Dr. Clinton, Pastor—Centenary, Rev. C. D. N. Campbell, Pastor—St. John's, F. A. Morris, Pastor—Kirkwood, Rev. Robinson, Pastor—The Autobiography of Rev. W. S. Woodward—Rev. J. C. Berryman Gives an Account of the Charleston District—Fort Scott—Sedalia—Travels of Rev. L. M. Lewis through South-east Missouri.

THE St. Louis Conference was held in the city of St. Louis September 1-8, 1869; Bishop Pierce, President; W. M. Prottsman, Secretary. The following preachers were admitted on trial: J. H. St. Clair, W. M. Shelton, J. R. Eddleman, R. J. Derrick, J. C. Alexander, W. C. Montgomery, J. A. Russell, G. W. Hull, S. Richmond, C. D. Davis, T. D. Payne, and A. J. Hartle. Remained on trial: G. H. Williamson, R. D. Poole,

T. P. Hill, W. E. Woodward, D. P. Meacham, C. C. Wright, and W. M. Bewley. Admitted into full connection: E. G. Frazier, C. C. Woods, and W. F. Graves. Re-admitted: W. T. Ellington. Traveling preachers ordained deacons: E. G. Frazier and D. P. Meacham. Ordained elders: G. H. Williams and S. A. Blakey.

Increase of membership, 1,841; Sunday-schools, 181; teachers, 567; scholars, 9,698. Contributed for Domestic Missions, $3,758.65; for Foreign Missions, $196.65. Baptized infants, 760; adults, 1,208.

After an harmonious session, while transacting the business of the Church, the preachers received their appointments gladly, and went away rejoicing in the privileges of preaching the everlasting gospel of the grace of God to a sinful and lost world.

The reader will find given below an interesting description of Bishop Marvin's travels in Southwest Missouri. The name of Marvin is enough to secure the reading of the piece without one word of commendation from any one. He was a man who never spoke without saying something of more than ordinary interest. Hence he drew crowds to hear him when he preached, and now that his voice is silent in death, his writings, his books are eagerly sought and read with avidity, because they contain his original, fresh, vigorous thoughts—thoughts that used to sway his audience as they came forth in utterances of clear, forcible, and fitting language. A man great in goodness and good in greatness, who photographed his image upon the age in which he lived, and which shall never be obliterated by the revolving cycles of time. He writes thus:

> Pleasant Hill furnishes one of many instances of towns which have suffered by the cupidity of railroad corporations. When the road is being located some man offers twenty or forty acres of land to have the depot established on his place, a mile from town. This being done, business forsakes the old town, property depreciates, and the company makes what the people lose. This has happened so uniformly in Missouri that it may be set down as a rule.
>
> As in many other cases, so at Pleasant Hill. The old town has the advantage for beauty of situation. It is on a commanding prairie eminence, while the depot town is on low land. Then a sort of straggling neck, in this as in other cases, connects the new and old towns, making of the whole an awkwardly arranged community. When a road is made where there is a town of two or three thousand inhabitants, more or less, they may take it for granted that if they get the depot in reasonable distance they will have to pay the company a good bonus for it.
>
> Within the last two or three years several new churches have been built in Pleasant Hill. The place was made a station last year, and Brother Horn was appointed there. He determined to build a church. It seemed almost impossible, after all that had so lately been done in the way of church-building, that he should succeed. But he did. The result of his efforts is a substantial, handsome brick edifice of good size, of neat, churchly appearance, and out of debt. It is situated on the side of the new town which lies in the direction of the old, so as to be accessible to both. The only objection that I could make was that it was on ground that was rather low. I like to see a church on a high and commanding site.
>
> On the last Sunday in July it was dedicated. A debt of seven hundred dollars was to be met. The subscription made for this purpose amounted to eight hundred and ten dollars.
>
> The congregation which assembled could not be accommo-

dated at all, and many who came were compelled to go away. There had been a meeting in progress during the week, and the Church was strengthened by several accessions. After a year of indomitable perseverance and great labor, the pastor was encouraged by evident and substantial fruit of his toil. The foundations are strongly laid here, and I think that prosperity will follow and will be permanent.

From Pleasant Hill I went out to Harrisonville on Monday, and preached there at night. The Church there seems to be in a good condition. It suffered a good deal during the war. Their house of worship was very much mutilated, but has been put in good repair since. A railroad is in course of construction, but the depot is to be a mile from town. Our church is on the side of the town which is nearest to the road.

At this place I found an old friend. During my first term at Centenary Church in St. Louis he was a clerk in a Main Street house. At a meeting at which Brother Watts assisted me he was awakened, and after a few days joined the Church. From the first he was a faithful member. The incidents of his awakening and conversion were such as to endear him to me very greatly. I found him on this visit in a comfortable house and doing a profitable business; at the head of a lovely family, an active and decided Christian. My heart was full of gratitude on his account. I shall not soon forget William H. Allen. We parted in tears. Such friendship, I make no doubt, will be renewed and perpetuated in the world to come.

From this point my travels in South-west Missouri fairly commenced. I was with Brother Webster in his buggy. This is a vehicle worthy of a place in history. The editor of the *Advocate* pronounced it the best buggy he ever rode in. The horses were made for the road, and the driver was equal to the rest of the outfit. On Tuesday night we reached Papinsville, in Brother Monroe's work, and found a meeting of considerable interest in progress. There was a very large congregation assembled in the open air just on the edge of town.

Brother Monroe has been blessed in his work this year, and has exerted an excellent influence in the community. He is held in honor for his work's sake, as a faithful minister of the Lord Jesus. There have been several members gathered in here, and a decided public interest is felt in the cause of God.

Our own Church is intrenched in the affections of the people. A movement is on foot for the erection of a house of worship. It will require a united and very earnest effort to accomplish it; such an effort as will bring out fully the resources of the country. I trust they may succeed. If this year's work shall be followed up faithfully hereafter, the Church will prosper within the bounds of this circuit.

We were received here with the most cordial hospitality. There are signs of the war here. The most enterprising men are just now beginning fairly to recover from the ruin in which the struggle left them. This state of things very much embarrassed Church enterprises.

From Papinsville we drove to Nevada City. This place bids fair to enjoy a prosperous existence. It is to be a sort of railroad center. It is already growing rapidly, and is a business center for a considerable scope of country. Our Church is strong here. Brother Murphy is the pastor, and is warmly supported in the work by faithful and efficient local preachers. We had preaching here on Wednesday night, in the court-house. People came to Church from remote portions of the country. The spacious audience-room was too small for the occasion. It was greatly crowded, while many persons failed to get in. There, as indeed in every place on the tour, the most profound attention was given to the word preached. I trust there was a salutary influence from the evening service.

On this circuit both a church and parsonage are in contemplation. The exigences of the Society demands a church in the town, and they are already prepared to build. A very great work has been done here since the war. God has been very gracious to his servants.

Our next point was Lamar. This is a mission field, and Brother Barneby is the missionary. On some portions of the work there has been a good degree of prosperity. The town of Lamar, however, has been regarded as inaccessible until very lately. A few members with one local preacher have moved in here, and a small Society may be organized. There is a Baptist Church in the place, in which I preached to a small congregation on Thursday night. There was good attention, and I trust some good was done.

A short day's drive on Friday brought us to the camp-ground

at Red Oak. Here we found a good area of comfortable seats, a brush arbor over them, a very tasteful pulpit, and a rather poor excuse for a preachers' tent. I found a home at Mrs. McCune's, about a mile from the ground. This family has had a sad war history. The saddest part of it, however, belongs to the *post-war* period. It is a case of outrage, crime, and executive clemency scarcely paralleled even in the war times. The murder of Mr. McCune and the subsequent history are facts well known in Missouri.

The hospitality I enjoyed with this excellent family will ever be remembered with a feeling of gratitude. The father was a most hospitable man. His son, though under pressure of heavy and malicious lawsuits, dispenses the same open-handed and generous hospitality. Although they are not members of our Church, they kept open house during the meeting, and received all comers with a heartiness that touched me. May the richest blessings of Providence and grace rest upon them!

The District Conference was held in connection with this meeting. There was a fair attendance, and some important business transacted. A convention was called to meet this fall in Sarcoxie, with a view of establishing a high school for the South-west. This convention has full authority to proceed with the enterprise. The measure is not premature. The demand for an academy here is urgent; indeed, I may say imperative.

Important measures were proposed with respect to missions in the district. Several changes of boundary between the circuits were suggested, with a view of giving the missions sufficient strength to be self-sustaining. Besides equalizing the strength of the various circuits, they say it puts them in better shape, and is altogether preferable in every respect. If this new adjustment of boundaries is accepted by the bishop, they are willing for every one of the charges to be stricken from the list of missions. They are more than willing: they greatly desire it. They desire it for these reasons:

1. All the circuits thus bounded will be able to support their preachers.

2. When there is a missionary appropriation the people become indifferent about the support of the preacher, thinking that there is no great need for them to do much, as he gets money from some other source.

3. The missionary treasury of the St. Louis Conference is bankrupt, and many of the preachers in wealthier portions of the work seem to be wholly indifferent about it. What little conscience they may have on the subject evaporates at Conference in the shape of solemn resolutions.

4. When the missionary goes to his work depending on what the preachers promise so solemnly, he is doomed to a bitter experience before the year is out. The people are easy because their pastor is to get help from abroad, and the preachers in those portions of the work from which the money is to come are easy because—because what?

5. When the preachers solemnly promise at Conference to raise missionary money *early in the year* it is a sure sign that they will not take collections until late, and then in a careless way, so as not to get much money. There are honorable exceptions, as will appear at Conference; but the dishonorable rule remains nevertheless.

One young brother who had not learned the ways of the St. Louis Conference took it for granted that the pledge of the preachers to raise the money was as good as money; so, on reaching his mission, to meet an exigence he contracted a debt, to be paid at his first quarterly meeting. The presiding elder came, but brought no money. Creditors were seen under embarrassment, such explanations were made as the case allowed, and they were put off until the second quarterly meeting, when, as he thought, the money would certainly be forth-coming. But, behold, when the time comes there is no money. This young brother, having a conscience about promising to pay, was mortified above measure. The case was laid before the presiding elder, who entered into it heartily and *borrowed* the money for the young brother; but the borrowed money remains unpaid to this moment, and from present prospects the generous borrower does not feel very certain that he will not himself have to pay it ultimately. It pains me to write these things, but they are matters of public notoriety, to the dishonor of the Church.

The camp-meeting at Red Oak was a season of grace. There were many conversions. The congregation on the first Sunday was, I think, the largest I ever saw at a camp-meeting. The latter part of the meeting was very much disturbed by rains, but on the last Sunday not less than four or five hundred persons collected in a drizzling rain. There had been heavy rains the night before; the ground was saturated, the seats were wet, the straw was literally soaked, and drops of water were falling from the arbor. Yet this large congregation assembled under the arbor, and remained two hours during service.

I have no doubt that the editor of the *Advocate* will tell his readers about this part of the meeting, as he was there the last two or three days. By the way, the people here conferred the doctorate on him. Henceforth let no one question the title. The voice of the South-west confers it. It comes directly from the fountain-head of all American honors—the people. I was present to congratulate the Doctor at this important epoch.

This meeting was in the bounds of Brother Tillery's circuit. The reorganization of our Church in this region began under his labors at Granby in the fall of 1865. At a time when no Southern Methodist preacher could call his life his own here he came, led by a strange providence. A wonderful revival at Granby attended his labors, by which he became so intrenched in the affections of all classes as not only to make his person safe, but also to secure to him an open door in every direction. His work is historic.

Brother Webster has also done a great work here. With the requisite good sense, enterprise, and courage for the work, he took the district three years ago. He has adventured into new regions, looked after Church property, and in many instances shown himself a father to the preachers. In many cases where the quarterage fell short he has given up his quota to the circuit preacher who was more needy than he. He has been self-possessed when threatened with the "boys in blue" if he did not forego the prosecution of property claims. Armed men in a Quarterly Conference, coming to enforce a surrender of property to the Northern Church, have failed to intimidate him. He and Tillery and Barnaby and others have conquered a peace.

It seems incredible, but my conviction is that our Church is this day the strongest in South-west Missouri. They are greatly in need of church-buildings, and will soon have them. Every preacher in this district promptly raised the amount assessed on his charge to pay arrearages on last year's missionary drafts.

E. M. MARVIN.

St. Louis, August 10, 1870.

1869-70. *St. Louis Conference.* 427

LEXINGTON DISTRICT.

There is a good report of the Lexington District by Rev. J. R. Bennett, the presiding elder, which the reader will no doubt peruse with pleasure. Brother Bennett was a high-toned Christian gentleman, whose influence was elevating in the Church and in society as well. He was an able and faithful expounder of the word of God, and was highly esteemed by those who knew him. His brother was a prominent minister of the Virginia Conference, whose high position in the Church was well known throughout the Connection. He did much in promoting the success and prosperity of Randolph-Macon College. Brother J. R. Bennett says:

I found all the preachers in their respective charges, having entered on their work with a determination to cultivate well that part of the Lord's vineyard committed to their care. I found on several of the circuits that we have not one Sabbath-school under the control of our Church, the few that are in operation being union schools. I urged the preachers to organize schools under our management. I expect on my next round to find several such organized and in running order. I found the finances in the following charges fully up, or nearly so, to the first quarter: Warrensburg Station, Warrensburg Circuit, Lexington and Waverly Stations. The remainder of the charges are greatly deficient, which ought not to be the case.

On the *Warrensburg Circuit* Brother W. J. Brown reports his charge in a good spiritual condition; had held a good meeting at Blackwater Chapel, with several conversions and accessions to the Church. The quarterly meeting was held at Knobnoster: a pleasant meeting and six additions to the Church.

Brother Wood is in charge of *Warrensburg Station.* He is doing a good work; has a fine Sunday-school. The congregation and Church embrace a large portion of the intelligent and business men of the place. He is well received and cared for, and will, I hope, accomplish much good this year.

Warsaw Circuit.—Brother Meek is in charge. This work he found in a feeble state, needing much pastoral care, which he is giving to it, and is pushing forward all the various interests of the Church.

Clinton Circuit.—Brother Wooldridge is on this circuit. This charge needs careful culture and the organization of Sunday-schools, that the children may be taught the pure doctrines of the word of God. The financial system here needs looking after by the Board of Stewards. I am looking forward to a most prosperous year for that circuit, under the pastoral care of so laborious and successful a minister as Brother Wooldridge.

Dover Circuit.—Brother Talbott is the pastor. He is very industrious in his pastorate, visiting from house to house. We have but one Sunday-school under the care of our Church. This is the one in the town of Dover, in a flourishing condition, under the superintendence of Brother W. Eastwood. The spiritual state of the Church reported good; finances low.

Saline Circuit is in charge of Brother Woodard. There are three Sunday-schools in this charge working successfully; others suspended during the winter months. The financial system adopted in this charge a few years ago works well while in operation, but owing to the classes not having the assessments for the year but little was paid on the first quarter. I hope the amount for Missions will be raised in full, as Brother Woodard is a working man.

Waverly Station was organized last March, and reported as a station at our last Conference. Brother Mister, a transfer from the Memphis Conference, has charge of this station; was well received by his people, and is working hard to build up the Church, looking after all its interests. We have had a flourishing Sunday-school, which is evidence that we ought, wherever practicable, to organize our own Sunday-schools. There was a union school taught in our church, which was dissolved early last year, and a school organized of our own under the excellent management of Brother A. T. Winsor. It is now by far the most flourishing school in town. This station has some noble men in it, willing to give of their substance to sustain the Church.

Lexington Station, under the pastoral care of Dr. Camp, is in a healthy spiritual condition: class and prayer meetings well attended and full of life. The pastor and the Church are praying and looking to God for a gracious revival of his work. Here all the interests of the Church are diligently attended to. The Sunday-school is prosperous and well conducted by the Superintendent, Brother E. Winsor.

St. Louis District.

We find the following brief sketch of the St. Louis District in the *Advocate* of February 16:

We date back to the beginning of the year, commencing with the solemn covenant of the watch-night meetings, which were held in all the city churches. Dr. Clinton made it the commencement of services at the First Church, which were protracted during the month of January and resulted happily in the edification of the Church and thirty-seven additions to the membership. During the same month protracted exercises were held at Wesley Chapel and St. Paul's Church with good results, and three accessions at the former and seven at the latter.

The removal of the Centenary congregation from their old place of worship has been already made known. The Sabbath services are held regularly at the Temple building, at the northwest corner of Fifth and Walnut Streets. A room in the new Centenary Church has been completed and fitted up for the regular official and social meetings. The room is the one to be used for the infant class of the Sunday-school. The first meeting held in the new building was that of the leaders and stewards on Monday night. The various services of the congregation have been interesting. Dr. Munsey preached for them on Sabbath last. The audience was larger even than his crowded congregation at the First Church. It was not our privilege to be present, but we hear that the occasion was one of transcendent interest. Dr. Munsey had been complaining during the week, but his effort was one sustained, and abounded in wonderful intellectual power and religious effectiveness.

Two protracted meetings have been held at St. John's Church, at both of which Bishop Marvin occupied the pulpit frequently.

The meeting commenced last week will continue through the present week. There has been considerable religious interest and a number of additions to the Church.

The presiding elder reports interesting and profitable quarterly meetings. The one now in progress at Bridgeton exhibits particular interest, and is continued this week. Brother Adkisson was present at our preachers' meeting on Monday. He reports five accessions to his charge, and his Church in a good spiritual condition.

The regular services at Kirkwood are kept up by Brother Robinson, the pastor, which continue well attended and otherwise sustained with interest. There is great sorrow felt among us on account of the precarious state of the health of Brother Axtell, who is known, with his excellent wife and a few others, to have originated the Church there. May God spare him to the Church and to his family yet longer!

We had the pleasure of spending the Sabbath at Mount Olive, where Brother Shumate is holding a protracted meeting with encouraging prospects. Brother St. Clair reports progress on the Maremac and St. Clair Bircuits. Thus all along the line God is blessing his Church with increasing religious interest.

Rev. W. S. Woodard.

Our friend whose name appears above has favored us with his autobiography, which reads as follows:

I was born on White's Creek, seven miles from Nashville, Tenn., March 31, 1829. In the autumn of that year my parents moved to Missouri and settled in Cooper County, near where Prairie Home now is. In 1856 we moved to Polk County, Mo., and settled on Sac River, not far from where Morrisville now is.

I was baptized in Cooper County by Jesse Green; was converted in August, 1846, at Ebenezer Camp-ground, in Green County, and gave my hand to David Ross for Church-membership, and was received into full fellowship in my grandfather's house in March, 1847, by Jesse Derrick; was licensed to preach at Lower Shady Grove Camp-ground, Polk County, April 6, 1850, by the Quarterly Conference of Bolivar Circuit, B. R. Johnson, presiding elder, and R. A. Foster, pastor; was admitted on trial as an itinerant preacher by the St. Louis Conference at its session held at Independence in July, 1850, and was appointed to Mount Vernon Circuit.

I left my father's house on the first day of August, 1850, for my circuit, since which time I have been a homeless wanderer, but am looking for a home in my heavenly Father's house, in the "city which hath foundations, whose builder and maker is God." My first circuit contained twenty-eight regular appointments, extending into five counties, and had in it two county seats, Mount Vernon and Greenfield. My second, third, and fourth appointments were also quite large.

Some time in the winter I visited Ben Johnson, whom I had known two years before in Steelville. I left an appointment, and on my next round I preached the first Methodist sermon ever preached in that town. I organized a class there in the early part of 1854. My fourth appointment was to Neosho Circuit, which I did not travel because of an accident in which my thigh was broken while on a visit to my parents immediately after Conference. I was not able to do anything till Christmas, after which I taught school the rest of the year.

In 1855 I was sent to Versailles; thence to Osceola, Wolf Island, Carthage, Stockton, De Soto. Here the war overtook me, and I remained on this circuit three and a half years. At the Conference which met at St. Louis in March, 1864, I was appointed to Steelville District. At the next Annual Conference the Steelville, Greenville, and Cape Girardeau Districts were all blended into one, and called Iron Mountain District, to which I was appointed. It embraced all of South-east Missouri. The next year the Greenville and Cape Girardeau Districts were restored, and I was assigned to the latter, which I traveled two years. At the Conference held at Kansas City in 1867 this was divided, and the upper end was called Potosi, to which I was returned. I had now been on this district four and a half years, changing its name every year. Bishop Kavanaugh, at my earnest request, reluctantly relieved me from district work, and sent me to Saline Circuit, which I served two years.

In 1870 Bishop McTyeire read me out to Rolla District. After the Conference adjourned I begged him earnestly to relieve me from the district, which he did and sent me to Chamois Circuit. This was the great mistake of my life. I should have gone to the Rolla District. For twenty years I have rued my rashness on that occasion. During all these years I have never had an appointment that has given me a support. The penalty of my rebellion has been protracted and painful.

In 1872 Bishop Pierce transferred me to the Western Conference and appointed me to the Council Grove District. From this I was relieved the next spring and returned to the Chamois Circuit; was next sent to Aullville Circuit, then to Lamonte, then to Neosho District. A kick from my horse put me on crutches until Christmas. My appointment for that year was Sunday-school Agent. Then I served Papinsville, Chilhowie, Wellington, and Chapel Hill Circuits. Since that I have been three years on the superannuated list, and served three years as Conference colporter. I am now on Herndon Circuit.

I was ordained deacon by Bishop Paine in September, 1852, in Lexington, and elder in Jefferson City by Bishop Kavanaugh in September, 1854.

I was married to Miss Eliza B. Spencer September 5, 1852. I have been preaching forty years; served twenty-five as pastor, seven as presiding elder, three as colporter, and one as Sunday-school Agent, making thirty-six years of effective work. The three years I rested were spent in writing a book which, if ever published, will be the best history of Methodism in Missouri ever written. I feel safe in saying that I have come nearer preaching in every county in the State than any other man now living. I have served the Church either as pastor or presiding elder in almost every county south of the Missouri River. Except W. B. McFarland, W. M. Prottsman, and H. N. Watts, I have been effective longer than any other man in the St. Louis Conference.

I know of no reason why I may not be effective yet twenty years longer. I am not conscious of having any bad habits. I drink only one cup of coffee a day. I do not use tobacco in any way—that bane of Methodist preachers—never did, and I honestly think that all preachers should have sense and grace enough to eschew the filthy weed.

The early part of my ministry was blessed with many gracious revivals of religion, and I received hundreds of persons into the Church. Recently my labors have not been so fruitful of immediate results.

The support and education of four sons and four daughters have burdened me, and I have been compelled to supplement an inadequate support by "serving tables." I have lived in a parsonage only three years during the forty years of my ministerial labors. I have always paid my house-rent out of what the Church paid me, and have never received all of the salary allowed me. I believe I have never failed to collect as much or more for Missions and other claims than the charge had ever paid before.

I have been assistant secretary of my Conference for thirteen years, twelve of which I was statistical secretary. I have tried to do my duty, but am conscious of many failures. I think I have done some good. The future of this life is overcast with clouds, but beyond all is fair and bright. God favored me with one of the best of women for a wife. We have walked in companionship with each other nearly thirty-eight years. She always has been, and still is, economy personified. But for her I never could have kept my head above the waves. My greatest grief to-day is that I cannot furnish her a home in which to spend her last days; but the "Lord will provide," and in his own good time, when our work is all done, he will take us home to bask in his smiles and rest forever beneath the shade of the tree of life.

CHARLESTON DISTRICT.

Though we adverted to the fact in our history of the Church in the Missouri Conference, its importance will justify a further remark here that we get more historic information from the reports made by the presiding elders of their respective districts than from any other source. When they make their reports as full as they should be they cover the ground and embrace almost the entire scope of Church history. They tell us all about the preachers, what they are doing; tell us what the Church is accomplishing in building houses of worship, parsonages, school-houses, colleges, and
28

orphan homes; tell us what they are doing for Missions, for Sunday-schools, for our religious literature, and every thing else relating to the interests of our beloved Zion. In view of these facts, we take pleasure in giving these reports a place in our history.

We find an interesting account of Charleston District from the pen of the presiding elder, Rev. J. C. Berryman, whose name is a household world in that part of the State, in which he has labored for scores of years. Thoroughly indoctrinated in the gospel of Jesus Christ and built upon his most holy faith, long has he been a strong pillar of the Church in South-east Missouri. He is one of the bright lights of the world—a living monument of the glorious achievement of Christianity in the salvation of man. Such faithful witnesses constitute a tower of strength in the cause of righteousness. Read his report:

> Having just closed the second round of quarterly meetings on the Charleston District, it might be interesting to your readers for the presiding elder to give a sort of general statement of the condition of our Church in this part of the St. Louis Conference. And what shall I say? God knows I have no disposition to say any thing that will do no good, and much less to say any thing that might do harm. There are a great many good and intelligent people here, and for the majority I can say *they gladly receive Southern Methodist preachers.* Presbyterians, Old School and Cumberlands, have some very good preachers and members within the bounds of this district; and between them and us there subsist the most amicable relations. The Baptists are more numerous, but here, as everywhere else, "Jordan lies between." Still they are doing a good work, and between us there is no strife. Methodist doctrines and usages,

however, are almost universally acceptable to the people of this region. Hence our ministry is generally well attended, and our membership respectable in numbers and social position.

But there is *one thing here that grieves me.* Family religion is woefully neglected by our people. After much inquiry, I feel sorry to say that not one in ten heads of families in our Church here pays any regard to the domestic altar. This I would not publish but with the hope of provoking them to think what they are doing. My parents were Methodists, but I confess that the utter neglect of family religion on their part would have impressed my young mind most unfavorably of the religion they professed, for I should naturally have argued that a religion which did not deeply and daily interest them for their children was not worth much. And in what way can parents so successfully manifest and carry out this interest for the salvation of their children as in reading the word of God and praying with them and for them daily? I confess my ignorance of any thing that can counteract the neglect of this duty in the education of the household. God has constituted each head of a family a priest to offer up the morning and the evening sacrifice for his domestic charge, and I hesitate not to say that the man who neglects this duty does so at the peril of his own soul. It may be a cross; but "must Jesus bear the cross alone, and all the world go free?"

Our *Sunday-schools* are very well sustained in a few places, but as a general thing this great auxiliary to the parental and ministerial duties and obligations is too much neglected—not for want of willingness on the part of the children to attend, but chiefly from a lazy indifference on the part of the pastors and parents. Where these two classes of persons take an interest in Sunday-schools they always succeed. To be sure there are many places in the country where serious difficulties have to be encountered.

We mention one of these difficulties: the want of suitable houses. I do suppose there is no part of the State of Missouri in which there is so great a destitution of church-buildings in proportion to membership and resources. There are a few good houses belonging to the Church here; but in the majority of cases we hold our meeting in school-houses, groves, and private dwellings. And I seriously fear that it will be a long time before there is any very great improvement in this particular. Nor it is for want of ability to do better. Other causes may have operated to retard the progress of our Church in this and in other interests, but I verily believe we, as a denomination, would have been far in advance of what we are if our preachers had not generally come to this part of our work with a pre-existing prejudice against the "swamp country," as it is called, with a determination to get out of it as soon as possible. The people here are aware of this fact, and it greatly damages their zeal in the upbuilding of the Church. I recently heard an excellent old brother express the wish that the Conference would send no preacher to the Charleston Circuit who did not want to come. We are doing something in several places to build new churches and repair and finish others.

Our finances are likely to be tolerably well sustained this year on most of the circuits. From my observation in regard to this interest I have come to the settled conclusion that as a rule the best cultivated fields repay the laborer most bountifully. I have seen no people among whom this rule worked more certainly than among the people of this district. I could give examples to prove that I am not mistaken. While one circuit reports quarterly almost a clean "balance-sheet," another equally able and willing is greatly in arrears. People want value received for their money. The man who goes straight forward doing his whole duty as one who must give account to God will be amply sustained here. But they expect us to do as we have promised, "to be men of one work."

The preachers from several of the circuits have reported some good meetings, a number of conversions and additions to the Church. I may say, without making distinctions which might give offense, that the circuit preachers on Charleston District are generally doing their work like men "constrained by the love of Christ" and love for the souls of the people to whom they preach. I do look for success and general improvement on almost all of the charges this year.

FORT SCOTT.

A correspondent of the *St. Louis Christian Advocate* writes about the affairs of our Church in and around Fort Scott in the following language:

The South-west is becoming considerably noticed in secular as well as religious papers. There is some little political excitement in this section, though it is hoped that peace and its attendant blessings will be entirely restored erelong. May God grant it! My work still moves on harmoniously. The presiding elder, Rev. H. W. Webster, has enlarged my field of operations, adding to my charge a portion of the Little Osage Circuit consisting of four appointments. I have visited every one of them. They are promising fields of labor, and a more hospitable and sociable set of people I have never seen. These Societies have been without a pastor quite awhile. In the neighborhood of Judge Weyand's residence they have had regular preaching; the judge, a man who is constantly alive to his duty, supplying the vacancy.

At another appointment a minister of another Methodism (North) than ours has been interfering wonderfully, telling our people that the two branches of Methodism are just about to unite. He came very near by his persuasive eloquence (?) destroying our Church, consisting of about thirty-five members. The above statement I make on reliable information. They could not have been so imposed upon if they had taken our *Advocate*. Of course they were not posted on the proceedings of our General Conference. The preposterous statements of these "unification" preachers ought by all means to be exposed. We have seen to our entire satisfaction what such preaching (?) has done. We have visited members where the M. E. Church, South, has been proclaimed "dead to all eternity."

How long will these things exist? Does such a course create and promote spirituality? Is it leading a life of quietness and peace in all godliness and honesty? Yet our membership holds fast with unflinching fidelity. This is written through no ill-will whatever, but just doing our duty in telling the truth. May God graciously bless us!

Our third quarterly meeting in Fort Scott was a pleasant introduction of Southern Methodism. We obtained the use of the Presbyterian Church on the condition that on Sabbath morning the service be conducted in the Presbyterian form—one of our ministers to preach. The appointment was well circulated. Rev. N. Duren, of Nevada City, was with us, and preached with great acceptability to a large and attentive audience. The writer of this tried to preach. May God bless his efforts to the good of the people! After preaching Brother Duren administered the sacrament; Rev. Mr. Gardener, pastor of the Prebyterian Church, and myself assisting. A large number of persons communed.

I regard this quarterly meeting as an omen of success. We will always thank God for the zealous interest and remarkably excellent discourse of Brother Duren. Pray for these "regions beyond," which you appropriately style the stereotyped signboard of Methodism.

SEDALIA.

As we have just given the reader an account of the organization of Southern Methodism in Fort Scott, he will here find a statement of its resuscitation and reorganization in the beautiful little city of Sedalia:

It is well known that our Church has had a mere nominal existence in this place for a long time. From the commencement various difficulties have embarrassed our efforts. We labored against wind and tide. Many of our professed friends, whose religious sympathies were with us, regarded our organization as unfortunate, our success hopeless, and failure and retreat only a question of time. Hence they followed afar off.

Furthermore, our Society had no "tabernacle" to worship in, no house of prayer they could call their own; had to wander from hall to court-house. So they were houseless, despised, and otherwise forsaken. Though never disbanded, yet from removals, dismissals, and other influences, the little Society had diminished to eight members; so something had to be done, or discomfiture and retreat were inevitable.

That something has been done. Through the zeal and efforts of Brother L. Pulliam, our pastor, it was arranged that our presiding elder and Dr. Jones, of Boonville, were to be with us one week, to be followed by Bishop Marvin the next week. The weather was delightful, the moonlight favorable. Large congregations greeted the ministers in the Presbyterian Church, and listened politely, attentively, and seriously to the preaching of the word. As Dr. Jones contrasted the advantages and superiority of the Christian's hope, his life, and his triumph with the gilded pageantry of earth and all the world worships as good and great the difference seemed, as it really is, immeasurable, and the claims of religion appeared irresistible. The judgments of many were deeply convinced, and some were moved and cried for mercy.

All felt that Christianity had in these men able and eloquent advocates, and that it was a rare privilege to attend upon their ministry. But duty called them to other fields. The brethren present, however, kept up the services and supplied the pulpit till Bishop Marvin arrived and took charge of the meeting. He was exhausted from continuous labors. Our situation was duly realized as a crisis in our history. His sympathy was fully enlisted, and animated his efforts in our behalf. Crowds unusually large for this place assembled to hear him. His preaching was in the spirit and with power, abounding in pointed application, persuasive eloquence, and impassioned appeal. The necessity of his departure from us was greatly deplored. Penitents multiplied as the meeting progressed, and the last night the altar was crowded. There were a number of conversions, eighteen additions to the Church, backsliders reclaimed, the people blessed and encouraged, and Southern Methodism, as a living reality, brought prominently before the people and established upon an enduring basis.

As another result of this meeting we have projected a plan for the erection of a house of worship—have already secured an eligible lot. With the favor of the great Head of the Church our little Society will enter upon a career of usefulness in the accomplishment of much good.*

Rev. L. M. Lewis gives, in the *St. Louis Christian Advocate*, an interesting description of his tour through South-east Missouri. We had the pleasure of making his acquaintance when he first came to this State, about thirty-five years ago. When

---

*Rev. P. Phillips, in *St. Louis Christian Advocate*.

we were in charge of Independence Female College he made our home his first stopping-place on reaching the far West. He seemed to think that he had reached his destination in Missouri, that this country was good enough for him, and that he would travel, with his interesting little family, no farther toward the setting sun. He impressed us favorably on first sight, and a more thorough acquaintance with him convinced us of the correctness of our early impression. He was cultured, talented—a philanthropist, a true patriot, a Christian gentleman, and an able and faithful minister of the gospel. We feel gratified that his name appears in this history, while our hearts were stricken with grief by the sad intelligence that he had fallen by the ruthless hand of the "last enemy." The reader will no doubt be pleased with his following historic sketch:

> Passing up the road from Pilot Knob one has to wait at Bismarck about three hours for the down train if he desires to go in the direction of Belmont; but, after enduring that agony quite a number of times, I have learned a trick. I now go up to Irondale, where the hospitable home of my quondam prison friend, Capt. Blackman, furnishes me a good supper and other comforts, and some pleasant talk of old scenes at Johnson's Island in 1863 and 1864, until the train comes along, when I get on board and off for the country below.
>
> On this trip I stopped at Fredericktown, which has greatly changed in the last few years, for in every direction new buildings are being constructed, and the limits extended until it is assuming quite a business appearance. I was soon in kind hands, meeting Gen. Rorzier, the indefatigable friend of progress in Missouri. He is a pleasant gentleman, and has large views on all subjects involving the development of the country. He is confident that a railroad from Ste. Genevieve or Grand

Tower through to Iron Mountain and Pilot Knob will be constructed in a few years, giving us access to the inexhaustible coal fields of Illinois. Lead, iron, and other minerals are being discovered in the vicinity of Fredericktown in vast quantities, and the attention of the capitalists is being directed to their development.

I attended the Sunday-school and got myself into business, for as they could do no better they made me superintendent. There seems to be some lethargy on this subject among our people here. Lack of teachers and want of regular and punctual attendance are slowly doing the work of destruction. On Sunday morning and also at night I bore my testimony to the truth of the gospel. I preached to them as best I could, and trust it may not be without fruit in the years to come.

Monday and Tuesday were spent in visiting the people and forming acquaintances. I dare not fail to make mention of the "Whittling Club" of Fredericktown. Many country towns possess the benefit of such an organization, but certainly this excels. I tender them my compliments.

I did not forget the *Advocate*, and I believe the number of subscribers will be increased from that section. I feel it as much my duty to urge its circulation as it is to attend to any other portion of the outside work imposed upon me by the Conference; especially when one has so good an argument as the excellence of said paper. As good as it now is, I did not fear to assert that it would be better still when the lengthy articles on debates, Campbellism, baptismal regeneration, and a few other like things shall be gotten through with. Has it not been a long investigation, that of Campbellism? It does seem to me that our people ought to be well posted by this time. How long has that war of words raged? It has been longer than I will make an effort to remember.

Education is appreciated in Madison County. Many of the youth in and around town will go off to school next fall. There is a considerable desire to secure the location of the School of Mines at this point, in connection with a seminary of learning, but what are its prospects of success the future must determine.

Dr. Joseph Dines ably represents our Church at Fredericktown, the place having been made a station last year. He found the house out of repair, the congregation run down to nothing, and the entire field generally embarrassing; but I learn that great improvement has taken place, and the prospects of the future are more cheering. They need a new house, on an eligible lot and well inclosed. I should like to say many things about the good people here; but I must prosecute my journey, according to my plan, down the road farther toward the south.

Certainly there will be no lack of food for man and beast next year. I have never seen a finer promise in my life. Corn will be abundant; and oats and grass, beyond computation, are being gathered, hauled in, stacked, and stored away. At every turn new fields of grain catch the eye, and all around men are busy cutting down the forests and preparing for more extensive planting and sowing next year.

This railroad is a great blessing to the section it traverses. People are coming in and buying property; towns are springing up; business of every sort is increasing. Now is the time that we, as a Church, should act. Let the losses sustained heretofore by our sloth teach us a lesson, and make us wise to-day. Eligible lots should be secured in all these prospective towns, whilst the proprietors are bidding for settlers, and offering, free of charge, building sites to all Christian denominations.

I stopped at Marble Hill, with Brother Rider. He is heroic in his devotion to Southern Methodism. Singly and alone he is preparing to build a church, where he and his neighbors may enjoy the preaching of the gospel. He intends to beg everybody he meets, and I bid him Godspeed, and would urge all persons to lend him a helping hand. I believe no nobler object can be presented than the one in which Brother Rider is engaged. The traveler who reaches this point is still in the world of minerals. Excavations and explorations are now being made in the hills around. The ministers of our beloved Methodism are earnestly engaged in their work, and I hear of success and of much good being done in various parts of this country.

At Allenville, through the munificence of a wealthy lady, our Church will soon be housed. I saw the foundation, the lumber, and the men at work. At present there is not a single place of worship in the town. Nothing seems to be doing in Church matters at Morley, a very interesting and important point. From this place I went to Commerce, where I was entertained by Sister Moore, who is most deeply interested in religious affairs. By her untiring industry and indefatigable perseverance, aided by a few faithful ones, a nice, neat, and comfortable brick church affords us a place of worship. This is in Brother Davis's charge. He is reported as a man of unflagging zeal and energy. He has lately had a gracious revival at Big Prairie, where he was aided by the active and indomitable agent of Bellevue Collegiate Institute, the *locum tenens* of South-east Missouri.

After preaching at Commerce on Sunday, and attending to some business on Monday, I turned my course again toward the railroad, passing through boundless fields of rustling grain, and over rich lands studded with the largest poplar trees I ever saw. After a short meeting with Gen. Watkins, whom I am glad to number among my best friends, I crossed the railroad and passed through many neighborhoods, terminating at last in Bloomfield. From this point Capt. E. W. Hill sent me in a nice buggy and behind a fast horse to Spring Hill.

Back again at home after a long absence, I feel like a new man. I find the foundation of the new college building completed. They will proceed at once to build the walls. I have been playing the antiquary a little of late, and will let you know the result of my research and investigations.

CHAPTER XIX.

EDUCATIONAL.

The Age in Which We Live Demands of the Church a High, Thorough, Christian Education, to Combat the False Theories of Scientific Infidelity and Materialistic Atheism—Historic Sketch of Central College, Located at Fayette, Mo.—Historic Sketch of Central Female College, Located at Lexington, Mo.—Historic Sketch of Woodlawn Seminary, Located near O'Fallon, Mo.—Brief Notices of Howard College, at Fayette, Mo., and St. Charles College, Located at St. Charles, Mo.—Other Institutions.

THE paramount importance of a Christian education has not been overlooked by the M. E. Church, South, in Missouri. For many years our Church has been making commendable advancement in this great and noble cause. She has seen the necessity of raising the standard of education in her institutions of learning to keep abreast with the progressive age in which we live—an age of unparalleled progress in the arts and sciences, in literature and philosophy, and in the application of steam and electricity to all kinds of machinery, thereby developing the various resources of the country in a manner hitherto unknown, and to the admiration of an astonished world.

Our people have been fully aware that Christian education, deep and high and thorough, is the bulwark of the Church and the safeguard of the Bible. This is another strong reason why the Church, in the acquisition of knowledge and in intellectual development, should not be a whit behind the learning of this wicked and godless world, whose boastful champions are now employing their learning, science, and philosophy to subvert Christianity and overthrow and destroy the Church of God.

Secular education, divorced from the Bible, tends to skepticism, infidelity, and bald atheism, in the form of rationalism, materialism, agnosticism, evolutionism, and all other false isms. When men repudiate the Bible they are out on a stormy sea, without pilot, chart, compass, or rudder, driven hither and thither by every wind of false speculation, false science, false philosophy, and will inevitably strand or wreck upon some ill-fated reef or rock. Such has been their destiny, and such always will be their destiny. The house builded on the sand cannot do otherwise than fall when the furious storm comes.

Secular education exclusive of the Bible is the devil's prime factor in the fearful work of human destruction. "Knowledge is power," just as much so when used for evil as when used for good. The devil, an intellectual giant, does his fatal work by knowledge, without which he could cut no figure in the wreck and ruin of our world. It was by knowledge he beguiled Eve, and the only way to conquer him is to meet his false knowledge with superior true knowledge.

The exclusion of the Bible from our public schools is an unmistakable demonstration of the controlling influence to which materialistic infidelity, aided by Roman Catholicism, has already attained. When this victory was achieved, and the Bible was excluded from our public schools, no doubt Satan and his fiendish hosts kept jubilee in hell for quite awhile, making the infernal regions reverberate with their vociferous shouts of victory.

To exclude all religious denominational books from the public schools is right and what might be expected; but the Bible is not a sectarian, not a denominational book. It says nothing about Roman Catholics, Episcopalians, Methodists, Baptists, Presbyterians, Campbellites, or any other sect or denomination. God, who is its Author, gave it to the *world as a universal benediction to all mankind* in all ages and places. Therefore, no human authority, legislative, judicial, or executive, has any right to interdict or prohibit its use in schools or anywhere else. To read the Bible is a God-given right to any person and to all persons, and what man or set of men shall dare say I shall not read the Bible when and where I please? Thus the reader cannot fail to see the imperative necessity of a thorough Christian education to confute all false notions and theories that antagonize the Bible.

It is well known that there have always been more learned men in the Church than out of it, more learned believers than learned infidels. The Church and education are companions. Philosophy is the handmaid of Christianity, and there is no antagonism between true science and the Bible, for God is the Author of both nature and revelation, and they must necessarily harmonize, though vigorous efforts have been made by certain scientists to show that they do not. Such attempts have always proved abortive, and will continue to do so. But now, perhaps more than ever before, is the Church called upon to defend the truth against the assaults of an artful, strategic, subtle infidelity, which wears the garb of Christianity and "steals the livery of Heaven in which to serve the devil."

INSTITUTIONS OF LEARNING.

The M. E. Church, South, has established in all parts of the State educational schools of all grades, from the elementary school to the college proper, whose curriculum in comprehensiveness and thoroughness will compare favorably with that of any literary institution in the country. As has always been the case in the history of education, some of these schools and seminaries have run their race and finished their course, and are now among the things that were; while others have been more permanent and durable, and are at this present writing accomplishing great good in educating the youth of the country to qualify them for the responsible duties of active life and to fit them for high and honorable stations in society and in the Church.

CENTRAL COLLEGE.

The following historic sketch of Central College,

at Fayette, Mo., has been sent to us through the kindness of Bishop E. R. Hendrix:

The Methodist Episcopal Church, South, after mature deliberation, and under the leadership of educated ministers and laymen who knew something of what it took to make a college, determined about the middle of the century to build in the State of Missouri one, and only one college, of the highest grade, upon which should be concentrated the energies of the entire denomination in the State. The proposition originated in the St Louis Conference at its session in Lexington, Mo., in September, 1852. The following extract from the report of the Committee on Education as adopted by the Conference shows the mind of the Church on the subject:

"In the judgment of your committee the time has come when the educational wants of our people require, and the resources of our people justify the establishment of a literary institution of the highest order in Missouri. But while we need and must have the facilities afforded by this order of institution, your committee are of the decided opinion that it is the true policy of the Church to unite upon and undertake the upbuilding of one such institution in Missouri, and but one. In accordance with these sentiments, your committee recommend that this Conference, in an official way, signify to the Missouri Conference our willingness to unite and co-operate with them in such a plan for the establishment of a college as shall be mutually agreed upon by the two Conferences."

This paper, which was drawn up by the Rev. Joseph Boyle, D.D., was brought before the Missouri Conference two weeks later in the city of St. Joseph, Mo., when Rev. E. M. Marvin, Chairman of the Committee on Education, brought in a report of hearty concurrence in the action of the St. Louis Conference, which report was adopted. D. R. McAnally, Joseph Boyle, and Nathan Scarritt, of the St. Louis Conference, and E. M. Marvin, William Holmes, and Dr. R. Bond, of the Missouri Conference, were appointed commissioners to mature the matter and to call an educational convention composed of one preacher and two laymen from each presiding elder's district in the two Conferences to inaugurate the proposed college.

This convention met in St. Louis April 13, 1853, and was

composed of twenty clerical and sixteen lay delegates. D. R. McAnally was elected President, and N. Scarritt was chosen Secretary. After a session of two days this convention located the college at Fayette, Mo., where there was already a flourishing high school under the auspices of our Church, with the largest attendance of students of any institution in the State, and determined to raise one hundred thousand dollars for the needs of the college, not less than fifty thousand dollars of the amount to be secured before the institution should commence operations. The two Conferences promptly approved the action of the convention, and appointed fifteen curators each to carry out these plans, and also appointed, each, an agent to bring the needs of the college to the attention of the people at large.

The charter of Central College, which was the name agreed on as designating the new institution, was granted by the Missouri Legislature in March, 1855; and the building having in the meantime been erected on the site of the high school at Fayette, which was burned in 1854, the doors of the college were opened to students on September 21, 1857. Rev. Nathan Scarritt, whose pen had done so much to awaken interest in the proposed college, was in charge as President *pro tempore* and Professor of Ancient Languages; Rev. Carr W. Pritchett was Professor of Mathematics; and Eli Offut was Principal of the Preparatory Department.

As has been the case with many an institution of world-wide fame, the early history of the college was a struggle for life on account of the lack of funds. The college had three Presidents in as many years, none of whom could supply funds necessary to pay the salaries of competent instructors. The needed funds were slower coming in on account of the financial panic the year of the opening of the college, and because of the anticipated outbreak of the Civil War. Despite all these difficulties, there was a fine attendance of students until the war troubles closed the doors of the college.

The close of the war found the college dismantled, but an heroic Church rallied in an educational convention at Fayette to re-establish it. Learning from the past, it was determined not to re-open the college until one hundred thousand dollars had been secured in good subscriptions for an endowment. In the meantime, while a classical seminary was being conducted in the college building, Rev. Dr. W. A. Smith, the newly elected President, amid much enthusiasm which he had awakened, addressed himself with success to the work of securing the needed endowment. He died in sight of the goal, but others took up the work until the glad result was reached. Rev. W. M. Rush secured some twenty thousand dollars, and was active in collecting the old subscriptions. Much of the new endowment was in subscriptions of amounts based on the supposed value of certain lots in several of our cities which decreased considerably in value before they were sold and funded.

Rev. J. C. Wills, D.D., was called to the presidency, which place he filled from 1871 to 1878, when his death filled all hearts with sorrow. He impressed himself on the students and the public as a superior educator, and a man of lofty personal character. A good reputation had been made for thorough scholarship and excellent discipline, when in 1878 Rev. Eugene R. Hendrix was elected to the presidency to succeed the lamented Wills. He gave the next two quadrenniums to the college, removing a debt of over twelve thousand dollars, besides making the final payment on the original building of seventeen thousand dollars, more than doubling the endowment, enlarging the campus from five acres to ten, in the very heart of the town, securing Stephen's Scientific Hall, a gymnasium, and Centenary Chapel—all at a cost of nearly fifty thousand dollars, besides building up a library of about five thousand volumes, adding several new chairs and greatly increasing the attendance of students. Wills Hall was erected during this period in memory of Dr. J. C. Wills, a most valuable friend of the college. Mr. Robert A. Barnes, of St. Louis, Mo., endowed two chairs, one bearing the name of his mother and the other his own name. Curators and other friends of the college subscribed liberally to endow a chair to be known as the Marvin Professorship of Moral Science and Christian Evidences.

In 1886, when Dr. Hendrix was elected one of the bishops of the Methodist Episcopal Church, South, Prof. O. H. P. Corprew, the Nestor of the Faculty, became acting President or Chairman of the Faculty until June, 1888, when Rev. J. D. Hammond, D.D., was unanimously chosen for the place which he has so ably filled as President of the college. The college has never lacked able professors, among whom may be mentioned F. X. Foster, W. G. Miller, E. A. Allen, and W. B. Smith, aside from the present members of the Faculty. In some departments, notably in the study of English according to the historical method, Central College was the pioneer among Western colleges. A religious atmosphere has pervaded the college since its opening, and hundreds of its students have been converted and many called to preach the gospel. Her alumni have always been in demand to man our institutions in this and adjoining States. It is believed that the college never was in better condition to realize the hopes of its founders of more than thirty years ago.

It would not be proper to close this sketch of Central College without making mention of the noble laymen whose cordial co-operation did so much to make possible the success already attained. Among these was Capt. W. D. Swinney, a man of as warm a heart as of great business capacity, and during his life-time no one else was thought of for President of the Board of Curators; Hon. Truston Polk, a graduate of Yale, a superior jurist, and an able statesman; Adam Hendrix, for twenty years Treasurer of the board, successful alike as an educator and banker; Nathan Coleman, who gave to the college the President's house, in recognition of Dr. Wills's loyalty to its interests when called to a chair in Vanderbilt; and the many noble men whose bow yet abides in strength in and out of the Board of Curators.

CENTRAL FEMALE COLLEGE.

A brief history of this institution came from the pen of Judge John E. Ryland, of Lexington, Mo. Judge Ryland is so well known in Missouri as a distinguished jurist and able statesman that no word of introduction is necessary from us. He was a citizen of Lexington before the college was organized, and has been a citizen ever since; hence he is a proper person to sketch its history. Read what he says:

This institution of learning is located at Lexington, in La

Fayette County, Mo., about two hundred miles west of St. Louis and about fifty miles east of Kansas City, on the Missouri Pacific railroad. The Missouri River flows by the foot of the bluffs on which the college is situated.

The college was organized in the year 1869, and incorporated under the laws of Missouri by the name of "Marvin Female Institute," in honor of that great and good man, Bishop E. M. Marvin.

The college is situated on the grounds known as the old Masonic College, about which the battle of Lexington was fought in the year 1861. The campus comprises some seven acres of ground, and is the highest point near the city of Lexington, and from which a commanding view of four or five counties is had, presenting to the beholder scenery charming and varied, such as should inspire love and gratitude and praise to Him who has so beautifully adorned our land.

The grounds and original building were donated to the college by the Grand Lodge of Masons in Missouri, upon condition that an institution of learning should be established and perpetuated there; and that as much as fifty thousand dollars be raised and expended on the grounds; which conditions have been fully complied with as far as can be. The money has been raised and expended in buildings and repairs, and there has been a flourishing and continually prosperous institution thereon.

In the year 1884 the Curators erected large additions to the original college building, and now a large three-story edifice, lighted with gas, heated by steam, and furnished with hydrant water in each story, affords a college home for nearly one hundred young ladies who are in pursuit of an education.

Dr. W. T. J. Sullivan, of Mississippi, was elected the first President of the college; but, he failing to accept the position, the place was filled for the first year by Dr. William Camp, who was then the pastor of the Church at Lexington, and who was greatly instrumental in organizing the college. Dr. J. O. Church, of Columbia, Tenn., was selected President for the second year, and was continued as such for nearly two years, when he was succeeded by Dr. Sullivan, who had been chosen the President of the college for the second time. He remained with the institution for four years, when he resigned; and Dr. W. G.

Miller, of Central College, Fayette, Mo., was elected to fill the vacancy. Dr. Miller retired at the end of the first year, and Rev. Marshall McIlhany succeeded him. He remained nearly two years, and was followed by W. F. Kerdolff, Jr., who continued in charge of the college for nine years. He resigned, and was succeeded by Prof. A. A. Jones, of Georgia, who is now the President of the college.

This institution has had a varied history of prosperity and adversity, of sunshine and of shadow. But since her doors were thrown open in the year 1869, and the daughters of our land invited to enter and partake of the rich benefits of Christian education under the auspices of our beloved Church, they have never been closed, and under the good providence of God they never shall be until time shall be no more.

For many years the success of the college was impeded by debt. But, through the liberality and noble efforts of some who love the Church and God and humanity more than they do money, this incubus was cut loose from the college and buried in the sea of oblivion. This college debt was disposed of in 1889, and the year succeeding this event was one of the most prosperous in all its history.

Central Female College is located in one of the most prosperous, healthful, and refined sections of our great State, and only needs an enlargement of the buildings and an increase of educational facilities in the way of more apparatus and an increase of books in the library, and a liberal endowment, to make her the leading college in the West for the education of the young women of the land.

Under Christian influences this college has already begun to perform the work designed by her founders, and has already graduated from her halls fifty-five young ladies, some of whom have gone to give light and knowledge to the benighted heathen and to tell them of Jesus and his great love.

Yes, indeed, nature has done much for this institution. Beautiful for situation is Central Female College—on a lovely eminence, lifted above surrounding objects, and commanding one of the finest scenic views that ever captivated the eye—a vast, grand, and picturesque landscape of flowery lawns and grassy meadows, of gorgeous fields of golden grain, of extensive woodlands adorning the rolling hills with their towering forest-trees, of the majestic Missouri River flowing through this variegated and expansive landscape, which includes the beautiful city of Lexington, giving additional attraction to the view.

After enjoying this fascinating environment until the soul is filled with the beautiful and the sublime, let the visitor enter the magnificent structure of the college, which displays the finest taste of modern architecture. He will at once perceive that art has done no less for the college than nature; that, beyond all doubt, they have vied with each other for the prize. Herein he will find every want anticipated, every convenience and accommodation of the latest style to make the inmates perfectly comfortable. Nothing has been omitted to render the college as attractive as the best home in city or country. As Central College proposes to furnish the young men with superior educational advantages, so Central Female College designs to give the very best literary facilities to the young ladies who are in pursuit of a liberal, thorough, and accomplished education. The two colleges belong to the three Conferences of this State, and in justice should share the patronage of those Conferences.

WOODLAWN SEMINARY, AT O'FALLON, MO.

We have received a brief sketch of this literary

institution by its founder and President, Prof. R. H. Pittman, which we give below:

In the winter of 1862 the sainted Robert Loving was boarding at our house, and teaching the public school in the neighborhood. Upon a call for recruits to the Southern cause he left for the army, upon the condition that I should teach the remainder of the term for which he was employed. This I did, and was thus led providentially to devote my life to the employment of teaching.

In the fall of 1863 I opened a school in my home at Fairview, St. Charles County, Mo., for the thorough Christian education of young ladies. The school increased year after year in numbers and interest, until the close of the term in June, 1874, when I accepted the presidency of Howard College, with the hope of accomplishing more good and building up that institution. But at the close of the second year failing health, both of myself and wife, forced me to give it up just when we began to realize our hopes of success.

Before resigning the position that I occupied in Howard College my former friends and patrons in St. Charles County proposed to move the buildings from Fairview to a small farm we owned near O'Fallon, if we would return and open school there —a more eligible location than the former.

This generous offer was accepted by me, and on September 1, 1876, I organized Woodlawn Seminary. The school here has continued to the present time (1890), increasing in numbers until the capacity of Woodlawn Seminary is filled to the uttermost.

As already stated, I believe it was providential that I was called to this work. God has graciously blessed our labors, and we have, year after year, had the great pleasure of seeing those committed to our care, with but few exceptions, brought to Christ and established in the Christian life. Hundreds have gone out from these halls of learning to honor God and be a great blessing to humanity.

Verily we feel that we owe a lasting debt of gratitude to God for leading us into such a field of usefulness, in which under his blessing so much good has been accomplished. To him who has been our wisdom and strength, our comforter and guide, be all the praise!

There are other institutions of learning in successful operation under the patronage of the M. E. Church, South, in Missouri—some that have a long and interesting history, but their friends have failed to furnish historical sketches of them; yet we must not pass them by in silence.

HOWARD COLLEGE

for young ladies, located at Fayette, well deserves a place in the history of " Methodism in Missouri." It is not only the oldest Methodist female college in the State, but more young ladies have been educated within her classic halls than in any other institution of the kind in this great and grand Commonwealth of ours. Other literary institutions have come and gone. They did good work, and flourished for a season; but they could not survive the trials, the vicissitudes, and the difficulties incident to educational institutions, and per consequence they went down and are numbered among the things that were. But Howard College, with a vitality that will not die, with a purpose that knows no change, with a will that always conquers, has moved right forward through misfortunes, disappointments, and financial embarrassments, in a successful career for about four decades of years. Her educated daughters are to be found in all parts of the State. Nor is that all: they are now sending their daughters to be educated at their *Alma Mater*, where they spent the happiest years of their lives in the culture of their heads and their hearts to fit them for the responsible duties awaiting them in the future.

The prospect of the college was never more promising and encouraging than at the present time. Though already a building of considerable magnitude, yet they find it necessary to increase its capacity by a new addition that is to cost about twenty thousand dollars. Should they succeed in this enterprise it will add very materially to the convenience and accommodation of the boarding department, and will give to the whole structure a more commanding appearance. We entertain no doubts respecting its completion, for it is in the hands of the indefatigable and indomitable Groves, who does not succumb to difficulties.

ST. CHARLES COLLEGE.

As Howard College is the oldest Methodist female college, so St. Charles College is the oldest Methodist male college in the State. Its history is varied and checkered. Formidable difficulties have been in the way of its success. It is in that part of the State where foreign population is largely in the ascendency, and continues to increase, while American population is all the time diminishing. The Lutherans and Catholics have their schools and colleges, and they adhere as rigidly to their system of education as they do to their religion. Indeed, it is a fundamental principle with them to educate their own children, not only in the arts and sciences, and literature and philosophy, but especially in the doctrines and usages of their own

Church. In this they act wisely, because by so doing they secure their children to their Church, and thereby perpetuate their own religious institutions. Thus we can account for the perpetuity and wonderful success of the Catholic Church during hundreds and hundreds of years. This accounts, too, for their strong opposition to our public schools, which tend to upset and overthrow their ecclesiastical system of education, which constitutes the foundation of their Church. Hence they fight the public school system with all their might and main, because it strikes at the very basic principles of their ecclesiastical fabric.

While our Church acts upon a much broader and more liberal basis, we might do well to imitate their example in educating our own children in our own schools and colleges, and thereby secure them to our Church. We are under the impression that the M. E. Church, South, is more liberal in the matter of education, as well as in some other things, than any other Protestant denomination in the country. Go to the schools of other denominations, and you will find the children of Methodists, but how many children of other denominations will you find in our schools? Send your children to other schools, and in nine cases out of ten they will return home in the faith of the school in which they were educated. Therefore, by sending them to other schools, they become lost to our Church. How many Protestants have sent their daughters to Catholic schools, who became Catholics and perhaps have taken the veil and are now in the nunnery for life!

St. Charles College has done good work, and a great deal of it. Before Central College or any other college west of the Mississippi River had an existence, St. Charles College was educating the young men of this State, commencing its career in 1834 under the presidency and management of such a man as Dr. Fielding; highly distinguished for his talents, his ripe scholarship, his administrative ability, and his eminent Christian character. The college opened under favorable auspices, and enjoyed great success and prosperity for a series of years. Many ministers, lawyers, physicians, and statesmen received their education in this old institution of learning. She may well boast of such men as Dr. H. A. Bourland, Dr. J. E. Godbey, Gen. Dent, Hon. D. P. Dire, J. C. Orick, Judge A. Krekel, and others. While this institution has elevated them to high positions of honor and trust, they in turn are reflecting no little credit and honor upon their *Alma Mater*. Any literary institution throughout this vast republic should not hesitate to own such men as those of whom we have just spoken.

The college is still in operation, and President Myers reports favorably of the last term ending in June, 1890. He says that they had about as many in the boarding department as they could well accommodate.

There are other educational institutions of the

Church in different sections of the State, both male and female, in a healthy condition, and faithfully performing the work for which they were organized. It is gratifying to know that our Church is not behind in this great cause, but is grandly moving forward in the establishment of schools, academies, and colleges sufficient to meet all the demands of our sons and daughters, and to give them a complete physical, intellectual, moral, and religious education to qualify them to take the places of their fathers and mothers, and to perform well their part in the responsible duties and battles of life. Parents who give their children such an education may reasonably expect to see them in high places of usefulness in society, in the Church, and in the State; and when their work is done, to meet them in the eternal, heavenly home of the true and the faithful.

THE END.

www.ingramcontent.com/pod-product-compliance
Lightning Source LLC
Chambersburg PA
CBHW032003300426
44117CB00008B/878